One Hundred Years of
THE NATION

One Hundred Years of
THE NATION

A CENTENNIAL ANTHOLOGY

Edited by HENRY M. CHRISTMAN

ABRAHAM FELDMAN, Poetry Editor

Introduction by CAREY McWILLIAMS

THE MACMILLAN COMPANY, NEW YORK
COLLIER-MACMILLAN LIMITED, LONDON

Contents

Contents

Contents

POETRY

Contents

Editor's Foreword

There is little that I can add to the excellent Introduction kindly provided by Mr. Carey McWilliams, Editor of *The Nation*, except perhaps to make a few brief remarks concerning the details of compiling this anthology.

First, I would emphasize the significant fact that *The Nation* has been publishing exceptional commentary on public affairs, books, and the arts weekly for one hundred years. Specifically, this means that more than 5,000 issues of *The Nation* have appeared—an inspiring publishing achievement that obviously cannot be fully encompassed within the scope of one anthology. Limitations of space precluded the inclusion of many additional selections of outstanding merit.

The reader will quickly recognize most of the names in this collection because, of course, many of the best and most famous minds of this country and abroad have contributed to *The Nation* throughout the past one hundred years. In addition, the reader will recognize the titles of a number of the selections themselves, for they have become accepted as classics of their kind. And, as the reader will soon discover, many of the articles from decades past deal cogently with problems that still are very much with us today at the time of the centennial of *The Nation* in 1965—further evidence of the perception of *The Nation* and its contributors in identifying and analyzing significant subjects and issues.

A word about the section on poetry. In its earlier years, *The Nation* resembled the original British reviews—that is, a journal that reviews and assesses developments on the political scene and in books and the arts, and does not solicit original work such as poetry or fiction. However, by the Twenties, *The Nation* was publishing much of the best poetry to be written in English and has continued to do so.

In an anthology that spans a century, and includes contributors not only of diverse backgrounds and views but also widely separated in time, a considerable variety of style, punctuation, capitalization, etc., is inevitable. No attempt has been made to introduce an over-all uniformity in this respect; on the contrary, care has been taken to present each contribution as originally intended by each individual author. Every selection is included complete and unabridged, of course.

I would like to take this opportunity to express my appreciation to Mr. Carey McWilliams, Editor of *The Nation*, and to Mr. George G. Kirstein, Publisher of *The Nation*, for their encouragement and assistance; to Mr. Abraham Feldman for his work on the poetry section and in other capacities; and to Mr. Edmund Wilson, who kindly gave me special permission for the use of his essay on Gogol.

HENRY M. CHRISTMAN

Introduction

The first issue of *The Nation*—"a weekly journal devoted to Politics, Literature, Science and Art"—opened on a minor note. The lead paragraph of the editorial section, which then as now opened the magazine, was disarmingly casual that first week of July 6, 1865:

> The week has been singularly barren of exciting events. It is curious to see, however, what a situation the return of peace has given to political agitation. As nothing is now dependent on the fortune of war, orators and writers are entering the arena with a confidence which they never displayed as long as their arguments and predictions were liable to revision or falsification at the hands of Lee or Grant.

In the years that followed there has been little cause to repeat the complaint. Two hundred bound volumes attest to the tumultuous character of the century which has now drawn to a close. These bound volumes are very much a part of the social and intellectual history of the period; on more than one occasion what was said in them exerted a significant, demonstrable impact on the course of events.

The second editorial paragraph in that same first issue also carries an ironic echo today:

> The negro's success [the "N" was not capitalized] in assuming a prominent position in the political arena, seems to be in the inverse ratio of the earnestness with which it is sought to suppress him and put him out of sight. Everybody is heartily tired of discussing his condition and his rights, and yet little else is talked about, and none talk about him as much as those who are most convinced of his insignificance.

The "talk" about the Negro, which continued down the years, has acquired a new urgency as the century has drawn to a close. The ebb and flow of national interest and concern with "the Negro problem" is faithfully recorded in the pages of *The Nation*—a publication which was largely founded because of the preoccupation of its sponsors with the future status of the freedmen.

After putting the first issue to bed, E. L. Godkin dashed off a note to Charles Eliot Norton—one of the sponsors—in which he said: "No. 1 is afloat, and the tranquility which still reigns in this city, under the circumstances, I confess amazes me." With the third number the circulation reached 5,000 copies and Godkin was elated. "We have got so much money," he wrote Frederick Law Olmsted, another sponsor, "that I don't think we can fail, unless by stupendous mismanagement. $100,000 *paid up*." For the times it was indeed a sizable capital. The initial subscription price was only $3, but the early issues carried a substantial volume of advertising: insurance, shipping, publishing, as well as advertisements for hoop skirts, both the plain and self-adjusting variety, steel pens, clothes wringers, pianos, stereoscopic views of the late war, mining stocks, safes, "demulcent soap, for chapped and tender hands," lock-stitch sewing machines, kerosene oil cooking stoves, furniture and harmonicas. At the end of the first three months, Godkin's optimism was still high. "We believe we are justified in asserting that no such reception has ever in this country been accorded to any weekly paper, not pictorial, as this journal has received." But in this same issue (October 5, 1865) the subscription price was increased to $6 per annum, "single copies fifteen cents" (a hundred years later, and despite an astronomic escalation in the general price level, the subscription price is only $10 and single copies sell for 35¢). Nor was it long before other familiar signs of magazine distress began to appear. The advertising abated. With Volume II the size was changed for a time. As another experiment, the magazine appeared semiweekly for a brief period. But nothing succeeded, and by the end of the first year the initial capital had been exhausted. Virtual liquidation followed, with Godkin finally emerging in full command. Miraculously, the paper never missed an issue.

And it has continued to appear week after week, through reorganizations, sales and the coming and going of editors and publishers but with remarkably few changes in format and general style: an opening editorial section, a body section made up of articles and correspondence and a "back-of-the-book" section devoted to literature and the arts. Walter Bagehot once said that newspapers were a good illustration of the doctrine of "persistence of type," but even so *The Nation* must be marked a special case. As Gustav Pollak wrote on the occasion of its fiftieth anniversary (*Fifty Years of American Idealism*, 1915): "Few periodicals in the history of journalism can claim, like *The Nation*, to have preserved their original features essentially unchanged during fifty years of continuous existence"—a statement that can now be extended for another giant step of fifty years. In addition, *The Nation* has preserved, as Alan Pendleton Grimes has noted (*The Political Liberalism of the New York Nation*, 1953), "a rare consistency in editorial policy over long periods of time. It is this longevity, constancy, and influence which make *The Nation*, within given periods of time, not unlike a consequential political treatise."

By the norms of American journalism, *The Nation* has exhibited an uncanny tenacity. With the exception of a brief period from 1938 to 1942, the magazine has never been self-sustaining, yet it has managed to pay its bills (it has always paid for contributions) and to carry on from week to week. How, then, can it be that a magazine with such a dismal financial history—a magazine that exhausted its initial capital the first year of publication—has managed to survive for a century when, in the same period, hundreds of publications were founded, flourished briefly or for a term of years, and then expired—some, in our time, with circulations running into the millions? The answer is to be found in a simple paradox: it is precisely because *The Nation* has always aimed at other objectives than success, measured in financial terms, that it has managed to survive. It is living proof of the bewildering truth—bewildering because it negates a major premise of the American credo—that "failure" can be the key to survival, and with magazines, in the long run, survival is the final proof of success. Oswald Garrison Villard was merely stating a fact when he wrote of the first editors: "To both Mr. Godkin and Mr. Garrison financial profits could naturally make no appeal"; a balanced budget was not their prime concern. Nor has it ever been a dominant concern with the handful of men —and women—of wealth who have backed the magazine. Uniformly their concern has been with policy and performance, not with profits. It has been what the magazine stood for, not what it earned, that has won their support. Without this kind of backing, *The Nation* could not have survived; but had it followed a policy of expediency, it would not have secured the kind of patronage that has kept it alive.

The cavalier attitude of the first editors toward profits was not a personal quirk but a matter of policy. The policy, as A. G. Sedgwick once wrote, was one of "attack . . . a policy that preserved it from the popularity for which, of course, it never made the smallest bid." Granted that the editors could afford to adopt this policy, still there must have been many temptations to depart from it. But the record shows that practice has remained consistent with policy. W. C. Brownell, for many years a member of the editorial staff, was like Villard, merely stating a fact, not boasting, when he wrote:

> There was not only no temporizing, compromising, compounding, with candor, in either major matters or in trifling; there was no partiality or ingenuity or bland indifference by which the devil may be, and so often is, whipped around the stump. There was in *The Nation's* field and conception of its function no temptation to anything of this sort, to be sure, which consideration may conceivably qualify its assessment of merit on the Day of Judgment —a day when we may hope the sins of daily journalism will, in consequence of the same considerations, be extended some leniency— but certainly cannot obscure the fact of its conspicuous integrity.

In an early editorial (October 24, 1867) the policy was proclaimed and the subsequent history of the publication shows that it was firmly adhered to:

> We never on any subject play the part of the Roman soothsayers. We do not put forward one thing in print and say another thing in private. We profess to supply opinions exactly as we have formed them, and not in the shape in which they will be likely to please or encourage or console. . . .
> We do not place an extraordinary value on our influence; but, as far as it goes, we are determined it shall only be exercised in a way that moralists—not party politicians—will approve. We treat our readers as grown-up men and women who can bear to hear the truth, and know how to reason from it with regard to their own duty, and not as children who have to have pretty stories told them and fine promises made to them to keep their courage up.

Consistent adherence to this policy accounts for the fact that *The Nation* has never had a large circulation, but it is also the key to its capacity to survive in a field in which many have failed.

The Nation was the brain child of a group of gifted men: E. L. Godkin, the Anglo-Irish journalist who came to this country in 1856 and undertook a tour of the South which he described in a series of vivid letters to the London *Daily News*; Frederick Law Olmsted, famous as the architect of New York's Central Park, who also wrote a series of classic reports on the antebellum South; Charles Eliot Norton, the Harvard scholar; and others. Just who it was that first suggested the idea of *The Nation* is somewhat uncertain—it may have been Olmsted—but Godkin was certainly the moving spirit. By his standards, which were essentially British, American journalism stood in dire need of reform, and he was convinced that a weekly critical journal of opinion could provide the best corrective. Whatever its origin, the idea of such a publication suddenly became a reality when James Miller McKim, the Philadelphia philanthropic abolitionist, decided to become a backer. McKim had been toying with the idea of founding such a publication in Philadelphia or Baltimore, in part because he wanted to create an editorial position for Wendell Phillips Garrison, a recent Harvard graduate, then literary editor of the *Independent*, who was about to marry McKim's daughter. Garrison was the third son of William Lloyd Garrison and Helen Eliza Benson ("the brightest and most independent of the sons," according to Walter M. Merrill, Garrison's biographer). The Garrison home had been, of course, a center of the antislavery agitation.

A key to the remarkable consistency of tone and policy of *The Nation* throughout the century is to be found in the continuity of certain family influences. Wendell Phillips Garrison had a major editorial responsibility for the paper from 1865 until his death in 1907, first as literary editor from 1865 to 1881 and then as editor. Henry Villard, the railway magnate, who purchased the paper in 1881—he also owned the New York *Post*—was a brother-in-law of Garrison and the father of Oswald Garrison Villard, who served as editor of *The Nation* from 1918 to 1932. From 1881 until 1932 the paper was owned, in one form or another, by the Villards. Thus the Garrison–Villard connection prevailed from 1865 to 1932, when Oswald Garrison Villard stepped aside as editor.

The founders of *The Nation* were young men: Olmsted, the oldest, was forty-three in 1865; Godkin was thirty-four; Norton, thirty-seven; Garrison, twenty-five; A. G. Sedgwick, who was connected with the paper for forty years, was not yet twenty-one when he joined the staff with the third number. They were all intense idealists and, fortunately, not so old as a group as to know better than to put their idealism to the test. What these men—and others of the original group—had in common was a deep interest in the welfare, civil rights and citizenship of the recently emancipated slaves or freedmen. They had other interests as well, but, as Godkin once said, the leading political aim was "to secure equality before the law in all parts of the Union"; all others were open questions. Olmsted and Godkin had written two of the finest reports on the antebellum South, and John Richard Dennett, who joined the staff when he was twenty-six—a recent Harvard graduate—and remained with the paper until his untimely death nine years later, wrote what is perhaps the finest account of the South in the immediate wake of the Civil War. The moment the South was reopened,

The Nation sent young Dennett on a tour of the region. A. G. Sedgwick was certainly not alone in his judgment that this series of articles published in the first two volumes under the title "The South As It Is" was "the most valuable contemporaneous picture of the South after the end of the Civil War." The London *Spectator*, for example, said that the series was "far the most instructive picture that has yet been furnished us of the condition of the Southern states." Even today the series makes remarkable reading. Another *Nation* staff contributor—William Francis Allen, who held the chair of ancient languages and history at the University of Wisconsin from 1867 until his death in 1889 and was one of the paper's most voluminous contributors—visited South Carolina in 1865 and noted down the old slave songs. His book, *Slave Songs of the United States*, was to remain for many years the best work of its kind. The continuity of *The Nation*'s concern with the so-called "Negro problem" has in fact remained constant through the years, although its pages also reflect the general slackening of national interest that came with the compromise of 1876. But all the old fervor reappeared in Oswald Garrison Villard's passionate advocacy and support of Negro rights. Villard, the biographer of John Brown, was one of the founders of the NAACP, which was first housed in *The Nation*'s offices at 20 Vesey Street.

If the leading political aim of the new publication was to secure full civil rights for the freedmen, Godkin's major personal interest was in the reform of American journalism. The original prospectus issued in 1865 set forth as the first aim of the new publication: "The discussion of the topics of the day, and, above all, of legal, economical and constitutional questions, with greater accuracy and moderation than are now to be found in the daily press." As a journalist, Godkin had very clear and definite ideas about the kind of magazine he thought *The Nation* should be and the role it should play in the reform of American journalism. His models were the *Spectator* (founded in 1828) of Robert S. Rintoul, John Stuart Mill, Richard Holt Hutton and Meredith Townsend, and the *Saturday Review* (founded in 1855). Both publications were products of the new age that began to open with the accession of Queen Victoria. "The rapidly increasing middle-class in all the new booming cities," writes D. W. Brogan, "as well as in London and Edinburgh, didn't want to wait three months for the latest views and reviews. The railway was altering the tempo of life and . . . the success of the independent weeklies . . . threatened to condemn the quarterlies to the fate of the horse and buggy or the stage coach."

Godkin was convinced that a weekly critical journal of opinion would not need to acquire a large circulation in order to exert a pronounced influence on the press. As he saw it, the function of such a weekly was not to explain or report or celebrate the national virtues but to take a consistently hard critical view of those aspects of the current scene that, in the judgment of its editors, stood most in need of critical scrutiny. He thought, too, that it should carry "sound and impartial criticism of books and works of art." But *The Nation*'s special function, as A. G. Sedgwick defined it, was to seek out and expose "the absurdity of the fallacies underlying the extreme view on either side—the faculty of seeing through the Idols of the Tribe. . . ." Its purpose was to evaluate critically the American achievement, to pronounce an informed judgment on "books and men and movements." It was to be scholarly but it was also to be journalistic—that is, topical. Godkin had the gift, as A. V. Dicey put it, of "appositeness"—that is, the habit of interesting himself "in the matters which are passing before everyone's eyes, and which at any given moment occupy the thoughts of his neighbors." Godkin, as Dicey noted, was no mere critic: "his thoughts lay near to action," as did Villard's. He was not a great editor—he lacked executive (organizing) ability—but he was a fine editorial writer and he had a sharp journalistic sense—and here too he was like Villard. To correct what Godkin regarded as the prevailing vices of the American press—inaccuracy and exaggeration—*The Nation* did not need—in fact should not have—a large circulation; a pin could puncture a balloon. His aim was to examine the dogmas of the week; the more widespread and inflated the dogma—the more everyone seemed inclined to accept it—the greater the need to examine it critically. In any future Godkin could forsee, he was convinced there would be need for such a publication. But he had no illusions that it was ever likely to be financially successful. If he did not get a certain minimum of irate cancellations each week, he was apt to feel that the magazine was slipping.

From the outset, Godkin knew that the influence of *The Nation* could not be exerted directly because its circulation—if it did its job well —would never be large. It was to be, as C. C. Nott, a staff contributor, put it, "an external conscience of other publications." "*The Nation*'s influence," wrote Rollo Ogden, "in shaping the American press was out of all proportion to the mere number of its readers. It did not strive nor cry. The effects it wrought were subtle and insinuated, never clamorous. A virtue went out from it which was unconsciously absorbed by many newspaper writers. They could scarcely have said where they got their new impulse to exercise a judgment independent of party. . . . The steady light which Mr. Godkin burned in *The Nation* . . . had its slow but cumulative radiations. Not merely did it become impossible to employ, with a grave face, the partisan shibboleths which he was continually holding up to ridicule but it was made easier for editors to refuse to give up to party what was meant for country. In this way, *The Nation* was as leaven in the lump of American journalism. Its primary appeal was to 'the remnant.' Yet those whom it taught and inspired were all the time going out to teach and inspire others. Thus the result was like a geometrical progression. *The Nation* reaped where apparently it had never sowed." The remnant may grow slowly but, fortunately, it is steadily renewed.

Years later, H. L. Mencken, a contributing editor, in an article in the Baltimore *Sun* (July 6, 1925), admirably restated the original Godkin conception: "*The Nation*," he wrote, "is unique in American journalism for one thing; it is read by its enemies. . . . That is, the more intelligent of them—the least hopeless minority of them. It is to such minorities that *The Nation* addresses itself, on both sides of the fence. It has penetrated to the capital fact that they alone count—that the ideas sneaked into them today will begin to sweat out of the herd day after tomorrow. . . . Editorial writers all over the land steal ideas from it daily. . . . It is my contention that *The Nation* has led the war in the reform of American journalism. . . . Its politics are outrageous. . . . It has no sense of decorum. . . . It is sometimes a bit rowdy. . . . But who will deny that it is honest? And who will deny that, taking one day with another, it is generally right—that its enthusiasms, if they occasionally send it mooning after dreamers, at least never send it cheering after rogues—that its wrongness, when it is wrong, is at all events, not the dull simian wrongness of mere stupidity."

It has always been its loyalty to Godkin's original intention that has, at one and the same time, limited *The Nation*'s circulation and ensured its survival. In the field of general ideas, one man's catnip is another man's poison. The reader who will cheer when the antifluoridationists are lambasted will cancel his subscription if the antivivisectionists are criticized. Many publications face this problem in some degree, but a magazine that is constantly *looking for trouble*—for which "trouble" or controversy is its meat and drink—will never win any popularity contests. But by the same token there are always *enough* readers—there always have been—who admire the spirit and intention to ensure the magazine's survival. "Your readers have not always adopted your opinions," Charles W. Eliot once wrote Godkin, "but if you have not convinced them yet, you have forced them to find some good reasons for holding opinions different from yours . . . you have pricked any number of bubbles and windbags, and have given us keen enjoyment in the process and how often you have exposed humbug and

cant to the great refreshment of sincere people!" Of Villard, William
Hard once said that he had "made more acres of public men acutely
miserable, per unit of circulation, than any other editor alive," and
the statement was probably true since Godkin was then dead.

Godkin and his associates were well aware that establishing a weekly
critical journal of opinion in this country would not be an easy task.
There was no precedent for it. He knew, too, that it would be necessary
to create his own audience—to bring it into being—which is exactly
what he did. His aim in this regard, as Charles Eliot Norton once observed, was "to quicken the conscience of the thoughtful part of the
community in regard to every important political question of the
time." He deliberately sought to limit his appeal to "the thoughtful
part of the community" because it was through this element, he was
convinced, that a small-circulation publication could exert an influence
out of all relation to its circulation. He could hope, too, to hold the
loyalty of such a readership once acquired. *The Nation*, wrote Lord
Bryce, was read by "the two classes which in America have most to do
with forming political and economic opinion—I mean editors and university teachers." Not all of these, of course, became or remained *Nation*
readers, but enough did to win for it the role that Godkin had envisaged.
Readership became, and still remains, a family tradition; there are today
numerous third- and fourth-generation *Nation* readers. No American
magazine has a more stable or a more loyal readership. In addition, it
has long enjoyed a reputation—a factor of its having been around for
such a long time—that has made it known to thousands of individuals
who have never been subscribers. Not a week passes that does not
bring to the editorial offices clippings, documents and miscellaneous
intelligence from all parts of the country, in many cases from individuals who, so far as our records indicate, have never at any time been
subscribers. In many cases, these communications are simply addressed
to "The Nation, New York."

Beyond all doubt, *The Nation* was a new journalistic creation which
brought new elements into the American press; there had never been
anything quite like it. While modeled on the *Spectator* and *Saturday
Review*, it was, as Lord Bryce said, "no mere imitation, either of those
journals or any other, but a new creation which brought new elements
into the American press." As a matter of fact, *The Nation* has always
had more than its share of imitators. By 1923, writes Alan Pendleton
Grimes, "there were, fashioned after the New York *Nation*, *Die Nation*
in Berlin, the London *Nation*, a Canadian *Nation*, a Mexican *Nation*,
and even a *Nation* in Lahore, India." There is no doubt that the new
magazine, as Rollo Ogden wrote, "fell happily upon the period." The

America of 1865 was still very provincial-minded, "more than a trifle crude, afflicted with Chauvinism." Political comment was violently partisan. To many bright young people in college, the new magazine was a revolution, a wonder and a delight. "I owe much to *The Nation*," wrote Francis Parkman, and he spoke for many others. When, in 1875, Richard Henry Dana, Jr., wrote to his son who was preparing to travel abroad that he would forward to him the New York *Nation* ("They will keep you well up in American affairs"), he was expressing a confidence that many of his generation shared.

The original prospectus for *The Nation* contained this promise: "*The Nation* will not be the organ of any party, sect, or body. It will, on the contrary, make an earnest effort to bring to the discussion of political and social questions a really critical spirit, and to wage war upon the vices of violence, exaggeration, and misrepresentation by which so much of the political writing of the day is marred." Down the years, this promise has been kept. On occasion, to be sure, *The Nation* has referred to itself in seemingly inconsistent terms. For example, under the editorship of Paul Elmer More, *The Nation* advertised itself as an "organ of thinking people, the exponent of sane progress, of wise Conservatism," whereas under O. G. Villard it referred to itself as "America's Leading Liberal Weekly Since 1865," and was once pronounced, by Karl A. Bickel, then president of the United Press, as "the best obtainable barometer on the state of liberal opinion in the United States" (1928). But advertisements to the contrary, *The Nation* has never been primarily a conservative or liberal publication; even under Villard and Frieda Kirchwey, it was never the house organ of what might be called the Liberal Establishment. A paper that supported Grover Cleveland and William McKinley, consistently took a dim view of William Jennings Bryan, refused to support Theodore Roosevelt, endorsed Taft, admired Hughes but twice supported Wilson (only to execrate him later—one of Villard's great editorials was captioned "The Madness of Versailles"), endorsed La Follette with enthusiasm, said either Al Smith or Norman Thomas in 1928, endorsed Thomas in 1932, then endorsed Roosevelt three times can hardly be accused of harboring partisan political affiliations. Yet there has always been a clear consistency of editorial purpose and intention which can be followed like a silver thread through the 200 bound volumes.

To grasp this purpose firmly, a minor clarification is required. Godkin was a thoroughly consistent thinker. When he came to this country in 1856 he had already adopted as his own "the political creed of the mid-Victorian era in its wisest and its noblest form"—to quote A. V. Dicey. He was, in brief, a Manchester liberal of the *laissez-faire* variety.

His gods were Mill, Grote, Bright and Gladstone. His liberalism or radicalism was of the variety that flourished in Great Britain from 1845 to 1880 or thereabouts. Its slogans were "peace, retrenchment and reform." He was not a pacifist, but he abhorred war and was always anti-imperialist. "Reform" meant to him, as it did to his colleagues here and in Europe, "the gradual, the considered, and therefore the effective, removal of every demonstrated evil which could be cured either by legislation or by the improvement of social habits and sentiments." A consistent advocate of a sound currency and of civil-service reform, he carried on a relentless campaign against Tammany Hall. This Mill–Grote variety of radicalism was not programmatic or ideological so much as it reflected an attitude; it stressed the rational, the critical, the idealistic. Manifestoes fade and programs date and ideologies ensnare, but the habit of relentless criticism—of seeing things "in a dry light"—remains a constant value—in journalism. By the turn of the century, of course, it was clear—and notably clear to Godkin himself—that the rising forces and pressures of industrialism had cut the ground from under the presuppositions of the mid-Victorian reformers. "Our present political condition," he wrote at the turn of the century, "is repulsive to me. I came here fifty years ago with high and fond ideals about America, for I was brought up in the Mill–Grote school of radicals. They are now all shattered, and I have apparently to look elsewhere to keep even moderate hopes about the human race alive." "In the politics of the world," *The Nation* observed in 1900, "Liberalism is a declining, almost a defunct force. Only a remnant, old men for the most part, still uphold the Liberal doctrine, and when they are gone, it will have no champions."

But Godkin was mistaken; "liberalism" of his variety—it might better be called "idealism"—came back with a great surge under the editorial leadership of Oswald Garrison Villard, who assumed the editorship of *The Nation* in 1918. It was *The Nation,* according to Alan Pendleton Grimes, that sustained the enfeebled progressive movement from 1918 to 1932 in its long season of exile and discontent, before it finally came to power under the New Deal of Franklin D. Roosevelt. It should be noted—the point is of major importance—that *The Nation* had never been a partisan of the progressive movement per se. For one thing, it could not abide the jingoism of Theodore Roosevelt any more than he could abide *The Nation.* Godkin was one of the editors, Henry F. Pringle noted, who "rarely failed to penetrate Roosevelt's gradually thickening hide." Of Roosevelt *The Nation* once said: "His view of his duties is essentially jovial. He loves to slap the country on the back with a 'bright' thought" (1906). As to what Roosevelt thought of

The Nation, I have framed in my office a letter dated April 21, 1894, that he wrote while a member of the Civil Service Commission in Washington to one of our subscribers (Professor George Elliott Howard of Stanford University). The letter reads:

> I thank you for your address on the American University. I have really enjoyed reading it. I was particularly glad to see the stand you took in reference to a servile following of Germanic methods in the matter. I have only one criticism to make. I see you quote the Nation as an authority. It is always possible that what the Nation says is true, but there is never any inherent probability of it; and I think it about the most unsafe guide in American politics that there is.

To *The Nation,* the "Americanism" of the 1890s, for which it held Roosevelt responsible in no small measure, was "a distinct reversion to archaic and barbarous forms of feeling and action. It calls for passionate and sudden action. It contemns and distrusts and impedes deliberation. It associates consideration for the feelings or interests of others with cowardice and want of patriotism. It makes national happiness and prosperity dependent on foreign misery and calamity. It tries to excite envy by exhibitions of brute strength. It covers weakness with ridicule. It minimizes and ignores domestic evils and abuses." (LVI, 1893, page 137.) But when Theodore Roosevelt's progressivism had broken up on the shoals of World War I, it was Villard who picked up the wreckage, invigorated it with the spirit of his own anti-imperialism and his intense antiwar idealism, and thereby managed to keep the progressive, reformist tradition alive until it triumphed in the New Deal. If Villard did not immediately recognize the leadership of Franklin D. Roosevelt, it was for the perfectly good reason that Roosevelt's best qualities were not apparent in 1932. In fact, Villard had good reason to be distrustful of the Roosevelt of 1932.

The thread of consistency that runs unbroken through the pages of *The Nation* from 1865 to the present time is, therefore, not "liberalism" but the kind of idealism for which the magazine has always stood. It has consistently taken not the partisan or ideological but "the moral view." It has been consistently against racism, against war, against imperialism, against the abuse of power, against the swinishness of political machines, against charlatanry, demagoguery, and superpatriotism of the flag-waving variety. Imperialism has always been anathema to *The Nation.* Godkin and Charles Eliot Norton were among the founders of the Anti-Imperialist League, and, after World War I, Villard carried on a superb campaign for independence for Ireland and India, for recognition of the USSR and for removal of imperialist controls in Haiti, Santo Domingo, Nicaragua, Samoa and the Philippines. He organized public hearings in Washington to expose the Black and Tan terror in Ireland and is credited with having helped to force a settlement of the Irish question. Almost single-handedly he forced the withdrawal of the Marines from Haiti; between 1918 and 1932 *The Nation* carried more than fifty articles and editorials on conditions in Haiti. Villard was a devoted advocate of civil rights for Negroes, of civil liberties, of woman suffrage. In the darkest period of McCarthyism, *The Nation* held its ground, refused to give an inch and would not concede that constitutional guarantees should be suspended so far as Trotskyites, "comsymps," "fellow travelers" and "reds" were concerned. It consistently criticized the underlying presuppositions of the cold war, looked askance at the cloak-and-dagger work of the CIA and felt that the FBI was not quite the perfect agency its director made it out to be. It was the first American publication to take a hard, cold view of "the military-industrial complex." Down the years, to quote Alan Pendleton Grimes, "*The Nation* continued as caustic and independent as before; it lambasted greed and corruption in politics wherever it was found. It had no mercy on friend or foe as it continued the holy war for public and private morality. It kept reason and conscience on their eighteenth-century pinnacle. It was, as before, a citizen of the world and met provincialism with an international approach." It was among the first American publications to call the turn on Mussolini and Hitler.

Its consistency, in a word, is to be found in its refusal to buy "the official line," in its insistence on the hard critical view, it its honesty and in its idealism. "Our criticisms . . . may be ill-founded or ill-judged," *The Nation* said in 1866 (Volume II, page 166), "but are always honest, and they shall certainly never be withheld; they shall go before our readers, like testimony before the courts, for what they are worth." Essentially the rare consistency in its editorial tone is to be found in its refusal to concede that idealism is futile. "There is no force so potent in politics as a moral issue," *The Nation* pointed out in an editorial of June 18, 1908. "Politicians may scorn it, ambitious men may despise it or fight shy of it, newspapers may caricature or misrepresent it; but it has a way of confounding the plans of those who pride themselves on their astuteness, and rendering powerless the most formidable enginery of party or boss."

Down the years *The Nation* has had a host of distinguished contributors. From them Henry M. Christman has made, for this centennial anthology, an excellent selection. For many years *The Nation* adhered to a policy of anonymity, to encourage the candor and rigor of its criticism. But from the first issue on, the early contributors included: Henry W. Longfellow, James Russell Lowell, John G. Whittier, Charles

Eliot Norton, Francis Parkman, Edmund Quincy, Daniel C. Gilman, Frederick Law Olmsted, Bayard Taylor, Charles Loring Brace, Richard Grant White, Sydney George Fisher, R. H. Stoddard, Lord Bryce, A. V. Dicey, Henry James, Sr., and Henry James, Jr. (barely twenty-two when he wrote his first *Nation* article), William James, Josiah Royce, W. C. Brownell, Paul Elmer More (editor from 1909 to 1914), George Perkins Marsh, Charles Sanders Peirce, Noah Porter, Russell Sturgis (who, beginning with the third number, wrote about the fine arts for *The Nation* until his death in 1909), W. D. Howells, Phillips Brooks, Jessie White Mario (for forty years *The Nation*'s correspondent in Italy; she is a character in one of Meredith's novels), Leslie Stephens, Asa Gray, Charles Francis Adams, Jr., A. F. Bandelier, Goldwin Smith, Henry T. Finck (music), Stuart P. Sherman, Thomas Wentworth Higginson, Henry C. Lea, Earl Shinn (art), Irving Babbitt, William Graham Sumner, Carl Schurz and many, many more. Since the policy of anonymity was set aside, no listing of distinguished contributors is needed. Of course, no one-volume collection can include all these remarkable contributors who have enriched *The Nation* with their writings from 1865 onward. Henry M. Christman, whose talents as an anthologist *The Nation* has had good reason to appreciate, has placed us once again in his debt for this fine selection—it is entirely his own—of the "best of the nation" over the first hundred years.

Those who, at any time, have been responsible for upholding *The Nation*'s good name have found themselves, to some extent, captives of its tradition. If they have been tempted to depart from that tradition, the pressure of the readership has brought them back to it. Nor can they ever escape entirely from an awareness of all that those 200 bound volumes imply. "Those . . . responsible for the conduct of *The Nation*," wrote Rollo Ogden, "look back . . . with a kind of proud humility. The secure past is not theirs, yet they, as inheritors of a high tradition, must not discredit it. As they think of the men who conceived *The Nation* and nourished its early years—both editors and contributors during the time when its fame was solidly built up—the sensation is like that of one walking through a gallery of the portraits of his famous ancestors. They are his, yet not his—his, if he lives worthy of the name they bequeathed to him; not his, if he fastens disgrace where they stamped only honor."

It is one of the superb facts about *The Nation* that it belongs to no one; you can no more "own" it than you can own the spirit it represents. It belongs to the dead as well as to the living; to all those who have written for it or read it; to those who have detested and cursed it as well as those who have loved and respected it. It is unique, anomalous and preposterous. By all the rules it should have expired with Volume I, yet it has survived for a century; and as it crosses into the second century of its existence it does so with the same spirit and confidence that animated its sponsors in 1865.

CAREY McWILLIAMS
Editor, *The Nation*

New York
July 6, 1965

Original Prospectus for *The Nation*

THE NATION

A WEEKLY JOURNAL OF POLITICS, LITERATURE, SCIENCE, AND ART WILL BE PUBLISHED JULY 6, 1865.

Terms:—Three Dollars per annum, in advance; Six Months, Two Dollars.

ITS MAIN OBJECTS WILL BE

First.—The discussion of the topics of the day, and, above all, of legal, economical, and constitutional questions, with greater accuracy and moderation than are now to be found in the daily press.

Second.—The maintenance and diffusion of true democratic principles in society and government, and the advocacy and illustration of whatever in legislation or in manners seems likely to promote a more equal distribution of the fruits of progress and civilization.

Third.—The earnest and persistent consideration of the condition of the laboring class at the South, as a matter of vital interest to the nation at large, with a view to the removal of all artificial distinctions between them and the rest of the population, and the securing to them, as far as education and justice can do it, of an equal chance in the race of life.

Fourth.—The enforcement and illustration of the doctrine that the whole community has the strongest interest, both moral, political, and material, in their elevation, and that there can be no real stability for the Republic so long as they are left in ignorance and degradation.

Fifth.—The fixing of public attention upon the political importance of popular education, and the dangers which a system like ours runs from the neglect of it in any portion of our territory.

Sixth.—The collection and diffusion of trustworthy information as to the condition and prospects of the Southern States, the openings they offer to capital, the supply and kind of labor which can be obtained in them, and the progress made by the colored population in acquiring the habits and desires of civilized life.

Seventh.—Sound and impartial criticism of books and works of art.

The Nation will not be the organ of any party, sect, or body. It will, on the contrary, make an earnest effort to bring to the discussion of political and social questions a really critical spirit, and to wage war upon the vices of violence, exaggeration, and misrepresentation by which so much of the political writing of the day is marred.

The criticism of books and works of art will form one of its most prominent features; and pains will be taken to have this task performed in every case by writers possessing special qualifications for it.

It is intended, in the interest of investors, as well as of the public generally, to have questions of trade and finance treated every week by a writer whose position and character will give his articles an exceptional value, and render them a safe and trustworthy guide.

A special correspondent, who has been selected for his work with some care, is about to start in a few days for a journey through the South. His letters will appear every week, and he is charged with the duty of simply reporting what he sees and hears, leaving the public as far as possible to draw its own inferences.

The following writers, among others, have been secured either as regular or occasional contributors:—

Henry W. Longfellow, James Russell Lowell, John G. Whittier, Samuel Eliot (Ex-President Trin. College, Hartford), Professor Torrey (Harvard), Dr. Francis Lieber, Professor Child (Harvard), Charles E. Norton, Judge Bond (Baltimore), Edmund Quincy, Professor W. D. Whitney (Yale), Profesor D. C. Gilman (Yale), Judge Daly, Professor Dwight (Columbia College), Judge Wayland, Frederick Law Olmsted, Rev. Dr. McClintock, Rev. Dr. Jos. P. Thompson, Rev. Phillips Brooks, Rev. Dr. Bellows, C. J. Stillé, Henry T. Tuckerman, Bayard Taylor, C. A. Bristed, C. L. Brace, Richard Grant White, William Lloyd Garrison, Sydney George Fisher, Theodore Tilton, James Parton, Gail Hamilton, R. H. Stoddard.

130 Nassau Street, N.Y.

JOSEPH H. RICHARDS,
Publisher.

Godkin's "Nation"

BY OSWALD GARRISON VILLARD

1940

Founded immediately after the greatest war in history up to that time, *The Nation* reaches its seventy-fifth anniversary with Europe in the middle of a devastating and needless conflict. I often wish that Godkin were alive now to scourge the British statesmen so largely responsible for this war, for he had the most powerful editorial pen ever wielded in this country—a pen backed by a fund of knowledge and a passion for righteousness and justice never surpassed in the history of daily and weekly journalism in the United States. No man ever entered upon an American editorial career better equipped for it than he, with wide knowledge of this country, Ireland, England, and the Continent, experience as a correspondent in the Crimean War, and a magnificent style.

Mr. Godkin's editorial associate in *The Nation's* establishment was Wendell Phillips Garrison, son of William Lloyd Garrison, and later son-in-law of J. Miller McKim, a Quaker Abolitionist of Philadelphia, who had gone with Mrs. John Brown to Harper's Ferry to bring Brown's body back to molder in the grave. McKim contributed to the financing of the new magazine. Few people realize, perhaps, that the main purpose behind the founding of *The Nation* was to champion the newly freed slaves and to work for a square deal for them. That our government did so little for the former slaves seems incredible in these days of social security, WPA, and so many other enterprises for keeping American citizens alive and creating employment for them. The government of Andrew Johnson thought the establishment of the Freedmen's Bureau under the direction of General O. O. Howard all that was necessary. Had there been the vision then to create educational institutions for the Negro throughout the South, to purchase land for the settlement of capable Negro farmers, and to supply them with the necessary working capital and equipment, the whole story of Reconstruction must have been different, especially if right-minded and just Southerners of the type of Robert E. Lee, P. T. Beauregard, and John B. Gordon had been drawn into such an undertaking.

The Nation editors themselves had no such far-reaching vision, but they did make every effort for elemental justice for the freedman. Gradually, however, this prime purpose of *The Nation* became less and less important. Godkin had a genius for politics, for analyzing issues and exposing political frauds, and was far too big a man to be tied down to one cause. He had his limitations, which I have often stressed; they were the limitations of the followers of the Manchester school in England, of Cobden and of Bright. Labor questions Mr. Godkin rarely judged aright. On the question of the enfranchisement of women his blind eye was at the telescope, though he fought bravely for their higher education and achieved a great deal, much more than he has been given credit for. He was one of the first American editors of the post-Civil War era to sound an authoritative note in dealing with foreign problems; his "leaders" on Europe never failed to attract attention on both sides of the Atlantic. The measure of his judgment and power in dealing with domestic affairs is found in the fact that no historian can write of the history of the United States from 1865 to 1905 without turning to the pages of this journal. There is not another weekly embalmed in our public libraries that is so often quoted by historians and so regularly treated as an authoritative source.

If Godkin was, as James Bryce called him, "a stringent economist" of the "old orthodox type," he was always clearness and courage personified. "The paper was the man, and the man was the paper." And the man never advocated anything that he did not believe in with passionate conviction. Never did he stop to consider the interests of the stockholders; so that the paper was often in financial difficulties and was perishing when it came into the hands of Henry and Fanny Garrison Villard in 1881. Bryce also pointed out that Godkin's judgments were severe because of the rigidity of his standards; he might have added that these standards were higher than any so far set up in American journalism. Bryce, often a politician himself, felt that they were at times too high; he remonstrated with Godkin for not allowing sufficiently for the "difficulties in which honorable and public-spirited men are placed by the exigencies of practical politics." But Godkin, being wholly outside the political game, was able to see how bitterly the American people often paid for those compromises, how many times they were unnecessary, how often politicians compromised before there was any exigency.

I defy any fair-minded man to read *The Nation* of Godkin and

Villard's "Nation"

BY LEWIS S. GANNETT

1940

I doubt that there was ever another such journalistic heaven as was *The Nation* in the early post-war years. I came back from France that autumn of 1919 with one ambition in all the world: to land a job on Villard's *Nation*. I knew what I wanted, and was blissful when I got it: half-time at first, and small pay.

Those were rousing days on Vesey Street. Every week's issue was a new adventure. The country was still in a state of war shock: it was blockading Germans, seeing Reds under every bed, crushing strikes in the name of freedom. And yet there was a breeze of hope in the air, a stirring all around the world. The British Labor Party seemed about to reshape England by a peaceful, democratic revolution; the new German Republic was giving women the vote and establishing works councils in every factory; Russia was a land of wild surmises, where every new and hopeful experiment might be tried out for an eager world to watch. Here at home we had the Plumb plan, a sort of industrial republic for the railroads; new unions about to organize the steel mills; labor banks booming, a hope of a great Farmer-Labor Party —in 1924 it seemed about to flower with La Follette. And there was exhilaration in fighting the whole wicked world.

Was there ever a day when the American press did quite as much lying? Even the "crusading" New York *World* waited until after the steel strike was crushed to tell a little truth about it; we on *The Nation* had fresh news, not printed in the big papers, almost every week. The *Times* and the other papers were killing off Lenin and Trotsky and crushing the Russian Revolution three times a week; we had our own reports. We were the first to print, in the International Relations Section, the new Russian constitution, the anti-imperialist treaties, new land laws in the border republics, as well as to expose secret treaties pre- and post-war, suppressed reports of pogroms in Poland, and documents on skulduggery in five continents. It is almost impossible to believe today that a world could ever have seemed so full of hope—or so full of such sinister machinations as *The Nation* was privileged to expose, week after week.

It was an exciting office in which to work. Most of us were young, and a little afraid of austere William MacDonald, who set our grammar straight and threw out our more extreme effusions. (But it was Mac-Donald himself who, when New Yorkers were sleeping in the streets, wrote that famous editorial, Seize Every Empty House, which so shocked Oswald Villard on his return from the West.) When, in 1922, the staff celebrated Villard's fiftieth birthday, it seemed to many of us that he was a phenomenally well-preserved old man. Among ourselves, we said that we admired him because he had had the courage to change his views on so many questions after reaching the hale old age of forty, when most men's minds were crusted; but when we tried to suggest that to our chief, he would thunder that he had never wavered from the true Godkin-Garrison-Villard tradition.

Albert Jay Nock was halfway on and halfway off the staff, dreaming of his brief and brilliant *Freeman;* he would read bits of "Wolfville" and of Artemus Ward at staff dinners. Henry Mussey, in one of his unprofessorial interludes, was our managing editor. Soon after Mussey returned to academic pastures, Ernest Gruening breezed into the office, charging in a dozen directions at once. We saved Haiti week after week, until the grateful Haitians proposed erecting a statue to Gruening's living memory. We got the troops out of Santo Domingo. It was Gruening who planned and carried out the famous series of articles on These United States. He was a man of sterling editorial principles. If memory serves me right, he persuaded both Carl Sandburg and Edgar Lee Masters to write articles on Illinois, and then rejected them both as not up to our penny-a-word standard. With difficulty we reverent juniors persuaded him not to reject Dreiser's article on Indiana.

It was Ernest Gruening's comfortable theory that an article, if you keep it long enough, always becomes timely. No matter what world-shaking event blazed in the newspaper headlines, he could always rummage in a desk drawer and come out with a "timely" article to meet the situation. In off weeks he went back to saving Haiti. Mr. Villard sometimes thought that Haiti wasn't really lead-article subject matter more than once or twice a month.

Gruening also was the staff lowbrow. Most of us were soundly in awe of Carl Van Doren and Ludwig Lewisohn; if they said a poem was good, we believed it, whether we could understand it or not. I once innocently spoiled one of Ernest's efforts to prove that we were wrong. I was closing the forms at the Nation Press one Tuesday morning, when a printer came to me querying a four-line poem at the foot of a column. It didn't make sense, he said. I thought perhaps a line had fallen out, and tried to find the original manuscript; I sought vainly to telephone Carl Van Doren. Finally, I took the quatrain out, and somehow filled the space. Carl, when located, said he had never seen the lines; Ernest Gruening, we discovered, had composed a little free verse of his own, with no meaning whatever, and believed that no reader would recognize it as different from the modern poetry selected by our literary editor.

Those were the days when "Hot Afternoons Have Been in Montana" won our poetry prize, Gruening and Villard's negative votes being outweighed by the enthusiastic juniors of the staff. Bob Benchley celebrated that poem with a famous parody, "Cold Mornings Have Been in Bensonhurst," and the prize-winner had cards printed reading, "Eli Siegel, Author of Hot Afternoons Have Been in Montana."

Norman Thomas was with us for two years; shy Arthur Gleason tried for a time to match his analytic spirit with our crusading zeal. George Soule, now of the *New Republic*, was briefly on the staff; so was Stuart Chase, but he had a flip way of throwing custard pies in his paragraphs which irked Mr. Villard's sense of the paper's dignity. Mr. Villard was a fighting liberal who yearned to be a sound conservative. He never wanted to do what Godkin and Garrison would not have done, and he always had to be persuaded into any break with tradition. Such liberals are often more effective than those who battle on all fronts at once, yet I still think that Stuart Chase writes rousing American English.

We all had a reverence for good writing though we differed in our definition of the word "good"; and in those days proofreading was an art. George Schumm, who had given his life to proofreading for lost causes, was our tutor. (He had worked for twenty years with Benjamin R. Tucker, that philosopher of American individualism who never rated a showing in "Who's Who" but had a half column in the "Encyclopedia Britannica," by Prince Kropotkin; Tucker died last year, without an obit in the newspapers of his own country.) I remember a succession of evening sessions—we were eager to work overtime—at which we hotly argued the more controversial uses of commas, colons, capitals, and italics. Under Carl Van Doren's leadership we reedited the University of Chicago Style Book; and Papa Schumm held us to it rigidly.

Carl Van Doren was, I still think, the greatest literary editor of this century. He had a genius for recognizing budding talent; the best young men and women in all the country's universities were proud to review for him; and when he painstakingly cut their prolix writing to the bone, and sent them proofs of his abridged versions of their scripts, they would write back thanking him, saying that they had not realized they could write so well. We believed in "editing," and learned to do it conscientiously. It was *The Nation*'s province, then as now, to recognize the important in a swamp of ill-written words, and to snake it out of the mire. *The Nation* never paid well; but people wrote avidly, from universities and from mining camps, eager to tell a story that the newspapers were missing. (Silas Bent coined the epigram: "To read *The Nation* is a necessity; to write for it is a luxury.") Freda Kirchwey developed a special genius at reworking manuscripts which at first seemed impossible, preserving the personality of the writer yet organizing a mushy text into new coherence and force.

It wasn't only the inarticulate who wrote for us; some of the best writers in America appeared in our pages, often as not anonymously. I understood what style meant when, making up the editorial pages, I found it necessary to add or subtract a line from Ludwig Lewisohn's copy, to bring the columns out even. Usually it was easy to insert or excise an adjective, or rephrase a sentence, to fill or cut a line. But the smallest word changed in Lewisohn's text obviously spoiled the rhythm. That was true only to a lesser extent of Joseph Wood Krutch's flowing prose.

Arthur Warner, best loved and most crotchety of the staff, had a special collection of hobbies. He hated the invading automobiles; and he loved to write of good American food. To that writing he brought a passion born of the fact that his own diet was perforce almost entirely restricted to milk toast, made with whole wheat bread. Warner was the staff handy man; it was he who exposed the "Myth of Calvin Coolidge" and therewith coined a phrase that became part of the language. Warner joined *The Nation* on his way out from the old New York *Evening Post*, then in the same building with us. He stopped on the fourth floor to report that he had been fired for writing a round-robin in behalf of a surreptitious newspapermen's union, and was promptly taken on *The Nation*'s staff. Later, from our office, he made another effort to organize such a union; Heywood Broun became its president, and so in a sense Warner as much as Broun was founder of the now flourishing Newspaper Guild. Broun too joined *The Nation* as a regular when the *World* dropped him, and his shambling presence added a new note to our Thursday morning editorial conferences.

The Nation had inherited plenty of causes from Godkin and Garrison; each week it took on new ones. It was avowedly and outspokenly a fighting, muckraking magazine. In the early years we worked at getting the Allies out of Russia; soon we were feeding the victims of famine. We were the first to denounce the Treaty of Versailles. Ernest Gruening lived in a perpetual anti-lynching crusade, and kept a special eye on Mexico and the Caribbean. Bill Hard came up from Washington and announced his expectation of blasting five members out of the Harding Cabinet; ably assisted by the elder La Follette, Wheeler, Walsh, and others, he almost succeeded. We were always eager to second that grandest of all the old Romans, George Norris of Nebraska, in what then seemed his almost hopeless crusade to save Muscle Shoals from the spoilsmen; few then dared to dream of such a Utopia as the TVA of today. The fabulous Paul Anderson, who succeeded Hard as our Washington correspondent, of course dared anything—dream or attack—and was miraculously effective.

One morning Dr. W. J. Maloney walked into conference with a plan to scare Britain into recalling the Black and Tans from Ireland. Before noon *The Nation's* Committee of One Hundred on Ireland was born; within a few months the famous Commission of Inquiry was sitting in Washington, and the Black and Tan atrocities were forced on public attention. The lovely Muriel and the fierce Mary MacSwiney came to America under our auspices, and in time the Republic of Eire was born. We felt partially responsible.

We sent Carleton Beals to Nicaragua to interview Sandino, the little rebel general for whom the American army was hunting in vain; Beals found him, and *The Nation* scored an impressive "scoop." Mr. Villard sent me off to China just in time to catch the leaders of both wings of the embryonic Nationalist state idling in Canton. Joseph Wood Krutch, Tennessee-born, interpreted Darrow, Bryan, and the "monkey trial" in Dayton as only an enlightened Tennessean could. Freda Kirchwey was always discovering and defending rebels in the colleges; she was also the New Woman editor, the Sex editor, and the Modern Morals editor. She edited the symposium on "Our Changing Morality" which later appeared in book form; she also assembled the series of anonymous autobiographies of "These Modern Women," which, had they been signed, would have produced an even bigger stir. Civilization was at the crossroads every week; some flip editor suggested that as a standing head for our lead editorial.

The noble succession of Van Dorens—Carl, Irita, Mark, and Dorothy—held the journal's literary standards high; there was a strange interlude when big-hearted John Macy dealt out books to reviewers selected rather for their need of money than for their authority. Macy's own criticism was incisive, his judgment of reviewers almost purely humanitarian.

Always "the Boss" was the heart of the paper. Villard's infectious moral indignation inspired us all; his natural gift for story-telling made his every return from an out-of-town crusade an adventure for the staff; his genius for friendship constantly brought new life into our pages. He had that capacity for perpetual excitement which is the essential of the good newspaperman. Sometimes we thought him too loyal to the Godkin-Garrison tradition; it was only after a long fight that Freda Kirchwey succeeded in introducing cartoons into the paper's chaste pages. When, in 1925, we actually printed a script for a "movie"—Mr. Villard insisted that we put that word in quotation marks, or else say "motion picture"—he felt we had betrayed him in his absence.

Sometimes, outvoted by his juniors, our democratic leader turned dictator, and vetoed our frivolous revolutions—in perspective one can see that he was often right. He wouldn't let us print an irreverent, rollicking piece that Bill Hard wrote about him, exposing him as a thunderer in public, who had "made more acres of public men acutely miserable, per unit of circulation, than any other editor alive," but a sunny story-teller in private, almost enjoying his own embittered indignations. Hard even burst into verse:

> When Oswald isn't following his employment—
> > his employment
> Of devastating all the public scene,
> His capacity for innocent enjoyment—
> > cent enjoyment
> Would make the joyous public man turn green.

We cussed him and loved him, listened and learned. *The Nation* of the nineteen twenties was a great school—for its editors and for America. What "Main Street," "Winesburg, Ohio," and "Spoon River" were in other fields of literature, *The Nation* was to journalism. It still is.

"Free Inquiry and Free Endeavor"

BY I. F. STONE

1940

To understand *The Nation's* past one must understand Edwin Law-rence Godkin. Godkin was more than the founder of *The Nation*. Though many other able and brilliant men contributed regularly to its pages *The Nation* for more than thirty years was synonymous with Godkin and Godkin with *The Nation*. His approach to economic problems, that of a laissez faire liberal, still dominated *The Nation* at its fiftieth birthday, thirteen years after his death. Godkin's moralistic approach to politics and politicians, which made him seem a Jeremiah to his admirers and a cantankerous perfectionist to his critics, was also Oswald Garrison Villard's and may still be found in the pages of *The Nation*. Godkin's most admirable characteristic as an editor was his independence, and this is still *The Nation's* ideal.

Godkin's independence was part of the atmosphere in which he was reared. His father was a Presbyterian minister in Catholic Ireland, but one whose devotion to Home Rule cost him his pulpit. Godkin's basic ideas on economics and society were acquired in the '40's. He entered Queen's College, Belfast, in 1846, and there, as he wrote many years later, "John Stuart Mill was our prophet, and Grote and Bentham were our daily food." These writers, fast becoming little more than names, were once new windows on the world. To a generation brought up on the history of Greece as written by Whig or Tory to illustrate "the dangerous turbulence of democracy," Grote's "History," with its glamorous picture of Athenian self-government as seen through the eyes of a philosophical radical, came as an inspiring revelation.

The outlines of a collectivist future that Godkin always regarded as the shadow of outworn fallacies rather than of coming truths were already visible in positivism and the first writings of socialism, in Mill's own budding doubts, and in the very rationale of utilitarianism itself. But to the young men of the British middle classes in Godkin's student days, and for many years after, laissez faire liberalism was almost a religious faith. The complex of ideas that now provides the toothless apologetics of an American Liberty League was then a rich and blooming hope. Like Marxism later, it seemed to promise an end of tyranny, poverty, ignorance, and war; and like Marxism it seemed no utopian dream but a body of inescapable conclusions from the observed facts of history and human nature. The visible embodiment of these ideals, the proof of their practicability, the guaranty of their ultimate achievement, was America, as Soviet Russia was to be for many radicals in our time. "I have said," Godkin wrote, "that John Stuart Mill was our prophet, but America was our promised land. To the scoffs of the Tories that our schemes were impracticable, our answer was that in America, barring slavery, they were actually at work." Their knowledge of America, as he recorded it, was drawn largely from de Tocqueville, and they could have had no better guide, for the latter's vision was distorted neither by millennial delusions nor by aristocratic antipathy.

These were the sources of the ideals and preconceptions with which Godkin, after turning down the editorship of the Belfast *Whig*, came to America in 1856, "on the eve of the Presidential election. The air . . . full of the discussion about slavery. The excitement . . . tremendous." Three months after Appomattox he launched *The Nation*, its name the product of a boyhood admiration for a weekly of the same name established in Dublin in 1842 and described as "remarkable for its talent, for its seditious tendencies, and for the fire and spirit of its political poetry."

When the first issue of *The Nation* appeared, on July 6, 1865, Godkin was thirty-three. He was to change little, but America much, before he relinquished the editorship in 1899. *The Nation* and its founder started under certain initial disadvantages. Their idealism could have found no more incongruous setting than the America of the Gilded Age. The laissez faire that *The Nation* was to preach, though one of the favorite optical illusions of American politics and constitutional law, was never really a dominant American philosophy. Business men opposed government aid to workers and farmers, and workers and farmers opposed government aid to business. But neither opposed government aid to themselves.

If Cobden symbolizes British capitalism, Hamilton symbolizes American, and Hamilton, with his plea for protective tariffs and subsidies, and his frank manipulation of governmental devices to encourage enterprise, was no follower of Adam Smith. Free trade itself began to seem a device for maintaining British industrial supremacy; French and German policy alike soon turned Hamiltonian to build up national industries. Our business interests have always found their political vehicle in parties which never permitted lip service to laissez faire to interfere with aid to business—the Federalists under Hamilton, the Whigs under Clay and Webster, the Republicans through McKinley to Hoover. The Jeffersonians, it is true, believed that government best which governs least, but our parties of the lower middle class, whether under Jefferson, Jackson, Wilson, or Franklin D. Roosevelt, were as ready as the Hamiltonians to use state power, when in office, for the advancement of their own class interests and economic welfare. Our early working class movements, as far back as the 1830's, were socialistic, and if British middle-class intellectuals in the '40's read Mill, American middle-class intellectuals in the '40's grew up in the shadow of Brook Farm, discussed Fourierism, and encountered socialism in Horace Greeley's *Tribune*.

Out of power each of the two major parties was wont to denounce the other for using the state for its own purposes, and laissez faire slogans came to be more and more strongly used to combat social legislation from the 70's on. Charles A. Dana set the fashion of preaching rugged individualism to workers while advocating higher tariffs for the manufacturers and bigger land grants for the railroad promoters. But to advocate laissez faire consistently and honestly, as *The Nation* and Godkin did, was to adopt a lonely and ineffectual attitude—hostile to the capitalist trend toward monopoly, hostile to the agrarian cry for regulation of railroads and business, hostile to the workers' attempts at collective action. In England the advocate of laissez faire marched in the triumphant ranks of the merchants and manufacturers; in America he fought a hopeless rear-guard action in the retreating forces of small business men, *rentiers*, and the Adams family. *The Nation* under Godkin attacked the Grangers, the Populists, the trade unions, the single-taxers, and the Socialists, as well as the trusts, the railroad barons, the tariff log-rollers, and the stockjobbing financiers. But the second group was to transform our economy and the first our politics until laissez faire liberalism, once a revolutionary and liberating force, became the slogan of reactionaries. *The Nation*, which was always liberal, thus grew less and less progressive. Finally, separated from the genteel and enlightened free-trade conservatism of the pre-war New York *Evening Post*, *The Nation* from 1917 on was to become what its founder would have termed "communistic."

SCHOLARS AND GENTLEMEN

Godkin and his pre-war successors labored under another disadvantage. They were not merely intellectuals; they were also gentlemen. They were fastidious to begin with, and history in the making is sadly unrefined. At their worst they grew querulous, and seemed to scold rather than instruct. Wendell Phillips Garrison, Horace White, Rollo Ogden, Harold de Wolf Fuller, Paul Elmer More, Hammond Lamont were all what it was once customary to term men of good family. Some of them, like Godkin himself as he grew older, tended to be snobbish. The pages of the old *Nation* are full of amusing illustrations of this tendency. It was always calling men it disliked "vulgar," and Dana found no better way to make Godkin writhe than by referring to him in print as "Larry" Godkin. To Godkin commenting on the Commune in Paris, "perhaps the most striking incident of the crisis" was that "veritable workingmen sit in council in the gilded saloons of the Hotel de Ville and are waited upon by lackeys in livery." Godkin could be more Tory than the Tories in his social prejudices. In 1900 we find him mourning the fact that since Peel's day the English upper classes "have never been content with a statesman of their own order" but had picked in Disraeli "a Jewish literary adventurer" (this was snobbery, not anti-Semitism) and in Joseph Chamberlain "a dealer in screws." Godkin wrote of Mill, "He suffered in his treatment of all the questions of the day from excess of culture and deficiency of blood"; but the judgment applies far better to Godkin and his pre-war successors than to Mill, for Mill's humanity in later years overcame his preconceptions and led him first to disavow the wage-fund theory and then to move toward socialism. It was easier for Godkin and his associates to see the absurdities than the strength of the new men and movements coming up about them: on the one hand the get-rich-quick vulgarians of capitalism, and on the other a procession of characters that seemed monstrosities to *The Nation*—Powderly and Debs, Donnelly and Bryan, a Coin Harvey and a Sockless Jerry Simpson.

Certain pages in the old *Nation* make strange reading. *The Nation* felt in 1865 that if the movement for an eight-hour day were successful, "the time is not far distant when all things will be in common and grass grow in Broadway." "Last winter," *The Nation* said in 1874 of the Granger movement for railroad regulation, "the Grangers came to the conclusion that what they wanted was reduction of the rates; next winter their fancy may take another turn, and they may think that each passenger ought to have a car for himself, with meals along the route furnished gratis by the company." In 1878 *The Nation* was worried because many newspapers, though "troubled by the growth of communism among the working classes in this country," yet favored the income tax. *The Nation* accused these newspapers of "forgetting that communistic ideas were started by the Western farmers in the Granger movement, and that nothing is more natural than that the doctrines about property which were promulgated passionately by persons who simply wished to impose on others part of the burden of carrying their goods to market, should have found expression in pillage and arson two or three years later among suffering operatives." In 1884 *The Nation* attacked the platform committee at that year's Republican convention for "catering to the tastes and dogmas of the Communists" because it proposed to bar contract labor, oppose acquisition of large tracts of land by corporations or individuals, and enforce the eight-hour law on government work. *The Nation's* advice on the Anarchist movement in 1887 was not to "be afraid of making 'martyrs' of their leading scoundrels by hanging them." "Debs Desperadoes" it named the Pullman strikers in 1894, and it called Altgeld "boorish, impudent, and ignorant" for objecting to the use of federal troops to break the strike. In Coxey's Army that same year it saw only "loafers and tramps." It defended Briand against Jaurès in 1911 after the former broke the French railway strike by martial law, and it disapproved when Lloyd George introduced a bill for sickness and unemployment insurance. It termed Theodore Roosevelt "reckless, cruel, and incendiary" in his attacks on the courts and supported Wilson in 1912, only to be disappointed when he surrendered to railway labor's demand for the eight-hour day in 1916. It thought the appointment of Louis D. Brandeis to the United States Supreme Court a mistake. *The Nation* felt that he had given no proof of possessing "the true judicial habit of mind."

LAISSEZ FAIRE PURITY

Labor didn't like the old *Nation*, but neither did Wall Street. The very first issue contained both an advertisement inserted by the leading financier of the time, Jay Cooke, and a criticism of him. In 1866, to those who would limit the franchise to men of property, it replied, "Wealthy men control our railroad corporations; what has been the degree of honor and regard for the public good with which these institutions have been managed?" Long before Matthew Josephson's "Robber Barons," *The Nation* was talking of our railroad magnates in the same terms. "No generation of feudal barons in the fourteenth century," *The Nation* said in 1868, ". . . ever . . . lived more openly or undisguisedly by force or fraud than do the railroad men of our time." Striking coal miners in 1871 seemed to *The Nation* to be engaged in an attempt to "corner" the public. But "the business of 'cornering' the public," *The Nation* pointed out, "that is, of extorting money from it by the sudden production of artificial scarcity for the benefit of one class or body, was first begun by capitalists for their own benefit, and they carried it on with the aid of legislation in nearly every civilized country for centuries, without admitting laborers to any share of the profits, or booty, whichever one pleases to call it." When Senator Hoar wrote Coxey that "5,000 or 10,000 men have no right to dictate to the other 65,000,000" in their demands for jobless relief, *The Nation* commented in a similar vein. "It is a pity," it said, "Senator Hoar did not find out sooner that he acted for a majority of the entire people, and not for 5,000 or 10,000 men. Since 1861 there have been twenty-two changes made in the tariff, all increases. Now nearly every one of these changes was made, not at the request of 65,000,000 people, but of small parties of men, sometimes solitary individuals."

In 1911 *The Nation* applauded when Justice Hughes for the Supreme Court held an Alabama peonage law unconstitutional, and when President Taft refused to pardon a rich man sentenced to prison for violation of the law. "Fines are not effective against men of wealth," *The Nation* declared, "imprisonment is necessary." In 1913 it attacked "our blatant Navy League" as formed in the interest of "battleship builders, organizers of ship trusts, and producers of nickel steel," and in a long editorial called attention to the revelations being made by "Dr. Liebknecht" in Berlin as to the part played by munitions makers in fomenting international ill-will. That same year, when the government opened its attack on George W. Perkins and the Harvester trust, *The Nation* dealt scornfully with the defenses customarily put forward by the trusts. "Out of court," *The Nation* commented, "the trust advocates never tire of inveighing against the outworn, medieval theory of competition in contrast with the new and 'inevitable' law of combination. In court they usually argue that there is no such thing as monopoly, and that equality of opportunity in business flourishes under the stimulus of scientific cooperation; cooperation being that principle of business by which George W. Perkins, instead of competing with his rivals, works harmoniously with himself."

The one public figure the old *Nation* really admired was Grover Cleveland, though it did not hesitate to criticize him sharply in the Venezuela incident. It stood as he did for a low tariff, economy, and clean government. In respect to this last issue *The Nation* was a little more than merely "goo-goo." It saw farther than the civil-service reformers with whom it went forth to battle against crooked politicians. It was not enough to place good men in public office. It was also necessary to strike at the causes of corruption. "The remedy," *The*

Nation said after the Credit Mobilier scandal, "is simple. The government must get out of the 'protective' business and the 'subsidy' business and the 'improvement' business and the 'development' business. It must let trade, and commerce, and manufactures, and steamboats, and railroads, and telegraphs alone. It cannot touch them without breeding corruption."

THE OLD AND THE NEW

The Nation after the World War, though still an organ of middle-class intellectuals, came more and more to draw its strength from contact with and sympathy for the labor movement, and to seek a counterpoise to big business in social legislation and in the organization of farmer and worker instead of hoping for a return to laissez faire. The old *Nation* applauded the hanging of the Chicago Anarchists; the new fought for Sacco and Vanzetti. The old denounced Debs; the new, in 1920, urged its readers to vote for him or Christensen. The old *Nation* saw in social legislation a reversion to a medieval world of fixed prices and wages; the new *Nation* saw in it the beginnings of a new society.

But between the old *Nation* and the new there are also many bonds. One of the principal purposes for which *The Nation* was founded was to defend the interests of the newly freed Negro. It consistently opposed American imperialism and spoke in behalf of the Latin American and Filipino peoples we have from time to time oppressed and exploited. It never permitted loyalty to party or person to outweigh loyalty to truth. It always resisted jingoism and war. The yellowing pages, with their vigor, their learning, their wit, their irony, can still inspire as well as exasperate. Godkin and his associates hated cant, falsity, tyranny, buncombe. Godkin dedicated *The Nation* to the defense of "free inquiry and free endeavor." "Free endeavor," in the sense that Godkin understood it, is no longer *The Nation's* ideal; but "free inquiry" still is its language, in 1940 as in 1865.

A Half-Hour at Herculaneum

BY WILLIAM DEAN HOWELLS

1866

The road from Naples to Herculaneum is, in fact, one long street; it hardly ceases to be city in Naples till it is town at Portici, and in the interval it is suburb, running between palatial lines of villas, which all have their names ambitiously painted over their doors. Great part of the distance this street is bordered by the bay, and, as far as this is the case, it is picturesque, as everything is belonging to marine life in Italy. Everywhere seafaring people go lounging up and down among the fishermen's boats drawn up on the shore, and the fishermen's wives making nets, and the fishermen's children playing and clambering over both, while over all flap and flutter the clothes hung on poles to dry. In this part of the street there are, of course, oysters, and grapes, and oranges, and cactus-pulps, and cutlery, and iced drinks to sell at various booths; and commerce is exceedingly dramatic and boisterous over the bargains she offers there; and equally, of course, murderous drinking shops lurk at intervals along the pavement, and lure into their recesses mariners of foreign birth, briefly ashore from their ships. The New York Coffee House is there to attract my maritime fellow-country-men, and I know that if I look into that place of refreshment I shall see their honest, foolish faces flushed with drink, and the excitement of buying the least they can for the most money. Poor souls! they shall drink that pleasant morning away in the society of Antonino the best of Neapolitans, and at midnight, emptied of every soldo, shall arise, wrung with a fearful suspicion of treachery, and wander away under Antonino's guidance to seek the protection of the consul; or, taking the law into their own hands, shall proceed to clean out, *more Americano*, the New York Coffee House, where Antonino shall develop into one of the landlords, and deal them the most artistic stab in Naples: handsome, worthy Antonino, tender-eyed, subtle, pitiless!

II

Where the road to Herculaneum leaves the bay and its seafaring life, it enters, between the walls of lofty, fly-blown houses, a world of maccaroni haunted by foul odors, beggars, poultry, and insects. There were few people to be seen on the street, but through the open doors of the lofty fly-blown houses we saw floury legions at work making maccaroni; grinding maccaroni, rolling it, cutting it, hanging it in mighty skeins to dry, and gathering it when dried, and putting it away. By the frequency of the wine-shops we judged that the legions were a thirsty host, and by the number of the barber-surgeons' shops that they were a plethoric and too full-blooded host. I think the latter were in the proportion of one to five of the former; and the artist who had painted their signs had indulged his fancy in wild excesses of phlebotomy. We had found that, as we came south from Venice, science grew more and more sanguinary in Italy, and more and more disposed to let blood. At Ferrara, even, the propensity began to be manifest on the barbers' signs, which displayed the device of an arm lanced at the elbow, and jetting the blood by a neatly described parabola into a tumbler. Further south the same arm was seen to bleed at the wrist also; and at Naples an exhaustive treatment of the subject appeared, the favorite study of the artist being to represent a nude figure reclining in a genteel attitude on a bank of pleasant green sward, and bleeding from his elbows, wrists, hands, ankles, and feet.

Phlebotomy and the manufacture of maccaroni may be distinct branches of industry at Naples, and I do not deny that they are; but I have never in my own mind been able to dissociate them since the day of my ride to Herculaneum.

III

In Naples everywhere one is surprised by the great number of English names which appear on business-houses, but it was entirely bewildering to read a bill affixed to the gate of one of the villas on this road: "This Desirable Property for Sale." I should scarcely have cared to buy that desirable property, though the neighborhood seemed to be a favorite summer resort, and there were villas, as I said, nearly the whole way to Portici. Those villas which stood with their gardens towards the bay would have been tolerable, no doubt, if they could have kept their windows shut to the vile street before their doors; but the houses opposite could have had no escape from its stench and noisomeness. It was absolutely the filthiest street I have seen anywhere outside of New York, excepting only that little street which, in Herculaneum, leads from the theatre to the house of Argo. This pleasant avenue has a stream of turbid water in its centre, bordered by begging children, and is either fouler or cleaner for the water, but I shall never know which. It is at a depth of some fifty or sixty feet below the elevation on which the present city of Portici is built, and is part of the excavation made long ago to reach the plain on which Herculaneum stands, buried under its half-score of successive layers of lava, and ashes, and Portici. We had the aid of all the virtuous poverty and leisure of the modern town—there was a vast deal of both, we found—in our search for the staircase by which you descend to the classic plain, and we found it a discovery involving the outlay of all the copper coin about us, while the sight of the famous theatre of Herculaneum was much more expensive than it would have been had we come there in the old time to see a play of Plautus or Terence. As for the theatre, "the large and highly ornamented theatre" of which I read, only a little while ago, in an encyclopædia, we found it, by the light of our candles, a series of gloomy hollows, of the general complexion of coal-bins and potato-cellars. It was never perfectly dug out of the lava, and it is known how it was filled up, together with other excavations, when they once threatened to endanger the foundations of worthless Portici overhead. I am amused to find myself so hot upon the poor property-holders of Portici. I suppose I should not myself, even for the cause of antiquity and the knowledge of classic civilization, like to have my house tumbled about my ears. But though it was impossible in the theatre of Herculaneum to gain any idea of its size or richness, I remembered then the magnificent bronzes which had been found in it, and did a hasty reverence to the place. Indeed, it is amazing, when one sees how small a part of Herculaneum has been uncovered, to consider the number of fine works of art in the Museo Borbonico which were taken thence, and which argue a much richer and more refined community than that of Pompeii. A third of the latter city has now been restored to the light of day; but though it has yielded abundance of all the things that illustrate the domestic and public life, and the luxury and depravity of those old times, and has given the once-secret rooms of the museum their worst attraction, it still falls far below Herculaneum in the value of its contributions to the treasures of classic art, except only in the variety and beauty of its exquisite frescoes. The effect of this fact is to stimulate the imagination of the visitor to that degree that nothing short of the instant destruction of Portici and the excavation of all Herculaneum will satisfy him. If the opening of one theatre, and the uncovering of a basilica and two or three houses, have given such richness to us, what delight and knowledge would not the removal of these obdurate hills of ashes and lava bestow!

Emerging from the coal-bins and potato-cellars, the visitor extinguishes his candle with a pathetic sigh, profusely rewards the custodian (whom he connects in some mysterious way with the ancient population of the injured city about him), and, thoughtfully removing the tallow from his fingers, follows the course of the vile stream already sung, and soon arrives at the gate opening into the exhumed quarter of Herculaneum. And there he finds a custodian who enters perfectly into his feelings; a custodian who has once been a guide in Pompeii, but now despises that wretched town, and would not be guide there for any money, since he has known the superior life of Herculaneum; who, in fine, feels towards Pompeii as a Bostonian feels towards New York. Yet the reader would be wrong to form the idea that there is bitterness in the disdain of this custodian. On the contrary, he is one of the best-natured men in the world. He is a mighty mass of pingueous bronze, with a fat lisp, and a broad, sun-flower smile, and he lectures us with a vast and genial breadth of manner on the ruins, contradicting all our guesses at things with a sweet "Perdoni, signori! ma——." At the end, we find that he has some medallions of lava to sell: there is Victor Emanuel, or, if we are of the *partito d'azione*, there is Garibaldi; both warm yet from the crater of Vesuvius, and of the same material which destroyed Herculaneum. We decline to buy, and the custodian makes the national shrug and grimace (signifying that we are masters of the situation, and he washes his hands of the consequences of our folly) on the largest scale that we have ever seen; his mighty hands are rigidly thrust forth, his great lip protruded, his enormous head thrown back to bring his face on a level with his chin. The effect is tremendous, but we, nevertheless, feel that he loves us the same.

IV

The afternoon on which we visited Herculaneum was in melancholy contrast to the day we spent in Pompeii. The lingering summer had at last saddened into something like autumnal gloom, and that blue, blue sky of Naples was overcast. So, this second draught of the spirit of the past had not only something of the insipidity of custom, but brought rather a depression than a lightness to our hearts. There was so little of Herculaneum: only a few hundred yards square are exhumed, and we counted the houses easily on the fingers of one hand, leaving the thumb to stand for the few rods of street that, with its flagging of lava and narrow border of footwalks, lay between; and though the custodian, apparently moved at our dejection, said that the excavation was to be resumed the very next week, the assurance did little to restore our cheerfulness. Indeed, I fancy that these old cities must needs be seen in the sunshine by those who would feel what gay lives they had once led; by dimmer light they are very sullen spectres, and their doom still seems to brood upon them. I know that even Pompeii could not have been joyous that sunless afternoon, for what there was to see of mournful Herculaneum was as brilliant with colors as anything in the former city. Nay, I believe that the tints of the frescoes and painted columns were even brighter, and the walls of the houses were far less ruinous than those of Pompeii. But no house was wholly freed from lava, and the little street ran at the rear of the buildings which were supposed to front on some grander avenue not yet exhumed. It led down, as the custodian pretended, to a wharf, and he showed an iron ring in the wall of the house of Argo, standing at the end of the street, to which, he said, his former fellow-citizens used to fasten their boats, though it was all dry enough there now.

There is evidence in Herculaneum of much more ambitious domestic architecture than seems to have been known in Pompeii. The ground-plan of the houses in the two cities is alike; but in the former there was often a second story, as was proven by the charred ends of beams still protruding from the walls, while in the latter there is only one house which is thought to have aspired to a second floor. The house of Argo is also much larger than any in Pompeii, and its appointments were much more magnificent. Indeed, we imagined that in this more purely Greek town we felt an atmosphere of better taste in everything than prevailed in the fashionable Roman watering-place, though this, too, was a summer resort of the "best society of the empire." The mosaic pavements were exquisite, and the little bed-chambers dainty and delicious in their decorations. The lavish delight in color found expression in the vividest reds upon the walls, and not only were the columns of the garden painted, but the foliage of the capitals was tinted of various hues. The garden of Argo's house was vaster than any of the classic world which we had yet seen, and was superb with a long colonnade of unbroken columns. Between these and the walls of the houses was a pretty pathway of mosaic, and in the midst once stood marble tables, under which the workmen exhuming the city found certain crouching skeletons. At one end was the dining-room, of course, and painted on the wall was a lady with a parasol. I thought all Herculaneum sad enough, but the profusion of flowers growing wild in this garden gave it a yet more tender and pathetic charm. Here—where so long ago the flowers had bloomed, and perished in the terrible blossoming of the mountain that sent up its fires in the awful similitude of nature's harmless and lovely forms, and showered its destroying petals all abroad—was it not tragic to find again the soft tints, the graceful shapes, the sweet perfumes of the earth's immortal life? And of them that planted and tended and plucked and

bore in their bosoms and twined in their hair these fragile children of
the summer, what witness in the world? Only the crouching skeletons
under the tables. Alas and alas! Master Poet, lend us your rhymes and
your handkerchief.

V

The skeletons went with us throughout Herculaneum, and descended into the cell, all green with damp, under the basilica, and lay
down, fettered and manacled, beside the big bronze kettle there in
which the prisoners used to cook their dinners. How ghastly the jolly
thought of it was! If we had really seen this kettle and the skeletons
there—as we did not—we could not have suffered more. They took all
the life out of the house of Perseus, and the beauty from his pretty
little domestic temple to the Penates, and this was all there was left in
Herculaneum to see.

"Is there nothing else?" we demand of the custodian.

"Signori, this is all."

"It is mighty little."

"Perdoni, signori—ma!"

"Well," we say sourly to each other, glancing round at the walls of
the pit, on the bottom of which the bit of city stands, "it is a good
thing to know that Herculaneum amounts to nothing."

The South As It Is—Vicksburg, Mississippi

BY JOHN RICHARD DENNETT

(From a special series in *The Nation*, "The South As It Is,"
by John Richard Dennett)

1866

VICKSBURG, Miss., March 8, 1866.

I set out from Baton Rouge for Vicksburg and the North on the steamboat *Columbian*. At the place where I went aboard, as at most other points, she followed the fashion of Mississippi steamboats, and made the landing with more haste than ceremony. It was pleasant to look on one Southern scene full of business-like activity and bustle—the bow scraped the bank, gangway planks were instantly pushed out, freight was rolled ashore in a hurry, people crowded aboard, jostling each other to beg a late newspaper from the clerk; the steam, all the time roaring and hissing, made the boat itself seem impatient to be off, and at the end of five minutes we were making for the middle stream.

The few passengers were mostly Northerners bound for St. Louis. One reads of the strange characters, of the gambling and hard drinking on these river boats, and I looked for something of the kind, but saw nothing of it; everything was orderly and commonplace. We were going up "against a rise," I was told, so that the water was thicker than usual with mud, and great quantities of driftwood were carried past us on the strong current, but our rate of speed was nearly eight miles an hour. Let the traveller forget that not unlikely he may be scalded to death or blown to pieces, and a voyage up the river is pleasant travelling, if only because one is constantly astonished at the grandeur and immensity of the stream, recognizes the river as a wonder of nature, and because, as he sails for days after days on into the heart of a continent, he is forced to see the vastness of the country and to think of its wealth and strength in the future.

I became acquainted with but one of my fellow-passengers. He was a man from Maine, and was then on his way home again from Texas, whither he had gone at the end of the war. He had been a photographer, he said, in Austin, and away down there that was a very profitable occupation; pictures commanded big prices. He'd have liked to stay there if the people had been a little more reasonable; but they were so down on Yankees that he was a little afraid to risk it, and, as he had been offered a good price for his gallery, he decided to sell out and get away. The soldiers were there now, but nobody knew how long they'd remain; as soon as they should go, all the Yankees that didn't want to turn rebels would have to go too. A regular Yankee soon finds out how he's looked down on, and he do' n't trust them. He himself had learned to carry a pistol all the time; everybody had to do it, and a Yankee in particular ought to go armed. Here was an example of the way in which they felt: One day he was in his back room, finishing a picture, and a couple of ladies walked into the reception room and began to examine the specimens. It so happened that he had photographed a good many of the officers, and he heard one lady say, "Why it 's a regular Yankee concern. 'Most every picture is some beast of a Yank." That was a kind of talk that always made him mad; he'd heard about enough of it, so he stepped out and said, "Madam, if those officers are Yankees, they are all gentlemen." The women walked off disgusted, and would n't have anything done. It was that style of thing that disgusted him with the Southerners. At one time they were decent, comparatively. "We 're whipped," you 'd hear 'em say—"fightin' 's played." But after the women folks got hold of them the men gave up all that, and now men and women were about alike—more disloyal than they were in '60. The niggers were going to have a good time.

This person's view of these matters was the same with that of an intelligent Northerner, whom I met in Baton Rouge. He had been travelling from Ohio to Louisiana, to seek for the remains of some unfortunate friends of his who had perished miserably in a steamboat explosion, and whose bodies, it was possible, might be found at some point between Vicksburg and the Gulf. His search had brought him into contact with all sorts of persons in several States, and he had endeavored to find out as much as possible about the opinions and feelings of the Southern people. I asked him to let me know his conclusions.

"You must understand," said he, "that in 1860 I was a strong Douglas man. I did n't like Lincoln, and the abolitionists I hated; but, of course, I was Union. As the war went on I began to believe in Lincoln, and, by the time the Emancipation Proclamation was issued, I had been educated up to it and endorsed it. As a war measure, I mean; that was how

Mr. Lincoln regarded it, and so did I. Well, since the war ended I 've been a conservative; I 've considered Stevens and Sumner dangerous men, who did n't understand the South, wanted to humble it and so on, and were standing in the way of peace. I believed what we used to hear, that the North did n't understand the South. I believe it yet, but in a very different sense. This journey has been the greatest that I ever experienced. I came out with the kindest feelings for these people down here; I wanted to see it made easy; we had whipped them, and I wanted it to rest there. I thought the South wanted it to end there. But I was tremendously mistaken. They hate us and despise us and all belonging to us. They call us cut-throats, liars, thieves, vandals, cowards, and the very scum of the earth. They actually believe it. They won't even allow that we won our own battles. 'We were overpowered by numbers,' they say; 'of course we could n't fight all Europe.' They 've said that to me more than fifty times within the last few weeks. And they say that they are the gentlemen; we are amalgamationists, mudsills, vandals, and so forth. And I 've heard and seen more brag, and lying, and profanity, and cruelty, down here, than I ever saw or heard before in all my life. The only people I find that a Northern man can make a friend of, the only ones that like the Government and believe in it, are the negroes. I 'm convinced they can vote just as intelligently as the poor whites. A Southerner would knock me down if I said that to him; but it 's true. I tell you I 'm going home to be a radical. Fight the devil with fire. I 've learned to hate Southerners as I find them, and they can hate me if they want to. I 'm a Sumner man after I get back, and I shall write out my experience for some of our papers. Every man that 's seen what I 've seen ought to let it be known. 'The North do n't understand the South,' you know, and I 'm going to help our people to see two or three things: that the chivalry hate us and despise us; that a 'nigger' they do n't consider human; that whatever harm they can do us without getting another whipping, they 've got the will to do, and mean to do, too. I wish every county in the North would send out two men, who have the confidence of their fellow-citizens, and make them travel through the South and report the true condition of things. They could n't make a true report without changing every honest administration man into a radical. I know what I was when I came out, but I could n't resist the evidence of my own senses."

It was eight o'clock in the morning when we reached Vicksburg, and it was not till the following morning that we could fully perceive the repulsiveness of the place. On that night, however, the landlord of the principal hotel assisted us to form a correct notion of it. He walked into the hall or office where most of his guests were assembled, and cried out in a loud voice as he walked up and down through the crowd, "Gentlemen, I warn you to take care of your money. Hardly a night passes that some gentleman in the house is not robbed. Let me beg you to look out for your money." Upon this my next neighbor said to me, "These d—d niggers, you see"—a reference to the waiters. But in fact the rooms contained two or three beds, and no one knew whether his room-mate was not a Vicksburg gambler or one of the people who make the city streets unsafe after nightfall.

On the next morning I walked about the place, observing with curiosity the singular bluff on which the town stands and overlooks many miles of the surrounding lowlands; and saw the semi-circular sweep of the Federal earthworks. In the streets there are still vestiges of the innermost lines of the besieged, and also of the caves or burrows in which people hid themselves from Grant's shot and shell. Not much, I suppose, has been done to remove the traces of the siege, and, if so, it is evident that the city suffered little by it.

The day was chilly, and in the afternoon I sat before the red-hot stove in one of the hotels and listened to one of those conversations which so displease most Northern travellers in the South. Perhaps a dozen people sat within hearing of the three speakers. Of the latter two were elderly men of good appearance, and the third was a young man of twenty-five or twenty-six, with a dyed moustache and insolent manners, who chewed tobacco and nursed one of his small feet, while, without modesty or hesitation, he engrossed the principal part in the conversation.

"Well," said one of the old men, "you were luckier than I was. They broke me up. I lost about fourteen thousand dollars worth of niggers, and they 've taken that lot of mine, and I 've got to go to work and make it up."

"They did n't make much out of me," the young man said. "Put a bullet through me at Baton Rouge; but I reckon they owed me that much, some of 'em. I had n't anything to lose. I was raised to work myself since I was that high."

"Ah, you were? At the North?"

"No, *sir*. Never was north of the Potomac till John Morgan went into Ohio, and if I live a hundred years I 'm never going again. Got no use for wooden hams."

"And these yer shoe-peg oats."

"What 's that?" said the other old man.

The young man explained to him: "Why, these Massachusetts and Connecticut Yankees make shoe-pegs by machinery, and they make 'em cheap, so whenever they can they shove 'em off for oats on some trader at a distance. Put a few sacks of pegs among the piles of oats, you know.

You go to New Orleans, and any of the grain-dealers will tell you all about it. Wooden nutmegs, wooden clocks, wooden hams—every d—n thing. I was talking to one of these fellows not long ago, and he beat round and would n't talk out openly. Trying to make me think he was a Southerner. Says I, 'How long have you been out from Boston?' 'Haow long have I been eout from Boston?' says he. 'Yes,' says I; 'I know a Yankee from Massachusetts whenever I see him. You 're no Southern man;' and then he owned he was n't."

"Ha! How did you know him?"

"His talk. And then they 've all got short fingers—picking up pegs, I tell 'em—and think more of half a dime than you would of a dollar. I can 't stand 'em."

"But, by George! though, I do n't see but what we 've got to stand 'em."

"Yes, if you stay here you have. What 's more, you 've got to stand nigger suffrage. You 'll have your niggers voting within a year."

"Oh, no; no, sir. That would n't be constitutional."

"Constitutional! How much constitution have you got left? Look at the nigger soldiers in the streets. You 'll have nigger suffrage in a year. Did n't you see that the niggers in Texas have sent up a petition for it? They have; and they 'll get it. Well, I expect to be in Mexico three months from now."

"You going to that new town some of our folks have got there? But a' n't the United States going to drive Maximilian out?"

"It's none of the United States's business."

"Oh, but there 's the Monroe doctrine. We've told Europe that our people a' n't going to have kings and monarchs on our soil, and you 'll see Maximilian 'll have to quit."

"Well, I a' n't in for monarchy myself. But the Mexicans are better than the Yankees and the niggers."

"Well, Johnson 's doing very well now. He do' n't believe much in the niggers, neither, and when we 're admitted into Congress we 're all right. The men that tyrannize over us now won't be in a majority then."

"All the men, North and South, that are conservatives, must unite together. There are some men at the North that behaved very well all through the war, and we must unite with them."

"All right; you gentlemen can try it."

"Well, if we can 't get in we can stay out, anyhow, and we 'll see how they can get along without us."

"If it was n't for these niggers. There 's the difficulty."

"They a' n't going to be in the way long. There a' n't half the niggers that there was. A heap of 'em 's dead. You may know that by it 's being so hard to hire 'em; there actually a' n't the niggers, and now they 're retaking 'em to Cuba, and selling 'em. Did you see that Toombs met his coachman in the street in Cuba, and found he 'd been sold there?"

"Yes," the other old man said; and Mr.——, of Hinds County, "had told him that he knew it for a fact that one cargo had gone over certain."

Then the talk went on about the injustice and folly of emancipation; how miserable the lot of the freedman must necessarily be; how cotton and sugar and rice never could be cultivated except by slave labor, and how the United States undoubtedly ought to pay the value of every emancipated slave. The young man for his part told of his battles, and, as I have repeatedly noticed on similar occasions, his audience received quite readily more than one story of cold-blooded cruelty, which, at the North, would not have been listened to by any circle of persons of equal intelligence and apparent respectability, if any one could be found to tell them there. For example, he and half a dozen of his companions being at some little distance from their command, came upon a straggling party of four Federal soldiers. Immediately after capturing the squad they stripped them of their shoes and hats. "We wanted them, you know; and if they had a fine watch or a roll of greenbacks, we wanted them too. Being on foot, they could n't keep up with us, and, of course, we were in a hurry about that time; so when we got into a piece of pine the Yanks did n't come out when we did. Do n't know whether any stray Yanks were seen round there after that. Maybe."

The headquarters of the Freedmen's Bureau for Mississippi is at Vicksburg. It is chiefly busied with a general supervision of the affairs of the colored people, and occupies itself with details only when its interference is necessary. The examination and approval of contracts is not a part of its work, and the relations between employer and employed are controlled, in the first instance at least, by the civil authorities. Through its subordinate officials, its influence is extended to every part of the State, and, as might be expected, it is not a popular institution. Every sub-assistant commissioner the assistant commissioner informs me, needs military force within call to sustain him. The freedmen are working very well, and are receiving good treatment; their labor being in great demand, it commands very good prices, and the planter finds it to his interest to use his laborers well. It is not from the oppressive acts of individuals, therefore, that the negroes suffer most injustice, but from the spirit in which the civil authorities enforce the laws. Under the provisions of the vagrant law, for example, a white man as well as a negro might be arrested; but in practice it is found

that while honest and industrious negroes are often arrested and pun-
ished, there is no arrest of notoriously idle and worthless white men.
For this state of things the spirit of public opinion is responsible; and
because this state of things exists the Bureau is a necessity. The hostility to schools for the negroes is very general, and often very bitter
and dangerous. In the middle of February a Dr. Lacy, an old man who
had started a school in Okolona, was four times shot at as he walked in
the street for no other reason than that he was a teacher of negroes.

Such cases, whenever they occur, are reported by the officers of the
Bureau to the military commander, General T. J. Woods. The case of
Dr. Lacy has been reported. As yet nothing has been done in reference
to it. In the town of Fayette the people will not permit schools to be
maintained, and in Grenada they will not permit them to be opened.

In the face of such opposition, 5,240 children have been gathered
into schools, and are receiving instruction from about 70 teachers, who
are paid in small part by their pupils, but mainly by the Northern
charitable associations. In the monthly reports returned by these teachers they are required, I notice, to give the number of pupils in their
charge whose blood is mixed, and the number of those whose blood is
purely African. Taking the returns of twelve schools which happened
to be first set down in the consolidated report, I find it stated that, in
the opinion of the teachers, the children of African blood number 287,
and those of mixed blood number 777. A majority of the scholars live
in the towns and cities.

In the office of the assistant commissioner, Colonel Thomas, I met
several gentlemen attached to the Bureau, and resident in different
parts of the State. They spoke of the conditions of the negroes as being
generally prosperous, but there is much hostility, they say, on the part
of the native white population to Northern men. The large landowners
are anxious for immigration, but it is not so with the mass of the
people. It is for their property rather than for their lives that the
new-comers fear; but in respect to their lives they are by no means at
ease. It would be easy to multiply instances, one gentleman told me; he
would give me two. Not long since Colonel S——, of Hinds County, a
Southerner, and a gentleman from the North were in treaty about
going into cotton-planting together, and probably would have done so.
But Colonel S——, after a little while, saw with regret that it would be
necessary to break off the arrangements. He informed his prospective
partner that he had reliable intelligence that more than a hundred men
in the neighboring county of Holmes had bound themselves to prevent
the settlement of Northern men among them, and had also determined
that no discharged negro soldier should be suffered to find employ-

ment in that section of country. My informant said it was beyond a doubt that Colonel S——acted in perfect good faith.

Another case was that of Mr. A——, of Boston. He moved into Mississippi after the war, with the intention of becoming a planter, and at first was very much pleased with his prospects—so much pleased that when a little while ago he made a visit to Massachusetts, he wrote a letter to the Boston *Post* and praised his new neighbors highly. Soon he came back, and it was not long before he began to think himself mistaken. By-and-by he became convinced that the people were too much opposed to Northern men for him to stay among them with safety. So he paid a considerable sum of money to the owner of the lands which he had intended to cultivate, was released from his bargain, and has left Mississippi.

On the last night of my stay in a Southern city I attended a political meeting, which had been called to endorse the President's recent veto message. It was held in the court-house, and was composed of about two hundred persons, who were by no means enthusiastic. Resolutions were passed, and many speeches were made, in all of which the President was lavishly praised, and the Senate and House of Representatives spoken of with great disrespect. "The war being over," said one speaker, "we were looking for peace, but it seems that the rebellion has only changed hands; that treason has reached the halls of the Congress of the United States. But there is a man at the head who is able to cope with it. President Johnson has put down the rebellion at the South, and he is now prepared to put down the rebellion at the North."

Another speaker warned the Southern people to remember that there was a party at the North, the Radical party, who would never be content till the last silver spoon was taken from them and their lands divided; but there was also in the North a Democratic party which needed the active cooperation of the Southern people, and only needed that to hurl the Radicals from power.

The evening was not very far advanced when Col. Joseph E. Davis, a brother of Jefferson Davis, was seen upon the floor and a committee was appointed to lead him to the platform. A speech from him was demanded, and he complied, speaking three or four minutes, when, as I think, at the suggestion of the chairman of the meeting he brought his remarks to an abrupt conclusion. The Vicksburg *Journal* says:

> "He fully endorsed the action of President Johnson in vetoing that accursed measure to enlarge the powers of the Freedmen's Bureau. The bill, if passed, would have caused a revolution equal to, if not more dreadful than, the one through which we have just

passed. We have a branch of the Freedmen's Bureau in our midst headed by officers of the most infamous character; who hold the offices for a given purpose; who gladly record the abuses and murders of negroes, and forward such information, rather than assist our people without homes and means in obtaining the necessaries of life. You have these officers among you. I charge you to look out for them. Mr. Davis's feeble health would not admit of any extended remarks."

I might give many passages from the various speeches, but they would be wearisome. I give but one.

Mr. McKee, formerly a general in the Federal army, stepped forward and said that he approved of the veto message of the President and endorsed it fully. "But in that hall on that night he had heard language used by some of the speakers that made his blood run cold."

Though it seemed to me not very successful as a political gathering, the meeting revealed very plainly the feeling which prevails in all the Southern country. The speakers represented the South as being cruelly injured, insulted, and oppressed, and the North as her wanton oppressor.

Mr. Emerson's New Course of Lectures

BY JAMES RUSSELL LOWELL

1868

BOSTON, November 4, 1868.

The readers of *The Nation*, who are interested in all good things, will perhaps like to hear a word of Mr. Emerson's new course of lectures now going on in Boston. The announcement that such a pleasure is coming, to people as old as I am, is something like those forebodings of spring that prepare us every year for a familiar novelty, none the less novel, when it arrives, because it is familiar. We know perfectly well what we are to expect from Mr. Emerson, and yet what he says always penetrates and stirs us, as is apt to be the case with genius, in a very unlooked-for fashion. Perhaps genius is one of the few things which we gladly allow to repeat itself—one of the few that accumulate rather than weaken the force of their impression by iteration? Perhaps some of us hear more than the mere words, are moved by something deeper than the thoughts? If it be so, we are quite right, for it is thirty years and more of "plain living and high thinking" that speak to us in this altogether unique lay-preacher. We have shared in the beneficence of this varied culture, this fearless impartiality in criticism and speculation, this masculine sincerity, this sweetness of nature which rather stimulates than cloys, for a generation long. At sixty-five (or two years beyond his grand climacteric, as he would prefer to call it) he has that privilege of soul which abolishes the calendar, and presents him to us always the unwasted contemporary of his own prime. I do not know if he seem old to his younger hearers, but we who have known him so long wonder at the tenacity with which he maintains himself even in the outposts of youth. I suppose it is not the Emerson of 1868 to whom we listen. For us the whole life of the man is distilled in the clear drop of every sentence, and behind each word we divine the force of a noble character, the weight of a large capital of thinking and being. We do not go to hear what Emerson says so much as to

63

hear Emerson. Not that we perceive any falling-off in anything that ever was essential to the charm of Mr. Emerson's peculiar style of thought or phrase. The first lecture, to be sure, was more disjointed even than common. It was as if, after vainly trying to get his paragraphs into sequence and order, he had at last tried the desperate expedient of *shuffling* them. It was chaos come again, but it was a chaos full of shooting-stars, a jumble of creative forces. The second lecture, on "Criticism and Poetry," was quite up to the level of old times, full of that power of strangely-subtle association whose indirect approaches startle the mind into almost painful attention, of those flashes of mutual understanding between speaker and hearer that are gone ere one can say it lightens. The vice of Emerson's criticism seems to be, that while no man is so sensitive to what is poetical, few men are less sensible than he of what makes a poem. Of the third lecture (and I have heard but three) I shall say something by-and-by.

To be young is surely the best, if the most precarious, gift of life; yet there are some of us who would hardly consent to be young again, if it were at the cost of our recollection of Mr. Emerson's first lectures during the consulate of Tyler. We used to walk in from the country to the Masonic Temple (I think it was), through the crisp winter night, and listen to that thrilling voice of his, so charged with subtle meaning and subtle music, as shipwrecked men on a raft to the hail of a ship that came with unhoped-for food and rescue. Cynics might say what they liked. Did our own imaginations transfigure dry remainder-biscuit into ambrosia? At any rate, he brought us *life*, which, on the whole, is no bad thing. Was it all transcendentalism? magic-lantern pictures, on mist? As you will. Those, then, were just what we wanted. But it was not so. The delight and the benefit were that he put us in communication with a larger style of thought, sharpened our wits with a more pungent phrase, gave us ravishing glimpses of an ideal under the dry husk of our New England; made us conscious of the supreme and everlasting originality of whatever bit of soul might be in any of us; freed us, in short, from the stocks of prose in which we had sate so long that we had grown well-nigh contented in our cramps. And who that saw the audience will ever forget it, where every one still capable of fire, or longing to renew in them the half-forgotten sense of it, was gathered? Those faces, young and old, a-gleam with pale intellectual light, eager with pleased attention, flash upon me once more from the deep recesses of the years with an exquisite pathos. I hear again that rustle of sensation, as they turned to exchange glances over some pithier thought, some keener flash of that humor which always played about the horizon of his mind like heat-lightning, and it seems now like the sad stir of the autumn leaves that are whirling around me. To some of us that long-past experience remains as the most marvellous and fruitful we have ever had. Emerson awakened us, saved us from the body of this death. It is the sound of the trumpet that the young soul longs for, careless what breath may fill it. Sidney heard it in the ballad of "Chevy Chase," and we in Emerson. Nor did it blow retreat, but called to us with assurance of victory. Did they say he was disconnected? So were the stars, that seemed larger to our eyes, still keen with that excitement, as we walked homeward with prouder stride over the creaking snow. And were *they* not knit together by a higher logic than our mere sense could master? Were we enthusiasts? I hope and believe we were, and am thankful to the man who made us worth something for once in our lives. If asked what was left? what we carried home? we should not have been careful for an answer. It would have been enough if we had said that something beautiful had passed that way. Or we might have asked in return what one brought away from a symphony of Beethoven? Enough that he had set that ferment of wholesome discontent at work in us. There is one, at least, of those old hearers, so many of whom are now in the fruition of that intellectual beauty of which Emerson gave them both the desire and the foretaste, who will always love to repeat—

> "Che in la mente m'è fitta, ed or m'accuora
> La cara e buona immagine paterna
> Di voi, quando nel mondo ad ora ad ora
> M'insegnavati come l'uom s'eterna."

I am unconsciously thinking as I write of the third lecture of the present course, in which Mr. Emerson gave some delightful reminiscences of the intellectual influences in whose movement he had shared. It was like hearing Goethe read some passages of the "Wahrheit aus seinem Leben." Not that there was not a little *Dichtung*, too, here and there, as the lecturer built up so lofty a pedestal under certain figures as to lift them into a prominence of obscurity, and seem to masthead them there. Everybody was asking his neighbor who this or that recondite great man was, in the faint hope that somebody might once have heard of him. There are those who call Mr. Emerson cold. Let them revise their judgment in presence of this loyalty of his that can keep warm for half a century, that never forgets a friendship, or fails to pay even a fancied obligation to the uttermost farthing. This substantiation of shadows was but incidental, and pleasantly characteristic of the man to those who know and love him. The greater part of the lecture was devoted to reminscences of things substantial in themselves. He spoke of Everett, fresh from Greece and Germany; of Channing; of the translations of Margaret Fuller, Ripley, and Dwight; of the *Dial* and Brook Farm. To what he said of the latter an undertone of good-humored irony gave special zest. But what every one of his hearers felt was that the protagonist in the drama was left out. The lecturer was no Æucas to babble the *quorum magna pars fui*, and, as one of his listeners, I cannot help wishing to say how each of them was commenting the story as it went along, and filling up the necessary gaps in it from his own private store of memories. His younger hearers could not know how much they owed to the benign impersonality, the quiet scorn of everything ignoble, the never-sated hunger of self-culture, that were personified in the man before them. But the older knew how much the country's intellectual emancipation was due to the stimulus of his teaching and example, how constantly he had kept burning the beacon of an ideal life above our lower region of turmoil. To him more than to all other causes together did the young martyrs of our civil war owe the sustaining strength of thoughtful heroism that is so touching in every record of their lives. Those who are grateful to Mr. Emerson, as many of us are, for what they feel to be most valuable in their culture, or perhaps I should say their impulse, are grateful not so much for any direct teachings of his as for that inspiring lift which only genius can give, and without which all doctrine is chaff.

This was something like the *caret* which some of us older boys wished to fill up on the margin of the master's lecture. Few men have been so much to so many, and through so large a range of aptitudes and temperaments, and this simply because all of us value manhood beyond any or all other qualities of character. We may suspect in him, here and there, a certain thinness and vagueness of quality, but let the waters go over him as they list, this masculine fibre of his will keep its lively color and its toughness of texture. I can never help applying to him what Ben Jonson said of Bacon: "There happened in my time one noble speaker, who was full of gravity in his speaking. His language was nobly censorious. No man ever spake more neatly, more pressly, more weightily, or suffered less emptiness, less idleness, in what he uttered. No member of his speech but consisted of his own graces. His hearers could not cough, or look aside from him, without loss. He commanded where he spoke." Those who heard him while their natures were yet plastic, and their mental nerves trembled under the slightest breath of divine air, will never cease to feel and say—

> "Was never eye did see that face,
>   Was never ear did hear that tongue,
> Was never mind did mind his grace,
>   That ever thought the travail long;
> But eyes, and ears, and every thought,
> Were with his sweet perfections caught."

The Tale of the "Ripe Scholar"

BY FRANCIS PARKMAN

1869

Not many years ago, a certain traditional prestige, independent of all considerations of practical utility, attached to the scholastic character, at least in New England, where the clergy long held a monopoly of what passed for learning. New England colleges were once little more than schools for making ministers. As the clergyman has lost in influence, so the scholar has lost in repute, and the reasons are not hard to find. The really good scholars were exceptions, and very rare ones. In the matter of theology some notable results were produced, but secular scholarship was simply an exotic and a sickly one. It never recovered from its transplantation and drew no vital juices from the soil. The climate was hostile to it. All the vigor of the country drifted into practical pursuits, and the New England man of letters, when he happened not to be a minister, was usually some person whom constitutional defects, bodily or mental, had unfitted for politics or business. He was apt to be a recluse, ignorant of the world, bleached by a close room and an iron stove, never breathing the outer air when he could help it, and resembling a mediæval monk in his scorn of the body, or rather in his utter disregard of it. Sometimes he was reputed a scholar merely because he was nothing else. The products of his mind were as pallid as the hue of his face, and, like their parent, void of blood, bone, sinew, muscle, and marrow. That he should be provincial was, for a long time, inevitable, but that he was emasculate was chiefly his own fault. As his scholarship was not fruitful of any very valuable results, as it did not make itself felt in the living world that ranged around it, as, in short, it showed no vital force, it began at length to be regarded as a superfluous excrescence. Nevertheless, like the monkish learning of the middle ages, it served a good purpose in keeping alive the tradition of

67

liberal culture against a future renaissance. We shall be told that we exaggerate, and, in one sense, this is true, for we describe not an individual, but a type, from which, however, the reality was rarely very remote, and with which it was sometimes identified. The most finished and altogether favorable example of this devitalized scholarship, with many graceful additions, was Edward Everett, and its echoes may still be heard in the halls of Congress, perplexing Western members with Latin quotations, profuse, if not always correct.

As the nation grew in importance and in sensitiveness, the want of intellectual productiveness began to trouble the popular pride, and an impatient public called on its authors to be "original." Spasmodic efforts were made to respond, and the results were such as may be supposed. The mountain went into convulsions of labor and produced a mouse, or something as ridiculous. After an analogous fashion some of the successors of our pallid, clerical scholars raise the cry, "Let us be strong," and fall into the moral and physical gymnastics of muscular Christianity. This, certainly, is no bad sign, in so far as it indicates the consciousness of a want; but neither originality nor force can be got up to order. They must spring from a deeper root and grow by laws of their own. Happily our soil has begun to put forth such a growth, promising in quality, but as yet, in quantity and in maturity, wholly inadequate to the exigent need.

In times of agitation, alive with engrossing questions of pressing moment, when all is astir with pursuit and controversy, when some are mad for gold, and some are earnest and some rabid for this cause or for that, the scholarship of the past is naturally pronounced not up with the times. Despite his manifold failings, "the self-made man," with his palatial mansion, his exploits in the gold-room, in the caucus, on the stump, in Congress, and in the presidential chair, flatters popular self-love and fills the public eye. Only a slight reason is wanted for depreciating the scholar, and a strong one is offered. Because the culture which our colleges supplied, and which too many of them still supply, was weak, thin, and unsuitable, it was easy to depreciate all culture. By culture we mean development, not polish or adornment, though these are its natural and by no means useless belongings. Using the word, then, in this sense, culture is with us a supreme necessity, not for the profit of a few but of all. The presence of minds highly and vigorously developed is the most powerful aid to popular education, and the necessary condition of its best success. In a country where the ruling power is public opinion, it is above all things necessary that the best and maturest thought should have a fair share in forming it. Such thought cannot exist in any force in the community without propagating its own image, and a class of strong thinkers is the palladium of democracy. They are the natural enemies of ignorant, ostentatious, and aggressive wealth, and the natural friends of all that is best in the popular heart. They are sure of the hatred of charlatans, demagogues, and political sharpers. They are the only hope of our civilization; without them it is a failure, a mere platitude of mediocrity, stagnant or turbid, as the case may be. The vastest aggregate of average intelligences can do nothing to supply their place, and even material growth is impeded by an ignorance of its conditions and laws. If we may be forgiven the metaphor, our civilization is at present a creature with a small and feeble head, a large, muscular, and active body, and a tail growing at such a rate that it threatens to become unmanageable and shake the balance of the vital powers.

The tendency of a partial education, such as the best popular education must of necessity be, is to produce an excess of self-confidence; and one of its results in this country is a prodigious number of persons who think, and persuade others to think, that they know everything necessary to be known, and are fully competent to form opinions and make speeches upon all questions whatever. As these are precisely the persons who make the most noise on the most momentous questions of the day, who have the most listeners and admirers, and who hold each other up as shining examples for imitation, their incompetency becomes a public evil of the first magnitude. If rash and ignorant theorizing, impulsive outcries, and social and political charlatanry of all sorts are to have the guiding of our craft, then farewell to the hope that her voyage will be a success. The remedy is to infuse into the disordered system the sedative and tonic of a broad knowledge and a vigorous reason. This means to invigorate and extend the higher education; to substitute for the effete and futile scholasticism which the popular mind justly holds in slight account, an energetic and manly development, trained to grapple with the vast questions of the present, and strong enough in numbers as well as quality to temper with its mature thought the rashness of popular speculation. Our best colleges are moving hopefully in this direction; none of them with more life and vigor than the oldest of them all. The present generation will see an increase in the number of our really efficient thinkers, but it is a positive, not a relative increase, and is far behind the fast increasing need. Powerful causes are at work against it, and we will try to explain what, to our thinking, some of these causes are.

Perhaps the most obvious of them is the ascendency of material interests among us. To the great mass of our population, the clearing of lands, the acquiring of new territory, the building of cities, the multiplication of railroads, steamboats, and telegraph lines, the growth of trade and manufactures, the opening of mines, with the resulting fine houses, fine clothes, and sumptuous fare, constitute the real sum and substance of progress and civilization. Art, literature, philosophy, and science—so far as science has no direct bearing on material interests— are regarded as decorations, agreeable and creditable, but not essential. In other words, the material basis of civilization is accepted for the entire structure. A prodigious number of persons think that money-making is the only serious business of life, and there is no correspond-ing number who hold a different faith. There are not a few among us who would "improve" our colleges into schools of technology, where young men may be trained with a view mainly to the production of more steamboats, railroads, and telegraphs; more breadstuffs; more iron, copper, silver, and gold; more cottons and woollens; and, conse-quently, more fine houses and fine clothes. All this is very well, but it does not answer the great and crying need of the time. The truth is, our material growth so greatly exceeds our other growth that the body politic suffers from diseases of repletion. A patient bloated with gen-erous living, and marked already with the eruptions of a perverted, diseased blood, is not to be cured solely by providing him with more food.

The drift towards material activity is so powerful among us that it is very difficult for a young man to resist it; and the difficulty increases in proportion as his nature is active and energetic. Patient and devoted study is rarely long continued in the vortex of American life. The dusty arena of competition and strife has fascinations almost irresistible to one conscious of his own vigor. Intellectual tastes may, however, make a compromise. Journalism and the lecture-room offer them a field midway between the solitude of the study and the bustle of the world of business; but the journal and the lecture-room have influences powerfully adverse to solid, mature, and independent thinking. There, too, is the pulpit, for those who have a vocation that way; but in this, also, a mighty and increasing temptation besets the conscientious stu-dent. As for politics, they have fallen to such a pass that the men are rare who can mingle in them without deteriorating.

Paradoxical as it may seem, the diffusion of education and intelli-gence is at present acting against the free development of the highest education and intelligence. Many have hoped and still hope that by giving a partial teaching to great numbers of persons, a stimulus would be applied to the best minds among them, and a thirst for knowledge awakened which would lead to high results; but thus far these results have not equalled the expectation. There has been a vast expenditure of brick and mortar for educational purposes, and, what is more to the purpose, many excellent and faithful teachers of both sexes have la-bored diligently in their vocation; but the system of competitive cramming in our public schools has not borne fruits on which we have much cause to congratulate ourselves. It has produced an immense number of readers; but what thinkers are to be found may be said to exist in spite of it. The public school has put money in abundance into the pockets of the dealers in sensation stories, sensation illustrated papers, and all the swarm of trivial, sickly, and rascally literature. From this and cheap newspapers thousands—nay, millions—draw all their mental improvement, and pamper their mental stomachs with adulterated, not to say poisoned, sweetmeats, till they have neither desire nor digestion for strong and wholesome food. But we would speak rather of that truly intelligent and respectable public which forms the auditories of popular preachers and popular lecturers, which is the lavish patron of popular periodical literature, which interests itself in the questions of the day, and has keen mental appetites of a certain kind. This public is strong in numbers and very strong in collective wealth. Its voice can confer celebrity, if not reputation; and it can enrich those who win its favor. In truth, it is the American people. Now, what does this great public want? It is, in the main, busied with the active work of life, and though it thinks a little and feels a great deal on matters which ought to engage the attention of every self-governing people, yet it is impatient of continuous and cool attention to anything but its daily business, and sometimes even to that. Indeed, the exciting events of the last ten years, joined to the morbid stimulus applied to all departments of business, have greatly increased this tendency; and to-day there are fewer serious and thoughtful readers than in the last decade. More than ever before, the public demands elocution rather than reason of those who address it; something to excite the feelings and captivate the fancy rather than something to instruct the understanding. It rejoices in sweeping statements, confident assertions, bright lights and black shadows alternating with something funny. Neither does it care much for a terse, idiomatic, and pointed diction, but generally prefers the flatulent periods of the ready writers. On matters of the greatest interest it craves to be excited or amused. Lectures professing to instruct are turned to a tissue of jokes, and the pulpit itself is sometimes enlivened after a similar fashion. The pill must be sugared and the food highly seasoned, for the public mind is in a state of laxity and needs a tonic. But the public taste is very exacting, and it offers great and tempting rewards to those who please it.

That which pleases it pays so much better in money and notoriety, and is so much cheaper of production, than the better article which does not please it, that the temptation to accept light work and high wages in place of hard work and low wages is difficult to resist. Nothing but a deep love of truth or of art can stand unmoved against it. In our literary markets, educated tastes are completely outridden by un-educated or half-educated tastes, and the commodity is debased accordingly. Thus, the editor of a magazine may be a man of taste and talents; but his interests as a man of letters and his interests as a man of business are not the same. "Why don't you make your magazine what it ought to be?" we once asked of a well-known editor. "Because," he replied, "if we did, we should lose four-fifths of our circulation." A noted preacher not long ago confessed to us that the temptation to give his audience the sort of preaching which they liked to hear, instead of that which it was best that they should hear, was almost irresistible.

The amount of what we have been saying is, that the public which demands a second-rate article is so enormously large in comparison with the public which demands a first-rate article that it impairs the quality of literary production, and exercises an influence adverse to the growth of intellectual eminence. Now, what is the remedy? It seems to us to be twofold. First, to direct popular education, not to stuffing the mind with crude aggregations of imperfect knowledge, but rather to the development of its powers of observation, comparison, analysis, and reasoning; to strengthening and instructing its moral sense, and leading it to self-knowledge and consequent modesty. All this, no doubt, is vastly more difficult and far less showy in its results than the present system of competitive cramming, and requires in its teachers a high degree of good sense and sound instruction. The other remedy consists in a powerful re-enforcement of the higher education, and the consequent development of a class of persons, whether rich or poor, so well instructed and so numerous as to hold their ground against charlatanry, and propagate sound and healthy thought through the community. He who gives or bequeaths money to a well-established and wisely-conducted university confers a blessing which radiates through all the ranks of society. He does a service eminently practical, and constitutes himself the patron of the highest and best utilitarianism.

Newport

BY HENRY JAMES

1870

SEPTEMBER, 5, 1870.

The season at Newport has an obstinate life. September has fairly begun, but as yet there is small visible diminution in the steady stream —the splendid, stupid stream—of carriages which rolls in the afternoon along the Avenue. There is, I think, a far more intimate fondness between Newport and its frequenters than that which in most American watering-places consecrates the somewhat mechanical relation between the visitors and the visited. This relation here is for the most part slightly sentimental. I am very far from professing a cynical contempt for the gaieties and vanities of Newport life: they are, as a spectacle, extremely amusing; they are full of a certain warmth of social color which charms alike the eye and the fancy; they are worth observing, if only to conclude against them; they possess at least the dignity of all extreme and emphatic expressions of a social tendency; but they are not so far from *"was uns alle bündigt, das Gemeine"* that I do not seem to overhear at times the still, small voice of this tender sense of the sweet, superior beauty of the local influences that surround them, pleading gently in their favor to the fastidious critic. I feel almost warranted in saying that here this exquisite natural background has sunk less in relative value and suffered less from the encroachments of pleasure-seeking man than the scenic properties of any other great watering-place. For this, perhaps, we may thank rather the modest, incorruptible integrity of the Newport landscape than any very intel· ligent forbearance on the part of the summer colony. The beauty of this landscape is so subtle, so essential, so humble, so much a thing of character and impression, so little a thing of feature and pretension, that it cunningly eludes the grasp of the destroyer or the reformer, and triumphs in impalpable purity even when it seems to condescend. I

73

have sometimes wondered in sternly rational moods why it is that Newport is so loved of the votaries of idleness and pleasure. Its resources are few in number. It is emphatically circumscribed. It has few drives, few walks, little variety of scenery. Its charms and its interest are confined to a narrow circle. It has of course the unlimited ocean, but seafaring idlers are of necessity the fortunate few. Last evening, it seemed to me, as I drove along the Avenue, that my wonderment was quenched for ever. The atmospheric tone, the exquisite, rich simplicity of the landscape, gave mild, enchanting sense of positive climate—these are the real charm of Newport, and the secret of her supremacy. You are melted by the admirable art of the landscape, by seeing so much that is lovely and impressive achieved with such a masterly frugality of means—with so little parade of the vast, the various, or the rare, with so narrow a range of color and form. I could not help thinking, as I turned from the great harmony of elegance and the unfathomable mystery of purity which lay deepening on the breast of nature with the various shades of twilight, to the motley discord and lavish wholesale splendor of the flowing stream of gentility on the Avenue, that, quite in their own line of effect, these money-made social heroes and heroines might learn a few good lessons from the daily prospect of the great western expanse of rock and ocean in its relations with the declining sun. But this is a rather fantastic demand. Many persons of course come to Newport simply because others come, and in this way the present brilliant colony has grown up. Let me not be suspected, when I speak of Newport, of the untasteful heresy of meaning primarily rocks and waves rather than ladies and gentlemen.

The ladies and gentlemen are in great force—the ladies, of course, especially. It is true everywhere, I suppose, that women are the central animating element of "society"; but you feel this to be especially true as you pass along the Newport Avenue. I doubt whether anywhere else women enjoy so largely what is called a "good time" with so small a sacrifice, that is, of the luxury of self-respect. I heard a lady yesterday tell another, with a quiet ecstasy of tone, that she had been having a "most perfect time." This is the very poetry of pleasure. In England, if our impression is correct, women hold the second fiddle in the great social harmony. You will never, at the sight of a carriage-load of mild-browed English maidens, with a presiding matron, plump and passive, in the midst of them, suspect their countrywomen of enjoying in the conventional world anything more than a fictitious and deputed dignity. They neither speak nor act from themselves, but from their husbands and brothers and lovers. On the Continent, women are proclaimed supreme; but we fancy them, with more or less justice, as maintaining their empire by various clandestine and reprehensible arts. With us—we may say it without bravado—they are both free and unsophisticated. You feel it most gratefully as you receive a confident bow from a pretty young girl in her basket-phaeton. She is very young and very pretty, but she has a certain delicate breadth of movement which seems to you a pure gain, without imaginable taint of loss. She combines, you reflect with respectful tenderness, the utmost of modesty with the least possible shyness. Shyness is certainly very pretty— when it is not very ugly; but shyness may often darken the bloom of genuine modesty, and a certain feminine frankness and confidence may often incline it toward the light. Let us assume, then, that all the young ladies whom you may meet here are the correctest of all possible young ladies. In the course of time, they ripen into the delightful women who divide your admiration. It is easy to see that Newport must be a most agreeable sojourn for the male sex. The gentlemen, indeed, look wonderfully prosperous and well-conditioned. They gallop on shining horses or recline in a sort of coaxing Herculean submission beside the lovely mistress of a phaeton. Young men—and young old men—I have occasion to observe, are far more numerous than at Saratoga, and of vastly superior quality. There is, indeed, in all things a striking difference in tone and aspect between these two great cities of pleasure. After Saratoga, Newport seems really substantial and civilized. Æsthetically speaking, you may remain at Newport with a fairly good conscience; at Saratoga, you linger on under passionate protest. At Newport, life is public, if you will; at Saratoga, it is absolutely common. The difference, in a word, is the difference between a group of three or four hotels and a series of cottages and villas. Saratoga perhaps deserves our greater homage, as being characteristically democratic and American; let us, then, make Saratoga the heaven of our aspiration, but let us yet awhile content ourselves with Newport as the lordly earth of our residence.

The villas and cottages, the beautiful idle women, the beautiful idle men, the brilliant pleasure-fraught days and evenings, impart, perhaps, to Newport life a faintly European expression, in so far as they suggest the somewhat alien presence of leisure—"fine old Leisure," as George Eliot calls it. Nothing, it seems to me, however, can take place in America without straightway seeming very American; and, after a week at Newport, you begin to fancy that, to live for amusement simply, beyond the noise of commerce or of care, is a distinctively national trait. Nowhere else in this country—nowhere, of course, within the range of our better civilization—does business seem so remote, so vague and unreal. Here a positive organic system of idleness or of active pleasure-taking has grown up and matured. If there is any poetry in the ignorance of trade and turmoil and the hard processes of fortune, Newport may claim her share of it. She knows—or at least appears to know—for the most part, nothing but results. Individuals here, of course, have private cares and burdens, to preserve the balance and the dignity of life; but these collective society conspires to forget. It is a singular fact that a society that does nothing is decidedly more picturesque, more interesting to the eye of sentiment, than a society which is hard at work. Newport, in this way, is infinitely more picturesque than Saratoga. There you feel that idleness is occasional, empirical. Most of the people you see are asking themselves, you imagine, whether the game is worth the candle, and work is not better than such toilsome play. But here, obviously, the habit of pleasure is formed, and (within the limits of a generous morality) many of the secrets of pleasure are known. Do what we will, on certain lines Europe is ahead of us yet. Newport falls altogether short of Baden-Baden in her presentment of the improprieties. They are altogether absent from the picture, which is therefore signally destitute of those shades of color produced by the mysteries and fascinations of vice. But idleness *per se* is vicious, and of course you may imagine what you please. For my own part, I prefer to imagine nothing but the graceful and the pure; and, with the help of such imaginings, you may construct a very pretty sentimental counterpart to the superficial movement of society. This I lately found very difficult to do at Saratoga. Sentiment there is pitifully shy and elusive. Here, the multiplied relations of men and women, under the permanent pressure of luxury and idleness, give it a very fair chance. Sentiment, indeed, of masterly force and interest, springs up in every soil, with a sovereign disregard of occasion. People love and hate and aspire with the greatest intensity when they have to make their time and privilege. I should hardly come to Newport for the materials of a tragedy. Even in their own kind, the social elements are as yet too light and thin. But I can fancy finding here the plot of many a pleasant sentimental comedy. I can almost imagine, indeed, a transient observer of the Newport spectacle dreaming momentarily of a great American novel, in which the heroine shall be infinitely realistic, and yet neither a schoolmistress nor an outcast. I say intentionally the "transient" observer, because I fancy that here the suspicion only is friendly to dramatic peace; the knowledge is hostile. The observer would discover, on a nearer view, I rather fear, that his possible heroines have too unexceptionally a perpetual "good time."

This will remind the reader of what he must already have heard affirmed, that to speak of a place with abundance you must know it, but not too well. I feel as if I knew the natural elements of Newport too well to attempt to describe them. I have known them so long that I hardly know what I think of them. I have little more than a simple consciousness of vastly enjoying them. Even this consciousness at times lies dumb and inert. I wonder at such times whether, to appeal fairly to the general human sense, the prospect here has not something too much of the extra-terrestrial element. Life seems too short, space too narrow, to warrant you in giving in an unqualified adhesion to a *paysage* which is two-thirds ocean. For the most part, however, I am willing to take the landscape as it stands, and to think that, without its native complement of sea, the land would lose much of its beauty. It is, in fact, a land exquisitely modified by marine influences. Indeed, in spite of all the evil it has done me, I could find it in my soul to love the sea when I consider how it co-operates with the Newport promontories to the delight of the eye. Give it up altogether, and you can thus enjoy it still, reflected and immobilized—like the Prussian army a month hence.

Newport consists, as the reader will know, of an ancient and honorable town, a goodly harbor, and a long, broad neck of land, stretching southward into the sea, and forming the chief habitation of the summer colony. Along the greater part of its eastward length, this projecting coast is bordered with lordly cliffs and dotted with seaward-gazing villas. At the head of the promontory the villas enjoy a magnificent reach of prospect. The pure Atlantic—the Old World westward tides —expire directly at their feet. Behind the line of villas runs the Avenue, with more villas yet—of which there is nothing at all to say, but that those built recently are a hundred times prettier than those built fifteen years ago, offering a modest contribution to our modern architectural Renaissance. Some years ago, when I first knew Newport, the town proper was considered extremely "picturesque." If an antique shabbiness that amounts almost to squalor is a pertinent element, as I believe it is, of the picturesque, the little main street at least—Thames Street by name—still deserves the praise. Here, in their crooked and dwarfish wooden mansions, are the shops that minister to the daily needs of the expanded city; and here of a summer morning, jolting over the cobble-stones of the narrow roadway, you may see a hundred superfine ladies seeking with languid eagerness what they may buy—to "buy something," I believe, being a diurnal necessity of the American woman of substance. This busy region gradually melts away into the grass-grown stillness of the Point, in the eyes of many persons the pleasantest quarter in Newport. It has superficially the advantage of being as yet uninvaded by fashion. When I first knew it, however, its peculiar charm was even more undisturbed than at present. The Point may be called the old residential, as distinguished from the commercial, town. It is meagre, shallow, and scanty—a mere pinch of antiquity—

but, as far as it goes, it retains an exquisite tone. It leaves the shops and the little wharves, and wanders close to the harbor, where the breeze-borne rattle of shifted sails and spars alone intrudes upon its stillness, till its mouldy-timbered quiet subsides into the low, tame rocks and beaches which edge the bay. Several fine modern houses have recently been erected on the water-side, absorbing the sober, primitive tenements which used to maintain the picturesque character of the place. They improve it, of course, as a residence, but they injure it as a spectacle. Enough of early architecture still remains, however, to suggest a multitude of thoughts as to the severe simplicity of the generation which produced it. It is picturesque in a way, but with a paucity of elements which seems to defy all effect. The plain gray nudity of these little warped and shingled boxes seems utterly to repudiate the slightest curiosity. But here, as elsewhere, the magical Newport atmosphere wins half the battle. It aims at no mystery. It clothes them in a garment of absolute light. Their homely notches and splinters twinkle in the sun. Their steep gray roofs, barnacled with lichens, remind you of old scows, overturned on the beach to dry. They show for what they are—simple houses by the sea. Over-darkened by no wealth of inland shade, without show or elegance or finish, they patiently partake of the fortunes of the era—of the vast blue glare which rises from the bay, and the storms which sweep inward from the ocean. They have been blown free of all needless accretion of detail—scorched clean of all graceful superfluities. Most of the population of this part of Newport is, I believe, of Quaker lineage. This double-salted Quakerism is abundant motive for this soundless and colorless simplicity.

One of the more recent movements of fashion is the so-called "New Drive"—the beautiful drive by the sea. The avenue, where the Neck abruptly terminates, has been made to prolong itself to the west, and to wander for a couple of miles over a lovely region of beach and lowly down and sandy meadow and salt brown sheep-grass. This region was formerly the most beautiful part of Newport—the least frequented and the most untamed by fashion. I by no means regret the creation of the new road, however. A walker may very soon isolate himself, and the occupants of carriages stand a chance of benefit quite superior to their power of injury. The peculiar charm of this great westward expanse is very difficult to define. It is in an especial degree the charm of Newport in general—the combined lowness of tone, as painters call it, in all the earthy elements, and the extraordinary elevation of tone in the air. For miles and miles you see at your feet, in mingled shades of yellow and gray, a desolate waste of moss-clad rock and sand-starved grass. At your left surges and shines the mighty presence of the vast immediate sea. Above the broken and composite level of this double-featured plain, the great heavens ascend in innumerable stages of light. In spite of the bare simplicity of this prospect, its beauty is far more a beauty of detail than that of the average American landscape. Descend into a hollow of the rocks, into one of the little warm climates of five feet square which you may find there, beside the grateful ocean glare, and you will be struck quite as much by their fineness as by their roughness. From time to time, as you wander, you will meet a lonely, stunted tree, into the storm-twisted multiplicity of whose branches all the possible grace and grotesqueness of the growth of trees seem to have been finely concentrated. The region of which I speak is perhaps best seen in the late afternoon, from the high seat of a carriage on the Avenue. You seem to stand just without the threshold of the west. At its opposite extremity sinks the sun, with such a splendor, perhaps, as I lately saw—a splendor of the deepest blue, more luminous and fiery than the fiercest of our common vespertinal crimsons, all streaked and barred with blown and drifted gold. The whole vast interval, with its rocks and marshes and ponds, seems bedimmed into a troubled mono-tone of glorious purple. The near Atlantic is fading slowly into the unborrowed darkness of its deep, essential life. In the foreground, a short distance from the road, an old orchard uplifts its tangled stems and branches against the violet mists of the west. It seems strangely grotesque and enchanted. No ancient olive grove of Italy or Provence was ever more hoarily romantic. This is what people commonly be-hold on the last homeward bend of the drive. For such of them as are happy enough to occupy one of the villas on the cliffs, the beauty of the day has even yet not expired. The present summer has been em-phatically the summer of moonlights. Not the nights, however, but the long days, in these agreeable homes, are what specially appeal to my fancy. Here you find a solution of the insoluble problem—to combine an abundance of society with an abundance of solitude. In their charm-ing broad-windowed drawing-rooms, on their great seaward piazzas, within sight of the serious Atlantic horizon, which is so familiar to the eye and so mysterious to the heart, caressed by the gentle breeze which makes all but simple, social, delightful *then* and *there* seem unreal and untasteful—the sweet fruit of the lotus grows more than ever succu-lent and magical. You feel here not more a man, perhaps, but more a passive gentleman and worlding. How sensible they ought to be, the denizens of these pleasant places, of their peculiar felicity and distinc-tion! How it should purify their tempers and refine their intellects! How delicate, how wise, how discriminating they should become! What excellent manners and fancies their situation should gener-ate! How it should purge them of vulgarity! Happy *villegianti* of Newport!

Chicago in Distress

BY FREDERICK LAW OLMSTED

1871

CHICAGO, November 2, 1871.

I have had an opportunity of looking at Chicago at the beginning of the fourth week after the fire, and, as you requested, will give you a few notes of my observation.

Chicago had a central quarter, compactly built, mostly of brick, stone, and iron, and distinguished by numerous very large and tall structures, comparable to, but often more ostentatious than, Stewart's store in New York. They were mostly lined, to the fourth, fifth, or sixth floor, with pine-wood shelves, on which, or in pine-wood cases, a fresh stock of—larger at the moment than ever before—dry goods, or other inflammable materials, was set up, with plentiful air-space for rapid combustion. This central quarter occupied a mile and a half square of land. On one side of it was the lake; on the other three sides, for the distance of a mile, the building, though irregular, was largely of detached houses, some of the villa class, with small planted grounds about them, and luxuriously furnished, but generally comfortable dwellings, of moderate size, set closely together. There were also numerous churches and tall school buildings, and some large factories. At a distance of two miles from the centre, and beyond, houses were much scattered, and within a mile of the political boundary there was much open prairie, sparsely dotted with cabins and a few larger buildings. It will be seen that a much larger part of the town proper was burned than a stranger would be led to suppose by the published maps.

The fire started half a mile southwest, which was directly to windward, of the central quarter, rapidly carried its heights, and swept down from them upon the comparatively suburban northern quarter, clearing it to the outskirts, where the few scattered houses remaining were protected by a dense grove of trees. The field of ruin is a mile in width, bounded by the lake on one side and mainly by a branch of the river on the other, and four miles in length, thus being as large as the half of New York City from the Battery to the Central Park, or as the whole of the peninsula of Boston. The houses burned set ten feet apart would form a row over a hundred miles in length. I judge that more than a third of the roof-space and fully half the floor-space of the city, the population of which was 330,000 was destroyed.

Familiar with these facts and comparisons before I came here, and having already seen many who had left the city since the fire, I now feel myself to have been able but slightly to appreciate the magnitude of its calamity. Besides the extent of the ruins, what is most remarkable is the completeness with which the fire did its work, as shown by the prostration of the ruins and the extraordinary absence of smoke-stains, brands, and all *débris*, except stone, brick, and iron, bleached to an ashy pallor. The distinguishing smell of the ruins is that of charred earth. In not more than a dozen cases have the four walls of any of the great blocks, or of any buildings, been left standing together. It is the exception to find even a single corner or chimney holding together to a height of more than twenty feet. It has been possible, from the top of an omnibus, to see men standing on the ground three miles away across what was the densest, loftiest, and most substantial part of the city.

Generally, the walls seem to have crumbled in from top to bottom, nothing remaining but a broad low heap of rubbish in the cellar—so low as to be overlooked from the pavement. Granite, all sandstones and all limestones, whenever fully exposed to the southwest, are generally flaked and scaled, and blocks, sometimes two and three feet thick, are cracked through and through. Marble and other limestones, where especially exposed, as in doors and window-dressings, especially if in thin slabs, have often fallen to powder. Walls of the bituminous limestone, of which there were but few, instead of melting away, as was reported, seem to have stood rather better than others; I cannot tell why. Iron railings and lamp-posts, detached from buildings, are often drooping, and, in thinner parts, seem sometimes to have been fused. Iron columns and floor-beams are often bent to a half-circle. The wooden (Nicholson) asphalt-and-tar-concrete pavements remain essentially unharmed, except where red-hot material or burning liquids have lain upon them. Street rails on wood are generally in good order; on McAdam, as far as I have seen, more often badly warped.

Where houses stood detached, and especially where they were surrounded by tall trees, there is less evidence of intense heat, charred wood and smoke-stains being seen in the ruins. I had heard it surmised that, by furnishing numerous small brands, the planted trees of the North Division would have helped to scatter the fire, but I find them generally standing to the smallest twigs, so inclined and stiffened, however, as to show perfectly the action upon them of the wind at the moment of death. It is evident that they would have been an efficient protection to the houses they surrounded had the buildings to windward been a little less tall, or the gale a degree less furious. For the wind appears not only to have been strong, but gusty and whirling. There is evidence of concentrated slants, eddies, and back-sets. This partly explains the small salvage. Many, a moment after they had been out to observe the flames in the distance, and had judged that they had still a chance to save their houses, were suddenly driven by a fierce heat, borne down upon them apparently from above, to flee, leaving even their choicest property, though previously packed and ready to be carried by hand. The radiated heat from the larger buildings was so strong that it scorched men ten rods away across the wind. Families were driven from one place of refuge to another—in several cases, to my knowledge, four times, and, finally, a few into the lake; many thousands into the open country. Some were floated or swam across the river.

Burning fragments of wooden parapets, sheets of roofing metal, signs, and scuttle-doors were carried great distances, and, with blazing felt, tarred paper, and canvas, and myriads of smaller sparks, sometimes swept down upon the fugitives with a terrific roar. Very sensible men have declared that they were fully impressed at such a time with the conviction that it was the burning of the world. Loose horses and cows, as well as people of all conditions on foot and in wagons, were hurrying half-blinded through the streets together, and it often happened that husbands and wives, parents and children, even mothers and infants, were forced apart and lost to each other. Sudden desolation thus added to the previous horrors, made some frantic who would otherwise have maintained composure. In general, however, the people, especially the households of the north side, appear to have manifested a greater degree of self-possession and of considerate thoughtfulness one for another, under these circumstances, than can be easily believed. Almost every one holds the remembrance of some instance of quiet heroism, often flavored with humor. The remains of only about one hundred human bodies have thus far been recognized in the ruins, and the coroner and others are of the opinion that not more than two hundred lives were lost. That the number should be so small can only be accounted for by the fact that there was an active volunteer rear-guard of cool-headed Christians, who often entered and searched houses to which they were strangers, dragging out their inmates sometimes by main force, and often when some, caught unawares, were bewildered, fainting, or suffocating. One still sees burned garments and singed beards.

Of course, a state of mind approaching insanity followed with many. After the lost had been found, as in most cases they soon were—children especially having been almost invariably taken up, tenderly cared for, and advertised by strangers—and after food and rest had been had, there was a reaction from desperation. For a time men were unreasonably cheerful and hopeful; now, this stage appears to have passed. In its place there is sternness; but so narrow is the division between this and another mood, that in the midst of a sentence a change of quality in the voice occurs, and you see that eyes have moistened. I had partly expected to find a feverish, reckless spirit, and among the less disciplined classes an unusual current setting towards turbulence, lawlessness, and artificial jollity, such as held in San Francisco for a long time after the great fire there—such as often seizes seamen after a wreck. On the contrary, Chicago is the soberest and the most clear-headed city I ever saw. I have observed but two men the worse for liquor; I have not once been asked for an alms, nor have I heard a hand-organ. The clearing of the wreck goes ahead in a driving but steady, well-ordered way. I have seen two hundred brick walls rising, ten thousand temporary houses of boards, and fifty thousand piles of materials lifting from the ruins; but, on Sunday, although there were other reports, in a walk of several miles among the ashes, I saw no hand-work going on, except that in two half-made cabins German women were holding boards while their husbands nailed them to the framing. It is obvious that the New England man is taking the helm.

There are respectable citizens who hold to the opinion that the fire was started and spread systematically by incendiaries, and I have seen one, lately from Paris, who is sure that it was part of a general war upon property. Numerous alleged facts are cited to sustain this view, but I believe them generally to be delusions growing out of the common excitement, or accidental coincidences. It is certain that the origin, progress, and all the unusual general phenomena of the fire can be reasonably accounted for in other ways.

You will have heard bad symptoms reported among the workingmen since the fire, but, on the whole, their conduct seems to have been as satisfactory as could have been reasonably expected. An unusual proportion of them are Germans, Swedes, and Norwegians, and, what is of great consequence, they were the owners of a lot and cottage. There has been an advance of about twenty per cent in wages, and this has occurred without strikes or any general ill-feeling. Laborers now command $2 a day, carpenters and masons $4 to $5. Good mechanics are wanted, and many hundred more than are now here will be required in the spring.

The responsibility of leading affairs is felt to be too great to be trifled with. Even in politics this is true; perhaps, on the principle of locking the stable-door after the horse is stolen. City officers are to be elected next week, and citizens who have heretofore been unable to spare time for public from their private business, are exhibiting some concern about the character of the candidates. The old knots of dirty, overdressed men waiting for something to turn up seem to have had enough, and have disappeared. I have seen no soldiers, nor the slightest occasion for them. The police, as usual, except those regulating the passage of the crossings, seem to have nothing on their minds but a lazy looking forward to the arrival of their reliefs.

Although few of those who were men of substance yet know where they stand, and the work of general permanent reconstruction must, from loss of land titles and other reasons, be postponed till next summer, there has been no delay in deciding upon and starting efficient temporary arrangements for nearly all the old business of the city, except that of the courts. The shipping, railways, telegraphs, are all doing more work than before the fire, and will probably continue to. The city is again supplied with water, most of it with gas; it is as well sewered and paved as before. Omnibuses and street-cars are running on all the old lines; newspapers are published, schools are open and full, and half the numerous churches of the past are working more than double tides—the sensible, economical Roman Catholic custom of successive congregations and relays of clergymen having been adopted; while every day in the week the most effective preaching of the Gospel, in the form of bread, beef, and blankets, is uttered from each. Theatres, concerts, and lectures are advertised, and a new public library is started in the basement of a Baptist meeting-house. Three hundred of the burnt-out business concerns advertise themselves in new quarters, and new stocks of goods are constantly seen coming from the Eastern railway stations. In but few respects will the market a week hence be much worse, either to buy or sell in, than before. There is no difficulty in handling the crops, and, fortunately, they are large and excellent. Chicago, in short, is under jury-masts, and yet carries her ensign union down, but she answers her helm, lays her course, is making fair headway, and her crew, though on short allowance and sore tried, is thoroughly sober and knows its stations.

You ask whether it is in the power of man adequately to guard against such calamities—whether other great cities are as much exposed as was Chicago? All the circumstances are not established with sufficient accuracy for a final answer, and one cannot, in the present condition of affairs, make full enquiries of men who must be best informed; but to such preliminary discussion as is in order, I can offer a certain contribution.

The prevailing drought was, I think, a less important element of the fire in Chicago—whatever may have been the case as to those other almost more terrific fires which occurred simultaneously in Wisconsin and Michigan—than is generally assumed; yet doubtless it was of some consequence. As to the degree of it, I learn that there had been no heavy rain since the 3d of July, and, during this period of three months, it is stated by Dr. Rauch, the Sanitary Superintendent, the total rain-fall had been but two and a half inches. The mean annual rain-fall at Chicago is thirty-one inches. With regard to the cause of the drought, it is to be considered that millions of acres of land hereabouts, on which trees were scarce, have been settled within thirty years by people whose habits had been formed in regions where woods abound. They have used much timber for building, for fencing, railroads, and fuel. They have grown none. They are planting none to speak of. The same is true of nearly all parts of our country in which a great destruction of forests has occurred or is occurring. If the reduction of foliage in any considerable geographical division of the world tends to make its seasons capricious, as there is much evidence, the evil both of destructive droughts and devastating floods is very likely to extend and increase until we have a government service which we dare trust with extensive remedial measures. It is not a matter which commerce can be expected to regulate.

I can obtain no scientifically definite statement of the force of the wind. Several whom I have questioned recollect that they found it difficult, sometimes for a moment impossible, to make head against it; but I think that no year passes that some of our cities do not experience as strong a gale, and that every city in the country must expect to find equal dryness coinciding with equal force of wind as often, at least, as once in twenty years.

The origin of the fire was probably a commonplace accident. The fire started in a wooden building, and moved rapidly from one to another, close at hand, until the extended surface of quickly-burning material heated a very large volume of the atmosphere, giving rise to local currents, which, driving brands upon the heated roofs and cornices of the tall buildings to leeward, set them on fire, and through the rapid combustion of their contents, loosely piled tier upon tier, developed a degree of heat so intense that ordinary means of resistance to it proved of no avail. Under an old law, wooden buildings had been forbidden to be erected in or moved to the locality were the fire started. In 1867, upon the motion of men who wished to dispose of buildings they had contracted to move out of the more compact part of the city, the Common Council consented to a modification of this law. The Board of Health at the time urged the danger of doing so, and was told to mind its business. Underwriters, merchants, and capitalists were silent.

Chicago had a weakness for "big things," and liked to think that it was outbuilding New York. It did a great deal of commerical advertising in its house-tops. The faults of construction as well as of art in its great showy buildings must have been numerous. Their walls were thin, and were often overweighted with gross and coarse misornamentation. Some ostensibly stone fronts had huge overhanging wooden or sheet-metal cornices fastened directly to their roof timbers, with wooden parapets above them. Flat roofs covered with tarred felt and pebbles were common. In most cases, I am told by observers, the fire entered the great buildings by their roof timbers, even common sheet-metal seeming to offer but slight and very temporary protection to the wood on which it rested. Plain brick walls or walls of brick with solid stone quoins and window-dressings evidently resisted the fire much better than stone-faced walls with a thin backing of brick.

There has been no court-martial called for the trial of the fire service of the city. I understand that it was under the same board with the police. Most of the so-called police force of Chicago whom I had seen before the fire appeared in dirty, half-buttoned uniforms, and were either leaning against a door-post in conversation with equally disreputable-looking friends, and incessantly spitting on the sidewalk, or were moving with a gait and carriage which can be described by no word but loafing.

No one can be sure that with reasonably solid brick walls, reasonably good construction, and honest architecture, this fire could, once under strong headway, with the wind that was blowing, have been stopped at any point in its career, even by good generalship, directing a thoroughly well-drilled and disciplined soldierly force of firemen and police. But that the heat thrown forward would have been less intense, the advance of the fire less rapid, the destruction of buildings less complete, the salvage of their contents greater, and the loss of life smaller, may be assumed with confidence.

The walls least dilapidated are those of the Post-Office. They are of brick faced with stone, and two to three feet thick. It is stated that the fire entered by the upper windward windows, which, strangely, were not protected by iron shutters. The interior is thoroughly burned out. The windward side of the exterior is scaled and seared with heat, but the leeward side is scarcely injured at all; the glass even remains in the windows, and the sidewalks, rails, and lamp-posts are essentially unimpaired. It appears to me that this one building stood for a time a perfect dam to the fiery torrent. It was far from fireproof; but had there been a dozen other as well-built walls standing in line across the wind, and had there been no excessively weak roofs and cornices to leeward of them, I should suppose that half of all that was lost might have been saved.

The two most important buildings in the city were the Court-House, which was also the City Hall, and the pumping-house of the Water-Works. The Court-House was a costly structure with a stone exterior, ostensibly fireproof, standing in the midst of a public square. No respectable structure in the same situation would have been seriously injured. Large additions had been made to it two years ago, and the design for them is said to have been bargained for under such conditions that no respectable architect could have been employed. The result, architecturally, was at all events very bad. There is much more beauty in the walls now, where they have been chipped and crumbled by the fire, than ever before. It has also been publicly charged that some of the legislators of the city were interested in the building contracts, and that much money was made on them. The first fall of snow after the roof was put on caused it to fall in, and other parts of the structure were so thoroughly shattered that it was feared that the whole would come down. A proposition to tear it down and rebuild it was seriously entertained, but, as one of the gentlemen who decided the question told me, in view of what it had already cost, the taxpayers would not have stood it, and it was determined to patch it up. On the top of it, a tall wooden, tin-clad cupola was set. The fire, true to its mission of instructive punishment, made a long leap forward to seize upon this; it soon fell in; and, before the nearest adjoining commercial blocks to windward had even taken fire, it had been completely burnt out with all its invaluable contents.

I have neither seen the Water-Works nor the justly distinguished engineer who is regarded as responsible for their construction, and who may be depended on to give the reason of their unfortunate breakdown with the utmost accuracy and candor. The roof of the pumping-house, of metal, I believe, is publicly stated to have been upheld by wooden timbering, which was charred by heat from firebrands which had fallen above. Breaking down, it broke some part of the pumping-engine, and thus the city was left without water. The main battle, such as it was, had been before this fought and lost, but that much might still have been saved had the flow of water continued, a single experience will sufficiently indicate.

A friend who had, with other treasures, a choice library of several thousand volumes, tells me that he had thought much of the danger of fire, and was prepared to meet it. His house stood apart from all others, and was surrounded by trees. He had a strong force of instructed assistants, with private hydrants, hose, wet carpets, and buckets, well distributed. He had horses and wagons ready, but to the last was confident in his means of resistance. All houses to windward of him had nearly burned down, and he had extinguished every spark that had fallen upon his own, when the water failed. Five minutes afterwards his roofs and walls were on fire in a dozen places, and he had all he could do to save the lives of his household.

Considering the circumstances under which the arrangements for relief were formed, they appear to be admirably good. In the midst of the most pressing demands of their private affairs, men of great good sense and well informed have taken time to devise and bring others into a comprehensive and sufficient organization, acting under well-guarded laws. Chicago, when all did well, exceeded all in her manner of providing for the sick and wounded, prisoners and refugees as well as friends; and now the bread she then floated is truly returning to her under natural laws; for men and women more fit to be trusted in every way than those to whom the control of the contributions for relief have at length, after, it is said, a hard struggle with political speculators, been given, could hardly be found in any other city. The most scrupulous caution is taken to guard against waste or imposition, and to avoid encouraging improvidence, indolence, or a disposition to mendicant habits. Among hundreds of women drawing rations, I saw few who did not appear to have been decent, tidy, motherly persons—nearly all were European born.

The most costly and best form of charity has been that of supplying, either as a loan or as a gift, a limited amount of building materials with printed plans for a rough cabin of two rooms to be made of it, together with a stove, mattresses, and blankets, to men having families, and able by their work to support them. This has already been done in 6,000 cases. Great eagerness is shown to obtain this favor, especially by those laboring men who were burned out from houses of their own, and who can thus at once reoccupy their own land. The thankfulness expressed by these men—thankfulness, as the Mayor says, "to all the world"—is sometimes very touching. The cost of the cabins, lined with heavy paper and supplied with a chimney, is, according to size, from $90 to $120. Besides the shelter thus provided, the public squares are filled with temporary barracks, and the whole number of those who have been housed by means of contributions received is, I believe, about 35,000. Wherever it is possible, persons not of families able to at least partly support themselves by labor, are helped to leave the city. The number of those to whom aid is thought needful to be administered has been rapidly reduced, every care being taken to obtain work for them and to avoid feeding those who avoid work. It is now a little over 60,000. With the coming on of winter, work will fail, and the number needing assistance increase. The funds thus far promised are not enough to meet the requirements of the barest humanity, and, especially if the winter should be severe, larger contributions than there is now reason to expect will be sorely needed.

Arrangements are made for searching out and privately and delicately administering to such sufferers as will not ask or be publicly known to receive charity. It is easy to see that the number of such must be very large. It was a maxim in Chicago that a fool could hardly invest in city real estate so badly that, if he could manage to hold it for five years, its advance would fail to give him more than ten per cent interest, while there was a chance for a small fortune. Acting on this view, most young professional men and men on small salaries, if they had families, bought a lot and built a small house for themselves, confident that by hook or by crook they should save enough to pay the interest as it fell due on the necessary mortgage, together with the cost of insurance. To accomplish this they lived pinchingly, and their houses and lots were their only reserves. In thousands of cases, they have lost their houses, their insurance, and their situations all at one blow. Fifty of the insurance companies doing business here have suspended payment, seven of them being Chicago companies, whose directors were men of local influence and often employers.

The Sanitary Department has a list, known to be as yet incomplete, of 180 regular physicians who were burned out. Many, if not most of these lost house and furniture, as well as office, instruments, and books, and the families in which they practised are dispersed. Judge Wilson reckons the number of lawyers, mostly young men, whose libraries were burned at five hundred. Many of both classes, for some days after the fire, took their places in the lines in order to get the rations of biscuits served out by the relief agents.

But even the condition of young men with families who have lost everything is hardly as sad as that of many of the older citizens, much overworked men who had fairly earned leisure and affluence. Owing to peculiar commercial conditions here, the number of such who have lost everything is larger than it would be in an older city. Cautious men averse to the general habits of speculation were most disposed to invest in buildings, and patriotic men, who had grown up with the city, and who had the most interest and pride in it, were most apt to insure in the local companies.

Amidst all the material prosperity of Chicago, there had always been a few of her citizens who had really bonded themselves to have no share in it, in devotion to higher pursuits. As examples of these, the Kinnicut brothers, as both are dead, may perhaps be named. There were others, their instructors, leaders, supporters, and followers, who, like them, had travelled frugally and far, studied devotedly, and who, aided by a few worthy men of greater wealth, were laying the foundations of a true seat and school of art, science, and learning. Several special collections had already been gathered which money can never replace. These, with libraries, many series of notes, the work of half a lifetime, and some unpublished books, more or less nearly complete, are lost; and most of those who had supplied the funds to sustain these most interesting and important bases of the higher civilization for the great Northwest, are thrown back to struggle again for the decent maintenance of their families.

But great as is this loss, it will be consciously felt by comparatively few. Even more appalling, in view of the long years of weary labor of many educated men involved, is the destruction of important papers, contracts, agreements, and accounts, notes of surveys, and records of deeds and mortgages. It is estimated that nine-tenths of the papers held by attorneys were kept in various patent safes on upper floors, and were destroyed. The same is true of those held by surveyors, real-estate agents, etc. The city and county records were, I believe, in vaults built, like those of the Custom-House and Post-Office, on stone slabs, supported on iron columns, which, soon yielding to the heat, tumbled them into a pit of fire, and all were lost. How the city is to recover from this blow no one can yet see, but the difficulty is engaging the study of its best and most conservative minds; and that in some way it will recover, and that it will presently advance even with greater rapidity, but with far firmer steps, than ever before, those most staggered and cast down by it have not a shadow of doubt.

Dante's Visual Images, and His Early Illustrators
AND
Botticelli's Illustrations to "The Divina Commedia"

BY BERNHARD BERENSON

1894 and 1896

FLORENCE, December 24, 1893.

Mere learning has perhaps done its very utmost with Dante by this time, and, if the subject is not to become stagnant, it must now be approached from other points of view, and the light of other than merely philological and philosophical erudition must be thrown upon it. Is it not rather extraordinary that thus far it has occurred to only one writer, and that not one of the corps enrolled to write on the subject, but a free-lance such as Vernon Lee is, to ask the question what visual images Dante had while giving his perfectly plastic descriptions of the exterior universe? Few students of Dante stop to wonder what correspondence there can be between his visual images while writing and those called up in our minds while reading him, and they are apt to fancy that the correspondence must be great. But those of us who visualize at all cannot read about Trajan and the Widow, let us say, without seeing an image based on some one or on a whole number of Roman bas-reliefs. Dante could not have such an acquaintance with the antique as we cannot help having, and his visual image of a scene taking place in Greece or Rome or Judea could have had no great likeness to ours. It could scarcely have been otherwise with the figure of Virgil himself. We cannot help dressing Virgil as a Roman, and giving him a "classical profile" and "statuesque carriage," but Dante's visual image of Virgil was probably no less mediæval, no more based on a critical reconstruction of antiquity, than his entire conception of the Roman poet. Fourteenth-century illustrators make

91

Virgil look like a mediæval scholar, dressed in cap and gown, and there is no reason why Dante's visual image of him should have been other than this.

That Dante had visual images, there can scarcely be a doubt. We have, in proof, besides the unequalled plasticity of all his descriptions, the detailed account in *Purgatorio*, Canto X., of the various reliefs representing acts of humility. These reliefs are simply the descriptions of the visual images called up in Dante's mind by the acts of humility. "To take plastic shape in the mind" has become a common phrase in criticism, but it can have no meaning unless that of *becoming visualized;* and as the phrase is applied to Dante, it means that Dante visualized everything that passed through his mind. Nothing, therefore, could bring us nearer to a knowledge of those contents of Dante's mind of which he was himself aware while writing, than if we could form some conception of his visual images.

Dante himself gives the clue. On the first anniversary of Beatrice's death, he says in the 'Vita Nuova,' he sat down and drew the figure of an angel. A student of early Tuscan art must know how this angel looked. Dante could not have invented this figure, but, like all amateurs, he drew an angel of the kind his favorite painter would have drawn, and in this instance the painter is Giotto. Dante's angel in all likelihood resembled one of Giotto's such as we see in Assisi, Padua, or Florence; and had Dante gone further and drawn a whole scene—that is to say, exactly rendered as only form and color can render a visual image—its relation to one of Giotto's whole pictures would have been the same. Dante's visual image of the Virtues, of the heavenly hosts, of Christ and the Virgin, of St. Francis, could not have been very different from Giotto's, nor even his image of Beatrice very different from one of the great painter's sleek-faced, almond-eyed, waistless women. Beatrice did not necessarily look like this. The visual image is not the direct impression of the object, but the memory of the impression more or less vague according to the varying powers of visualization; and in a lover of the arts such as Dante was, visualization is largely determined by the works of art with which he is intimately acquainted. It is Giotto whom Dante knew best and loved best, and it is the study of Giotto, therefore, and of kindred painters (some even closer in spirit to Dante, such as Duccio, Simone Martini, and the Lorenzetti) that will enable us to form a clear conception of Dante's visual images.

None of these painters shows trace of direct Dantesque inspiration, and none of them has left what would have been the most valuable of all commentaries on the real Dante, a series of illustrations to the 'Divina Commedia.' But they frequently dealt with subjects fringing on Dante's, and a systematic study of these would be a great help in reconstructing the poet's visual images. Illustrations, moreover, by their followers, the heirs of their conceptions, exist in plenty. After these contemporaries of Dante, no painter at all on a level in genius with him appeared until Signorelli, but by that time visual imagery had changed from mediæval to modern. To a certain extent, the antique had already been critically reconstructed. Still, Signorelli's illustrations in the chapel of S. Brizio at Orvieto have an interest not only as interpretations by a great artist, but as the visual images suggested by Dante to a person much nearer the poet than we are, for the attitude of the Renaissance towards antiquity was still subjective—far less than Dante's, but endlessly more than our own. The Renaissance viewed antiquity not with our feeling of its being for ever past, but with longing and the hope of wholly restoring it to a living present. It is this which gives that fascinating tinge of romance to Renaissance reconstructions of antiquity. Michelangelo's attitude is already quite like our own, and his visual images could give no clue to Dante's; but as interpretations they would be invaluable, for he is the only artist of modern times whose genius was of a kind and of a quality to be compared with Dante's. That a series of illustrations by Michelangelo to the 'Divina Commedia' existed there can be but little doubt, and their loss is one of the greatest the study of Dante has incurred. Botticelli's sketches are scarcely to be considered, for, great as they are as works of art, Botticelli was too subjective to give his illustrations a greater connection with the subject that can be had in lineal rhapsodies. Zuccaro and Stradano, working when the Renaissance was rotten-ripe, far from being a help, are as much in the way as Doré. They were even farther from suspecting the difference between their own and Dante's visual images. The next great event in the study of Dante will probably be an edition of the 'Commedia' with illustrations chosen from the finest of the fourteenth and fifteenth centuries, and from the best by Signorelli and Botticelli, supplemented by such parallel conceptions as may be found in Dante's contemporaries, and even in Michelangelo and Tintoretto. The editor of such an edition of the 'Commedia' will find that the ground has been well prepared by Dr. Ludwig Volkmann, in his pamphlet on early illustrations to Dante.*

Dr. Volkmann has examined more than seventy illustrated codices in Germany and Italy, not having extended his studies beyond these countries. France and England would have increased the list considerably. He divides the codices into two classes, those containing illuminations and such as have water-color or lineal illustrations. The

---

* *Bildliche Darstellungen zu Dantes Divina Commedia bis zum Ausgang der Renaissance.* Leipzig; Breitkopf & Härtel, 1892.

Inferno, as might have been expected, attracted the greatest number of illustrators, the *Purgatorio* fewer, and the *Paradiso* least of all. Traditional compositions, therefore, as for ecclesiastical subjects, sprang up for the first, while the illustrator of the last had to rely on his own invention. But it seems to have taken a whole generation before illustrators found out what parts of the 'Commedia' they could handle. At first they tried all the cantos.

Illuminated codices contain, as a rule, miniatures for the initial letters only at the beginning of each of the three sections, and these miniatures soon became stereotyped. In the initial of the *Inferno* Dante is represented either at his desk, or with Virgil in the forest. The P of the *Purgatorio* contains either Virgil and Dante sailing up to the Mount, or a picture of souls aflame. The L of the *Paradiso* gives a bust of Christ, the Trinity, or Dante and Beatrice. A few of the illuminated codices contain elaborate and very complete illustrations. Of the fourteenth century, the best of all is one in the Nazionale at Florence, dating from about 1333. Here Minos, Pluto, and Cerberus are represented not as we who have been brought up on Smith's 'Classical Dictionary' think of them, but as creatures with hoofs, claws and horns, and flaming eyes, as Dante in all probability saw them in his mind. A codex in the Angelica at Rome is almost on a level with one in Florence. Among miniatured codices of later days the most valuable is certainly the one in the Vatican that was begun for Frederic of Urbino by some follower of Giovanni Bellini, and finished at a much later date by some one who was no stranger to Lorenzo Lotto's works. This codex would yield a number of plates for an illustrated edition of Dante.

The great difference between the illustrations in miniature and those in outline or water-color is that the former never represent the same person more than once in the same illustration, while the latter tend to be panoramic, crowding several events in which the same person is concerned into one composition. This, by the way, was a practice common in Italian painting in general. The best of this latter series is a codex in the Marciana at Venice, with 245 large illustrations, for the most part in outline, by an artist who shows great affinities with the Florentines of the Trecento. At the beginning of the *Paradiso* he has represented Dante at the feet of Apollo, who appears here as a young, fair-haired knight fiddling to his heart's content. Most of the other illustrations are equally remote from our own conceptions and probably equally close to Dante's visual images. At Altona there is a valuable codex of about 1400.

The early engravings, such as Baldini's, have small value except as playthings, and the early woodcuts are scarcely better, although they often have inimitable traits of naïveté; but the conceptions of their authors are too infantile to touch Dante at all. The first edition of Dante with woodcuts appeared at Brescia in 1487. Repetitions and improvements of this were published at Venice in 1491, 1493, and 1497. But it is the illustrators of the fourteenth century, and not these late people, who bring us close to Dante's visual image. These scarcely deserve attention.

FLORENCE, October 22, 1896.

The publication in a form almost popular of Sandro Botticelli's drawings for Dante's 'Divina Commedia' has long been called for, and is at last accomplished.* Something has been lost in reducing the illustrations to half the size of the originals. One or two have become quite inextricable in their entanglement, and the first sketching in with silver point has nearly disappeared. But these slight losses are more than recompensed by the comparatively small price and the extreme handiness of the present edition, bound in book form. Dr. Lippmann's introduction and commentary leave little or nothing to be desired in the way of information or elucidation.

To many these illustrations will be disappointing. They have heard that Botticelli was a great artist, and they expect him to give them, to an even intenser degree, feelings of the kind and quality that they have had in reading Dante. None of the gloom, the chill dread, the passion, the despair, the luridness of the "Inferno" will be brought home to them as they turn over Botticelli's designs. They will find scarcely an attempt at dramatic expression; they will find many more instances of the unconscious grotesque than of the realized sublime; and, throughout, conceptions as infantile as Fra Angelico's, but seldom so winning. Nor, taken as real illustration, are matters much improved in the "Purgatorio." There is no trace in Botticelli of the feeling of hope and convalescence and early morning which penetrates you as you read these cantos of Dante. And Sandro's "Paradiso" fails no less in communicating the one essential quality of this part of the poem—its sublimity. Here again the artist remains shut up in the Fra Angelico world. All in all, Rossetti's "Blessed Damozel" would have been a fitter subject for Botticelli's fancy than Dante's 'Divina Commedia.'

As illustrator, then, to the 'Divina Commedia,' Botticelli, it must be

* *Drawings by Sandro Botticelli for Dante's Divina Commedia.* Reduced facsimilies after the originals in the Royal Museum, Berlin, and in the Vatican Library, with an Introduction by F. Lippmann. London: Lawrence & Bullen; New York: Dodd, Mead & Co. 1896. Imperial quarto.

acknowledged, disappoints, partly because his genius was not at all Dantesque, but chiefly because the poem does not lend itself to satisfactory illustration. Although Dante describes with a vividness and tangibility surpassing all other poets', his effects seldom result from an appeal to vision only. Yet visual form, so small a part of the poet's outfit, is the illustrator's entire tool-chest. All his effects must come through it, and can come by it only. Think of making mere outline, as in the case of Botticelli's illustrations, convey all the manifold sensations, all the passions and emotions, which rapidly succeed each other in Dante's verses! One might as well attempt to render Beethoven's Ninth Symphony or Berlioz's "Dies Iræ" with no other instrument than the French horn.

And even if it were possible to make outline convey feelings as full and penetrating as Dante's, which episodes should the illustrator choose? They follow each other in bewildering number, with no connection in the realm of visually representable things, held together by nothing more tangible than the emotional tone of each canto. The fact is that Dante is not a great epic or dramatic poet. He has none of those stretches of culminating narrative, none of the working up to a climax, which lend themselves so admirably to the exercise of the visual imagination. In spite of the fact that he wrote one of the longest real poems in existence, and that this is apparently a narrative, Dante as a poet is great only as a master of the lyric, or (to make a concession) of the "dramatic lyric." Now the lyric is beyond the reach of the illustrator.

Dante does not lend himself to illustration; and, even if he did, Botticelli was not the man for the task. Then, pray, what is the value of these drawings? The answer is simple enough. Their value consists in their being drawings by Botticelli, not at all in their being drawings for Dante. And at this point the honest showman should warn the public that a drawing by Botticelli is something very peculiar. It does not so much as attempt to be correct; it is not a faithful reproduction of anything whatsoever. A hundred "artist-journalists" now at work publish daily drawings which are far more exact, more life-like, more clever, and more brilliant than any you will find in Botticelli's designs for the 'Divina Commedia.' If that is the only kind of drawing you care for, you will be no less disappointed in Sandro than if you went to him for interpretative illustration. His real place as a draughtsman is not among great Europeans, but with the great Chinese and Japanese, with Ririomin, Haronobu, and Hokusai. Like these, he is a supreme master of the single line. He gives it a swiftness and a purity which in the whole world of sensation find their analogy only in some few ecstatic notes of the violin, or in the most crystalline *timbre* of the soprano voice. His universe was of the simplest. It consisted of things

that could and of things that could not furnish themes for rhapsodies
in swift, pure lines. Dante happened to find himself among the blessed
in this simple division; hence Botticelli chose him as a subject for his
art. These illustrations required of our artist no coloring—with him
always an afterthought—and scarcely any sterotyped composition.
Here he could be free as nowhere else, and here, therefore, we see him
in his most unadulterated form. The value of these drawings consists in
their being the most spontaneous product of the greatest master of the
single line that our modern Western world has yet possessed.

Now let us look at a few of these designs, beginning with the "Inferno," where Botticelli, feeling himself most weighed down by the
story, is least himself. What do we see as we turn to the drawing for
the opening canto? In the first place, a fretwork arrangement of exquisite pen strokes, by itself as pleasant as light on rippling water.
Looked at closer, this smiling fretwork becomes a wood of graceful
stems, whose branches cross and recross like the rapiers of courteous
fencers. In rhymic balance to the mass of this dainty forest you have
a tangle of flower-bushes. Between, ramp three heraldic beasts, performing a figure with four men whose long cloaks fall into lines as
swift and almost as pure as those of the tree stems. I defy any one to
read gloom and terror into this piece of lineal decoration. Or turn to
the illustration for Inf. xiii. Again a marvellous fretwork of lines
which, seen closer, resolve themselves into a tangled wood where
decorative dogs leap at decorative nudes, while even more decorative
harpies sit upon the branches. We are in the round of the suicides, but
it would take a child with a feverish imagination to get a shiver out of
this design. I will not deny that, in other sheets—indeed, in many of
those for the "Inferno"—there is somewhat more correspondence with
the text, but I doubt whether it ever is enough to be satisfactory as
expression, while it is precisely in such drawings that the artist is least
satisfactory as pure art. What does occur at times is a fortunate accord
between the way Botticelli would naturally treat a subject and Dante's
feeling about it. This occurs rarely in the "Inferno," where it would be
hard to instance another example than that of the hypocrites under
their copes of lead (singularly Japanese, by the way, in movement of
line); but, out of the "Inferno," as we shall see, this accord gets more
and more frequent.

But Botticelli's strength was not in arrangement alone. He was, above
everything, master of the line in movement. He loved to make it run
and leap, to make it whirl and dance. He was truly great only when he
had a theme which permitted the exercise of this mastery. Such themes
the "Purgatorio" and "Paradiso" offered him in plenty. Examples
become too many to cite, and I shall confine myself to a few of the

best. You will rarely see a frieze of greater decorative beauty than is formed by the nudes leaping into the purgatorial flames, as if they were the waters of the Fountain of Youth, while Virgil and Statius and Dante pass by discoursing on the relation between soul and body. This is the illustration to Purg. xxv, and, after this one, every consecutive drawing becomes, if possible, more and more beautiful. The flames leap even higher, and the nudes are worked in with them even more harmoniously. And presently you come to a design whose beauty keeps you spellbound: rare trees shoot up with exquisite grace, and between them you see the poets breathing gladly and gazing at the pure ether. One lady, with fascinating movement of figure and flutter of drapery, is gathering flowers, and another addresses the poets. Are we in Dante's terrestrial Paradise, or in Poliziano's Realm of Venus? No matter which, it could not be more lovely. This is followed by a succession of scenes in which Botticelli's talents find their completest satisfaction: the car of the Church, the grandly draped elders, the dancing, flower-scattering angels, the torch-bearers, the streaming smoke, the heraldic beasts—each and all so many exquisitely drawn laughing, leaping, whirling lines in wonderful arrangement. But the crown of the whole work is still to come: it is the design for Par. i. The daintiest trees ever drawn wave softly over a smooth meadow wet by the water of Eunoe's placid stream. Behind the rare leafage of the reed-like trees, Beatrice and Dante, with faces of ecstasy, are wafted gently up to the higher spheres. To convey in words a sensation corresponding to the singular beauty of this page would require Dante himself, or perhaps Shakespeare or Keats. Line, movement, and pattern can go no further. None of the remaining illustrations can be put beside this one; yet they are all lovely. The type of them is the one for Par. vi—a pure circle studded with exquisite flamelets, Beatrice pointing upward as she floats, and Dante with his face and hands expressive of the utmost ecstasy. The flicker of the flamelets, the flutters of the draperies, the bending towards each other of the two figures, with the whole enclosed in a pure circle, form one of those happy patterns which, for the very reason of their childlike simplicity, one can gaze at for hours, being soothed and refreshed.

To the few scores, or let us hope, hundreds the world over, who feel the difference between art and illustration, as well as between art and fidelity to nature or mere dexterity, Dr. Lippmann's publication is one of the great events of recent years.

Strauss and His "Elektra"

BY ERNEST NEWMAN

1910

Judging from the tone of a number of last Monday's articles, our musical critics, as a whole, are still a little doubtful as to the propriety of saying what they must really feel about Strauss. They cannot possibly like a great part of what they hear, but at the back of their heads is the thought that, as Wagner was abused by the critics of his own day for extravagances that time has shown to be no extravagances at all, so time may show that Strauss was right in *his* extravagances, and that the critics who objected to them were wrong. So a number of the prudent gentlemen stay the flood of ridicule that is almost on their lips, and, instead, talk darkly of the future showing what it will show, and utter other safe commonplaces. All the while there is no real comparison between the Wagnerian case and the Straussian. All new music, from the mere fact that it *is* new, is apt to be misunderstood, and an idiom may seem wild or incoherent merely because we are not yet accustomed to it. But because the human ear has sometimes disliked a new thing and afterwards liked it, it does not follow that it will some day like everything that to-day it cordially dislikes. There are other things to be considered, and one of these is the fact that nowadays we are much better placed than our fathers were for judging new music accurately. They had, for the most part, to listen to it without the slightest previous knowledge of it, and to express an opinion upon it probably after one hearing of the work. In these days we can generally study the score of the work long before we hear it. To talk of hearing "Elektra" for the first time on Saturday last is nonsensical. The vocal score has been at our service for twelve months or more, and it was open to any critic to have it by heart before he went into Covent Garden on Saturday. A piano arrangement, it is true, does not tell us all about a complex modern work; but it tells us a great deal, and with that knowledge we can listen to a first performance on the stage in a better state of preparation than the Wagnerian critics could do at a tenth performance. All this critical timidity, then, is not very creditable. Anyone who had taken the trouble to study the score of "Elektra" could easily gather from Saturday's performance whether the parts he had marked out as requiring elucidation sounded as bad as he had expected them to do, or better. And, after the performance, he should be quite able to relieve posterity of the trouble of making up his mind for him on nine points out of ten. Anyhow, it would be better to make the attempt.

All but the Strauss fanatics will admit that, though he is undoubtedly the greatest living musician, there is a strong strain of foolishness and ugliness in him, that he is lacking in the sensitive feeling for the balance of a large work that some other great artists have, and that consequently there is not one large work of his, from "Don Quixote" onward, that is not marred by some folly or some foolery. If it were not for this strain of coarseness and thoughtlessness in him, he would never have taken up so crude a perversion of the old Greek story as that of Hugo von Hofmannsthal. One does not in the least object to a modern poet looking at ancient figures through modern eyes, so long as he can see them convincingly and make them live for us. But to make a play a study of human madness, and then to lay such excessive stress upon the merely physical concomitants of madness, is to ask us to tune our notions of dramatic terror and horror down to too low a pitch. Strauss, of course, revels in this physical, and therefore more superficial, side of the madness, with the result that, instead of impressing us, he generally either bores us or amuses us. We have only to look at a pathological study of human morbidity such as Dostoievsky gives us in "Crime and Punishment," so fine, so unobtrusively true to life, and then listen to the vulgar din by which Strauss tries to convey to us that a woman's brain is distraught, to realise the difference between a man of genius and one who, for the moment, has become merely a man of talent. For the real complaint against the excited music in "Elektra" is that it mostly does not excite you at all; you are rather sorry, in fact, that the composer should take so much trouble to be a failure. For he is so violent that, as a rule, you cannot believe in the least in his violence. He has the besetting Teutonic sin of over-statement, of being unable to see that the half is often greater than the whole; and all this blacking of his face, and waving of his arms, and howling "bolly-golly-black-man —boo!" at us leaves us quite unmoved, except to smile and wish he wouldn't do it. One could easily name a hundred passages in ancient and modern music that thrill us far more horribly, and with far simpler means, than all the clatter that breaks out when Orestes, for example, is murdering Aegisthus. The mere recollection of the stories of ghosts in the churchyard, or of his own fears when, as a child, he was left alone in a dark room, might have told Strauss that horror and the creeping of the flesh are not necessarily associated with noise and fury. His orchestra doth protest too much.

Nor do we need to wait for posterity to tell us that much of the music is as abominably ugly as it is noisy. Here a good deal of the talk about complexity is wide of the mark. The real term for it is incoherence, discontinuity of thinking. "The three angles of a triangle are equal to two right angles" sounds absurdly simple, but really represents a good deal of complex cerebral working; so does the G minor fugue of Bach. But "the man in the moon is the daughter of Aunt Martha's tom-cat," though it sounds very complex, is incoherent nonsense; and so is a good deal of "Elektra." Unfortunately, while we have obvious ways of testing the sense or nonsense of the remark about the man in the moon, it is not so easy to test the sense or nonsense of a passage of music; and so a good deal of quite confused thinking gets the credit for being hyper-subtle thinking. What awestruck worshippers call complexity in "Elektra" would often be more correctly described as impudence at its best and incompetence at its worst. As for the more normally lyrical pages in "Elektra," there are very few of them worthy even of a smaller musician than Strauss. The first solo of Chrysothemis, for example, is merely agreeable commonplace; the theme of triumph in the finale is so cheap that it must have been picked up on the rubbish-heap of Italian or French opera. Nothing marks so clearly the degeneration of the musician in Strauss from what he was fifteen years ago than the average melodic writing in "Elektra."

What saves the opera is, first of all, the wonderful beauty of parts of the scene between Elektra and Orestes, especially when, ceasing to be a maniac and becoming a normal woman, she pours out her soul in love for her brother. There is grandeur again—spasmodic, of course, but none the less unescapable—at a hundred points in the score. It may last merely a moment or two, and then flicker off into ugliness or commonplace, but while it is there we are mastered by it. Elektra's cry of "Agamemnon," whenever it occurs, always holds us in this way. Strauss in "Elektra," indeed, is like a huge volcano spluttering forth a vast amount of dirt and murk, through which every now and then, when the fuming ceases and a breath of clear air blows away the smoke, we see the grand and strong original outlines of the mountain. And when Strauss puts forth his whole mental strength, it is indeed overwhelming. We may detest the score as a whole for its violence and frequent ugliness, but the fine things in it are of the kind that no other man, past or present, could have written—the monologue of Elektra just mentioned, for example, or the wailing themes that dominate the section preceding it, or the tense, fateful gloom of the finish of the opera. The result of it all is to give far more pain to Strauss's admirers than it can possibly do to those who have always disliked him. In spite of the pathetic way in which he wastes himself, playing now the fool, now the swashbuckler, now the trickster, you cannot be in doubt that you are listening to a man who is head and shoulders above all other living composers. One still clings to the hope that the future has in store for us a purified Strauss, clothed and in his right mind, who will help us to forget the present Strauss—a saddening mixture of genius, ranter, child, and charlatan. As it is, one would hardly venture to prophesy more than a few short years of life for "Elektra," for the public will not long continue to spend an hour and three-quarters in the theatre for about half an hour's enjoyment.

A Great French Philosopher at Harvard

BY WILLIAM JAMES

1910

The Hyde lectureship, which has year after year brought to Harvard some splendid object-lesson of the way in which popular lectures may best be given, has never till this year taken a philospher as its example-setter. This year we have been having Prof. Emile Boutroux, and the occasion seems to me so well worthy of commemoration that I venture to set down a brief account of it for *The Nation's* readers.

The whole enterprise of international exchange of professors is still in its tentative infancy, and one may hear as many arguments against it as reasons for it. The Hyde foundation requires all lectures to be in the French tongue, and the first thing that has been disclosed is the appalling rarity of ability to understand spoken French, even in a centre of learning like Cambridge.

M. Boutroux's auditors this year should preëminently have been our students of philosophy; but, victims of the deplorable manner in which they have been taught foreign languages, hardly half a dozen of them have shown their faces. Few, even of our instructors, follow a French lecture easily—though many more can follow German—and what with "other engagements," and the terrors of the title, "Contingence et Liberté," of M. Boutroux's course, their number proved so small that the bulk of the audience consisted of world's people from Boston and elsewhere, including a good number of French visitors attracted, I am sure, less by the particular subject, than by the rare pleasure of hearing any intelligible discourse whatever in the language of the far-off native country.

It is obvious that the institution of professorial exchange needs overhauling. It ought to be a means of vital stimulation, of making our somewhat torpid youth aware of the presence of a wider world about them, human and social as well as intellectual. So far it has missed fire in this respect. Our young fogies in the graduate schools continue working for their Ph.D. examinations by moving, like Faust's Wagner, "von Buch zu Buch," "von Blatt zu Blatt," and remain for the most part quite unconscious that an opportunity has been lost to them.

M. Boutroux is one of the veterans of his country in the sphere of philosophy, and an extraordinarily influential personage in all academic lines of activity. Almost every philosopher of the younger generation has been his pupil; one finds him sitting as a judge at every *soutenance de thèse* for the doctorate in philosphy; he attends congresses; has been since its foundation *directeur* of the Institut Thiers, and is president this year of the Academie des Sciences Morales et Politiques, where he will shortly have to welcome Mr. Roosevelt as an *associé étranger*. He is a somewhat ascetic looking figure, with a very French and rather military physiognomy, but with the kindliest of manners, a power of extraordinarily clear statement, and, above all, a great air of simplicity and sincerity while lecturing.

M. Boutroux, like almost all his compatriots, thinks it no praise to say of a lecturer that "he talks like a book." German and Anglo-Saxon lecturers may talk like books, but the idea of a public lecture in France is different. It ought not to furnish information of details as a book does. It ought rather to confine itself to tracing perspectives, defining tendencies, bringing out contrasts, and summing up results. It ought, above all, to generalize and simplify, and it ought to avoid technicality of language. Needless to say that, for this task, complete mastery of the subject is an indispensable condition, and only the great masters have succeeded greatly as popular expositors. M. Boutroux's single lectures on Pascal and on Comte showed the breadth and simplicity which result from absolute mastery of a subject.

His continuous course, entitled "Contingence et Liberté," consisted of eight lectures, and the high originality of his position here is what, in my eyes, entitles his visit to notice beyond the immediate circle of his listeners. M. Boutroux is, by virtue of priority, the leader *de jure* of the reaction against the abstract, and in favor of the concrete point of view in philosophy, which in the last few years has got under full headway in all countries. The leader *de jure*, I say, meaning the historic leader or precursor, for the leadership in loudness has passed in England and this country to more strident voices, and in France to those more radically revolutionary in tone. Boutroux is above all a liberal, grants cheerfully to the opposing side what it can fairly claim, harbors no enmities, and makes no enemies, so that many a convert to "pragmatism" or to "Bergsonism" has remained ignorant that the ball was set rolling by his first publication, "La Contingence des lois de la nature," away back in 1867. His freedom from polemic virulence, his indisposition to flourish a party flag, have kept his name more in the shade than has been just. The most important features of "pragmatism" and "Bergsonism" find clear expression in that early work. And the *Weltanschauung* of that work, matured and reinforced, but in no wise altered, was what this course of lectures reaffirmed. Deemed paradoxical when it first appeared, that *Weltanschauung* is now recognized as possibly discussable, to say the very least, and is evidently about to enter on a powerful career.

I can only sketch the essence of it briefly, without following the lecturer's own order, or going into any detail. The quickest way to get at the character of anything is to know what to contrast it with. The best term with which to contrast M. Boutroux's way of looking at the world is the "scholastic" way of taking it. When I say "scholastic," I don't use the word historically, but as common-sense uses it when it makes of it a reproach. In this sense scholasticism is found in science as well as in philosophy. It means the pretension to conceive things so vigorously that your definitions shall contain all that need be known about their objects. It means the belief that there is but one set of thoughts which absolutely tell the truth about reality, and it means the claim to possess those thoughts, or the more essential part of them. If the word "scholastic" be objected to, let the word "classic" be employed. M. Boutroux's bugbear would then be the classic spirit, and he might be treated as a "romantic" in philosphy.

H. Taine has attributed the misfortunes of France in the revolutionary and Napoleonic periods to the rule of the classic spirit, with its trust in immutable principles and rigorously logical applications; but Taine himself, so far as his general view of man and nature went, cherished classic ideals. If we look back to his time, we find a different idea of the meaning of "Science" from that which the best investigators have now come to believe in. Taine, Berthelot, Renan, and the other great influencers of public opinion during the Second Empire, thought of science as an absolute dissipator of the mysteries of nature. It stripped reality naked of disguise, revealed its intimate structure, was destined to found a new morality and to replace religion. Its votaries were to be the high priests of the future, and the destinies of our planet were to be committed to their keeping. John Fiske's favorite word "deanthropomorphization" serves as a good summary of this whole way of thinking.

Carried away by the triumphs of chemistry, physics, and mathematics, these men imagined that the frame of things was eternally and literally mechanical, and that truth was reached by abstracting from it everything connected with personality. Personal life is a mere by-product, it was said, and its categories, though we have to live in them practically, have no theoretic validity. At the present day, however, concepts like mass, force, inertia, atom, energy, are themselves regarded rather as symbolic instruments, like coördinates, curves, and the like, for simplifying our map of nature and guiding us through its jungle. But the whole undivided jungle, with our personal life and all, is the reality immediately-given; and though it is given only in small bits at a time to any one, yet the whole content and quality of it is more completely real than that of any of those conceptual substitutes.

This was the central thesis of Professor Boutroux's lectures. Whereas the classic and scholastic tradition is that reality is above all the abstracted, simplified, and reduced, the inalterable and self-identical, the fatal and eternal, Boutroux took the diametrically opposite view. It is the element we wholly live in, it is what Plutarch's and Shakespeare's pages give us, it is the superabounding, growing, ever-varying and novelty-producing. Its real shape is biography and history, and its "categories," far from sterilizing our world for all purposes of living reason, keep fertilizing it infinitely. "Reason" is a term which Professor Boutroux rescues from its purely classic use of tracing identities, concealed or patent. It is for him the faculty of judgment in its widest sense, using sentiments and willingnesses, as well as concepts, as its premises, and abounding in power, as everything else does, the more abundantly it is exercised.

The practical gist of his whole contention was that reality means novelty, elementary and genuine, and not merely apparent. For the classic rationalism, elementary novelty would be synonymous with Absolute Chance at the heart of things, and that is inadmissible. "Pure irrationalism and sentimentalism" would then be the verdict on Professor Boutroux's *Weltanschauung*. But Boutroux is above all things a liberal and mediating mind, and loves not harsh oppositions. If novelties came abruptly "out of whole cloth" and juxtaposed themselves to the existent, like dominoes against dominoes in a game, the world would be as bad a field of rattling bones as the "irreducible" categories and concepts of classical philosophy make it. Not chance, therefore, but "contingency," is the idea which Professor Boutroux prefers to work with; and by contingency he means the element of spontaneity which characterizes concrete human life—where the consciousness of the present is ever of *many* future possibilities, and contains always enough causality for either of them, when realized, to be regarded as its natural effect. Which *shall* be realized is meanwhile uncertain until our living reason makes its choice. Ever something new, but never anything entirely new. No literal imitation like that which is postulated as the "uniformity of nature," yet always imitation in the midst of the variation; and an "order" unlike that "logical" order, where the same comes only from the same, and which is all that mathematical science can imagine—an order satisfying other kinds of demand, and yet not disappointing the intellectual demand that the effect shall in *some* way grow out of and continue all that went before it.

In this sense the entities of science, the molecules or energies, and the equations that express their laws, are previous in reality only in the way in which "grams" and "metres" are, or only as a statue is previous in its rock. The creative touch of human reason was needed in each case for the extrication; and that those particular creations resulted rather than a hundred others just as possible, is one of those selective interactions between living minds and their environment which can be "understood" when once it has occurred, but which no acquaintance with the previous conditions can show to an outsider that it was the sole thing possible. Theories result from psychological variations, just as Roosevelts and Rockefellers result from biological variations. Both variations are adapted partly, and partly non-adapted. They change the world-situation and are changed by the world-situation; but the resultant new situation is always a unique one, and none but the agents of its production are in a position vitally to understand why or how it comes into being.

With such a view it would seem natural to interpret the non-human environment as enjoying also an interior life. Panpsychism of some kind, although the lecturer did not enter into that consequence, would seem, in other words, to be a rightful part of his system.

The great originality of M. Boutroux throughout all these years has been his firm grasp of the principle of interpreting the whole of nature in the light of that part of it with which we are most fully acquainted, namely, our own personal experience. The filling in of the picture will require endless research of detail, but the working direction, once given, cannot be easily forgotten; and it seems not unlikely that at a future not remote the whole earlier efforts to substitute a logical skeleton of as few "immutable" principles and relations as we can dissect out cleanly for the abounding richness and fertility of the reality we live in, and to call this skeleton the deeper truth, will seem an aberration. It is essentially a view of things from the outside, and knows nothing of how they *happen*. M. Boutroux has steadily called his generation to take the inside view of how things really happen.

Even less than I expected, have I followed his own order or language, but it is too late to re-write. Those readers who know something of present-day philosophy will recognize in my account the same call to return to the fulness of concrete experience, with which the names of Peirce, Dewey, Schiller, Höffding, Bergson, and of many minor lights are associated. It is the real empiricism, the real evolutionism, the real pluralism; and Boutroux (after Renouvier) was its earliest, as he is now its latest, prophet. It keeps us on cordial terms with natural life, and refuses to divorce our "philosophy" of men from the world of our bosoms and our business.

The Making of a Red

BY ROBERT C. BENCHLEY

1919

You couldn't have asked for anyone more regular than Peters. He was an eminently safe citizen. Although not rich himself, he never chafed under the realization that there were others who possessed great wealth. In fact, the thought gave him rather a comfortable feeling. Furthermore, he was one of the charter members of the War. Long before President Wilson saw the light, Peters was advocating the abolition of German from the public-school curriculum. There was, therefore, absolutely nothing in his record which would in the slightest degree alter the true blue of a patriotic litmus. And he considered himself a liberal when he admitted that there might be something in this man Gompers, after all. That is how safe he was.

But one night he made a slip. It was ever so tiny a slip, but in comparison with it De Maupassant's famous piece of string was barren of consequences. Shortly before the United States entered the war Peters made a speech at a meeting of the Civic League in his home town. His subject was: "Inter-Urban Highways: Their Development in the Past and Their Possibilities for the Future." So far 100 per cent American. But, in the course of his talk, he happened to mention the fact that War, as an institution, has almost always had an injurious effect on public improvements of all kinds. In fact (and note this well; the Government's sleuth in the audience did) he said that, all other things being equal, if he were given his choice of War or Peace in the abstract, he would choose Peace as a condition under which to live. Then he went on to discuss the comparative values of macadam and wood blocks for paving.

In the audience was a civilian representative of the Military Intelligence service. He had had a premonition that some sort of attempt was going to be made at this meeting of the Civic League to discredit the war and America's imminent participation therein. And he was not disappointed (no Military Intelligence sleuth ever is), for in the remark of Peters, derogatory to War as an institution, his sharp ear detected the accent of the Wilhelmstrasse.

Time went by. The United States entered the war, and Peters bought Liberty Bonds. He didn't join the army, it is true, but, then, neither did James M. Beck, and it is an open secret that Mr. Beck was for the war. Peters did what a few slangy persons called "his bit," and not without a certain amount of pride. But he did not hear the slow, grinding noise from that district in which are located the mills of the gods. He did not even know that there was an investigation going on in Washington to determine the uses to which German propaganda money had been put. That is, he didn't know it until he opened his newspaper one morning and, with that uncanny precipitation with which a man's eye lights on his own name, discovered that he had been mentioned in the dispatches. At first he thought that it might be an honor list of Liberty Bond holders, but a glance at the headline chilled that young hope in his breast. It read as follows:

PRO-GERMAN LIST BARED BY ARMY SLEUTH
Prominent Obstructionists Named at Senate Probe

And then came the list. Peter's eye ran instinctively down to the place where, in what seemed to him to be 24-point Gothic caps, was blazoned the name "Horace W. Peters, Pacifist Lecturer, Matriculated at Germantown (Pa.) Military School." Above his name was that of Emma Goldman, "Anarchist." Below came that of Fritz von Papen, "agent of the Imperial German Government in America," and Jeremiah O'Leary, "Irish and Pro-German Agitator."

Peters was stunned. He telegraphed to his Senator at Washington and demanded that the outrageous libel be retracted. He telegraphed to the Military Intelligence office and demanded to know who was the slanderer who had traduced him, and who in h—l this Captain Whatsisname was who had submitted the report. He telegraphed to Secretary Baker and he cabled to the President. And he was informed, by return stage-coach, that his telegrams had been received and would be brought to the attention of the addressees at the earliest possible moment.

Then he went out to look up some of his friends, to explain that there had been a terrible mistake somewhere. But he was coolly received. No one could afford to be seen talking with him after what had happened. His partner merely said: "Bad business, Horace. Bad business!" The elevator starter pointed him out to a subordinate, and

Peters heard him explain: "That's Peters, Horace W. Peters. Did'je see his name in the papers this morning with them other German spies?" At the club little groups of his friends dissolved awkwardly when they saw him approaching, and, after distant nods, disappeared in an aimless manner. After all, you could hardly blame them.

The next morning the *Tribune* had a double-leaded editorial entitled "Oatmeal," in which it was stated that the disclosures in Washington were revealing the most insidious of all kinds of German propaganda—that disseminated by supposedly respectable American citizens. "It is not a tangible propaganda. It is an emotional propaganda. To the unwary it may resemble real-estate news, or perhaps a patriotic song, but it is the pap of Prussianism. As an example, we need go no further than Horace W. Peters. Mr. Peter's hobby was inter-urban highways. A very pretty hobby, Mr. Peters, but it won't do. It won't do." The *Times* ran an editorial saying, somewhere in the midst of a solid slab of type, that no doubt it would soon be found that Mr. Peters nourished Bolshevist sentiments, along with his team-mate, Emma Goldman. Emma Goldman! How Peters hated that woman! He had once written a letter to this very paper about her, advocating her electrocution.

He dashed out again in a search of some one to whom he could explain. But the editorials had done their work. The door-man at the club presented him with a letter from the house-committee, saying that, at a special meeting, it had been decided that he had placed himself in a position offensive to the loyal members of the club, and that it was with deep regret that they informed him, etc. As he stumbled out into the street, he heard someone whisper to an out-of-town friend, "There goes Emma Goldman's husband."

As the days went by things grew unbelievably worse. He was referred to in public meetings whenever an example of civic treachery was in order. A signed advertisement in the newspapers, protesting, on behalf of the lineal descendants of the Grand Duke Sergius, against the spread of Bolshevism in Northern New Jersey, mentioned a few prominent snakes in the grass, such as Trotzky, Victor Berger, Horace W. Peters, and Emma Goldman.

Then something snapped. Peters began to let his hair grow long, and neglected his linen. Each time he was snubbed on the street he uttered a queer guttural sound and made a mark in a little book he carried about with him. He bought a copy of "Colloquial Russian at a Glance," and began picking out inflammatory sentences from the *Novy Mir*. His wife packed up and went to stay with her sister when he advocated, one night at dinner, the communization of women. The last prop of respectability having been removed, the descent was easy. Emma Goldman, was it? Very well, then, Emma Goldman it should be! Bolshevist, was he? They had said it! "After all, who is to blame for this?" he mumbled to himself. "Capitalism! Militarism! Those Prussians in the Intelligence Department and the Department of Justice! The damnable bourgeoisie who sit back and read their *Times* and their *Tribune* and believe what they read there!" He had tried explanations. He had tried argument. There was only one thing left. He found it on page 112 of a little book of Emma Goldman's that he always carried around with him.

You may have read about Peters the other day. He was arrested, wearing a red shirt over his business cutaway and carrying enough TNT to shift the Palisades back into the Hackensack marshes. He was identified by an old letter in his pocket from Henry Cabot Lodge thanking him for a telegram of congratulation Peters had once sent him on the occasion of a certain speech in the Senate.

The next morning the *Times* said, editorially, that it hoped the authorities now saw that the only way to crush Bolshevism was by the unrelenting use of force.

The Centennial of Herman Melville

BY RAYMOND M. WEAVER

1919

"If ever, my dear Hawthorne," wrote Melville from Pittsfield in the summer of 1851, "we shall sit down in Paradise in some little shady corner by ourselves; and if we shall by any means be able to smuggle a basket of champagne there (I won't believe in a Temperance Heaven); and if we shall then cross our celestial legs in the celestial grass that is forever tropical, and strike our glasses and our heads together till both ring musically in concert: then, O my dear fellow mortal, how shall we pleasantly discourse of all the things manifold which now so much distress us." This serene and laughing desolation of Herman Melville's —a mood that steadily deepened into a less tranquil despair—is a spectacle to inspire with sardonic optimism those who gloat over the vanity of human wishes. At this time Melville was thirty-two years old: happily married, living in the lovely quiet of the Berkshires, surrounded by an admiring group of *literati*, widely distinguished as a novelist on both sides of the Atlantic, and at the very pinnacle of his creative genius; yet did he luxuriate in tribulation. "Dollars damn me," he wrote to Hawthorne; "and the malicious Devil is forever grinning in upon me, holding the door ajar. The calm, the cool, the silent grass-growing mood in which a man *ought* always to compose—that, I fear, can seldom be mine. What I feel most moved to write, that is banned— it will not pay. Yet, altogether, write in the *other* way I cannot. So the product is a final hash, and all my books are botches." Just as Petrarch's sonnets, which he pretended to despise as "silly boyish things," have alone survived to fame, while his great works in Latin, that cost him such excessive toil, have been forgot, so Melville's earliest novels, "Typee" and "Omoo," have left in comparative obscurity the other fourteen volumes that he considered more characteristic of himself.

"Think of it!" he writes to Hawthorne. "To go down to posterity is bad enough, any way; but to go down as a 'man who lived among the cannibals'! When I think of posterity in reference to myself, I mean only the babes who will probably be born in the moment immediately ensuing upon my giving up the ghost. I shall go down to them, in all likelihood. 'Typee' will be given to them, perhaps, with their ginger-bread." One pauses to wonder if in the fulness of celestial bliss the shades of Melville and Petrarch pause in the eternal quaffing of their Elysian champagne to reflect maliciously on the blind ingratitude of mortals.

The High Gods, in a playful and prodigal mood, gave to Melville, to Whitman, to Julia Ward Howe, to Lowell, to Kingsley, to Ruskin, and to Queen Victoria, the same birth year—doubtless with an eye to later convivialities in Heaven. Herman Melville was born in New York City on the first of August, one hundred years ago. He was the third of eight children. Melville's father, an importing merchant, died when Melville was still a boy, and the family, in none too flourishing circumstances, settled near Albany. But Melville carried with him reminiscences of the evenings he and his brother used to spend by the sea-coal fire in old Greenwich Street, listening to their father's rapturous accounts "of the monstrous waves at sea, mountain high; of the masts bending like twigs; and all about Havre and Liverpool, and about going up into the ball of St. Paul's in London." Melville's boyhood was neither easy not protected; he has said that he learned to think much and bitterly before his time. So at the age of eighteen, undefiled by the horrors of "education," goaded by hardship to migration, and pathetically lured by the glamorous mirage of distant lands, Melville planned a hegira. He shipped to England on a merchantman as a common sailor.

A wiser if a sadder boy, Melville returned home in 1838, to work on his uncle's farm, and to drift into that last haven of tame or baffled souls—the drudgery of teaching school, an experience that fired Melville to the mood of extremest desperation. He fled from the plow and the ferrule, and shipped from New Bedford on board the *Acushnet*, a whaler bound for the sperm fisheries of the Pacific. After eighteen months of barbarism at sea; after four months among the amiable cannibals of the valley of Typee (Taipi) on the island of Nukuheva (Nukahiva) of the Marquesas group; after a stirring escape and a cruise aboard the *Julia*, with its "cockroaches in the forecastle"; after a mutiny, an imprisonment, and some months of drifting in Honolulu among the savages both native and missionary, Melville shipped back home on the frigate *United States*. He received his discharge in Boston in 1844. For the next two years he lived at his mother's home near Troy, New York, and took to making books.

During four wild and adventurous years Melville had wandered with devil-may-care desperation over strange seas, and under bland and persuasive skies had drifted beyond the outmost reaches of civilization. And he returned to Puritan New England, to the same pump in the yard, and to the same intolerable monotony of relatives and friends. Literature was an adventure and an escape. In "Typee" (1846) he lived over again in joyous imagination his idyllic sojourn among the cannibals; in "Omoo" (1847) he retold his adventures in the *Julia* and the ensuing vagabondage ashore. These two books have enjoyed all the successes: they have been indiscriminately praised; they have been imitated; their authenticity has been hotly debated; the identity of the author has been contested; they have basked in the full venom of ecclesiastical vituperation; and among the orthodox they have enjoyed the felicity of a *succès de scandale*. The success of Melville's virgin attempt at letters determined his career; he made the startling discovery that literature sometimes pays. Inspired with a deceptive sense of security by this discovery, he married the daughter of Chief Justice Shaw of Massachusetts.

His third book was "Mardi" (1849), which starts off, according to Melville's intention, as an amusing block of South Sea adventure. But even before he had finished the first two hundred pages he abandoned himself with wholehearted exuberance to the demon of perversity. The result is one of the most dazzling curiosities of literature, a baffling but glorious chaos of adventure, rhapsody, epigram, allegory, satire, and mysticism—like "Gargantua," a mad book of burlesque and ecstasy. The reviews of "Mardi"—the French reviews in particular—make a bulky chapter in the comedy of criticism.

"Dollars damn me," wrote Melville. The result was "Redburn" (1849) and "Whitejacket" (1850), both autobiographical accounts of Melville's life at sea, modelled after Richard Henry Dana's "Two Years Before the Mast" (1840), and worthy successors of their very noble original.

In 1850 the Melville family moved to Pittsfield, Massachusetts, and soon developed the closest intimacy with Hawthorne, then living in Lenox. On June 29, 1851, Melville sent Hawthorne this piquant revelation of diabolism: "Shall I send you a fin of the 'Whale' by way of a specimen mouthful? The tail is not yet cooked, though the hell-fire in which the whole book is boiled might not unreasonably have cooked it ere this. This is the book's motto (the secret one): *Ego non baptiso te in nomine* —— — make out the rest for yourself."

Born in hell-fire, and baptized in an unspeakable name, "Moby-Dick, or the Whale" (1851), reads like a great opium dream. The organizing theme of the book is the hunting of Moby-Dick, the abhorred white whale, by the monomaniac Captain Ahab. To Ahab, this ancient and vindictive monster is the incarnation of all the vast moral evil of the world; he piles on the whale's white hump the sum of all the rage and hate of mankind from the days of Eden down. There are in "Moby-Dick" long digressions, natural, historical, and philosophical on the person, habits, manners, and ideas of whales; there are long dialogues and soliloquies, such as were never spoken by mortal man in his waking senses, conversations that for sweetness, strength, and courage remind one of passages from Dekker, Webster, Massinger, Fletcher, and the other old dramatists loved by Charles Lamb; perhaps a fifth of the book is made up of Melville's independent moralizings, half essay, half rhapsody; withal, the book contains some of the most finished comedy in the language. If one logically analyzes "Moby-Dick," he will be disgusted, just as Dr. Johnson, who had no analysis but the logical, was disgusted with "Lycidas." And so with Melville's novel. If one will forget logic and common sense, and "abandon himself"—as Dr. Johnson would contemptuously have said—to this work of Melville's, he will acknowledge the presence of an amazing masterpiece. But neither "Lycidas" nor "Moby-Dick" should be read by philistines or pragmatists.

Melville's later novels mark a deepening of despair. "Pierre, or the Ambiguities" (1852), while worthily comparable to Meredith's "Egoist" in elaborate subtlety and mercilessness of pyschological analysis, is a prophetic parody of Hardy's most poisonous pessimism. The intention of this dark, wild book of incest and death seems to be to show the impracticability of virtue: that morality is a luxury occasionally to be indulged in by a strolling divinity, but for man a dangerous form of lunacy. "Pierre" is a book to send a Freudian into ravishment. "Israel Potter" is a story of the days of Franklin and John Paul Jones, both of whom appear in the novel. The unnecessary degradation of the hero with which the book closes is utterly inexcusable both in art and in probability; it is a cruel practical joke. "Piazza Tales" (1856) gives proof that Melville had not yet, with Coleridge, buried his wand in a grave of metaphysical speculations, to conjure no more, as witness the story "Benito Cereno." Melville's last novel, "The Confidence Man" (1857), is a very melancholy performance, and is not, even by transcendent charity, a novel at all. It is a series of episodes on a Mississippi river-boat among people of superhuman conversational endurance. The book seems to have been written by one who believed in the saying of Thrasea: "He who hates vice, hates humanity."

In 1857, in ill health, Melville went abroad. He visited Hawthorne in Southport, indulged in an orgy of "ontological heroics," and moved on to the Mediterranean, to Constantinople, and the Holy Land. What his reflections were in the Holy Land he has recorded in the poem "Clarel" (1876).

In 1863 Melville with his wife and four children moved to New York. Here he spent the remaining twenty-eight years of his life in most sedulous obscurity. Invited in 1882 to be one of the charter members of the Authors' Club, he declined, preferring the company of his family, of his grandchildren, of his books, of his prints, of his thoughts. He published five volumes of verse during these years, but as a poet Melville is not distinguished. To turn from his great novels to his poetry is to be reminded of a star that drops a line of streaming fire down the vault of the sky—and then the heavy shapeless thing that sinks into the earth.

It was Melville's abiding craving to achieve some total and undivined possession of the very heart of reality; his was the quest for the lost Atlantis, the ancient eternal desire of man for the unknown. In the promiscuous exuberance of youth Melville venturesomely sought his El Dorado on the world's rim. But his beckoning Hesperides ever retreated before him. After his final disillusionment in the Holy Land, he broke faith with geography, and retreated completely into meta-physics—metaphysics, which is but misery dissolved in thought. Dr. Titus Munson Coan has left a record of a visit to Melville in 1859: "In vain I sought to hear of Typee and those Paradise Islands; he preferred to pour forth instead his philosophy and his theories of life. The shade of Aristotle arose like a cold mist between myself and Faraway. He seems to put away the objective side of life and to shut himself up as a cloistered thinker and poet." Superficially it would seem that whale-hunting, sea-roving, and mutiny are incompatible with monasticism and metaphysics. But, more closely considered, they are but two ges-tures for the same emotion; both are ventures into mystery, into un-certainty, into "strange surmise." Dante pilgrimaged farther than did Ulysses, but the wanderings of Melville outstripped them both.

"Like a frigate," Melville once wrote of himself, "I am full with a thousand souls; and as on, on, on, I scud before the wind, many mari-ners rush up from the orlop below, like miners from caves; running shouting across my decks; opposite braces are pulled and boisterous speaking trumpets are heard, and contending orders, to save the good ship from the shoals. In my tropical calms, when my ship lies tranced on Eternity's main, the many, many souls in me speak one at a time, then all with one voice, rising and falling and swaying in golden calls and responses." Because of this multiplicity of personality, Melville

eludes summary classification. In his composite achievement he is sev-
erally a gentle Smollett, a glorified Whitman, an athletic Coleridge, a
dandified Rabelais, a cynical Meredith, a doubting Sir Thomas Browne.
Essentially was he a mystic, a treasure-seeker, a mystery-monger, a
delver after hidden things spiritual and material. The world to him was
a darkly figured hieroglyph; and if he ever deciphered the cabalistic
sign, the meaning he found was too terrible, or else too wonderful, to
tell. Whenever he sat down to write, at his elbow stood ever the
chosen emissary of Satan, the Comic Spirit—a demoniac familiar that
saved him in many a trying pass. The versatility and power of his
genius was extraordinary. If he does not eventually rank as a writer of
over-shadowing accomplishment, it will be owing not to any lack of
genius, but to the perversity of his rare and lofty gifts.

Minnesota: The Norse State

BY SINCLAIR LEWIS

1923

On May 9, 1922, Mr. Henry Lorenz of Pleasantdale, Saskatchewan, milked the cows and fed the horses and received the calls of his next farm neighbors. Obviously he was still young and lively, though it did happen that on May 9 he was one hundred and seventeen years old. When St. Paul, Mendota, and Marine, the first towns in Minnesota, were established, Henry was a man in his mid-thirties—yes, and President Eliot was seven and Uncle Joe Cannon was five. As for Minneapolis, now a city of four hundred thousand people, seventy-five years ago it consisted of one cabin. Before 1837, there were less than three hundred whites and mixed breeds in all this Minnesotan domain of eighty thousand square miles—the size of England and Scotland put together.

It is so incredibly new; it has grown so dizzyingly. Here is a man still under forty, born in a Minnesota village. Twenty-two years before he was born, the village was a stockade with two or three log stores and a company of infantry, a refuge for the settlers when the Sioux came raiding. During a raid in 1863, a settler was scalped within sight of the stockade. Yet so greatly had the State changed in those twenty-three years that not till he was sixteen did the man himself ever see an Indian. That Indian was on a train, bound East to continue the study of Latin which he had begun on the reservation.

On the spot where the settler was scalped in 1863 is a bungalow farmhouse now, with leaded casement windows, with radio and phonograph, and electric lights in house and garage and barns. A hundred blooded cows are milked there by machinery. The farmer goes into town for Kiwanis Club meetings, and last year he drove his Buick to Los Angeles. He is, or was, too prosperous to belong to the Nonpartisan League or to vote the Farmer-Labor ticker.

Minnesota is unknown to the average Easterner, say to a Hartford insurance man or to a New York garment-worker, not so much because it is new as because it is neither definitely Western and violent, nor Eastern and crystallized. Factories and shore hotels are inevitably associated with New Jersey, cowpunchers and buttes with Montana; California is apparent and Florida and Maine. But Minnesota is unplaced. I have heard a Yale junior speculate: "Now you take those Minnesota cities—say take Milwaukee, for instance. Why, it must have a couple of hundred thousand population, hasn't it?"

This would be a composite Eastern impression of Minnesota: a vastness of wind-beaten prairie, flat as a parade ground, wholly given up to wheat-growing save for a fringe of pines at the north and a few market-towns at the south; these steppes inhabited by a few splendid Yankees —one's own sort of people—and by Swedes who always begin sentences with "Vell, Aye tank," who are farmhands, kitchenmaids, and ice-men, and who are invariably humorous.

This popular outline bears examination as well as most popular beliefs; quite as well as the concept that Negroes born in Chicago are less courteous than those born in Alabama. Minnesota is not flat. It is far less flat than the province of Quebec. Most of it is prairie, but the prairie rolls and dips and curves; it lures the motorist like the English roads of Broad Highway fiction. Along the skyline the cumulus clouds forever belly and, with our dry air, nothing is more spectacular than the crimson chaos of our sunsets. But our most obvious beauty is the lakes. There are thousands of them—nine or ten thousand—brilliant among suave grain fields or masked by cool birch and maples. On the dozen-mile-wide lakes of the north are summer cottages of the prosperous from Missouri, Illinois, even Texas.

Leagues of the prairie are utterly treeless, except for artificial windbreaks of willows and cottonwoods encircling the farmhouses. Here the German Catholic spire can be seen a dozen miles off, and the smoke of the Soo Line freight two stations away. But from this plains country you come into a northern pine wilderness, "the Big Woods," a land of lumber camps and reservation Indians and lonely tote-roads, kingdom of Paul Bunyan, the mythical hero of the lumberjacks.

The second error is to suppose that Minnesota is entirely a wheat State. It was, at one time, and the Minneapolis flour-mills are still the largest in the world. Not even Castoria is hymned by more billboards than is Minneapolis flour. But today it is Montana and Saskatchewan and the Dakotas which produce most of the wheat for our mills, while the Minnesota farmers, building tall red silos which adorn their barns like the turrets of Picardy, turn increasingly to dairying. We ship beef to London, butter to Philadelphia. The iron from our Mesaba mines is in Alaskan rails and South African bridges, and as to manufacturing, our refrigerators and heat-regulators comfort Park Avenue apartment-houses, while our chief underwear factory would satisfy a Massachusetts Brahmin or even a Chicago advertising-man.

Greatest error of all is to believe that Minnesota is entirely Yankee and Scandinavian, and that the Swedes are helots and somehow ludicrous.

A school principal in New Duluth analyzed his three hundred and thirty children as Slovene, 49; Italian, 47; Serbian, 39; American, 37; Polish, 30; Austrian and Swedish, 22 each; Croatian, 20; colored, 9 (it is instructive to note that he did not include them among the "Americans"); Finnish, 7; Scotch, 6; Slav unspecified 5; German, French, Bohemian, and Jewish, 4 each; Rumanian, Norwegian, and Canadian, 3 each; Scandinavian, unspecified; Lithuanian, Irish, Ukrainian, and Greek, 2 each; Russian and English, 1 each—60 per cent of them from Southern and Eastern Europe!

Such a Slavification would, of course, be true only of an industrial or mining community, but it does indicate that the whole Mid-Western population may alter as much as has the East. In most of the State there is a predomination of Yankees, Germans, Irish, and all branches of Scandinavians—Icelanders and Danes as well as Swedes and Norwegians. And among all racial misconceptions none is more vigorously absurd than the belief that the Minnesota Scandinavians are, no matter how long they remain here, like the characters of that estimable old stock-company play "Yon Yonson"—a tribe humorous, inferior, and unassimilable. To generalize, any popular generalization about Scandinavians in America is completely and ingeniously and always wrong.

In Minnesota itself one does not hear (from the superior Yankees whom one questions about that sort of thing) that the Scandinavians are a comic people, but rather that they are surly, that they are Socialistic, that they "won't Americanize." Manufacturers and employing lumbermen speak of their Swedish employees precisely as wealthy Seattleites speak of the Japs, Bostonians of the Irish, Southwesterners of the Mexicans, New Yorkers of the Jews, marine officers of the Haitians, and Mr. Rudyard Kipling of nationalist Hindus—or nationalist Americans. Unconsciously, all of them give away the Inferior Race Theory, which is this: An inferior race is one whose members work for me. They are treacherous, ungrateful, ignorant, lazy, and agitator-ridden, because they ask for higher wages and thus seek to rob me of the dollars which I desire for my wife's frocks and for the charities which glorify me. This inferiority is inherent. Never can they become

Good Americans (or English Gentlemen, or Highwellborn Prussians). I know that this is so, because all my university classmates and bridge-partners agree with me.

The truth is that the Scandinavians Americanize only too quickly. They Americanize much more quickly than Americans. For genera-tion after generation there is a remnant of stubborn American aboli-tionist stock which either supports forlorn causes and in jail sings low ballads in a Harvard accent, or else upholds, like Lodge, an Adams tradition which is as poisonous as communism to a joy in brotherly boosting. So thorough are the Scandinavians about it that in 1963 we shall be hearing Norwegian Trygavasons and Icelandic Gislasons say-ing of the Montenegrins and Letts: "They're reg'lar hogs about wages but the worst is, they simply won't Americanize. They won't vote either the Rotary or the Ku Klux ticket. They keep hollering about wanting some kind of a doggone Third Party."

Scandinavians take to American commerce and schooling and jour-nalism as do Scotsmen or Cockneys. Particularly they take to Ameri-can politics, the good old politics of Harrison and McKinley and Charley Murphy. Usually, they bring nothing new from their own experimental countries. They permit their traditions to be snatched away. True, many of them have labored for the Nonpartisan League, for woman suffrage, for cooperative societies. The late Governor John Johnson of Minnesota seems to have been a man of destiny; had he lived he would probably have been President, and possibly a President of power and originality. But again—there was Senator Knute Nelson, who made McCumber look like a left-wing syndicalist and Judge Gary like François Villon. There is Congressman Steenerson of Minnesota, chairman of the House postal committee. Mr. Steenerson once pro-duced, out of a rich talent matured by a quarter of a century in the House, an immortal sentence. He had been complaining at lunch that the Nonpartisan League had introduced the obscene writings of "this Russian woman, Ellen Key" into the innocent public schools. Some one hinted to the Swedish Mr. Steenerson, "But I thought she was a Swede."

He answered: *"No, the Key woman comes from Finland and the rest of Red Russia, where they nationalize the women."*

Good and bad, the Scandinavians monopolize Minnesota politics. Of the last nine governors of the State, six have been Scandinavians. So is Dr. Shipstead, who defeated Senator Kellogg in the 1922 election; so is Harold Knutson, Republican whip of the House. Scandinavians make up a large proportion of the Minnesota State Legislature, and while in Santa Fe the Mexican legislators speak Spanish, while in Quebec the representatives still debate in French, though for generations they have been citizens of a British dominion, in Minnesota the politicians who were born abroad are zealous to speak nothing but Americanese. So is it in business and the home. Though a man may not have left Scandinavia till he was twenty, his sons will use the same English, good and bad, as the sons of settlers from Maine, and his daughters will go into music clubs or into cocktail sets, into college or into factories, with the same prejudices and ideals and intonations as girls named Smith and Brewster.

The curious newness of Minnesota has been suggested, but the really astonishing thing is not the newness—it is the oldness, the solid, traditionalized, cotton-wrapped oldness. A study of it would be damaging to the Free and Fluid Young America theory. While parts of the State are still so raw that the villages among the furrows or the dusty pines are but frontier camps, in the cities and in a few of the towns there is as firm a financial oligarchy and almost as definite a social system as London, and this power is behind all "sound" politics, in direct or indirect control of all business. It has its Old Families, who tend to marry only within their own set. Anywhere in the world, an Old Family is one which has had wealth for at least thirty years longer than average families of the same neighborhood. In England, it takes (at most) five generations to absorb "parvenus" and "profiteers" into the gentry, whether they were steel profiteers in the Great War or yet untitled land profiteers under William the Conqueror. In New York it takes three generations—often. In the Middle West it takes one and a half.

No fable is more bracing, or more absurd, than that all the sons and grandsons of the pioneers, in Minnesota or in California, in Arizona or Nebraska, are racy and breezy, unmannerly but intoxicatingly free. The grandchildren of the men who in 1862 fought the Minnesota Indians, who dogtrotted a hundred miles over swamp-blurred trails to bear the alarm to the nearest troops—some of them are still clearing the land, but some of them are complaining of the un-English quality of the Orange Pekoe in dainty painty city tea-rooms which stand where three generations ago the Red River fur-carts rested; their chauffeurs await them in Pierce Arrow limousines (special bodies by Kimball, silver fittings from Tiffany); they present Schnitzler and St. John Ervine at their Little Theaters; between rehearsals they chatter of meeting James Joyce in Paris; and always in high-pitched Mayfair laughter they ridicule the Scandinavians and Finns who are trying to shoulder into their sacred, ancient Yankee caste. A good many of their names are German.

Naturally, beneath this Junker class there is a useful, sophisticated, and growing company of doctors, teachers, newspapermen, liberal lawyers, musicians who have given up Munich and Milan for the interest of developing orchestras in the new land. There is a scientific body of farmers. The agricultural school of the huge University of Minnesota is sound and creative. And still more naturally, between Labor and Aristocracy there is an army of the peppy, poker-playing, sales-hustling He-men who are our most characteristic Americans. But even the He-men are not so obvious as they seem. What their future is, no man knows—and no woman dares believe. It is conceivable that, instead of being a menace, in their naive boosting and their fear of the unusual, they may pass only too soon; it is possible that their standardized bathrooms and Overlands will change to an equally standardized and formula-bound culture—yearning Culture, arty Art. We have been hurled from tobacco-chewing to tea-drinking with gasping speed; we may as quickly dash from boosting to a beautiful and languorous death. If it is necessary to be Fabian in politics, to keep the reformers (left wing or rigid right) from making us perfect too rapidly, it is yet more necessary to be a little doubtful about the ardent souls who would sell Culture; and if the Tired Business Man is unlovely and a little dull, at least he is real, and we shall build only on reality.

The nimbler among our pioneering grandfathers appropriated to their private uses some thousands of square miles in northern Minnesota, and cut off—or cheerfully lost by forest fire—certain billions of feet of such lumber as will never be seen again. When the lumber was gone, the land seemed worthless. It was good for nothing but agriculture, which is an unromantic occupation, incapable of making millionaires in one generation. The owners had few of them acquired more than a million, and now they could scarcely give their holdings away. Suddenly, on parts of this scraggly land, iron was discovered, iron in preposterous quantities, to be mined in the open pit, as easily as hauling out gravel. Here is the chief supply of the Gary and South Chicago mills. The owners of the land do not mine the ore. They have gracefully leased it—though we are but Westerners, we have our subsidiary of the United States Steel Company. The landowners themselves have only to go abroad and sit in beauty like a flower, and every time a steam shovel dips into the ore, a quarter drops into the owner's pocket.

This article is intended to be a secret but flagrant boost. It is meant to increase civic pride and the value of Minnesota real estate. Yet the writer wonders if he will completely satisfy his chambers of commerce. There is a chance that they would prefer a statement of the value of our dairy products, the number of our admirable new school-buildings, the number of motor tourists visiting our lakes, and an account of Senator Nelson's encouraging progress from poverty to magnificence. But a skilled press agent knows that this would not be a boost; it would be an admission of commerce-ruled barrenness. The interesting thing in Minnesota is the swift evolution of a complex social system and, since in two generations we have changed from wilderness to country clubs, the question is what the next two generations will produce. It defies certain answer; it demands a scrupulous speculation free equally from the bland certitudes of chambers of commerce and the sardonic impatience of professional radicals. To a realistic philosoper, the existence of an aristocracy is not (since it does exist) a thing to be bewailed, but to be examined as a fact.

There is one merit not of Minnesota alone but of all the Middle West which must be considered. The rulers of our new land may to the eye seem altogether like the rulers of the East—of New England, New York, Pennsylvania. Both groups are chiefly reverent toward banking, sound Republicanism, the playing of golf and bridge, and the possession of large motors. But whereas the Easterner is content with these symbols and smugly desires nothing else, the Westerner, however golfocentric he may be, is not altogether satisfied; and raucously though he may snortle at his wife's "fool suffrage ideas" and "all this highbrow junk the lecture-hounds spring on you," yet secretly, wistfully he desires a beauty that he does not understand.

As a pedant, to hint that our society has become somewhat involved in the few years since Mr. Henry Lorenz of Saskatchewan was seventy, let me illogically lump a few personal observations of Minnesota:

Here is an ex-professor of history in the State University, an excellent scholar who, retiring after many years of service, cheerfully grows potatoes in a backwoods farm among the northern Minnesota pines, and builds up cooperative selling for all the farmers of his district.

Here is the head of a Minneapolis school for kindergartners, a woman who is summoned all over the country to address teachers' associations. She will not admit candidates for matriculation until she is sure that they have a gift for teaching. She does something of the work of a Montessori, with none of the trumpeting and anguish.

Here is the greatest, or certainly the largest, medical clinic in the world—the Mayo clinic, with over a hundred medical specialists besides the clerks and nurses. It is the supreme court of diagnosis. Though it is situated in a small town, off the through rail routes, yet it is besieged by patients from Utah and Ontario and New York as much as by Minnesotans. When the famous European doctors come to

America, they may look at the Rockefeller Institute, they may stop at Harvard and Rush and Johns Hopkins and the headquarters of the American Medical Association, but certainly they will go on to Rochester. The names of "Charley" and "Will" have something of the familarity of "R. L. S." and "T. R."

Here is a Chippewa as silent and swart as his grandfather, an active person whom the cavalry used to hunt every open season. The grandson conducts a garage, and he actually understands ignition. His farm among the lowering Norway pines he plows with a tractor.

Here is a new bookshop which is publishing the first English translation of the autobiography of Abelard.

Here are really glorious buildings: the Minneapolis Art Institute, the State Capitol, the St. Paul Public Library, and Ralph Adams Cram's loveliest church. Here, on the shore of Lake of the Isles, is an Italian palace built by a wheat speculator. Here where five years ago were muddy ruts are perfect cement roads.

Here is a small town, a "typical prairie town," which has just constructed a competent golf course. From this town came an ambassador to Siam and a professor of history in Columbia.

And here are certain Minnesota authors. You know what Mid-Western authors are—rough fellows but vigorous, ignorant of the classics and of Burgundy, yet close to the heart of humanity. They write about farmyards and wear flannel shirts. Let us confirm this portrait by a sketch of nine Minnesota authors, eight of them born in the State:

Charles Flandrau, author of "Harvard Episodes" and "Viva Mexico," one-time Harvard instructor, now wandering in Spain. Agnes Repplier has called him the swiftest blade among American essayists. Scott Fitzgerald, very much a Minnesotan, yet the father of the Long Island flapper, the prophet of the Ritz, the idol of every Junior League. Alice Ames Winter, president of the General Federation of Women's Clubs. Claude Washburn, author of "The Lonely Warrior" and several other novels which, though they are laid in America, imply a European background. He has lived for years now in France and Italy. Margaret Banning, author of "Spellbinders." Woodward Boyd, whose first novel, "The Love Legend," is a raid on the domestic sentimentalists. Carlton Miles, a dramatic critic who gives his Minnesota readers the latest news of the continental stage. He is just back from a European year spent with such men as Shaw, Drinkwater, and the director of La Scala. Brenda Ueland, who lives in Greenwich Village and writes for the *Atlantic Monthly*. Sinclair Lewis, known publicly as a scolding corn-belt realist, but actually (as betrayed by the samite-clad, Tennyson-and-water verse which he wrote when he was in college) a yearner over what he would doubtless call "quaint ivied cottages."

Seventy-five years ago—a Chippewa-haunted wilderness. Today—a complex civilization with a future which, stirring or dismayed or both, is altogether unknowable. To understand America, it is merely necessary to understand Minnesota. But to understand Minnesota you must be an historian, an ethnologist, a poet, a cynic, and a graduate prophet all in one.

Indiana: Her Soil and Light

BY THEODORE DREISER

1923

There is about it a charm which I shall not be able to express, I know, but which is of its soil and sky and water—those bucolic streams and lakes which so charm those who see them. And where else will one find such beech and sugar groves, so stately and still and serene—the seeming abodes of spirits and elves that are both friendly and content? Rains come infrequently and then only in deluging showers. Corn and wheat and hay and melons flourish throughout the State. Spring comes early. Autumn lingers pleasingly into November. The winters are not, in the main, severe. Yet deep, delicious snows fall. And a dry cold in the northern portion makes sleighing and skating a delight. The many lakes and streams afford ample opportunity for house-boats, lakeside cottages, and bungalows as well as canoeing and fishing and idling and dreaming. In the beech and sugar groves are many turtle doves. The bluejay and the scarlet tanager flash and cry. Hawks and buzzards and even eagles, betimes, soar high in the air. Under the eaves of your cottage are sure to be wrens and bluebirds. Your chimneys are certain to shelter a covey of martins. And to your porches will cling the trumpet vine, purple clematis, and wistaria. From the orchard and woodlot of your farm will sound the rusty squeak of the guinea hen and the more pleasing cry of the peacock, "calling for rain."

One should not conclude from this, of course, that the State is without manufacture, or that, size for size, its cities and towns are not as interesting as those of other States. To me they are more so. There is something in the very air that sustains them that is of the substance of charm. What it is I cannot say. You will find it suggested in the poems of Riley and the stories of Tarkington, a kind of wistfulness that is the natural accompaniment of the dreams of unsophistication. To be sure the State is lacking in urban centers of great size which somehow, regardless of character, manage to focus the interest of the outside world. Apart from Indianapolis, a city of three hundred thousand, there is no other of even a third of its size within its borders. Evansville, on the Ohio, and at the extreme southwest corner of the State, has possibly eighty thousand. Ft. Wayne, in the northern portion of the State, the same. Terre Haute, the most forthright of its several manufacturing centers, had, until recently at least, a population of seventy thousand. And because of the character of its manufactories which relate to steel and coal it is looked upon by many who are not a part of it as grimy. Its smaller cities such as Gary, Hammond, South Bend, Kokomo, Richmond, Muncie, and several others literally resound with manufacture, being centers for steel, packing, automobiles, engineering supplies, farm machinery, and so forth. Yet contrasted with the neighboring States of Ohio, Michigan, and Illinois—in particular the latter's northern portion—it pales as a center of manufacture. Ohio can boast quite ten centers to its one. In passing from any of these States into Indiana one is reminded of the difference between Holland and Germany or France, the one with its canals, its windmills, and level fields, dotted with simple homes, the other with its plethora of cities and factories and, in the old days, its ever-present army. The one is idyllic, the other almost disturbingly real and irritatingly energetic.

Yet to my way of thinking the State is to be congratulated rather than not upon this limited commercial equipment. Not all of our national domain need to be commercial, I trust, however much we may wish it. A few such pastoral areas might prove an advantage. Besides, as I have indicated, there is running through the mood of the State something which those who are most intimate with it are pleased to denominate "homey" or "folksy"—a general geniality and sociability. And with this I agree. The automobile and the phonograph, plus the dancing which the latter inspires, have added so much to the color of the small town and the farm in these days. Or, if it be the lone cottage, far from any town, with neither automobile nor phonograph, then the harmonica and the accordion are found to be in service. And one may sing and dance to those. Is it the light, or the soil, or what?

In this connection the church life of Indiana, as well as its moral taboos, have always interested me. Morality one might well assume by now, as well as all important social regulations, are best and most understandingly based upon and regulated by the Golden Rule. Beyond that, among the intelligent, restrictions and compulsions are few. Neither theory nor dogma nor ritual nor custom nor creed are disturbingly binding. Yet in my native State, and despite the steady growth in scientific knowledge, devotion to denominational liturgy and dogma appears to be unmodified. Go where you will, into any city or town you choose, and there will be not one but four or five or six or more churches of the ultra sectarian type and each with a lusty and *convinced* following. Nowhere, considering the sizes of the various cities and towns and hamlets, will you see larger or more attractive edifices of this character. And not infrequently the Bible school attachments or additions are almost as impressive as the church themselves. In short, sectarian religion appears to flourish mightily. It is the most vigorous and binding of all local social activities. The affairs of the church are not only spiritually but socially of the utmost importance. Nearly everyone belongs to one or another of the various denominations and the rivalry between the several sects is not infrequently keen, especially in the smaller places. And in the main, and despite all science, they are still imperialistic in their claim to revelation and devotion. Religious innovations are taboo. Even modern liberalizing theologic tendencies, though sanctioned by a stray soul here and there, are not in the main either understood or approved of. To this day in many orthodox quarters the youths of the hour are still discouraged from attending the State or any other university on the ground that they are "hotbeds of infidelity and irreligion." And the local press, running true to form, as it does everywhere, editorially sustains this contention.

And yet, as the world knows, Indiana has its "genius belt" geographically delimitated even, as "south of a line running east and west through Crawfordsville." And, locally at least, and until recently there was no hesitation in stamping the decidedly successful literary and art products of the State as the effusions of genius. Well, there's neither good nor ill but thinking makes it so. Certainly the State may well be proud of George Ade and Booth Tarkington and William M. Chase, the artist, to say nothing of those distinguished elders James Whitcomb Riley and General Lew Wallace, the author of "Ben Hur." Whether as much may be said for some others still remains to be seen. Certainly from the point of view of current popularity they have nothing to complain of. And as for posterity, well, posterity pays no grocer's bills. There are many aspiring writers who would gladly change place with George Barr McCutcheon or Charles Major, who wrote "When Knighthood Was in Flower."

Yet apart from these the State is not without a few personalities whose names will awaken responsive and other than literary thought beyond its borders—William Henry Harrison, the "Indian fighter" and quondam President, for instance, and Thomas B. Hendricks, once a Vice-President. Also Oliver P. Morton, an efficient early Governor; John Hay, diplomat, author, and cabinet officer of his day; and John

Clark Ridpath, the historian. As a true and loyal Hoosier I suppose I should add that James B. Eads, the distinguished engineer, once lived in Brookville, Indiana, that Robert Owen founded his human brotherhood experiment at New Harmony, in Posey County, that Henry Ward Beecher was once pastor of the Second Presbyterian Church of Indianapolis, and that Abraham Lincoln is supposed to have studied those few books and caught that elusive something that later gave character and beauty to his utterances somewhere in a log cabin in Spencer County.

But beyond these, what? Well, beyond an agreeable and respectable and kindly social world in which to be and pass one's brief and changeful days, what more is needed? Trusts? There are several in active operation, ye tin-plate and ye steel trust, for instance; the former organized at Kokomo, Indiana, the latter in full and dictatorial swing at Gary and Hammond, where only so recently as July, 1919, a number of very respectable employees on strike were promptly and in true liberty fashion shot to death upon the streets of Hammond, their crime being, apparently, opposition to insufficient wages and certain (as they seem to have assumed) unsatisfactory piece-work conditions. The moral entanglements resulting from this method of adjusting labor difficulties are before the courts of Indiana at this very time. Large industries? Indianapolis, Kokomo, and South Bend are assumed to be automobile manufacturing centers of the greatest import, nationally and internationally speaking. The steel interests of Gary, Hammond, and Terre Haute are assumed, not only locally but nationally, to be second to none in America. Indianapolis has not one but several enormous packing plants. The underlying coal-beds of southwestern Indiana—especially about Terre Haute—are listed as among the important resources of the Central West. The melon- and fruit-bearing powers of the climate and soil of that same area have brought about not only specialization and intensive cultivation but a trade-mark which is of the greatest value. In addition the State has scenic wonders such as the caves about Wyandotte and such natural scenery and curative springs as have given rise to French Lick, West Baden, Mud Lavia, The Glades, and all the delightful lake life that characterizes its northern half.

But perhaps, after all, this is not the type of thing that should be registered of Indiana. Despite a long and happy intimacy with it, it is entirely possible that I have not even suggested or have entirely missed its truer spiritual significance as we are wont to say of so much that is but deeply human. Going south through Indiana once with a friend and fellow Hoosier, we two fell into a solemn and almost esoteric, I might say, discussion of the State and its significance, intellectually, emotionally, and otherwise. Previous to what I am about to set down I had been pointing out a number of things—not only those that have always appealed to me, the poetic and folksy charm of the State and its inhabitants—but also a number of other things that rather irritated me, its social devotion to dogmatic religion, for one thing, its rather pharisaical restfulness in its assumed enlightenment and knowledge of what is true and important to the world at large, its political somnolence as suggested by its profound and unchanging devotion to the two ancient and utterly platitudinous parties. With all of this he most solemnly agreed. Then, having done so, entered not so much upon a defense as an interpretation of the State which I will here set down as best I can.

"You should go sometime to an automobile speed contest such as is held annually at the Speedway at Indianapolis, as I have often, year after year; in fact, since it was first built. There, just when the first real summer days begin to take on that wonderful light that characterizes them out here—a kind of luminous silence that suggests growing corn and ripening wheat and quails whistling in the meadows over by the woods, you will find assembled thousands from this and other countries, with their cars and at times their foreign tongues, individuals interested in speed or fame or the development of the automobile. And this might cause you to feel, as it has me, that as rural as it all is, at times Indiana is quite as much of a center and more so even, than places which, by reason of larger populations, set themselves up as such. As I say, I have been there often, and getting a bit tired of watching the cars have gone over into the woods inside the course and lain down on the grass on my back.

"There, about me, would be the same familiar things I have always known and loved since I was a boy here, but that getting out into the world for a time had made me think that I had forgotten, though I hadn't—the sugar and hickory and beech trees, the little cool breezes that come up in the middle of the day and cool the face and hands for a moment, and rustle the leaves—the same fine blue sky that I used to look up into when a boy. But circling around me continuously, just the same, to the south and the north and the east and the west, where were the banks of the track beyond the woods, were these scores of cars from all parts of the world, with their thunder and dust, the thunder and dust of an international conflict. Then I would get up and look to the south along the immense grandstand that was there and would see, flying in this Indiana sunlight, the flags of all the great nations, Italy and England, France and Belgium, Holland and Germany, Austria and Spain. And it came to me then that the spirit that had been instrumental for some reason in distinguishing this particular State from its sister States, as it unquestionably has been distinguished, was and still is, I think, effective. It has won for Indiana a freedom from isolation and mere locality which is worldwide. It has accomplished here, on this quiet Hoosier soil, a very vital contact with universal thought."

"Universal thought is a pretty large thing to connect up with, F——," I contended genially. "And this is all very flattering to dear old Indiana, but do you really believe yourself? It seems to me that, if anything, the State is a little bit sluggish, intellectually and otherwise. Or, if it isn't that, exactly, then certainly there is an element of self-complacency that permits the largest percentage of its population to rest content in the most retarding forms of political, religious, and social fol de rol. They are all, or nearly all, out here, good and unregenerate Democrats or Republicans, as they have been for, lo! these seventy years, now—come next Wednesday. Nearly all belong to one or another of the twenty-seven sure-cure sects of Protestantism. And they are nearly all most heartily responsive to any -ism which is advertised to solve all the troubles of the world, including those of our own dear nation. I call your attention to the history of the Millerites of southeast Indiana, with their certain date for the ending of the world and their serious and complete preparation for the same; the Spiritualists and free lovers who fixed themselves in northwestern Indiana, about Valparaiso, if I am not mistaken, and Mormon fashion ruled all others out; the something of soil magnetism which drew Robert Owen from Scotland to New Harmony and there produced that other attempt at solving all the ills to which the flesh is heir. Don't forget that the Dunkards—that curious variation of Mennonism—took root out here and flourished mightily for years, and exists to this day, as you know. Also the reformed Quakers. And now I hear that Christian Science and a Christianized form of Spiritualism are almost topmost in the matter of growth and the enthusiasm of their followers. I have no quarrel with any faith as a means to private mental blessedness. But you were speaking of universal and creative thought. Just how do you explain this?"

"Well, I can and I can't," was his rather enigmatic reply. "This is a most peculiar State. It may not be so dynamic nor yet so creative, sociologically, as it is fecund of things which relate to the spirit—or perhaps I had better say to poetry and the interpretative arts. How else do you explain William M. Chase, born here in Brookville, I believe, General Lew Wallace, James Whitcomb Riley, Edward Eggleston and his 'Hoosier Schoolmaster,' Booth Tarkington, George Ade, John Clark Ridpath, Roswell Smith, who founded the *Century Magazine*, and then Lincoln studying and dreaming down in Spencer County? All accidents? I wonder. In fact I am inclined to think that there is much

more to soil and light in so far as temperament and genius are concerned than we have any idea of as yet. There may be, and personally
I am inclined to think there is, a magnetic and also generative something
appertaining to soil and light which is not unrelated to the electro-
magnetic field of science in which so much takes place. I look upon
them as potent and psycho-genetic even, capable of producing and
actually productive of new and strange and valuable things in the
way of human temperament. Take little Holland, for instance, and
its amazing school of great painters. And Greece, with its unrivaled
burst of genius. Or Italy, with its understanding of the arts. Or,
England, with its genius for governing. There is something about
the soil and light of certain regions that makes not only for individuality
in the land but in the people of the land.

"For instance," he continued. "I insist that the Hoosier is different
mentally and spiritually to the average American. He is softer, less
sophisticated, more poetic and romantic. He dreams a lot. He likes to
play in simple ways. He is not as grasping as some other Americans and
some other nationalities. That may be due to the fact that he is not as
practical, being as poetic and good natured as he is. If he be poor and
uneducated he likes to fish and play an accordion or sing. If he is better
schooled he likes to read, write verse, maybe, or books, and dream. In a
crude way, perhaps, he has the temperament of the artist, and so I still
look to Indiana, or its children, at least, to do great things, artistically.
And all this I lay to the soil and light. Why? I don't know. I just guess
that they have something to do with it.

"Nothing else explains to me Edward Eggleston and his turning to
letters at that early time and in the region from which he hailed—the
extreme southeastern part of Indiana. Or General Lew Wallace writing 'Ben Hur' there in Crawfordsville, under a beech tree. Neither will
anything else explain to me why the first automobile this side of
France was built right here at Kokomo, and almost at the same time
that the first one was perfected in France. Nor why the first automobile course, after Brooklands, England, was built here at Indianapolis—not near New York or Chicago, as one might have expected,
perhaps. Or why an adventurer like La Salle should come canoeing up
the Maumee and the St. Joseph into this particualr region. The French,
who first had this territory, chose to fortify at Terre Haute and
Vincennes. Why? They might just as well have fortified at other
points beyond the present State borders.

"What I am trying to get at is this: Via such a soil and such light as
is here cooperating you have a temperament more sensitive to the
resource above mentioned. In the case of those who wandered in here,
like La Salle and Lincoln, you have sensitives affected by the condi-

tions here. Their dreams or aspirations were here strengthened. This is a region not unlike those which produce gold or fleet horses or oranges or adventurers. There are such regions. They are different. And I look upon Indiana as one such."

"Bravo!" I applauded. "Very flattering to dear old Indiana, to say the least, and as an honest native, and moved by self-interest, I hereby subscribe. But—" And then I went back to the churches, the hard-headed conventionalities, the fact that the "inventor" of the first auto-mobile here was accused of robbing the French of their patents, that Robert Owen was a canny Scot who saw to it that he never lost a dollar in his idealistic enterprise but held the whole town of New Harmony and all that thereunto appertained in fee simple, so that when the idea proved groundless he was able to shoo all his assembled theorists off the place and sell it for what it would bring. But my friend was not in the least abashed. He reproached me with being incurably materialistic and clung to his soil and light theory, which, I may as well admit, appeals to me very much. His final rebuke to materialism was that human nature in toto is nothing but a manifesta-tion of forces which unavoidably assume opposite phases, which same we label good or evil, but which really are found to be supplementing each other in any manifestation which can be labeled life. So you may see how far Indiana, with its temperament carried us.

But admiring and even revering the State as my native heath I am perfectly willing to admit all of his claims and even more of such as may be in its favor.

H. L. Mencken

BY H. L. MENCKEN

1923

Ask a professional critic to write about himself and you simply ask him to do what he does every day in the practice of his art and mystery. There is, indeed, no criticism that is not a confidence, and there is no confidence that is not self-revelation. When I denounce a book with mocking and contumely, and fall upon the poor author in the brutal, Asiatic manner of a drunken longshoreman, a Ku Kluxer, or a midshipman at Annapolis, I am only saying, in the trade cant, that the fellow disgusts me—that his ideas and his manners are somehow obnoxious to me, as those of a Methodist, a golf-player, or a clog-dancer are obnoxious to me—in brief, that I hold myself to be a great deal better than he is, and am eager to say so. And when, on the other hand, I praise a book in high, astounding terms, and speak of the author as if his life and sufferings were of capital importance to the world, then I am merely saying that I detect something in him, of prejudice, tradition, habit of mind, that is much like something within myself, and that my own life and sufferings are of the utmost importance to me.

That is all there ever is in criticism, once it gets beyond cataloguing. No matter how artfully the critic may try to be impersonal and scientific he is bound to give himself away. In fact, his very effort to be impersonal and scientific is a form of giving himself away, as the writings of my eminent colleague, Prof. Dr. Erskine, well demonstrate. I have never had the honor of being presented to Erskine, but I know quite as well as his grandmother that he is essentially a shy man—that the winds of doctrine alarm him and he has no stomach for rough adventure. Hence his plea for decorum and tradition, i.e., for what has passed the stage of experiment and danger, i.e., for safe harbors and refuges. He can no more get himself out of his criticism than he can get himself out of his skin. Nor can, at the other pole, the critical Bolsheviki of Greenbaum Village—all of them as foreign and as loathsome to Erskine, I daresay, as so many Nietzsches or Beethovens. When these bright young men print profound aesthetic treatises upon the art of Fatty Arbuckle, Gertrude Stein, and the "Parisian Widows" burlesque troupe, they say, of course, nothing that is pertinent to aesthetics, but they do say something extremely amusing about their own tastes, and hence about themselves. More, they say something even more amusing about the seminaries where they were bred to the humanities.

With criticism thus so transparent, so unescapably revelatory, I often marvel that the gentlemen who concern themselves with my own books, often very indignantly, do not penetrate more competently to my essence. Even for a critic I am excessively garrulous and confidential; nevertheless, it is rare for me to encounter a criticism that hits me where I live and have my being. A great deal of ink is wasted trying to discover and denounce my motive in being a critic at all. I am, by one theory, a German spy told off to flay, terrorize, and stampede the Anglo-Saxon. By another I am a secret radical, while professing to admire Coolidge, Judge Gary, and Genghis Khan. By a third, I am a fanatical American chauvinist, bent upon defaming and ruining the motherland. All these notions are nonsense; only the first has even the slightest plausibility. The plain truth is—and how could it be plainer?—that I practice criticism for precisely the same reason that every other critic practices it: because I am a vain fellow, and have a great many ideas on all sorts of subjects, and like to put them into words and harass the human race with them. If I could confine this flow of ideas to one subject I'd be a professor and get some respect. If I could reduce it, say, to one idea a year, I'd be a novelist, a dramatist, or a newspaper editorial writer. But being unable to staunch the flux, and having, as I say, a vast and exigent vanity, I am a critic of books, and through books of *Homo sapiens*, and through *Homo sapiens* of God.

So much for the motive. What, now, of the substance? What is the fundamental faith beneath all the spurting and coruscating of ideas that I have just mentioned? What do I primarily and immovably believe in, as a Puritan believes in hell? I believe in liberty. And when I say liberty, I mean the thing in its widest imaginable sense—liberty up to the extreme limits of the feasible and tolerable. I am against forbidding anybody to do anything, or say anything, or think anything so long as it is at all possible to imagine a habitable world in which he would be free to do, say, and think it. The burden of proof, as I see it, is always upon the policeman, which is to say, upon the lawmaker, the theologian, the right-thinker. He must prove his case doubly, triply, quadruply, and then he must start all over and prove it again. The eye

through which I view him is watery and jaundiced. I do not pretend to
be "just" to him—any more than a Christian pretends to be just to the
devil. He is the enemy of everything I admire and respect in this
world—of everything that makes it various and amusing and charming.
He impedes every honest search for the truth. He stands against every
sort of good-will and common decency. His ideal is that of an animal
trainer, an archbishop, a major general in the army. I am against him
until the last galoot's ashore.

This simple and childlike faith in the freedom and dignity of man—
here, perhaps, stated with undue rhetoric—should be obvious, I should
think, to every critic above the mental backwardness of a Federal
judge. Nevertheless, very few of them, anatomizing my books, have
ever showed any sign of detecting it. But all the same even the dullest
of them has, in his fashion, sensed it; it colors unconsciously all the
diatribes about myself that I have ever read. It is responsible for the
fact that in England and Germany (and, to the extent that I have ever
been heard of at all, in France and Italy) I am regarded as a highly
typical American—in truth, as almost the archetype of the American.
And it is responsible equally for the fact that here at home I am often
denounced as the worst American unhung. The paradox is only apparent. The explanation of it lies in this: that to most Europeans the
United States is still regarded naively as the land of liberty *par excel-
lence,* whereas to most Americans the thing itself has long ceased to
have any signifiance, and to large numbers of them, indeed, it has of
late taken on an extreme obnoxiousness. I know of no civilized country, indeed, in which liberty is less esteemed than it is in the United
States today; certainly there is none in which more persistent efforts
are made to limit it and put it down. I am thus, to Americans, a bad
American, but to Europeans, still unaware of the practical effects of
the Wilson idealism and the Roosevelt saloon-bouncer ethic, I seem to
be an eloquent spokesman of the true American tradition. It is a joke,
but the joke is not on me.

Liberty, of course, is not for slaves: I do not advocate inflicting it on
men against their conscience. On the contrary, I am strongly in favor
of letting them crawl and grovel all they please—before the Supreme
Court of the United States, Gompers, J. P. Morgan, Henry Cabot
Lodge, the Anti-Saloon League, or whatever other fraud or combination of frauds they choose to venerate. I am thus unable to make the
grade as a Liberal, for Liberalism always involves freeing human beings
against their will—often, indeed, to their obvious damage, as in the
cases of the majority of Negroes and women. But all human beings are
not congenital slaves, even in America. Here and there one finds a man
or a woman with a great natural passion for liberty—and a hard job

getting it. It is, to me at least, a vast pleasure to go to the rescue of such a victim of the herd, to give him some aid and comfort in his struggle against the forces that seek to regiment and throttle him. It is a double pleasure to succor him when the sort of liberty he strives for is apparently unintelligible and valueless—for example, liberty to address conventions of the I.W.W., to read the books of such bad authors as D. H. Lawrence and Petronius Arbiter, to work twelve hours a day, to rush the can, to carry red flags in parades, to patronize osteopaths and Christian Science healers, to belong to the best clubs. Such nonsensical varieties of liberty are especially sweet to me. I have wrecked my health and dissipated a fortune defending them—never, so far as I know, successfully. Why, then, go on? Ask yourself why a grasshopper goes on jumping.

But what has liberty to do with the art of literary criticism, my principal business in this vale? Nothing—or everything. It seems to me that it is perfectly possible to write profound and valuable literary criticism without entering upon the question of freedom at all, either directly or indirectly. Aesthetic judgments may be isolated from all other kinds of judgments, and yet remain interesting and important. But this isolation must be performed by other hands: to me it is as sheer a psychological impossibility as believing that God condemned forty-two little children to death for poking fun at Elisha's bald head. When I encounter a new idea, whether aesthetic, political, theological, or epistemological, I ask myself, instantly and automatically, what would happen to its proponent if he should state its exact antithesis. If nothing would happen to him, then I am willing and eager to listen to him. But if he would lose anything valuable by a *volte face*—if stating his idea is profitable to him, if the act secures his roof, butters his parsnips, gets him a tip—then I hear him with one ear only. He is not a free man. Ergo, he is not a man. For liberty, when one ascends to the levels where ideas swish by and men pursue Truth to grab her by the tail, is the first thing and the last thing. So long as it prevails the show is thrilling and stupendous; the moment it fails the show is a dull and dirty farce.

Zionism—Alive and Triumphant

BY CHAIM WEIZMANN

1924

Of all the concepts which are associated with the Jewish problem and the outstanding effort which is being made toward its solution, perhaps none has become involved in obscurer controversy than "political Zionism." So keen and even acrimonious have the debates become that the doctrine which this phrase inadequately represents has been torn out of its setting of history and reality, like a sentence wrenched out of its context, and has become a sort of *Ding an sich*, a self-inclosed system of ideas, or, better still, an incantation, capable of effecting a wonderful transformation in the relationship of Palestine to the Jewish people.

Yet political Zionism can no more be dissociated from practical affairs than law from natural process. For us there is only Zionism—and "cultural Zionism," "practical Zionism," "political Zionism" are only convenient figures of speech, arbitrary approaches or methods of discussion. To talk of political Zionism as something which the Zionist can either accept or deny is to talk of granting permission to two and two to make four. Political Zionism is not something outside of the process of building up a homeland in Palestine which may be added to that process or withheld from it. It is inherent in every step. Every affirmative act in the creation of a Jewish center in Palestine is political.

Political Zionism, in brief, is the creation of circumstances favorable to Jewish settlement in Palestine. The circumstance most favorable to Jewish settlement in Palestine is the existence of a Jewish settlement in Palestine. The larger the Jewish settlement the greater the ease with which it can be increased, the less the external opposition to its increase; the smaller the Jewish settlement in Palestine the more difficult its increase, the more obstinate the opposition.

One does not create political Zionism by affirming it, any more than one destroys it by denying it. Men who have never heard the phrase, and others who have combated it, have been political Zionists. Those first pioneers of nearly half a century ago, who went out to Palestine and founded the first modern colonies, who laid the foundations of the still small but flourishing Jewish settlement, were actually the founders of political Zionism. They built up positions, they furnished proof of the practicality of the scheme, they gave the most convincing demonstration of the will behind the demand; their work, whatever they intended, reached beyond the immediate achievement and beyond the Jewish people. The world respects the settlements in Palestine more than all the protestations of the Jews.

Those who believe, or who affect to believe, that some sort of system can be devised whereby Palestine can be "given" to the Jewish people are talking of a Zionism which is not political but metaphysical. A country is not a thing done up in a parcel and delivered on demand. England can no more "give" Palestine to the Jews than it can give them history or a culture. All that England can do—and is making serious efforts to do—is to create conditions whereby the Jews cannot "take" Palestine but can grow into it again, by natural and organic process.

England could not even give Palestine to the Jews if that country were entirely uninhabited. It could permit Jewish immigration "as of right and not on sufferance"—which is precisely what it is doing now. The rest is in the hands of the Jewish people. That Jewish immigration into Palestine should be recognized as being "of right and not on sufferance" is the triumph of political Zionism. The preamble to that part of the British Mandate over Palestine which says: "Whereas recognition has been given to the historical connection of the Jewish people with Palestine and to the grounds for reconstituting their National Home in that country," is the triumph of political Zionism. This recognition is not British alone, but is common to all the nations which combined to give the Mandate, and to America, which indorsed the essential part of the Mandate in a special resolution.

But the idea that England should "give" Palestine to the Jews is particularly crude and Utopian when it is linked up with the suggestion of expropriation or removal of the Arabs. Fortunately no such suggestion has ever come from a responsible Zionist leader. For apart from its inherent impracticality and immorality, the idea again betrays a complete dissociation from the realities of the situation. England would not commit such an act even if the Jewish people were to demand it. And the Jewish people would not demand it because it realizes that, in laying the foundations of its old-new home, it must not tolerate even a suspicion of faith in those vicious imperialist principles which have been the source of half its woes.

If there is any significance at all in the rebuilding of a Jewish homeland, it must be made evident first in the attitude of the Jewish people toward the nations in the midst of which that homeland is being built. Friendliness with the Arabs is not simply a matter of convenience or expedience; it is a cardinal doctrine; it is an essential part of the Jewish outlook, an aspect of the spiritual dream which the Jewish homeland is to embody. If we reject the vicious shifts and tricks of what is inaccurately called *Realpolitik* it is not only because of its essential stupidity and ineffectiveness, but because our entire history has been a living protest against it. To solve one problem by the creation of two others is a method which is not unapproved in the world of practical men. Perhaps it pays in the case of fly-by-night nations, though even most of these live long enough to witness the undoing of their practical wisdom. In the case of the Jews, who are, as it were, a permanent institution, there is a reputation to be cherished and maintained. Nor is Jewish-Arab cooperation a new concept. The ideal already has an illustrious history. It is not so long ago—as history, and particularly Jewish history, goes—that Jews and Arabs worked hand in hand from Granada to Bagdad in founding and spreading one of the most brilliant civilizations: when the rest of Europe was still steeped in the dark slumber of the Middle Ages, Spain, Mesopotamia, and Northern Africa were brightly illumined by a great Arab Jewish culture. That culture has never disappeared; it survived, transmuted and disguised, in the Renaissance to which it contributed generously; its unacknowledged issue today forms part of our Western civilization.

For I would make it clear that the primal appeal of the Jewish homeland in Palestine is spiritual. Zionism cannot solve immediately, it can only relieve to some extent, the Jewish world problem. If Palestine were empty today, if it could absorb fifty thousand immigrants a year (and by the way these two conditions are not supplementary: an empty Palestine could not absorb Jews more rapidly than Palestine as it is), it would still fail to solve the problem of eight million of Jews subject to the moods and caprices of unfriendly surrounding nations. But even at that the refugee problem in its relation to Palestine has another aspect. Our plea to the Western world to open its gates to the persecuted Jews loses much of its cogency if that part of the problem which is in our own hands remains unsolved. When we are sending as many refugees into Palestine as that country can absorb, we have a double claim on the sympathy of the world.

One must not, of course, talk of "sending Jews into Palestine" as though this were purely an arithmetical problem. Jews "sent to Palestine" cannot stay there unless they can be absorbed healthily into the economic life of the country. Preparation must be made for every Jew who wishes to enter Palestine. In the last three years we have sent over thirty thousand Jews into the country. Tens of thousands more await the opportunity to enter it. They cannot be admitted pell-mell and at random, lest the emigration from Palestine finally counterbalance the immigration into it. And by preparation we mean of course the growth and development of the country's resources and the integration of newcomers with its economic life. Money is needed for this task; but we need equally a sense of organic construction. Restriction of immigration into Palestine has nothing to do with political conditions. Given the means we could double and treble the immigration, though we must understand that even unlimited means would not enable us to ship a hundred thousand Jews a year to Palestine. It takes time for a small country like Palestine to digest and assimilate fifteen or twenty thousand newcomers.

It would be false to see the ultimate possibilities of the Zionist experiment in terms of Palestine alone. The peculiar position of Palestine fits it to play a role of extraordinary importance in the Near East—a role which it has already entered on. The development of Palestine is the key to the development of a vast territory once the most fruitful in the world, today cut off from the centers of civilization and given over to neglect and decay. Unfortunately hunger is impatient, and the immense resources of the Mesopotamian hinterland are neglected because they cannot be developed in a day. Yet the first steps toward this development have already been taken. The linking up of Bagdad with Haifa is the tangible evidence. The carrying of mail in seven hours between these two points—separated hitherto by three and a half weeks of laborious traveling; the immediate prospects of a railway track which will carry freight back and forth in three days, these are both symbols and achievements. Their creation was made possible only with the awakening of Palestine by Jewish enterprise, and Jewish enterprise is perhaps destined to play an exceedingly important part in the economic reconstruction of the Near East.

Yet I must repeat that if the question of the Jewish refugee gives a new spur to the Zionist effort, it is not and never was the primal motive. There was something more affirmative behind the first stirrings of the movement—and that something became more coherent and self-conscious the movement gathered momentum and power. Zionism envisages more than the negative relief of suffering, more than philanthropic effort, and Palestine to the Zionist was never merely a last desperate opportunity to escape the persecution of the world. Indeed, whatever fortuitous cooperation there has been between anti-Semitism and Zionism, it would be quite wrong to make the two interdependent. The Jew does not depend on anti-Semitism for his existence, and Zionism is the strongest expression of the Jewish will to live.

The hope and lure of Palestine, its special appeal to the Zionist, lay in the authentic Jewish life and culture which could again develop there, after an interruption of twenty centuries. The concept of Jewish culture—and even Jewish culture in Palestine—has too often been of a "literary" nature. It is true that Zionist effort has succeeded in reviving the Hebrew language so that throughout an entire public-school and high-school system Hebrew is the language of tuition, so that Jewish children again use Hebrew as their natural medium. It is equally true that within a few months the Hebrew University is to be opened. It is equally true that concomitant with the Zionist renaissance there has come an extraordinary resurgence of Hebrew poetry—certainly the finest we have produced since the time of the Spanish singers—and perhaps the finest since the days of the Hebrew prophets. But culture must not be dissociated from life, and when we talk of a renewed Jewish culture, an authentic Jewish culture, in Palestine, we are not talking only of schools and literary people.

A civilization is whole and complete. The Jewish village in the valley of Jizreel, the Jewish cooperative colony under the shadow of Mount Hermon, the Jewish merchants of Tel-Aviv and Jerusalem, the young men and women who are building roads and draining marshes— these are, after all, the material of the new Jewish culture. These people, working in a world of their own, from clean and unspoiled beginnings, are apt to produce that now forgotten value—the purely Jewish culture. In all other countries, in all other colonies, the Jew comes to add and to adapt. He is nowhere free to be himself; he must be that which an established civilization will permit him to be. With the best will in the world a nation welcoming the Jew cannot remove the tacit pressure and demand of its civilization and culture on the individuality of the Jew. But in Palestine the Jew can, for the first time since his dispersion, enter again into direct relation with his foundations. No one there stands between him and the first principles of life. He is back on the soil in every sense of the word: it would perhaps be better to say that he is back on the earth.

It is idle to speculate as to the forms which Jewish life in Palestine will take in two or three generations from now. To say that the Jew will give this or that to the world, as the result of a restoration of Palestinian Jewish life, is to indulge in vicarious generosity. We must say frankly that we cannot foresee the end of the experiment. We can only say that its beginnings are extraordinarily auspicious, that all circumstances combine to convince us of the value of the effort, that the vitality and richness of the Jewish people precludes the fear that the final product will be either commonplace or meaningless. Given a chance to be himself, the Jew will certainly not serve the world less than when forced to be everybody but himself. And that restoration to himself implies, too, the rehabilitation of his reputation in his own eyes and in the eyes of the world.

Last Days of the Charming Lady

BY ALLEN TATE

1925

The Charming Lady will most likely be where you would have her, under the lilacs, with magnolias, if it is spring (and it is sure to be), heavy on the air not far away. She will not fail, being what she is—the typical Charming Lady—to talk quietly about the age at once heroic and golden in the history of the States of the Secession. Her conversation will be deft and serious but not too serious, because it will be cast in a whimsicality of fortitude before the intimate rumor of raped magnificence: It is certain to be an elegy on the perished amenities of the Old South, done much after the manner in which Mr. T. S. Eliot a few years ago lamented the decay of all modern culture. It is a scattering tradition, and its last living authority will scarcely survive the present decade.

Yet now the Lady is not too hard to find. You may meet her, if you are eligible, in Nashville or Charleston or . . . But mostly her grandfather tested the qualities of inertia in Virginia "before the war" and was a part of the Tradition, and used words like tradition and aristocracy with a disarming contempt for accuracy. The Old South was never greatly distinguished for a culture of ideas.

The bookish culture of ante-bellum Southerners was the accident of a charmed idleness. The native literary product, whether it was Cable or Sims or Timrod, Lanier being not a very notable exception, came mostly after the war, but the substance of the old order was in it; it evinced charm without energy. And it came to a typical conclusion in the books of Thomas Nelson Page, shallow like him and diverting for those not disaffected by a sense of humor, fraught with no critical awareness of relative social values; it was formed out of a taste that required very little beyond the prettily decorative verse of, say, Edward Coate Pinkney. There remains not a trace of even an intimation

that one function of literature is passage and *bon voyage* to intellectual
and spiritual adventure.

For adventure by all accounts was romantically yet decently physical. The venturesome mind seldom observes the rules of any game but
its own. It notoriously sets politics and economics to quaking, and
doubtless in the South it was an embarrassing Gorgon to be throttled
or at least hidden away. The South was proprietor of a particular
mechanism of truth: it had to protect the mechanism against the removal of old parts and the fitting in of new. It was set upon being a
One-hoss Shay forever. Mastered by its one idea and so master of none,
it fought four years—in a fashion which a contemporaneous Cervantes,
as well as a Thomas Nelson Page, might have owned to be his proper
milieu—to preserve this single, all-embracing idea.

Southern culture consisted, in essence, in a reflowering of eighteenth-
century English manners and in the backwash, sterilized, of liberal
thought from that century; a delight in English landscape reveries
stimulated by Collins and Cowper and a little of Gray, and reproduced, with a few local trees and shrubs substituted for their British
originals, in the verse of Henry Timrod; and eighteenth-century political and humanitarian catchwords bandied innocuously enough except
by Thomas Jefferson, the urbane heretical democrat—undetected in
that role—which ideas ironically contributed to the economic and spiritual bankruptcy of the next generation in his own regime. Most literate persons did lip service to Shakespeare. All of them knew something
of Pope, or should have—that whatever is is right, if it was what you
approved of. And the novels and poems of Walter Scott were a complete repository of manners and of the spirit of manners which is
morals.

The Old South was strictly a political and economic aristocracy. It
would have shuddered could it have grasped the first implications of a
French critic's assertion that only through the abolition of truths,
through the dissociation and repudiation of outmoded general notions
which have lost their roots in an existing reality, can a society create
new forms for the perpetuation of its strength. The South was beau-
tifully devoted unto the death to its one idea—the permanence of a
special politico-economic order. An essential literature was impossible.
The South could not afford to look at itself critically; and it is a
commonplace in the history of intelligencce that spontaneous self-
examination—which the Charming Lady permits to neither herself nor
her visitor—is the initial moral attitude which must preface the exacting business of beautiful letters. It implies the recognition of a relation
extra-social: the relation of man to a god. The South, before the Civil
War, probably had little more than incidental commerce with the

name of Deity. Its aristocracy needed but few of the privileges of which the sole storehouse, according to the best imaginative opinion, stands in some empyrean; it was an aristocracy of social privilege founded in a rigid social order. Deprived of that order, the Old South has degenerated into and survives only as a sentiment susceptible of no precise definition.

For the privilege is long over and done with. While New England has preserved to some extent a culture of ideas in spite of its thorough absorption of industrialism—it articulated in the beginning a system of ideas of which the apical notion was a God—it is significant that after the Civil War the South became, equally with the Middle West, rich soil for the growth of the secular and vulgar and moralistic churches. The hope of the South lay always in a secular order and made few requisitions of literature and religion—of Petronius and God! Its spiritual needs did not conspicuously exceed the supply of sentimental chivalry. And lest the supply find nowadays no market Mr. James Branch Cabell has sophisticated it with deathbed agonies, the corpse dressed out in the glittering jerkin, or, for that matter, the tweeds of a pretentious erudition. Mr. Cabell's comedies, Koschkei the Deathless notwithstanding, contain not so many universal ideas as Southern elegiacs conducted in the name of destiny. They are commentaries on the decadence of an emotion. Their escape from realism—this is not a judgment on their aesthetic value, or lack of it—is identical in origin with the historical Southern escape from ideas.

And so it is not surprising that the second generation after the Civil War is whooping it up in boosters' clubs along with the veritablest descendant of carpet-bagger and poor white. For this second generation, like its forebears, has no tradition of ideas, no consciousness of moral and spiritual values, as an inheritance; it has simply lost a prerogative based on property. As a result it is now almost indistinguishable from the classes it would have held in nice contempt before 1865. Thus, the grandfather of our Charming Lady was a civilized person chiefly, but not entirely in certain ante-bellum towns, because he and the other grandfathers happened to be the gentlemen who got together in the matter and agreed that it was so.

Yet it is doubtful whether there have been other societies in the United States so distinguished for the graces of living as the two flourishing simultaneously in Charleston and in the counties of Virginia between Charlottesville and Washington from about 1800 to 1850. These societies were already in disintegration before the Civil War; for the invention of the cotton gin had put their commercially more zealous cousins west of the mountains on a very nearly equal economic footing with them; and the amenities were gradually released for the more pressing activities of economy.

It is a loss to American letters that these sections in the Old South were not so intelligent as they were gracious, that they never saw their cultural limitations critically enough to be creatively aware of their perfections and to produce their Henry James. This failure is precisely the failure to produce a "historian of fine consciences" that had almost realized their maturity. Now, in our own time, Miss Frances Newman, a Southerner at last who discovers "sophistication" to be the essence of literature—whatever she means by that: it is hardly preciosity, as she would imply—knows her Meredith, has read immoderately in Henry James, is superior to the tribal morality, and attributes to the present social life of Atlanta a casuistry so sensitized and complex that the Atlantans, reading it, will find in themselves not so much cultivation as bewilderment. Miss Newman might more profitably look elsewhere. For the tribal sentiment, though discharged of late from economic captivity by a goodly Mammon, has not yet devoted enough leisure to the dissociation of its insularity.

It was out of this sentiment that the so-called literature of the South was written. Its criticism has not felt dissimilar promptings. Criticism in the South was concerned with expository encomium of almost any writing which satisfied the complacent criterion of exhibiting an indispensable subject matter: the properties inherent in the defeatist attitude created by the eventuality of 1865. There was no suspicion of the necessity for a revaluation of those properties as a maieutic to the dormant or undirected creative mind until the *Double Dealer* and the *Reviewer* were established about five years ago. But the suspicion has not been extended into a usable conviction, into a current of ideas in which an intelligence could find immediate and productive direction. The South has not yet performed the first function of literary criticism, which was Matthew Arnold's in the England of Victoria. It has waited for an outsider to begin it with much vehemence, considerable acumen, and little justice. But Mr. Mencken has roused a person like Gerald W. Johnson, and that is an important business of satire.

The South of the first generation after the Civil War has had at least one social critic not wholly ancillary to the idols of the tribe. Yet the vigor of his attack, in the *South Atlantic Quarterly* and elsewhere, was not alone sufficient to the purpose. Mr. Edwin Mims's writings betray an inadequate sense of the ante-bellum Southern consciousness, and a sensitiveness to that temperament is the critical requisite prior to all scholarship. His criteria are obscured by a cultural deficiency due, probably, to the influence of the secular and vulgar and moralistic churches. So when he came to summarize Southern poetry, in "The South in the Building of the Nation," this cultural astigmatism, in a specific form of unrealized moral and social values, permitted the tribal sentiment to emerge in him almost pure; he succumbed to the sentimental local-color fallacy—the ingenuous opinion that a particular setting is intrinsically more "poetic" than another. And this is the best in criticism the South of the old school can offer.

The sensitive person from the South in this age approaches literature with few or none of the prepossessions, or benefits, derived from the interdependency of a religion and a society. His mind is open for experiment in form, for curiosity about world literature. In 1919 a Southern mind, of those now writing in verse the most important for the national literature, put itself on record:

> Cursed the paternity that planted me
> One green leaf in a wildernes of autumn;
> And wept, as befitting such a fruitful spirit
> Sealed in a yellow tomb.

The modern Southerner does not inherit, nor is he likely to have, a native culture compounded of the strength and subtlety of his New England contemporary's. But he may be capable, through an empiricism which is his only alternative to intellectual suicide, of a cosmopolitan culture to which his contemporary in the East is emotionally barred. . . . T. S. Eliot is not living in St. Louis. For reasons only slightly different, Conrad Aiken and John Gould Fletcher are living permanently abroad.

In 1828 Goethe wrote: "Left to itself every literature will exhaust its vitality if it is not refreshed by . . . the contributions of a foreign one." In 1925 the American man of letters, according to Mr. Van Wyck Brooks, is still in search of a tradition. His proper tradition, which is somewhere in the United States, may yet be discovered in an instrumental experience elsewhere. It is pretty certain that the Southern variety of American writer must first see himself, if at all, through other eyes. For he of all Americans is privy to the emotions founded in the state of knowing oneself to be a foreigner at home.

Poor Me and Pure Boston

BY UPTON SINCLAIR

1927

Everybody admires "Lindy" because he does not talk about himself. I wish I could follow the same charming practice in telling about Boston and its censorship, but unfortunately all I know about it is what it has done to me.

Behold me, therefore, an author who had been known most of his life as the prize prude of the radical movement; a man who can say that he has never told a smutty story in his life, and who was once described by his former marital partner, through the newspapers of the civilized world, as "an essential monogamist"—a very old-fogyish thing to be. I am the author of some thirty books, and a Boston police magistrate has decreed that the last one "manifestly tends to corrupt youth." Let me say at once that "Oil!" is no different in this respect from any of the others. Judged by the Boston method, they are all equally vicious. They are being read throughout the rest of America and in other civilized lands, and Boston alone thinks they are obscene.

It is rather a joke on an author—sitting at his typewriter at home, engaged in work upon a book denouncing what he considers the really obscene writers of his country and time—to have his labors interrupted by a telegram advising him that his own book has fallen under the ban. I am happy to be able to say that I was not calling for the police, but for the moral forces of society to make war upon true obscenity. I wrote that "every time you get a censor, you get a fool, and worse yet, a knave, pretending to be a guardian of morality while acting as a guardian of class greed." And now the Boston censor has arisen to provide me with the proofs!

How does it work here? An Episcopal clergyman stopped me on the street yesterday and told me he knew the man who made the com-

151

plaint to the police about "Oil!" The clergyman gave me his name, and added: "I have suppressed two reports damaging to his moral character." It is, you see, the old story of "Honi soit qui mal y pense."

The next step, under Boston practice, is that two detectives are sent to a bookstore to buy the book about which a complaint has been made. In this case they chose a bookseller who has the hard luck to be only a few doors from the courthouse. They bought the book from Mr. John Gritz, a clerk, who happens to be only twenty years of age and the nearest approach to a cherub that you can find wearing trousers.

The book is then turned over to an inspector. He is a busy man, and his business isn't reading. Here is a book of something over a quarter of a million words; naturally, he says, "What the hell?", passes the book to a clerk in his office, and says, "Hey, Joe, here's a juicy one." I am telling this not as a fiction writer, but as one who has been hanging round the courthouse for the past week, listening to the men on the inside gossiping about what did actually happen.

Next, "Joe" takes the book home and marks the passages which he thinks corrupted his morals. The book is returned to the inspector and he reads these passages and says: "Holy smoke, here this guy has a girl say to a fellow that she knows how to keep from having babies." Boston is 70 per cent Roman Catholic, you understand, and the percentage prevails in the police department. So the inspector goes before a magistrate, and the magistrate takes the book home overnight, and reads the marked passages. If he is an especially fair-minded man, he may have an impulse to read the whole book; but the law does not require him to do so. The law provides for the condemnation of a book "containing" anything, and under the governing decision only the passages complained of are required as evidence. "You are not trying any book except this," said the trial judge in a charge which the Supreme Court of Massachusetts upheld, "and only such parts of this as the Government complained of. . . . It makes no difference what the object in writing this book was, or what its whole tone is." The test is whether it contains, anywhere, anything "manifestly tending to corrupt the morals of youth." You can see that this confines modern writers to the juvenile department, and makes it impossible for them to write for adults.

For my part, I am not going to be bound by this limitation. I believe that grown people have experiences and needs which have to be dealt with in fiction. I will not deliberately corrupt anyone, of course, but if young people read my books they will learn what is going on in the modern world; also they will learn what I consider to be the cause of this moral breakdown, the presence of parasitism and exploitation in our society—the fact that a class of idlers are permitted to have enormous wealth without doing anything to earn it.

In the case of "Oil!" there are 527 pages, and the police object to nine; that does not seem to indicate an abnormal interest in the sexual aspects of life. The first scene they object to begins on page 193, and anyone who buys the book looking for obscenity—a great many people are now doing so—will find it rather slow in starting. There are four or five pages about a "petting party," and that is very bad, according to the Boston police; but on the other hand there are twenty-six pages about how to lease a tract of ground for a drilling-site, and really that does not seem to be giving undue emphasis to the "petting party" aspects of the life of a young "oil prince."

Of course, when a born preacher like myself puts such a scene into a novel, it is for a purpose. I am showing my young "oil prince" groping his way out of the customary life of his class and into a better one. The next time he is invited to a "petting party," he does not go—because he is looking for a better kind of love. Curiously enough, I was rebuked by the reviewer of *The Nation* for these little preachments. "To inject a paragraph of moralizing into the piquant incident of Mrs. Thelma Norman's attempt to be seduced in Bunny's cabin is absurdly priggish." I had hoped that what displeased *The Nation* reviewer might help me out with the magistrate, and I took a copy of the review to court, but alas, I was not allowed to show it, or to say a word. It can never be introduced, under the law, nor can the "petting party" scene be judged in the light of what comes after, what lessons are drawn from it, what repudiation it meets with from the author and the hero later on in the book. Speaking strictly, I may get such testimony in if the Superior Court sees fit to admit it, but the court is under no obligation to admit it, and if it declines to do so the Supreme Court will not call it an error: such is the governing decision, brought out by a trial of the novel "Three Weeks."

I wanted to be the defendant in this case, instead of the cherubic Mr. Gritz. But alas, the police department of Boston does not want me. Mr. George E. Roewer, the unwearying defender of unpopular causes in Boston, approached the authorities with the customary proposition for a test case with a minimum fine upon conviction, but it appears that the police consider the birth-control utterance of my flapper, Eunice Hoyt, especially bad, and I am to go to jail for a year if they can get me. What I am going to do I will not say until after I have done it, but I can assure you I am not going to spend a year on Deer Island.

It is obvious that under this law very little standard English literature can be sold. Consider Smollett or Fielding, "Tess of the D'Urbervilles" and "Ann Veronica." Or consider Shakespeare and the Bible.

One of the newspapermen here tells me that the public is sick of Shakespeare and the Bible, because every publisher of a book, obscene or claimed to be obscene, always proposes these tests. Nevertheless, poor Boston will have to go on hearing about it, until it changes its laws so that these two books can be legally sold and so that modern writers may be free to produce great literature if they can. I have called a meeting at Byron Street House, headquarters of the Community Church of Boston, for the morning of June 16, and I am there going to read the very offending passage of Act III, Scene ii of "Hamlet," and offer this book to the police at bargain prices. Then I am going to read the quite horrible piece of obscenity in Genesis 19, 30-38, and see if the police will buy that.

POSTSCRIPT—JUNE 16. *I offered a copy of the Bible to the police this morning. They would not buy it. I sold it to a Boston rationalist of very high moral standards who is distressed by the thought of how such a passage will corrupt youth and promises to appear before a magistrate and demand a warrant for my arrest. I then offered the police what they thought was a copy of "Oil!" I did not say it was "Oil!" All I did was hold it up before the audience. The police bought it and notified me to appear in court tomorrow. Then they examined the volume and found they had bought the Bible bound in a cover of "Oil!" They demanded their money back, and I was too polite to keep it. The only way to fight this law is to make a monkey of it.*

JUNE 21. *At last I have found a policeman willing to buy a copy of "Oil!" and have sold him one.*

The Passport Nuisance

BY EZRA POUND

1927

"The American people does not think." Very well, no mass of 120,000,-000 people ever has thought; it takes but the most rudimentary knowledge of crowd-psychology, unanimism, etc., to know that thought does not occur in such aggregates. Why expect our nation to surpass, all so easily and so undesigningly, the records of the past and "great nations of antiquity"?

"The American people does not remember." Another age-old quality or defect of the populace, the traditional populace. Americans under thirty do not remember pre-war Europe, for the natural reason that they mostly never saw it; and in consequence they cannot be expected to become especially enraged over particular imbecilities that have developed in Europe since 1914 or 1918.

Elder American tourists have not all of them been in Europe before; and we are, let us suppose, the most patient and nebulous race of beings that have ever moved on this planet. The majority of tourists appear to believe that European conditions were always as bad as they now are; their historic perspective does not reach back to, let us say, the causes of Wilson's first election. We are, as a nation, educated to look not to the past but the future; as the simple-minded freshman is told to look up—while you slip a bit of ice down the front of his collar.

The post-war annual exodus to Europe is divisible roughly into three or four parts: (1) The studious, I mean the young, actively acquisitive explorers; (2) the cultural, I mean the patient old ladies who have been saving up for some time; (3) the drunks (a post-war phenomenon—this—in any such quantity as to demand special treatment), and (4) the shoppers. I suppose these are all particularly patient classes. The old ladies have learned patience; the young are still accustomed to being interfered with by college deans and other such formenifera; the drunks are so relieved by the prevalence of certain facilities that they are ready to put up with anything; the shoppers are notably idiots, and besides they usually have attendants to take trouble for them. (So also have the envoys of the Standard Oil and other legendary monsters with whom the bureaucracy distinctly does *not* monkey.)

While Europe still "groaned under tyranny" I wandered about the face of this continent, I went on foot into its by-ways for sixteen years with no "papers," that is to say with no brass checks, no government's petty officials' permission, nothing in fact, but for one year (1911, I think it was) an unstamped membership card to the Touring Club de France, and a tin button of that fraternity which helped me to get into a small inn at Chalus when covered with twenty miles of mud.

This comfortable period is "over"; not permanently, if I can help it, but at any rate suspended; and this suspension has continued for six or eight years too long. To trace the remote causes of any ill odor is a thankless task, especially if the search reveal such national treasures and sources of civic pride as the late Bryan, the late Wilson, and the unfortunately still extant personnel of the United States Department of State. It is, alas, almost wholly forgotten that Bryan gave Wilson to America; and that Wilson subsequently introduced into international affairs an academic mind; a mind used not to dealing with adults, but to administering petty formalities to an adolescent scholastic body. And whatever ultimately be said by Mr. Wilson's apologists, and whatever final praise be given to his aims and aspirations, there remains at least one private conviction that during his rule the civic organization of America suffered very great damage; that the individual welfare of the citizen went by the board; that the powers of all classes of officials were extended beyond the limits of decency, and beyond limits compatible with the permanent safety of the commonwealth.

Yes, these are very large words. Let 'em stand. What, gentle reader, *are* bureaucrats? Hired janitors who think they own the whole building. The French, being more given to speculation than we, have recently produced several students of bureaucracy, several authors who have studied the *fonctionnaire* as one studies other poisonous insects, and even tried to explain and account for his actions, his inhibitions. The result is not encouraging. One can sympathize with a tyrant, led on by some megalomania or some dream of ultimate benefit to the race or some decoration of his own personal glory; one can sympathize with the crook who does it for excitement, or the poor devil who steals to feed himself or his family; but for the *rond-de-cuir* who sits in an office devising, in perfect safety, some inane means of annoying others, one can have no tolerance.

Mr. Wilson might have made a fairly successful Emperor of By-
zantium; in the year 853 few of his habits would have greatly annoyed
the populace of that city. But a President who exceeds his functions
naturally encourages the small fry to follow suit. There had been,
before Wilson's election, very few Democrats; the supply for normal
appointees was short, and for the abnormal war demands, still shorter.
The war produced, if not a new ruling class, at least a new zealous
bossiness.

I had my first meeting with the new civic order during the armi-
stice. I was living in London. I was told that I "could not go to France
unless I had business." I naturally had business. I received a lot of other
improbable information from the under-sub-vice-assistant. My wife
could not possibly accompany me unless she were ill. I naturally produced doctors' certificates. I could not move about in France; I must
go to one place and stay there. At this point I was rescued by an
elderly intelligent official from another department who took two
hours off and swore to several contradictory statements in a manner
showing great familiarity with the mind-ersatz of officialdom.

I went to France. When I got to Toulouse I found, as I has suspected, that the under-sub-vice-assistant's information was false. The
young chap at the *mairie* told me I could do as I liked, and that I was
free to walk into the Pyrenees. A few miles from the Spanish border
an officer on horseback rode up behind me and asked where was I
going. I said "Mt. Segur." He said "All right, go there. I am looking
for French deserters."

This was, you perceive, before the so-called Peace of Versailles, and
before all Europe had gone crazy over formalities. I had no trouble till
I got back to Paris and entered the American consulate. There the vice-
assistant-second-sub categorically forbade me to return to my home in
London. I said: "I live there," and suggested that he ask the assistant-
first-vice or some one higher up concerning the regulations. He disappeared behind a partition, and returned with a request that I "get a
letter" from my employer, evidently knowing no strata of life save one
where *everyone* has an employer. It was next suggested that I find
some sort of "reference" for myself. Every American I had known in
Paris before the war had left. I knew no one save the Ambassador
whom I had met two days before. I thought vaguely that he might
have other things to do—at that particular time—than look after pass-
ports. However, I stepped into a taxi and drove round to the embassy.
The embassy dealt with the consulate, and I proceeded about my
lawful occasions.

That was 1919, and Europe was, confessedly, in a mess, and errors
might be exceptions. But what in heaven's name has that temporary

confusion to do with 1924, 1925, 1926, 1927? What has it to do with the unending boredom of waiting an hour, a half-hour, three hours, in countless bureaus, for countless useless visas, identities, folderols?

England is not richer than we are; England is not less exposed to the immigration of undesirable units. The British passport costs seven shillings, sixpence (less than two dollars); it is good for seven years. Visas to other countries have either been mutually abolished or their cost reduced to a trifle.

The American official and executive group does not desire the comfort and convenience of the American individual. And what is more, we have one of the clumsiest systems of communication between individuals, and unorganized groups of individuals, that exists in any allegedly representative government. Apart from our tendency to put up with anything, and our instilled duty to be humorous instead of taking action, the normal American has no idea whatsoever as to how he should or can deal with any executive infamy. That, I take it, is part of the price we pay for having our national capital tucked away in a corner. The English who do most things badly are at least able to get at their rulers. Someone takes little Whiff or old Jiblet out on a golf-links and wrings his figurative neck; someone knows so-and-so and the matter gets a few moments' attention. Anything causing inconvenience to ten or twenty thousand literate people can be got on the floor of the House of Commons in, I should say, forty-eight hours. In the United States this could only happen if the issue affected some very large organized business.

Our ideal public servant was given a one-column-wide, four-inch newspaper boost some months ago: "Aged 70 and a bachelor, has not taken a vacation for 20 years, has never indulged in sports or other games, but occasionally enjoyed a good cigar."

I have left out the international aspects of the passport nuisance. The mass of mutual irritation between individuals of one state and officials of another ought to be weighed; but for the space of this article I have tried to consider only the relation of the American to his own government, and more particularly the government's attitude to the individual, as summed up let us say by a little dialogue between one American (not myself) and his consul.

The American, gently: "Forty dollars is a bit heavy for (passport and visa fees for) a little trip of six weeks."

Consul: "Aw! We dun' care wether yuh trevul er not."

Lift Up Thine Eyes

BY SHERWOOD ANDERSON

1930

It is a big assembling plant in a city of the Northwest. They assemble there the Bogel car. It is a car that sells in large numbers and at a low price. The parts are made in one great central plant and shipped to the places where they are to be assembled. There is little or no manufacturing done in the assembling plant itself. The parts come in. These great companies have learned to use the railroad cars for storage.

At the central plant everything is done on schedule. As soon as the parts are made they go into railroad cars. They are on their way to the assembling plants scattered all over the United States and they arrive on schedule.

The assembling plant assembles cars for a certain territory. A careful survey has been made. This territory can afford to buy so and so many cars per day.

"But suppose the people do not want the cars?"

"What has that to do with it?"

People, American people, no longer buy cars. They do not buy newspapers, books, foods, pictures, clothes. Things are sold to people now. If a territory can take so and so many Bogel cars, find men who can make them take the cars. That is the way things are done now.

In the assembling plant everyone works "on the belt." This is a big steel conveyor, a kind of moving sidewalk, waist-high. It is a great river running down through the plant. Various tributary streams come into the main stream, the main belt. They bring tires, they bring headlights, horns, bumpers for cars. They flow into the main stream. The main stream has its source at the freight cars, where the parts are unloaded, and it flows out to the other end of the factory and into other freight cars.

The finished automobiles go into the freight cars at the delivery end of the belt. The assembly plant is a place of peculiar tension. You feel it when you go in. It never lets up. Men here work always on tension. There is no let-up to the tension. If you can't stand it get out.

It is the belt. The belt is boss. It moves always forward. Now the chassis goes on the belt. A hoist lifts it up and places it just so. There is a man at each corner. The chassis is deposited on the belt and it begins to move. Not too rapidly. There are things to be done.

How nicely everything is calculated. Scientific men have done this. They have watched men work. They have stood looking, watch in hand. There is care taken about everything. Look up. Lift up thine eyes. Hoists are bringing engines, bodies, wheels, fenders. These come out of side streams flowing into the main stream. They move at a pace very nicely calculated. They will arrive at the main stream at just a certain place at just a certain time.

In this shop there is no question of wages to be wrangled about. The men work but eight hours a day and are well paid. They are, almost without exception, young, strong men. It is, however, possible that eight hours a day in this place may be much longer than twelve or even sixteen hours in the old carelessly run plants.

They can get better pay here than at any other shop in town. Although I am a man wanting a good many minor comforts in life, I could live well enough on the wages made by the workers in this place. Sixty cents an hour to begin and then, after a probation period of sixty days, if I can stand the pace, seventy cents or more.

To stand the pace is the real test. Special skill is not required. It is all perfectly timed, perfectly calculated. If you are a body upholsterer, so many tacks driven per second. Not too many. If a man hurries too much too many tacks drop on the floor. If a man gets too hurried he is not efficient. Let an expert take a month, two months, to find out just how many tacks the average good man can drive per second.

There must be a certain standard maintained in the finished product. Remember that. It must pass inspection after inspection.

Do not crowd too hard.

Crowd all you can.

Keep crowding.

There are fifteen, twenty, thirty, perhaps fifty such assembling plants, all over the country, each serving its own section. Wires pass back and forth daily. The central office—from which all the parts come—at Jointville is the nerve center. Wires come in and go out of Jointville. In so and so many hours Williamsburg, with so and so many men, produced so and so many cars.

Now Burkesville is ahead. It stays ahead. What is up at Burkesville? An expert flies there.

The man at Burkesville was a major in the army. He is the manager there. He is a cold, rather severe, rather formal man. He has found out something. He is a real Bogel man, an ideal Bogel man. There is no foolishness about him. He watches the belt. He does not say foolishly to himself, "I am the boss here." He knows the belt is boss.

He says there is a lot of foolishness talked about the belt. The experts are too expert, he says. He has found out that the belt can be made to move just a little faster than the experts say. He has tried it. He knows. Go and look for yourself. There are the men out there on the belt, swarming along the belt, each in his place. They are all right, aren't they?

Can you see anything wrong?

Just a trifle more speed in every man. Shove the pace up just a little, not much. With the same number of men, in the same number of hours, six more cars a day.

That's the way a major gets to be a colonel, a colonel a general. Watch that fellow at Burkesville, the man with the military stride, the cold steady voice. He'll go far.

Everything is nicely, perfectly calculated in all the Bogel assembling plants. There are white marks on the floor everywhere. Everything is immaculately clean. No one smokes, no one chews tobacco, no one spits. There are white bands on the cement floor along which the men walk. As they work, sweepers follow them. Tacks dropped on the floor are at once swept up. You can tell by the sweepings in a plant where there is too much waste, too much carelessness. Sweep everything carefully and frequently. Weigh the sweepings. Have an expert examine the sweepings. Report to Jointville.

Jointville says: "Too many upholsterers' tacks wasted in the plant at Port Smith. Belleville produced one hundred and eleven cars a day, with seven hundred and forty-nine men, wasting only nine hundred and six tacks."

It is a good thing to go through the plant now and then, select one man from all the others, give him a new and bigger job, just like that, offhand. If he doesn't make good, fire him.

It is a good thing to go through the plant occasionally, pick out some man, working apparently just as the others are, fire him.

If he asks why, just say to him, "You know."

He'll know why all right. He'll imagine why.

The thing is to build up Jointville. This country needs a religion. You have got to build up the sense of a mysterious central thing, a thing working outside your knowledge.

Let the notion grow and grow that there is something superhuman at the core of all this.

Lift up thine eyes, lift up thine eyes.

The central office reaches down into your secret thoughts. It knows, it knows.

Jointville knows.

Do not ask questions of Jointville. Keep up the pace.

Get the cars out.

Get the cars out.

Get the cars out.

The pace can be accelerated a little this year. The men have all got tuned into the old pace now.

Step it up a little, just a little.

They have got a special policeman in all the Bogel assembling plants. They have got a special doctor there. A man hurts his finger a little. It bleeds a little, a mere scratch. The doctor reaches down for him. The finger is fixed. Jointville wants no blood poisonings, no infections.

The doctor puts men who want jobs through a physical examination, as in the army. Try his nerve reactions. We want only the best men here, the youngest, the fastest.

Why not?

We pay the best wages, don't we?

The policeman in the plant has a special job. That's queer. It is like this. Now and then the big boss passes through. He selects a man off the belt.

"You're fired."

"Why?"

"You know."

Now and then a man goes off his nut. He goes fan-toed. He howls and shouts. He grabs up a hammer.

A stream of crazy profanity comes from his lips.

There is Jointville. That is the central thing. That controls the belt.

The belt controls me.

It moves.

It moves.

It moves.

I've tried to keep up.

I tell you I have been keeping up.

Jointville is God.

Jointville controls the belt.

The belt is God.

God has rejected me.

You're fired.

Sometimes a man, fired like that, goes nutty. He gets dangerous. A strong policeman on hand knocks him down, takes him out.

You walk within certain definite white lines.

It is calculated that a man, rubbing automobile bodies with pumice, makes thirty thousand and twenty-one arm strokes per day. The difference between thirty thousand and twenty-one and twenty-eight thousand and four will tell a vital story of profits or loss at Jointville.

Do you think things are settled at Jointville, or at the assembling plants of the Bogel car scattered all over America? Do you think men know how fast the belt can be made to move, what the ultimate, the final pace will be, can be?

Certainly not.

There are experts studying the nerves of men, the movements of men. They are watching, watching. Calculations are always going on. The thing is to produce goods and more goods at less cost. Keep the standard up. Increase the pace a little.

Stop waste.

Calculate everything.

A man walking to and from his work between white lines saves steps. There is a tremendous science of lost motion not perfectly calculated yet.

More goods at less cost.

Increase the pace.

Keep up standards.

It is so you advance civilization.

In the Bogel assembling plants, as at Jointville itself, there isn't any laughter. No one stops work to play. No one fools around or throws things, as they used to do in the old factories. That is why Bogel is able to put the old-fashioned factories, one by one, out of business.

It is all a matter of calculation. You feel it when you go in. You feel rigid lines. You feel movement. You feel a strange tension in the air. There is a quiet terrible intensity.

The belt moves. It keeps moving. The day I was there a number of young boys had come in. They had been sent by a Bogel car dealer, away back somewhere in the country. They had driven in during the night and were to drive Bogel cars back over country roads to some dealer. A good many Bogel cars go out to dealers from the assembling plants, driven out by boys like that.

Such boys, driving all night, fooling along the road, getting no sleep.

They have a place for them to wait for the cars in the Bogel assembling plants. You have been at dog shows and have seen how prize dogs are exhibited, each in his nice clean cage. They have nice clean cages like that for country boys who drive in to Bogel assembling plants to get cars.

The boys come in. There is a place to lie down in there. It is clean. After the boy goes into his cage a gate is closed. He is fastened in.

If a country boy, sleepy like that, waiting for his car, wandered about in a plant he might get hurt.

There might be damage suits, all sorts of things.

Better to calculate everything. Be careful. Be exact.

Jointville thought of that. Jointville thinks of everything. It is the center of power, the new mystery.

Every year in America Jointville comes nearer and nearer being the new center. Men nowadays do not look to Washington. They look to Jointville.

Lift up thine eyes, lift up thine eyes.

What I Believe

BY BERTRAND RUSSELL

1931

The answer to such a question as What do you believe? is generally expected to consist of two parts: the first explaining one's views as to the nature of the world, the second one's opinions as to how human life should be conducted. The man who invents some fallacious and fantastic argument to show that since the world is such and such, conduct ought to be so and so is considered to show greater profundity than the man who perceives that the two questions have nothing to do with each other. Academic philosphers, ever since the time of Parmenides, have believed that the world is a unity. This view has been taken over from them by clergymen and journalists, and its acceptance has been considered the touchstone of wisdom. The most fundamental of my beliefs is that this is rubbish. I think the universe is all spots and jumps, without unity, without continuity, without coherence or orderliness or any of the other properties that governesses love. Indeed, there is little but prejudice and habit to be said for the view that there is a world at all. Physicists have recently advanced opinions which should have led them to agree with the foregoing remarks; but they have been so pained by the conclusions to which logic would have led them that they have been abandoning logic for theology in shoals. Every day some new physicist publishes a new pious volume to conceal from himself and others the fact that in his scientific capacity he has plunged the world into unreason and unreality. To take an illustration: What are we to think of the sun? He used to be the glorious lamp of heaven, a golden-haired god, a being to be worshiped by Zoroastrians and Aztecs and Incas. There is some reason to think that the doctrines of Zoroaster inspired Kepler's heliocentric cosmogony. But now the sun is nothing but waves of probability. If you ask what it is that is probable, or in what ocean the waves travel, the physicist, like the Mad Hatter, replies, "I have had enough of this; suppose we change the subject." If, however, you press him, he will say that the waves are in his formulae, and his formulae are in his head, from which, however, you must not infer that the waves are in his head. To speak seriously: such orderliness as we appear to find in the external world seems to be due to our own passion for pigeonholes, and it is quite doubtful whether there are such things as laws of nature. It is a curious sign of the times that religious apologists welcome this view. In the eighteenth century they welcomed the reign of law, since they thought that laws implied a Lawgiver, but religious apologists in the present day seem to be of opinion that a world created by a Deity must be irrational, on the ground, apparently, that they themselves have been made in God's image. The reconciliation of religion and science which professors proclaim and bishops acclaim rests, in fact, on grounds of quite another sort, and might be set forth in the following practical syllogism: science depends upon endowments, and endowments are threatened by bolshevism, therefore science is threatened by bolshevism; but religion also is threatened by bolshevism; therefore religion and science are allies. It follows, of course, that science, if pursued with sufficient profundity, reveals the existence of a God. Nothing so logical as this penetrates, however, to the consciousness of the pious professors.

The odd thing is that, at the very moment when physics, which is the fundamental science, is undermining the whole structure of applied reason and presenting us with a world of unreal and fantastic dreams in place of the Newtonian order and solidity, applied science is becoming peculiarly useful and more able than ever to give results of value to human life. There is here a paradox of which possibly the intellectual solution may be found hereafter, or, equally possibly, no solution may exist. The fact is that science plays two quiet distinct roles: on the one hand as a metaphysic, and on the other hand as educated common sense. As a metaphysic it has been undermined by its own success. Mathematical technique is now so powerful that it can find a formula for even the most erratic world. Plato and Sir James Jeans think that because geometry applies to the world, God must have made the world on a geometrical pattern, but the mathematical logician suspects that God could not have made a world containing many things without exposing it to the skill of the geometer. In fact, the applicability of geometry to the physical world has ceased to be a fact about that world, and has become only a tribute to the geometer's cleverness. The only thing that the geometer needs is multiplicity, whereas the only thing the theologian needs is unity. Of unity, however vague, however tenuous, I see no evidence in modern science considered as a metaphysic. But modern science considered as common sense remains triumphant, indeed more triumphant than ever before.

In view of this state of affairs, it is necessary to make a sharp distinction between metaphysical beliefs and practical beliefs in regard to the conduct of life. In metaphysics my creed is short and simple. I think that the external world may be an illusion, but if it exists, it consists of events short, small, and haphazard. Order, unity, and continuity are human inventions just as truly as are catalogues and encyclopedias. But human inventions can, within limits, be made to prevail in our human world, and in the conduct of our daily life we may with advantage forget the realm of chaos and old night by which we are perhaps surrounded.

In human beings three things seem to me to be particularly desirable. They are scientific method, friendly feelings, and interest in life or the world. Let us begin with scientific method.

The ultimate metaphysical doubts which we have been considering have no bearing whatever upon the practical uses of science. If a Mendelian develops a variety of wheat which is immune from diseases that are destructive to the older varieties, if a physiologist makes a discovery about vitamins, if a chemist makes a discovery about the scientific production of nitrates, the importance and usefulness of their work is quite independent of the question whether an atom consists of a miniature solar system, or a wave of probability, or an infinite rectangle of integers. When I speak of the importance of scientific method in regard to the conduct of human life, I am thinking of scientific method in its mundane forms. Not that I would undervalue science as a metaphysic, but the value of science as metaphysic belongs in another sphere. It belongs with religion and art and love, with the pursuit of the beatific vision, with the Promethean madness that leads the greatest men to strive to become gods. Perhaps the only ultimate value of human life is to be found in this Promethean madness. But it is a value that is religious, not political or even moral, and at the moment it is morals and politics of which I wish to speak.

Scientific method as an ingredient in everyday life consists of the habit of basing opinions upon evidence rather than upon emotion or tradition. The agriculturist who employs the methods that he learned from his father and his grandfather is likely to be indignant with the urban whippersnapper who sets to work to instruct him. Frequently the latter is ignorant of something essential and is apparently overwhelmed by the shrewd man of practical experience. Nevertheless, he is likely to possess some new piece of knowledge which, if it can be incorporated with experience, will lead to an important improvement on traditional methods. Uneducated mothers imagine that nature has taught them how to bring up their infants, and are indignant when male experts offer them advice. No doubt the male experts would be a failure if they tried to bring up infants themselves. Nevertheless, on many points, such as fixed hours of feeding, their advice has now been accepted by all intelligent women. The main principle of the scientific method is that emotion, like what the soldier said, is not evidence. If this could be more widely recognized, it would not only improve the technique of the arts and of education, but would go far to solve international problems, which are rendered intractable by the substitution of patriotic emotion for a sober survey of facts. Emotion has its sphere, since it decides the ends to which our activities are to be devoted, but it should not be allowed to obscure our vision as to the means for realizing those ends.

Scientific method is closely connected with the social virtue of impartiality. Piaget, in his book on "Judgment and Reasoning in the Child," contends that the reasoning faculty is a product of the social sense. Every child, he says, begins with a dream of omnipotence, in which all facts are bent to his wishes. Gradually, through contact with others, he is forced to the realization that their wishes may be opposed to his, and that his wishes are not invariably arbiters of truth. Reasoning, according to Piaget, develops as a method of arriving at a social truth upon which all can agree. This condition is, I think, largely valid, and emphasizes one great merit of the scientific method—namely, that it tends to avoid those intractable disputes which arise when private emotion is regarded as the test of truth. Piaget ignores another aspect of scientific method—namely, that it gives power over the environment and also power of adaptation to the environment. It may be, for example, an advantage to be able to predict the weather, and if one man is right on this point while all his companions are wrong, the advantage nevertheless remains with him, though a purely social definition of truth would compel us to regard him as in the wrong. It is success in this practical tests of power over the environment, or adaptation to it, which has given science its prestige. The Chinese emperors repeatedly refrained from persecuting the Jesuits because the latter were in the right as to the dates of eclipses when the Chinese astronomers were in the wrong. All modern life is built upon this practical success of science, at any rate where the inanimate world is concerned. It has had hitherto less success in direct applications to man, and it therefore still meets with opposition from traditional beliefs where man is concerned, but it cannot well be doubted that if our civilization survives, man also will soon come to be viewed scientifically. This will have a great effect upon education and the criminal law, perhaps also on family life. Such developments, however, belong to the future.

The power over the environment which science gives is not necessarily a good thing; the stock instance to the contrary is war. If science gives a nation the power to wipe out an enemy capital within a few hours of the outbreak of war, the gain to mankind is problematical. Whether scientific power is to be a boon or a curse depends upon the dominant emotions of those who wield it. Hitherto hatred and cruelty have always played a very large part in human life. Education and the criminal law have at most times been so ferocious as to defeat their supposed ends; that is to say, boys have been stupider, and criminals more criminal, than they would have been if they had been more kindly treated. Similarly, when nations go to war nominally for economic ends, both sides are impoverished, and it is clear that hatred has blinded them as to their true interests. The more scientific power men acquire, the more important it becomes that they should wield this power for good rather than for evil. How they will wield power depends upon their dominant emotions: if these emotions are friendly, they will wield it well; if hostile, badly.

The problem is therefore presented to the men of science to devise a method of generating friendly feeling in the mass of mankind and more especially in the holders of power. The method of direct exhortation, which has been favored by the founders of religions, has not proved very effective, and it is clear that quite other methods are required. A considerable period of experimentation will be necessary before anything can be said positively on this subject, but it is clear that among the factors concerned are diet, instinctive satisfaction, and skill in constructive work. Probably a radical transformation of the economic system is also necessary. I have no doubt whatever that methods could be devised for creating a world in which most men had friendly feelings toward other men, but I think rivers of blood will have to flow before the holders of power will allow such a world to be created, and I am doubtful whether rivers of blood are the right kind of rivers to water the tender plant of human kindness.

When I speak of the necessity of friendly feelings, I emphatically do not mean unselfishness. Unselfishness is, of course, a vague word which is incapable of any precise meaning, but at any rate is always involves control of the feelings by the will. Traditional ethics emphasize the will far too much; emotions and sentiments are far more important than will. The type of person that should be produced is a type that spontaneously, without self-control, wishes to do what in fact is in the general interest, not the type that is filled with destructive wishes kept in check by an iron self-control. Destructive wishes, where they exist strongly, will find an outlet somehow, usually by generating beliefs which justify cruel actions. Useful emotions are produced not by preaching, but by physiological means and by wise conditioning.

This technique applies not only to friendly feelings but also to interest in life. There are many moderns in whom zest is lacking: they live more or less virtuously, but with a minimum of enjoyment. This is usually due to the fact that they force themselves by an effort of will to live in a way which is contrary to powerful emotions, of which they may or may not be conscious. An indispensable psychological condition for interest in life is a certain emotional harmony which makes it unnecessary to suppress certain emotions in order to gratify certain others. The most frequent conflict is between sexual emotions and desire for the respect of neighbors. Wherever such conflicts are strong, they are likely to produce either listlessness or rage: a man will either lose all interest in life or will find his chief pleasure in punishing those who have enjoyed the pleasures which he has denied himself. To keep alive the spontaneous play of interest and the flow of friendly feeling, it is necessary that as far as possible such fundamental emotional conflicts should be avoided. This requires partly an adaptation of the individual to the community, but partly also an adaptation of the community to the individual. To avoid emotional conflicts in the individual, it is sometimes best to adopt such methods of education as will prevent certain desires from growing up, but at other times it is best to alter public morality in such a way that desires previously incompatible shall cease to be so. The latter is the best method wherever public morality condemns acts which would be harmless if they were not condemned.

I believe that the substitution of a scientific for a religious technique in the production of virtue may prove to be of enormous importance. Moralists hitherto have been extraordinarily unsuccessful in producing the type of character that they said they desired. The growth of psychology and biochemistry is likely to give us in the not too distant future a far greater power of molding character than mankind has ever hitherto possessed. Like the power over inanimate nature, this new power over human nature may be used either for good or for evil. I do not profess to know in which way it will be used, but if it is used for evil, our scientific civilization will not long survive.

"Hire Learning" at Ohio State

BY NORMAN THOMAS

1931

A splendid laboratory for the study of what has been called the "hire learning" in America is to be found on the campus of the great Ohio State University at Columbus. Not for many years has there been so clear a demonstration that a board of trustees, dominated by the usual business ideals, expects its students to be docile Babbitts in embryo, its university president to be a high-grade office manager, and its faculty to conform or get out.

Two highly pertinent editorial paragraphs in *The Nation* for June 3 called attention to the refusal of the trustees to renew their contract with Professor Herbert Adolphus Miller, together with its apparent background of student—and some faculty—opposition to military training, and its aftermath of the most naively frank statements of a university board's conception of its relations to a faculty that have been written in recent years. The story is worth telling at more length.

Ohio State University is one of three State-maintained universities in a State more generously sprinkled with colleges, public and private, than Jack Horner's pie with plums. Until the beginning of this century the material development of Ohio State University, at least in comparison with the development of the corresponding institutions in Wisconsin, Illinois, and Michigan, was retarded by various academic, local, and rural jealousies. Within the last generation, however, it has received large appropriations, and has forged far ahead of its former rivals, the other State-supported colleges, in equipment and attendance. Moreover, until recently the superficial observer and also, I think, the more careful student of American universities would have placed Ohio State University among the more competent and liberal of our great State institutions. It had a very active military department and compulsory training, it is true, but it had also a more lively opposition to such training than existed in most universities; in the critical departments of history, political science, economics, and sociology it boasted a somewhat unusual group of able men, apparently entirely free to speak their minds. Among them Professor Herbert A. Miller stood out, less, perhaps, by reason of his academic work than because of his public interest in problems of race and nationality, and his real services to President Masaryk of Czecho-Slovakia in the war days when that country's declaration of independence was written.

During all this time the university was under the control of a board of seven which had expressly reserved the right to make yearly contracts, and only yearly contracts, with the staff from president to the youngest instructor. This board, in turn, has been completely dominated, not by the president of the university, Dr. George W. Rightmire—a personally likable man, vigorous in neither health nor spirit —but by Julius F. Stone (born Stein), president of the board, of which he has been a member since 1909.

Nobody doubts that in his own way Mr. Stone loves the university, and has something more than the usual layman's interest in some forms of scientific research. But that is not why he is president of the board of a great university. The appropriate reason for his position is his standing as an industrialist and banker. He is today head of the Wolfe interests in Columbus, and these interests control one of Columbus's largest banks (Mr. Stone is a director), the BancOhio chain of banks (Mr. Stone is president), and two Columbus newspapers, the *Ohio State Journal* and the Columbus *Dispatch*. Mr. Stone is also chairman of the board of the Seagrave Corporation, which makes fire engines. In general the Wolfe interests dominate Columbus business, and until very lately have had tremendous political power in the city and at the State Capitol no matter which party was in control. Who, then, by American standards, could be more fit than this big-business leader for a high educational post? Well, he has it, and by universal testimony he, who is a strong-minded person, dominates the board to which the new Democratic governor, the supposedly liberal Mr. White, has recently reappointed him.

But things haven't been going so well in these hard times. Candidates in Columbus supposedly backed by the Wolfe crowd went down to defeat last November. The present legislature, now in session, is wrestling with a muddled tax situation in Ohio; it wants to save money, and a cut in the appropriation for Ohio State University might recommend itself to legislators some of whom come from cities with municipal universities of their own, or from towns and counties friendly to other colleges, public or private.

To add to Mr. Stone's worries, while everything was up in the air, some 700 pesky students, after a lot of discussion freely permitted on the campus, signed a petition asking for optional military drill. Still worse, the faculty indorsed the petition by the close vote of 83 to 79. The vote was taken before the head of the fifty-two military men assigned to teach the young to shoot, Colonel Grosvenor Townsend, had made his speech. Ostensibly for this reason President Rightmire called another faculty meeting. Things weren't pleasant. The Colonel was talking about Communists as the authors of anti-militarism. Some patriot in the legislature had introduced a resolution to investigate "those faculty members supporting the optional-drill movement." That faculty meeting was the biggest in years. Under some sort of pressure men came who had to have a Boy Scout show them the way to the meeting place. There were many motions, and on the real test votes the supporters of compulsory drill won about two to one. But the vote given out to the press was not the vote on the vital issue, but on a formal motion to transmit the student petition with the unfavorable recommendation of the faculty. This vote, understood to be simply a registering of the facts, was passed 144 to 9, and was deliberately announced to the press to give the impression of an overwhelming reverse for opponents of compulsory drill.

But even this victory for compulsory drill, exaggerated by the Wolfe press, was not enough to ease Mr. Stone's mind. He put through the trustees a statement rejecting the student petition about drill and moralizing on the purposes of the university. Compulsory military drill was declared to be among "those educational activities that have stood the test of time." The statement ended with the extraordinary "if you don't like it, get out" paragraph which *The Nation* has already quoted. Never was the duty of professors to conform more baldly stated:

> The board feels that the university should not be subjected to emotional criticism because of the unripe vociferations of a small group of students and a very few members of the faculty, who are under no compulsion to come here and under none to remain unless they can subscribe to the fundamental purposes of this university.

No wonder that fifty-six professors and seventy-seven instructors formally protested, and that five deans have declared the innocence of the whole faculty of communism or any offense against academic propriety! The docile Dr. Rightmire had to back up his bosses, the trustees, by a statement of his own amplifying the argument of the board.

Then, perhaps as a warning that papa could spank as well as lecture naughty little professors, Professor Herbert A. Miller was notified that his contract would not be renewed. Mr. Miller had been somewhat active against compulsory drill, but the statement concerning his discharge gave other reasons and alleged that the decision to get rid of him had been reached months previous to the fight on militarism and had been, supposedly, communicated to Mr. Miller by President Rightmire. The latter had, indeed, talked to Mr. Miller in the fall, but by no means in terms of anything more than a desire to clear up some misunderstandings. Hence Mr. Miller had taken no step either to defend his cause or to get another place.

And what were the alleged reasons for eliminating in this offhand fashion a man of real distinction for many public services? These: that Professor Miller's teachings on race relations had brought complaints from parents, and that in India he had expressed an improper degree of sympathy for Gandhi! With regard to the first charge, of itself impertinent, irrelevant, and unsupported by evidence, the head of Mr. Miller's department (sociology) has said that he had received and heard of no complaints from parents. The second is one of the most ridiculous reasons ever given for discharging a professor. It appears that the German-born Mr. Stone and company are more zealous for British supremacy in India than the British, for the British government has never made any complaint concerning Professor Miller. And the particular speech which so shocked Mr. Stone, both in its summary version as given by Mr. Miller and its longer version as discovered by the trustees in a Bombay paper, is a mild expression of interest in Gandhi's tactics, the kind of interest felt by hundreds of thousands of Americans. To discharge a professor for it is a most contemptible truckling, unasked, to foreign imperialism. Of course it is inconceivable that the Gandhi episode is anything but a pretext. Now the Stone crowd have found other pretexts, equally weak: (1) that when Mr. Miller spoke in Korea before a meeting arranged by some of his former students in America, the Japanese police ended the meeting while Mr. Miller was explaining the Czecho-Slovakian independence movement (true, but not at all discreditable to a professor in the land of Jefferson and Lincoln); and (2) that he had been unwelcome at Oberlin, where he formerly taught (emphatically false, as his Oberlin friends proved).

Mr. Stone's dictatorship did not neglect his press. The *Ohio State Journal* and the *Dispatch* by cartoons and editorials and columnist chatter have tried to make out that the university trustees are saving the institution from the "reds." The columnist, Hugh Fullerton, with an eye on the rural vote, waxes sentimental over the glories of the American farm—he forgets the mortgage and the price of wheat—and sees the youthful red from the university redeemed from the error of his ways by a combination of hard work and home cooking. In a *Dispatch* cartoon a mother sheep labeled Common Sense consoles herself with thinking how her errant lambs, gone after a Billy Goat Professor to red pastures, will miss her at "dinner time"—a naive commentary on the strictly utilitarian purposes of education.

It is fair to say that Mr. Stone has not found his university students or faculty or even public opinion so docile as his university president and his papers. Three thousand students, without delay, signed a petition for Professor Miller's reinstatement. A special petition was presented by graduate students with equal enthusiasm. A formal demand has been presented by faculty members for an investigation of the situation by the Association of University Professors. Altogether I found on the campus during a recent visit a livelier degree of social and intellectual interest than is usual in that annex to the stadium which we call the college campus in America. Mr. Stone must rejoice that the end of the academic year is near.

Aside from college sentiment, newspaper comment in the principal papers—especially the Scripps-Howard papers in Ohio—has inclined toward support of Professor Miller. His own varied activities have given him the friendship and support of such diverse groups as the Negroes, many recent immigrant groups, notably the Czecho-Slovaks, who are strong in Cleveland, and some of the best leaders of Protestant and Jewish thought. Sixty-eight Columbus clergymen have sent to the board a letter criticizing its action with great severity. Resolutions for an investigation of the dismissal of Professor Miller and of the business administration of the university, the latter aimed at certain alleged transactions involving members of the board of trustees, have been introduced into the legislature. Governor White may have reason to be less nonchalant than he was when he told the student committee which waited on him and an insistent photographer: "Oh, no, I don't want a picture taken. If I did, why Rightmire, or whatever his name is, might come down here and want his picture taken, too. You've got your publicity now and that's enough."

There can be no solution of this situation which does not reinstate Professor Miller, rescind the limitations upon faculty freedom implied in the trustees' statement, and permit student discussion on such pertinent issues as college militarism. Anything less will leave Ohio State University a school for "hire learning" in the most literal sense.

The situation is particularly a challenge to youth and to the teaching profession. Unless things are changed in Columbus, every young man or woman who goes to Ohio State will know that he and his professors on certain vital matters must think—or at any rate talk—as Mr. Julius Stone thinks proper or get out. Education will be crassly a process of getting certain information for the sake of "success" in a world in which bankers, with the approval of the legislators, are the final authority on militarism, race relations, and economic wisdom.

At least equally concerned must be the whole academic profession. Acquiescence in the Ohio situation is unadorned prostitution of loyalty to truth, to be excused only for the same economic reasons that excuse the women who follow the oldest of professions. If to teach sociology at a university one must refrain from offending the race prejudice of any parent, must express no interest in Gandhi's technique of revolution, and must stimulate no students to question compulsory militarism, then to teach sociology is an intellectual slavery worse than the devotion of any theologian to a rigid creed; for a theologian's creed has at least a nobler background than the prejudices and self-interest of the particular Babbitts who are the fount of academic power. At the very least it must be understood that a man taking Professor Miller's place becomes by that act an outcast and pariah from his own profession. In general, an academic blacklist against an unrepentant university would be a salutary and in the long run a very powerful thing.

Finally, the situation at Ohio State University raises once more the question of the competence of democracy and the validity of its ideals. Our State universities at best are proof of a genuine hunger of democracy for education. That is not education which subordinates the quest for truth to the service of existing prejudice. Democracy fastens on itself its own chains whenever in the name of patriotism or any popular prejudice it lets its own friends and servants, the seekers after truth, be made the victims of that sort of disguised economic dictatorship which Mr. Julius Stone of the Wolfe interests so conspicuously typifies.

The President and Unemployment

BY ROBERT M. LA FOLLETTE

1931

The Administration of Herbert Hoover began on March 4, 1929, with his inspiring declaration that "the larger purpose of our economic thought should be to establish more firmly stability and security of business and employment, and thereby remove poverty still further from our borders." Although he acquiesced in the laissez faire philosophy of his immediate predecessors in office by voicing a hope that this purpose would be attained largely through the spontaneous cooperation of individuals, President Hoover added the significant pledge that his Administration would "assist and encourage these movements of collective self-help by itself cooperating with them."

For eighteen months unemployment has been spreading poverty and acute suffering through industrial and agricultural areas alike. No one yet knows when the present economic disaster will be brought to an end. The illusory prosperity and feverish optimism which marked preceding years have given way to fearful economic insecurity and to widespread despair. These eighteen months have revealed the hypocrisy of the President's pledge of cooperation toward the attainment of economic security. The Administration's efforts to attain economic security have consisted of attempts to minimize the seriousness of the depression, of bold assurances that steps which would restore prosperity were about to be taken, and of a woefully unsuccessful program to stimulate private or local agencies to undertake tasks which the Administration was determined to shirk.

The utter inadequacy of the President's plan to muddle through the depression was increasingly evident as time went on. Instead of adopting constructive measures to meet the issues confronting us, the President in his Valley Forge speech of May 30 last abandoned all pretense of economic leadership. He counseled his fellow-citizens to await with resignation and individual fortitude the day when good fortune might again bring better economic conditions. Abandoning all thought of controlling the complexities of modern economic society, he urged that we "pin our faith upon the inventiveness, the resourcefulness, the initiative of every one of us."

President Hoover entered office with a widely accepted reputation as an economic expert. For years he had indicated his interest in preventing and mitigating unemployment. After appointment by President Harding in 1921 to the chairmanship of the Conference on Unemployment, Mr. Hoover said: "There is no economic failure so terrible in its import as that of a country possessing a surplus of every necessity of life, in which numbers, willing and anxious to work, are deprived of these necessities. It simply cannot be if our moral and economic system is to survive."

Pledges to bring about security of employment and to "abolish poverty" marked the campaign of 1928. The election of Herbert Hoover, the country was assured, would mean the adoption of constructive and aggressive measures to cope with the problem of unemployment. Three months after the inauguration these pledges were recalled to the President's mind by the head of the Iowa State Federation of Labor, who suggested that a national conference be called to consider the unemployment problem. The President replied that he "hoped that we will be able to take it up when some of the momentarily pressing problems of the Administration are out of the way." These "momentarily pressing problems" continued to dominate the President's attention down to the day on which a stock-market crash warned even the unwary that the nation's economic structure had been undermined.

President Hoover's first recognition of the situation was a reassuring statement, on October 25, 1929, that the country was still "on a sound and prosperous basis." Events soon exploded this theory and on November 15 the President temporarily avowed a sounder view by saying that "words are not of any great importance in times of economic disturbance; it is action that counts."

Action was to proceed along five fronts. The first involved the maintenance of credit stability and of ample supplies of capital through the Federal Reserve system, a task which the long-established banking organization readily accomplished, especially since it soon became evident that the country had an over-supply rather than a shortage of capital. Other points in the program, including the revival of construction activities, the stimulation of exports, and assistance to agriculture, were defeated by more permanent Administration policies which ran in a contrary direction. The fifth point, a reduction of income taxes to reassure business, was jammed through Congress only to demonstrate the hollowness of the Administration's glib description of the depression as merely psychological.

By way of doing something more specific, the President on the same day announced that he called a series of conferences with industrial, financial, and labor leaders, not so much to meet as to "head off an emergency." The eminent gentlemen who visited the White House seemed to agree with the President that no attempt should be made to reduce wages, and pledged increased capital expeditures to maintain employment.

An increasing wave of unemployment soon followed, and the President again declared that it was slight in volume and that it would soon be over. On March 8, 1930, he issued his justly famous statement:

> All the evidences indicate that the worst effects of the crash upon employment will have been passed within the next sixty days, with the amelioration of seasonal unemployment, the gaining strength of other forces, and the continued cooperation of the many agencies actively cooperating with the government to restore business and to relieve distress.

On June 4, 1930, the President was waited on by a delegation of bishops, bank presidents, and manufacturers, described by Mr. Amos Pinchot in *The Nation* of January 14, 1931. The President assured the delegation that they must be misinformed concerning the seriousness of the unemployment situation. In Mr. Pinchot's words:

> With calm confidence he spoke of the results that were being gained through the conference he had called of great business leaders and of their fine response to his appeal not to curtail the volume of their activities. He showed us, in authoritative style, that every agency of both the federal and State governments was working at top capacity to relieve the situation. "Gentlemen," he said, "you have come six weeks too late."

Ironically enough, it was at this time that the President reached his decision to sign the Hawley-Smoot tariff bill, which contributed greatly to the almost complete ruin of our export trade.

Demands that the Administration adopt a constructive program became more and more insistent as the fall of 1930 came on. Optimistic statements and announcements of small increases in the volume of federal public works failed to conceal the growth of unemployment, and the protracted drought further enlarged the area of disorganization.

Admission that the unemployment problem had not been met came on October 17, 1930, when President Hoover announced a new series of conferences to draw up more effective plans, on the ground that "as a nation we must prevent hunger and cold to those of our people who are in honest difficulties." The immediate result was the creation of the President's Emergency Committee on Employment, with Colonel Arthur Woods as its chairman. The Woods committee collected information for the President's guidance and made suggestions to private employers and to States and municipalities of ways in which they might alleviate unemployment. The major public-works expansion program recommended to the President by the Woods committee, which would have thrown the powerful resources of the federal government into the breach and substantially reduced unemployment, never saw the light of day because of the President's opposition to legislative action and his blind faith that "the spirit of voluntary service" would be strong enough to cope with the problem "in full measure of the need."

Throughout the following session of Congress, from December, 1930, until March, 1931, the President successfully prevented enactment of more adequate measures to relieve unemployment. Federal assistance to meet the relief of actual distress was blocked through the subserviency of the leaders of a bi-partisan majority in the Senate to the influence of large income-taxpayers, and through the responsiveness of a majority in the House of Representatives to the pressure of the Administration. Instead of an emergency public-works program upon a scale sufficiently great to reduce substantially the volume of unemployment, the Administration's emergency public-works program was limited in the main to an appropriation of $116,000,000, most of which will be available only until September 1.

In harmony with the Administration's general attitude toward unemployment, the session ended with the President's pocket veto, based upon untenable grounds, of the Wagner employment-exchange bill, which almost alone among the measures passed by the Seventy-first Congress might have made some permanent contribution toward the alleviation of the evils of unemployment. The virtual disintegration of the Woods committee, whose members had accepted appointment in the belief that their expert knowledge would receive at least courteous attention from the President, followed within a few weeks. Although the chairman of the committee refused to comment upon his departure from Washington, one of his admirers, Edward A. Filene, remarked that "Colonel Woods is a man of action who refuses to follow a road which leads windingly or not at all to the goal."

A review of the Hoover Administration's unemployment policy demonstrates that the President has lacked either the understanding or the courage to press toward the goal of alleviating the distress of the unemployed and of reducing the number out of work. Timidity and disingenuousness have marked the course of the Administration at a time when heroic courage and bold frankness were necessary. Vigor and firm leadership have been displayed by the President at times, but only to resist proposals which would have mitigated suffering but which necessarily involved an additional levy upon wealthy income-taxpayers.

No informed person has charged the President with full responsibility for the disaster which overtook the United States in 1929. It was produced by factors which had long been working, although President Hoover, like his predecessors, lacked the vision or the will to control those forces. No one has maintained that the federal government alone could solve all the economic problems which now confront the nation. The failure of President Hoover during his Administration is revealed, however, by his attitude toward the measures which would have at least partially ameliorated the unemployment crisis, and which had been under discussion since the unemployment conference over which he presided in 1921. Some of these proposals had again been recommended only a few days before President Hoover's inauguration by the Senate Committee on Education and Labor, which under the chairmanship of Senator Couzens had carried on a thorough study of unemployment.

Instead of frankly informing the country concerning the actual state of affairs, the President repeatedly gave out misleading statements. He clung vehemently to his assertions that the depression would soon be over, and that the number of unemployed was smaller than informed observers had been led to believe.

His Cabinet members for months continued to place the number out of work at 2,000,000, even after official figures had shown the total to be far greater. Finally the Woods committee, in order to obtain a sounder basis for its own guidance, induced the Metropolitan Life Insurance Company to make an independent survey in January, 1931, which resulted in an estimate placing the number out of work at more than 5,000,000. Characteristically the Administration withheld this information until it had been demanded by a resolution of the Senate. A second and more detailed survey, conducted by the Bureau of the Census early in 1931, showed 6,050,000 persons unemployed. It too was withheld by the Administration, this time until after the adjournment of Congress had made it impossible to pass relief appropriations. Strange light is cast upon the Administration's good faith in this connection by Secretary of Commerce Lamont's announcement in March, 1931, that in accordance with a change of Administration policy the public would henceforth be given "all the facts." For more than a year, in other words, the facts had been suppressed.

Despite this assurance, unwarranted optimism continues to emanate from the White House. Late in May, 1931, the President informed the country that he and his Cabinet had found "many factors they considered favorable." A week later Fred C. Croxton, vice-chairman of the Woods committee, felt it necessary to issue a warning that there must be no let-up in relief activities and that almost certainly millions of unemployed would need assistance next winter.

For a hundred years the federal government has granted financial aid to communities temporarily unable to cope with relief problems created by disaster. In spite of his inaugural declaration in favor of cooperation with "movements of self-help," the President devoted much of his energy during the past winter to the defeat of proposals to cooperate with local communities by supplementing out of federal revenues their relief funds, which were rapidly being exhausted. To defend his position, the President drew an arbitrary distinction between "natural" disasters and economic disasters, although the suffering created by the present economic disruption probably far exceeds the burdens imposed by all the "natural" disasters of the last century. He insisted that relief for the unemployed must be locally and privately financed, although official figures finally disclosed that during 1930, 72 per cent of the meager assistance given the unemployed was contributed by local governments and was therefore out of local taxes. The net result of this policy was to throw the burden upon direct, local taxpayers and to relieve the big income-taxpayers of their fair share of the relief levy.

Expansion of public works to afford temporary employment in times of depression had been favorably discussed for more than ten years. Appropriations large enough to initiate an effective emergency program were urged by President Hoover's own advisers. He insisted upon a meager appropriation of $116,000,000. To satisfy the demand for a larger program of public works, he has sponsored misleading statements which lumped expenditures for the purchase of land with expenditures for actual construction, which failed to distinguish between the volume of work normally undertaken prior to the depression and the amount now under way, which obscured the amount of employment actually afforded, and which combined federal and State outlays.

Senator Wagner's bill setting up a permanent organization to regulate federal public works in accordance with business conditions was enacted only after long delay on the part of Administration leaders, and a director to guide its operations is yet to be appointed. Creation of an organization for effective cooperation between federal and State employment offices was proposed in a bill passed by Congress only to be pocket-vetoed, after the adjournment, on specious grounds. Instead, the President set up a system of federal employment directors who have already begun to antagonize and disrupt existing State employment offices. Measures to encourage the establishment of employment reserves or to create a national system of employment insurance were ignored by the Administration, and when the Senate nevertheless authorized a special committee to consider this problem during the present adjournment, Senator Wagner, who had sponsored the creation of the committee, was deposed from the chairmanship by Administration influence.

Other long-range measures—to abolish child labor, to revise the Smoot-Hawley tariff in order to stimulate export trade, to increase federal income and inheritance taxes to provide funds for an expansion of the government's construction program and to enable it to relieve suffering, and to bring about intelligent planning of our economic life in order to prevent a repetition of the situation into which we drifted —have met with Presidential indifference or hostility.

The third winter of unemployment is approaching. Responsibility for the failure of the federal government to provide a program for the relief of distress among millions of our people rests squarely upon President Hoover. The bankruptcy of his leadership in the worst economic crisis in our history reveals the tragic failure of rugged individualism and places the major cost of deflation upon those least able to bear it—the unemployed.

Revolutionary Interlude in France

BY LEON TROTSKY

1936

NORWAY, *July 9*

We must repeat once again that the serious capitalist press like the Paris *Temps* or the London *Times* has made a much more correct and penetrating evaluation of the meaning of the June events in France and Belgium than has the press of the People's Front. While the Socialist and Communist official organs, tagging behind Blum, talk about the beginning of the "peaceful transformation of the social regime in France," the conservative press insists that in France a revolution has begun and that it will inevitably assume violent forms during the next stages. It would be a mistake to view this prognosis as solely or chiefly intended to frighten the property owners. The representatives of big capital are capable of following the social struggle very realistically. Contrariwise, petty bourgeois politicians readily incline to accept their own desires for reality. Standing between the principal classes, finance capital and the proletariat, the Messrs. "Reformers" propose that both of the opponents accept the middle course which they have greatly labored to elaborate in the General Staff of the People's Front, and which they themselves interpret differently. However, they will shortly have occasion to convince themselves that it is much easier to reconcile class contradictions in leading articles than in governmental activity, especially in the very heat of a social crisis.

In parliament an ironical charge has been hurled against Blum that he carried on negotiations concerning the demands of the strikers with representatives of the "200 families." "And who else was there for me to negotiate with?" wittily replied the Premier. In point of fact, if any negotiations are to be carried on with the bourgeoisie, then it is necessary to choose the real masters, those capable of deciding for themselves and of issuing orders to others. But in that case, it was pointless to have so noisily declared war against them! Within the framework of the bourgeois regime, its laws and mechanics, each one of the "200 families" is incomparably more powerful than the Blum Government. The financial magnates represent the crown of the bourgeois system of France, while the Blum Government, despite all its electoral successes, "crowns" only a brief interlude between the two contending camps.

At the present moment, in the first half of July, it might superficially seem as if everything had more or less returned to normal. As a matter of fact, within the depths of the proletariat, as well as among the summits of the ruling classes, a well-nigh automatic preparation for a new conflict is now going on. The very essence of the matter lies in the fact that the reforms, very meager as they are in substance, upon which the capitalists and the leaders of the labor organizations agreed in June, are not viable, because they are already beyond the powers of declining capitalism, taken as a whole. The financial oligarchy, which did a swimming business in the very heat of the crisis, could, of course, abide both with the forty-hour week, paid vacations, and so on, but the hundreds of thousands of middle and petty entrepreneurs, upon whom finance capital leans and upon whose shoulders it now is loading the costs of its agreement with Blum, must either submit docilely to ruin or seek, in their turn, to load the costs of social reforms upon the workers and peasants, as consumers.

Blum, to be sure, has more than once expatiated in the Chamber and in the press upon the enticing prospect of a general economic revival and of a rapidly expanding turnover which will make it possible to lower considerably the general productive costs and therefore allow of increased expenditures for labor power without a rise in commodity prices. In point of fact such combined economic processes were frequently to be observed in the past. They mark the entire history of rising capitalism. The only trouble is that Blum is trying to project into the future what has irrevocably receded into the past. Politicians, subject to such an aberration, may call themselves socialists and even communists but they fix their eyes not ahead but behind them, and they are therefore a brake upon progress.

French capitalism with its celebrated "equilibrium" between agriculture and industry entered into the stage of decline later than Italy and Germany but no less irresistibly. This is not a phrase from a revolutionary proclamation, but a statement of incontrovertible fact. The productive forces of France have outgrown the bounds of private property and the boundaries of the state. Governmental intervention on the foundations of a capitalist regime can be of assistance only in shifting the unprofitable expenditures of the decline from one class to another. Which class would that be? When the Socialist Premier has to carry on negotiations about a "more just" distribution of the national income, he is unable, as we have already learned, to find any worthy partners other than the representatives of the "200 families." Holding in their hands all the basic levers of industry, credit, and commerce, the financial magnates shift the costs of the agreement upon the "middle classes," compelling them by reason of this very thing to enter into a struggle with the workers. In this now lies the crux of the situation.

The manufacturers and the merchants present their ledgers to the ministers and say, "We cannot do it." The government, calling to mind old textbooks of political economy, replies, "It is necessary to cut down the costs of production." But this is easier said than done. More-over, in the given conditions technological improvements would mean increased unemployment, and ultimately a deepening of the crisis. The workers, on their part, are protesting against the fact that the incipient increases in prices threaten to devour their conquests. The government issues orders to the prefects that they launch a campaign against the high cost of living. But the prefects know from long experience that it is much easier to lower the tone of an oppositionist paper than to lower the price of meat. The wave of mounting prices still lies ahead.

The small manufacturers, tradesmen and, in their wake, the peasants will become more and more disillusioned with the People's Front, from which they expected immediate salvation far more directly and inno-cently than did the workers. The fundamental political contradiction of the People's Front lies in the fact that the politicians of the Golden Mean at its head, in their fear of "scaring" the middle classes, do not transgress the bounds of the old social regime, that is, the historical blind alley. Meanwhile, the so-called middle classes—not their summits, of course, but the lower ranks—sense the impasse at every step and are not at all afraid of bold decisions, but on the contrary demand them as a riddance from the noose. "Do not expect miracles from us!" the pedants in power keep repeating. But the gist of the matter lies pre-cisely in the fact that without "miracles," without heroic decisions, without a complete overturn in property relations—without the con-centration of the banking system, of the basic branches of industry, and of foreign trade in the hands of the state—there is no salvation for the petty bourgeoisie of the city and country. If the "middle classes" in whose name the People's Front was expressly created are unable to find revolutionary audacity from the left, they will seek it on the right. The petty bourgeoisie is gripped by fever and must inevita-bly toss from side to side. Meanwhile, the big capitalists are confi-dently watching for such a turn as will make a beginning for fascism not only as a semi-military organization of bourgeois papas' sons with automobiles and airplanes but as a real mass movement in France.

The workers in June exerted colossal pressure upon the ruling classes, but they did not carry it to its conclusion. They evinced their revolutionary might but also their weakness: the lack of a program and of a leadership. All the props of capitalist society and all of its incurable ulcers remain intact. Now the period is unfolding of the preparations for a counter-pressure: repressions against the left agitators, the increasingly envenomed agitation on the part of the right agitators, experimentation with rising prices, mobilizations of manufacturers for mass lockouts. The trade unions of France which on the eve of the strike hardly numbered one million members are now approaching the five million mark. This unprecedented mass influx is indicative of the feelings that inspire the labor masses. There cannot even be talk that they will permit the costs of their own conquests to be loaded upon themselves without a struggle. The ministers and the official leaders are indefatigable in urging the workers to remain seated peacefully and not to hinder the government while it is working over the solution of problems. But inasmuch as the government, in the nature of things, is incapable of solving any problem whatever; inasmuch as the June concessions were gained thanks to the strike and not patient waiting; inasmuch as every new day will expose the bankruptcy of the government in the face of the developing counter-offensive of capital, these monotonous exhortations will soon lose their potency. The logic of the situation which flows from the June victory, or, rather, to put it more correctly, from the semi-fictitious character of this victory, will compel the workers to accept the challenge, to embark once again upon a struggle. Taking fright at this prospect, the government shifts to the right. Under the direct pressure of the radical allies, but, in the last analysis, upon the demand of the "200 families," the Socialist Minister of Internal Affairs announced in the Senate that no further occupations of factories, stores, and farms by the strikers would be tolerated. A warning of this sort cannot, of course, put a halt to the struggle, but it is capable of making it infinitely more decisive and acute.

An absolutely objective analysis, which proceeds from facts and not desires, thus leads us to the conclusion that a new social conflict is being prepared from two sides, and that it must break out with an almost mechanical inevitability. It is not difficult even at the present time to define in general the nature of this conflict. During all revolutionary periods in history, two successive stages may be established which are closely linked together: first, the "elemental" movement of the masses which catches the opponent off-guard and which extorts serious concessions, or, at any rate, promises; and then the ruling classes, sensing that the foundations of their rule are being threatened, prepare for their revenge. The semi-victorious masses evince impatience. The traditional left leaders, who, like the opponents, were caught unawares by the movement, hope to save the situation by means of conciliatory eloquence, and end by losing their influence. The masses are drawn into a new struggle almost leaderless, without a clear program and without understanding the difficulties ahead. Such a conflict ineluctably arising from the first semi-victory of the masses has often led to their defeat—or semi-defeat. An exception to this rule will hardly be found in the history of revolutions. However, the difference (and it is no slight one) lies in the fact that sometimes the defeat assumes the character of a *rout:* such for example were the June days, in 1848 in France, which put an end to the revolution; in other cases, however, the semi-defeat proves only a *stage toward victory:* such a role, for example, was played by the defeat of the Petrograd workers and soldiers in July, 1917. It was precisely the July defeat that accelerated the rise of the Bolsheviks, who were not only able to estimate correctly the situation without any illusions or embellishments but also did not break away from the masses during the most difficult days of failure, sacrifice, and persecution.

Yes, the conservative press is making a sober analysis of the situation. Finance capital with its auxiliary political and military organs cold-bloodedly prepares for revenge. Among the summits of the People's Front there is nothing except confusion and internal strife. The left newspapers are smothered in moral preachments. The leaders choke with phrases. The ministers vie to show the Bourse that they are mature statesmen. Together, all this implies that the proletariat will be drawn into the impending conflict not only *without* the leadership of its traditional organizations, as was the case in June, but also *against* them. But there is no generally recognized new leadership in existence as yet. Under such conditions one could hardly count upon immediate victory. An attempt to probe into the future would rather lead one to the following alternative: either June days, 1848, *or* July days, 1917. In other words: either a rout for many years to come, with the inevitable triumph of fascist reaction, or only a severe lesson in strategy as a result of which the working class will mature, renew its leadership, and prepare the conditions for future victory.

The French proletariat is no novice. It has behind it a great number of epoch-making struggles. True, the new generations have to learn each time from their own experience—but they do not begin from the beginning, nor do they learn everything all over again, but through an abbreviated course, as it were. The great tradition permeates the very marrow of the workers and facilitates the selection of the road. Already in June the anonymous leaders of the awakened class had found methods and forms of struggle with magnificent revolutionary tact. The molecular process of mass consciousness is not being suspended now for a single hour. All this enables us to conclude that the new layer of the leaders not only will remain true to the masses in the days of the inevitable and, probably, not far distant conflict, but will also be able to lead the inadequately prepared army from the battle without a rout.

It is not true that the revolutionists in France are allegedly interested in precipitating the conflict, or "artificially" provoking it. Only the dullest police minds are capable of thinking so. Marxist revolutionists see their duty in looking clearly into the face of reality and calling things by their names. To make a timely deduction from the objective situation concerning the prospectives of the second stage is to help the advanced workers not to be caught unawares, and to introduce as much clarity as possible into the consciousness of the struggling masses. In this consists at present the task of a serious political leadership.

Big Parade—1936 Model

BY JOHN DOS PASSOS

1936

CLEVELAND, *September 24*

Through the swirl of dust and torn strips of last year's phone books and old mail-order catalogues that fly into your eyes and mouth and find their way down the back of your neck, they come, marching between hedges of faces, sweating in their cheap shimmery costumes out of old romantic musical comedies—the bands, the bands, the junior bands, cowboy bands, the redskin bands, the ladies' auxiliary bands (every lady has a fresh permanent frizzle, every lady sucks in in front and sticks out behind); cheeks puff, snare drums rattle, cymbals clash, and in front of every band stalks, minces, goosesteps, hobblewalks the inevitable drum major. There are tall drum majors, short fat drum majors, male and fairy drum majors, tiny-tot drum majors, pretty-girl drum majors. Their pants are tight, they suck in in front and stick out behind. There are the natty police bands, and cops, more cops than you can imagine, cops on motor cycles, cops on horseback, cops afoot, cops in radio cars; plenty of firemen, too, and the cheerful little locomotives and freight cars of the Forty and Eight societies; painted-up cars with bells and saluting cannon; various automotive whimsies—and it takes them eleven and a half hours to pass a given point.

On the sidewalks behind the ranked backs of the gazing public, in front of the plate-glass windows the storekeepers have protected with lattice and chicken wire, in the boom and tinkle of the old marching tunes, the boys keep up the traditional Legion whoopee now nineteen years stale; but all the same, in an intonation or a wisecrack, in the gesture of a man in shirt sleeves carefully measuring the contents of a pint into paper cups and at the same time popping his eyes at a girl, a trace remains perhaps of the old Battle of Paree, the kidding, the feeling of being on the loose in a town full of food and drink and women and comic adventures when next week you're just as likely as not to have your block blown off, and looking forward to telling tall stories to the guys in the outfit when they come back from leave—whatever it was that made the A. E. F. bearable nineteen years ago. Two men, each a little high, are wrangling about whether something happened at St. Quentin or in the Argonne. In the way they look now you can see how they looked then, nineteen years ago. "You better keep still till you find out what you're talkin' about, buddy." "Hell, boy, twenty years from now you'll be tellin' 'em you won the war."

In the convention hall it's not so much fun. There's a prayer. A bald-headed representative of the Legion of Valor refers to some communistic business (the C. L. U. pamphlet it must have been) that he found on the seats, and says he'd be sorry for them if they showed their ugly heads in this crowd, and goes on, amid ill-suppressed titters and finally hearty laughter, to a long-winded account of how the legionnaires had given him a royal welcome just like he'd entertained the Duke and Duchess of Kent when he was on a government post in Haiti. He was led away from the mike with difficulty. More addresses. The head of the Veterans' Bureau. A traffic-safety expert. Representative Rankin, white-haired, silver-tongued, from Alabama, quotes Tennyson on peace. A letter from Josephus Daniels, signed your old shipmate. Mr. Pratt of the American Educational Association makes a sensible conservative speech on the schools which is received with little enthusiasm except when he says that teachers should not teach subversive doctrines in the schools. He gets a big hand before he has time to continue that, nevertheless, in the opinion of American school teachers, it is their duty to give their pupils a fair picture of the pros and cons of social change. Then comes William Green, looking more like Uncle Wiggly than ever with his pink cheeks and gleaming glasses, to make a vague plea for peace in general and for cooperation between the A. F. of L. and the American Legion in particular.

The speeches, except for Mr. Pratt's unexpected note of good sense, were cut-and-dried occasional oratory. The main business of the day was the choosing of the next convention city. In spite of the pleas of Los Angeles, Denver, and Montreal (where, a little prematurely it turned out, they had named a street for Ray Murphy, the retiring national commander), New York, represented by Governor Lehman, Mayor LaGuardia, and 90,000 first-class hotel rooms, won the day.

Then everybody hurried out to lunch in spite of the fact that the committees on Americanism and National Defense were reporting resolutions. A voice droned off a long set of vaguish resolutions in favor of a big navy, officers' training, a better army, aviation, a return to dirigibles, that were passed by acclamation without any comment by the few delegates left. The Americanism Committee came out with resolutions against relief for aliens, for cutting down immigration, against sedition, and home loans to non-citizens, for deportation of reds and jailing of subversive influences, but the hall was getting emptier and emptier. Finally merely the titles of the resolutions were read off and they were passed in bunches. It's lunch time. Sure, Mr. Hearst, it's O. K. by us—but the boys' hearts don't seem to be in their work.

What has happened is that in spite of the hopes of the founders that the Legion would be an aggressive arm against labor unionism and dangerous thoughts and a defense for the vested interests, it has settled down in this its year of greatest membership, of its biggest parade and smoothest convention—not a controversial matter reared its head from the floor—to being just another fraternal organization with its clubrooms and bridge parties and social work and poker evenings and fascinating internal politics. As such it is the field for the careers and supplies the meal tickets of thousands of professional organization workers. The legionnaires' interests, and those of the increasingly important women's auxiliary, lie in the bands and the parades and the junior baseball teams and in the comfortable feeling of belonging so necessary to people now that small-town life is broken up and the family is crumbling and people live so much by themselves in agglomerated industrial masses, where they are left after working hours with no human contact between the radio and the car and the impersonal round of chain stores and picture palaces. The fraternal organizations give people a feeling of belonging to something outside themselves. They are the folk life of America. We've got to have it. It's lonely being a unit in a parade that takes eleven and a half hours to pass through the public square. Makes you feel too small. Until something else more urgent arises to draw people together and as long as the little fellow can pay his dues, the professional organizers will continue to lead Elks and Redmen and Veiled Prophets and Mystic Shriners and legionnaires and their wives and little ones in brainless antics, decked in fatuous costumes, behind really excellent marching bands (that's one thing we do well) from convention city to convention city across the country. And steadily the American passion for a smooth-running machine, if nothing else, will tend to eliminate troublesome ideas, outstanding personalities, and dissenters who ask awkward questions about how and in what direction the parade is being led.

Forging Man's Fate in Spain

BY ANDRÉ MALRAUX

1937

Speaking before people whose very calling is the defense and maintenance of culture, I want my talk to be limited to the function of trying to make you understand why so many Spanish writers and artists are fighting on the side of the loyal Spanish government, why so many foreign artists are today behind the Madrid barricades, why the only one of the great writers of Spain who joined the Fascists, Unamuno, died at Salamanca discarded by them, hopeless, and alone.

On December 27 one of the planes of my squadron was brought down in the Teruel region—behind our lines. It had fallen very high, at about 2,000 meters above sea level, and snow covered the mountains. In this region there are very few villages; it was only after several hours that the peasants arrived and began constructing stretchers for the wounded and a coffin for the dead.

When all was ready, the descent began. There were no roads, only mule paths. The old peasant women, who in this region almost all have sons in the militia, had decided to accompany the wounded. But it was not only the peasant women. The entire populace followed behind us, coming single file down the narrow mountain path. At each one of the villages through which we passed the people were waiting; and each village, when the wounded had passed by, was emptied of its inhabitants. When we reached the first large settlement in the valley, there too the people stood waiting before the low walls of the Spanish town. They gazed in silence at the first wounded—those wounded in the legs; they were used to such things. But when those who had been wounded in the face were carried past—men with flat bandages where their noses should have been, their leather tunics still covered with coagulated blood—then the women and children began to cry. I raised my eyes; the file of peasants extended now from the heights of the mountain to its base—and it was the grandest image of fraternity I have ever encountered: those abandoned villages, that entire people following men wounded for their sake, men whom they had never seen before, descending like a procession out of ancient times, while their sobs, mounting in the great silence of the gorge, made a sound like the roar of an underground river.

The Fascist aviators who were wounded the same day were given military escort. And I could not help thinking that these men of ours, lying on stretchers made by the hands of peasants, had been willing to risk their lives in the specific hope that no military escort but the strong fraternity of the people themselves would henceforth accompany those who fight for their ideas.

On the way back, as we passed near the lines where the Moorish machine-gunners, in the depths of the night, were playing an accompaniment to the sound of our ambulance, I reflected that something was happening here that was of far greater significance than our wounded men, something without precedent since the first war of the French Revolution: the world civil war had begun.

What is the positive element in the various forms of fascism? I think it is the exaltation of differences that are essential, irreducible, and constant, such as race or nation. In National Socialism there are two words, national and socialism, but we happen to know that the best way to achieve socialism is not to shoot the Socialists, and that the significant word here is "national." The fascist ideologies, by their very nature, are static and particular. As for democracy and communism, they disagree in respect to the dictatorship of the proletariat, but not in respect to their values, since the dictatorship of the proletariat is, in Marxist eyes, the concrete means for obtaining real democracy—all political democracy being a delusion so long as it does not rest on economic democracy. But what unites us all is that by the general movement now carrying works of art and learning toward a greater and greater number of men, we aim to preserve or to recreate, not static and particular values, but humanist values—humanist because they are universal and because, myth for myth, we do not want the German or the Nordic, the Italian or the Roman, but simply *man*.

In Madrid on the first day of January toys which had been sent from every country in the world were distributed to the children. The distribution took place at the center of the great bull ring; the toys were heaped up in little piles, each like a tangled mass of insects. For an hour the children passed in silence among these little piles of toys; and it seemed as if the generosity of all the world was also accumulated there. Then came the sound of the first bomb. A squadron of Junkers was bombarding the city. The bombs fell six hundred meters away; the attack was very short, and the bull ring is very large. By the time the children reached the gates, the Junkers had departed, and the children turned back to get the last toys.

When all was over, there remained in the immense empty space one little heap, untouched. I approached to examine it; it was a pile of toy airplanes. It lay there in the deserted bull ring, where any child could have helped himself. The little boys had preferred anything, even dolls, and had kept away from that pile of toy airplanes, not with fear, but with a sort of mysterious horror.

That scene has stayed in my memory. We and the Fascists are forever separated by that little heap of abandoned playthings.

I well know that war is violence. I know too that a government bomb might by accident miss its military objective, and fall into a city and wound civilians. What I wish to draw your attention to in the most emphatic way is this: We destroyed the airdrome of Seville but we did not bombard Seville. We destroyed the airdrome of Salamanca, but we did not bombard Salamanca. I destroyed the airdrome of Avila at Olmedo, but I did not bombard Avila. For many months now the Fascists have been bombarding the streets of Madrid.

I have always been struck by the absolute inability of the fascist arts to portray anything but the struggle of man against man. Where in fascist countries is the equivalent of the Soviet films or of the novels dealing with the creation of a new world? A communist civilization, which turns over the instruments of production to the collectivity, can pass from civil life to military life, but a fascist civilization, which maintains the structure of capitalism, cannot do so. Between the collective farmer and a soldier of the Red Army there is no essential difference; both for the artist and for themselves they belong to the same living order. Each of them can pass from one function to the other. But between a German storm trooper and a German peasant there is a difference in nature. The peasant lives on the inside of capitalism: the soldier on the outside. A communion that is real, disinterested, and authentically fascist exists only in the military order. And the result is that fascist civilization, at its extreme point, leads to the total militarizing of the nation—just as fascist art, when it comes to exist, will lead to the aestheticizing of war.

Now, the enemy of a soldier is another soldier, is part of mankind—another man; whereas for the democrats and the Communists the adversary of mankind is not other men but nature. In the struggle against nature, in the exaltation arising from the conquest of things by men, lies one of the strongest traditions of the Occident, extending from "Robinson Crusoe" to the Soviet films. Determined to fight, since fighting is the only safeguard of the meaning we want to give our lives, we nevertheless refuse to make fighting a fundamental value. We desire a philosophy, a political structure, and a hope that lead toward peace and not toward war. In the most serene peace there are still enough combats, tragedies, and exultations for centuries of art.

I was sitting in a cafe in Valencia with one of our comrades who had been blinded in the first month of this war. From month to month he had hoped to recover his sight, and each time his hopes had been in vain. Suddenly he said to me, "How is it that I see turning lights?" And a moment later, "They are stopping." There was so much conviction in his voice that I turned around. Behind me, in the street, the horses of a merry-go-round were revolving with their lights. The blind man had in truth begun to see once more.

I think that each of us is a little like my comrade who, from the depths of his darkness, saw lights returning. There is much suffering in the world, but there is one kind of suffering which it is a privilege to endure, the suffering of those who suffer because they want to make a world worthy of man—the suffering of those who know that defending the realm of the mind means imparting culture to an ever-growing number—of those who know that the realm of the mind is not for the privileged, that possessing culture is not a question of privilege, and who know that the life of culture throughout the centuries, if it depends first on those who create it, depends less on those who inherit it than on those who desire it.

It is for the men who are defending this concept, consciously or unconsciously, that I have come to ask your help. I ask it in the name of the dignity which culture has conferred upon you. Let each man choose his own way of alleviating this suffering; relieve it he must. That is our responsibility to man's destiny—and perhaps to our own hearts.

Those Charming People

BY HEYWOOD BROUN

1937

Whenever the newspaper publishers of America arrogate to themselves the right to take an inch they immediately proceed to give some innocent party the most outlandish sort of ell. At the moment the front pages and the editorial pages of very many newspapers in America are devoted to the brave deeds of the publishers in preserving a "free press." This traditional and undeniably vital right was saved by a little group of owners and agents who met in secret conclave in Chicago and at the end of their session gave out a short canned statement as to just what they had done to preserve the integrity of the news.

I believe that the working newspapermen and women of America have an even greater interest in free press and news integrity than any owner, and it worries us to learn that the complete custodianship of this sacred right should have been intrusted solely to such a small and secretive group. And the number of Swiss guards is growing smaller all the time. Every day brings the news that one or two or three more papers have collapsed or combined with their rivals. Whether this curtailment of the avenues of information is due to economic pressure or editorial ineptitude I couldn't say. The truth lies somewhere between the two and constitutes a most unhappy medium. It may be that within the next five or ten years all American newspapers will be owned or controlled by four or five men. They will still be vociferous in their devotion to free press and the integrity of the news (although publishers seldom talk of this latter right), but in any case the question of what is true, and just where freedom lies, will rest with a definite oligarchy of the best minds or the biggest purses.

To a very considerable extent this condition already exists. The flourishing city of Cleveland has but one morning paper—the *Plain Dealer*. It is not a bad paper at all, although definitely on the conservative side, but if the *Plain Dealer* makes up its mind to use its editorial page or its news columns (such things have been known) to favor a particular cause the opponents of the proposition must wait until the afternoon to see what the Cleveland *Press* of the liberal Scripps-Howard chain has to say in rebuttal. And if the liberal Scripps-Howard chain does not rebut, then the inquiring Clevelander is left wholly to the mercies of Dan Hanna's Cleveland *News*.

Memphis, Tennessee, although smaller than Cleveland, is not precisely a river village and it has two newspapers, one in the morning and one in the afternoon. Both belong to Scripps-Howard. Possibly one ought to argue that Memphis is extremely lucky now that both its newspapers belong to a liberal chain, even though it happens to be the same one. I am not the person to argue the point, since as a Scripps-Howard employee I am naturally disposed to feel that my employers are wiser and more righteous than other newspaper owners. I can remember numerous good fights which they have made, but just for the sake of the argument and objectivity, I might admit the dim contingency that on some particular point at some future time they could be wrong. If this be treason, make the least of it. If by the widest stretch of the imagination anybody can imagine the Scripps-Howard chain being wrong, then it will have to be granted that when this legendary day comes, Memphis, Tennessee, will be out of luck. Only one version will be served to it.

After the recent convention of the publishers in Chicago a statement and a set of resolutions were issued which were prominently displayed in practically all the papers of the country. The statement announced that the Newspaper Guild was seeking to force the "closed shop" on American newspaper publishers. This is not accurate, and since the subject has been discussed at such length in so many conferences, it is difficult to believe that the publishers of America reported falsely through some inadvertence. The Guild is seeking the Guild shop, and there is a tangible difference. The linotypers' union (the I. T. U.) is a closed shop. A newspaper cannot hire anybody to work in its composing room unless he belongs to the union. I certainly am not quarreling with this arrangement. The I. T. U. trains men for the difficult craft which it represents. Indeed the union controls and assigns the jobs. Obviously the American Newspaper Guild does not and could not, if it so desired, have within its membership all men and women who potentially might be good reporters or copy readers. Accordingly the Guild is freely admitting that the publisher should have the right to hire whomsoever he pleases with the stipulation that at the end of a given period that person must become a member of the

Guild. You may argue that the system is good or bad if you will, but it is not the "closed shop" as that phrase is familiarly applied.

In response to the publishers' statement I made a reply which was much shorter than their blast. It was approximately 200 words in length. A very large number of newspaper owners who had beaten their breasts as evidence of their devotion to a "free press" promptly threw the Guild statement into the waste basket and printed not a line of it. The *Herald Tribune* went to the fantastic lengths of printing an editorial in which it said that "Guild leadership" was working with President Roosevelt to muzzle the press. I think I have a right to claim a share in Guild leadership. I have seen Mr. Roosevelt just once in two years. We talked for two minutes. I said, "Mr. President, you are looking very well." One may not quote the President, but I hope I violate no tradition if I state that in his brief answer he made no suggestion of any kind that the American Newspaper Guild should proceed to muzzle the press. Far from having any such desire, I wish it were possible to unmuzzle the press so that it would construe "free press" to mean an obligation to report the other side of all controversies, even those in which the publishers themselves are parties.

Two Visions of Peace

BY THOMAS MANN

1940

It is generally agreed, *consentio omnium*, that in Europe the old order cannot persist unaltered. The statesmen of the democracies, especially British statesmen, have evinced a complete realization of the necessity and inevitability of profound changes in the political and economic structure of our world. It is not only the dictators who are "dynamic." But when it comes to considering what form this future world is to take, aims and concepts are separated by a gap so wide and deep that clearly war alone could arbitrate between them. The two ideas of change at issue in this war are a European Confederation or supreme domination by a gigantic absolute state.

It should be pointed out that in announcing their decision not to make peace with the present German government the great democracies have taken a more important step than might appear at first glance. Actually it entails the epoch-making renunciation of a principle to which Europe with fateful conservatism has long held fast, although it has been obvious that it was outworn and doomed to perish—the principle of non-intervention, whose underlying concept is the absolute sovereignty of nations. The principle of non-intervention is based on an idea of democracy and freedom which no longer meets the social demands of our time. Democracy is a legal relationship between liberty and equality, between the claims of the individual and of society, a relationship which is labile and must be constantly reconstituted; and today everyone free to think for himself feels that in the union of liberty and equality the weight has shifted toward the side of equality and economic justice—from the individual, therefore, toward the social. Today social democracy is on the agenda; only as liberty which has matured to include social values, while preserving individual values by voluntary concessions to equality, only in this spiritual form, can democracy survive—within countries and between them.

For the inner life of a people is in exact, though often unrecognized, accordance with its behavior within the community of nations, and it is an error to believe that what goes on in any one country—for example, all that has happened in Germany since the year 1933—need concern nobody but its own people. In the future, relations between peoples must be controlled by a new concept of liberty as individualism subject to social bonds and limitations. Only through the victory of this idea, the idea of a democracy which transcends the national, can Europe win happiness, peace, and order in place of anarchy, which leads, again and again, to bloody wars and is the death of civilization. Anarchy is individualism without social limitations, and insistence on the limitless sovereignty of nations is anarchy which imperils the very existence of Europe. It must disappear. The egotism of nations must make sacrifices which imply the break-up of the idea of national sovereignty, yes, of the national idea itself. The goal of this war, and its fruits, must be a peace which is at last worthy of the name; a peace which no longer serves as a shield for atavistic "history-making" mummery but is the firm foundation of a community of free peoples who are yet responsible to one another under a commonly binding moral law.

One side in the struggle takes these thoughts as the basis of its conception of the future. Brief hints of them, expressed without utopian extravagance but not to be misunderstood, are found in the assertions of British statesmen before and since the outbreak of the war. "We shall use all our influence when the time comes," said Lord Halifax in his radio address at the beginning of November, 1939, "in the building of a new world . . . on a basis of *human equality, self-respect,* and mutual tolerance. We shall have to think out again many things that lie at the root of international contacts—social, political, *economic* —and find means of reconciling the *necessity of change in a constantly changing world* with security against the disturbance of the general peace through resort to violence. To this order that we shall create *all nations will have their contribution to make,* and a great responsibility both in thought and action will rest upon our people. *We, not less than others,* have *our lesson to learn* from past failures and disappointments."

Here I have stressed not only what is significant but also what is appealing. It is both appealing and significant when the British Foreign Secretary explains that England not less than others has its lesson to learn. This does not indicate self-righteousness or any intention of seeking the role of schoolmaster, even in a moral sense, in Europe, but rather the realization that "in a constantly changing world" the democracies too must change, must be ready to embrace the new necessities of the time. When one considers the directions in which, according to the speaker, this readiness to change extends—"social, political, economic"—one may well call it a dynamic program of progress. If the new world is to be built, the world to which "all nations will have their contribution to make," everything depends not only on Germany's emerging from this war a different country, but on its opponents, too, being no longer what they were; and here unquestionably there is a certain danger, and a doubt about what we are to hope for. For if the war is short, as from a human viewpoint one must hope, then it is to be feared that the general changes effected by it will not be sweeping enough to form the groundwork for a really new world. But if it is long and bloody, then the feelings of hate and revenge it will leave behind might become a deadly danger to all good resolutions. At least one has a right to hold the second to be the graver danger. Before the war these realizations and resolutions were just developing; its outbreak has sharply intensified them. They are almost identical with the decision to fight it out, and they have a better prospect of surviving at the end of a war of moderate duration than in the moral and physical desolation that a long and cruel war would bring with it.

HIERARCHY OF HELOTS

I have attempted above to characterize one of the two views of the future at issue in this war. The second view is not wanting in boldness and magnificence either; in fact, in these respects it is superior to the first, granted that gloomy enmity and contempt for mankind may come under the head of magnificence. This conception of the future has unfortunately nothing to do with a human desire for an equilibrium of liberty and equality, of individual and social values; it is on the contrary allied to an unqualified and rancorous belief in the necessity of mastery and servitude. It conceives the world as in the process of division into a few great "living spaces," *Gross-Lebensräume*, which must be self-sufficient, or "autarchic." These realms are to be established by force—which the master-peoples who create them are by natural prerogative entitled to use—through the subjugation and annexation of surrounding small nations which, lacking military strength and a large population, are denied this claim to freedom; and which, if they resist absorption by the great realm, become guilty of a criminal assault against the majesty of numbers. Here the idea of race plays an important part. The "great," in other words the numerous, people is endowed at the same time with the quality of superior race, while the

small ones are of lesser manhood and born to slavery. Their subjugation and annexation admit them to the great community of the master-
race only in so far as the latter adds them to its numbers, which thus
become still more majestic; pillaged and deprived of their rights, they
enter the estate of helots, constrained to pay homage to the ruling race
and kiss the boots that tread upon them. That this master-race is itself
composed of disfranchised slaves whose masters, the inventors of the
whole regime, inspired by the deepest contempt for humanity, rule
them by terror and stultifying propaganda is small consolation for the
slaves of the slaves.

Altogether there is no denying that the system is pretty desperate. It
admits no hope whatever—indeed, one is ashamed to pronounce this
weak and insipid word in connection with it. Dark threats, inexorable
cruelty intensified by lust, hard and bloody oppression, uninterrupted
warlike tension are its very essence, essentials without which it could
not be maintained. Every faintest stirring of a wish for the precious
blessings of peace, and so for freedom, for the benefits of civilization
and the serene enjoyment of life, for pure uplifting thought beyond
the spheres of power or politics—these must count for it as high treason. How could it be otherwise? The subjugated smaller peoples, in
whom a tendency to shake off the yoke will always be present, must be
kept in bowed submission by every means of terror; so too must the
master-race, which is almost as little to be trusted. In relation to other
countries war remains the constant watchword: the very condition of
autarchy requires the command, independent of any foreign supply, of
all raw materials, which further requires the possession of all strategic
points necessary to the "security" of the great sovereign realm, necessary, that is, to its capacity for aggression—all of which would be
beside the point if peace were the question. Peace cannot, it dare not,
ever be the question; this heroic snarling philosophy of life does not
permit it. After all, there are still several of these great realms. The
world is divided up—but, it goes without saying, not for good. Among
the master-peoples there must be a super-lordly people, singled out
by its racial superiority to abuse the others, and the eschatological
consummation will be the abuse of all the world by this one: probably,
God willing—it must be His will, we shall know how to hold Him to
it—it will be the German people.

VICTORY WITHOUT PEACE

Poor German people, how do you feel in the messianic role for
which not God, not fate, but a handful of maniacal scoundrels has
singled you out? The goal they set will be fearful wretchedness to

pursue, would be utter horror to attain. All that innately you most love and prize, all your need to love and be loved, you will have to deaden and deny; all that is harsh, bitterly cruel, and unnatural is to be your lot: isolation, the enmity of the world, disfranchisement, loss of intellectual freedom, the extinction of culture, and every possible deprivation. To these, thoroughly tried out in the years of National Socialist rule, you are doomed forever, for only under these conditions can you be "in form" for your horrible mission, and to win the world as your scoundrels intend, you must put from you all that the world has ever won for a people.

You are committed to this not only for the duration of the march toward the goal but forever, even after the victory. For such a victory gives no one peace; the eschatology of your scoundrels is utterly impossible and untenable, and a world which has only been abused without being won over will be in eternal revolt against the wretches who overcome it. Its state of mind will be that of those "hot-headed" Czech students ("hot-headed" is what, with a nauseating pretense of reasonableness, your scoundrels chose to call them) who in a quite hopelessly evil hour threw themselves barefisted against the iron machines of tyranny and were shot with the air of idiotic implacability on which German rule prides itself. "Rather die than endure it"—what is to become of you, German people, when the whole world takes the desperate watchword of these hot-heads for its own?

And has it not already done so? The war, which your seducers, firmly relying on the desire of others for peace, promised to spare you, has no other watchword, and in no other way can *"Il faut en finir"* be translated. You would believe no one who proclaimed to you the hopelessness of your struggle, for you still feel yourself strong. If only you could be made to realize that when victory can bring no hope the battle must be hopeless!

THE OTHER "NEW EUROPE"

Of the two concepts of the future, the two projects for a new order in Europe, one has been tried out; as yet the other has not. Temporarily and in limited measure the ultra-powerful empire of mastery and servitude, the empire of the self-enslaved superior race which sets its heel upon the subjugated helot races, has been tried out: the whole world knows approximately what it will be like. The picture of this peace stands before our eyes in the shape of a "Greater Germany" and its protectorates, set up by villainous madmen. In the unspeakable atrocities which are taking place in Poland and the Bohemian Protectorate those "subjects of the German people" who are still at liberty—

the Danes, the Dutch, the Swiss, and whoever else may be regarded as occupying the German "living space"—can envisage their own fate.

The other "new world" has not been tried out; it is only a promise, and a precarious promise, of a peace to which each country would have to make equal sacrifices of national sovereignty and national self-determination, of a world of international cooperation, political and economic, where liberty is subject to social bonds and limitations, the Commonwealth, the Confederation of Europe. It is an optimistically humanitarian prospect of welfare, freedom, regard for law, individual happiness, the blossoming of culture; and consequently—for one must realize with what harshness and self-contempt man is apt to look upon himself—it is at a certain moral and intellectual disadvantage as against the tragically pessimistic and realistic idea of a black, bloody, and violent future.

An optimistic view of the world is easily associated with shallowness, thinness, and weak varnishing of the truth, while the pessimistic view which denies "happiness" appears to be deeper, more knowing, braver, and manlier. The German mind and temperament in particular are disposed to see optimism and pessimism in this light. But there are two ways of "denying" happiness, and there is a great moral difference between the pessimism which grows out of life's sufferings, out of painful sympathy for man's dark lot, and that which is malevolence and recalcitrance toward better things as such. There is a difference—and more than a difference—between the pessimism that says, Things will never be any better, and that which says, May they never be any better. The former leaves moral room for a readiness to oppose the will of man to the fatality of nature and to save for him as much of happiness and honor as possible. But a pessimism which says in bitter anger: What, is this earth to be a better and brighter place? I'll know how to handle that! So far as I can, I shall see to it that it will be still darker, crueler, and bloodier—a pessimism such as that has nothing to do with profundity, morality, or manliness; it is sheer opposition, base deviltry. And when, contrary to its longing for a world where better, saner, and happier circumstances prevail, a people advocates this pessimism, then that people is not heroic but base, and deserves the name of an enemy of mankind.

Does the German people propose to charge itself with this name, which is not so much a name as a curse? It is understood and agreed that those now in power in Germany are the sole obstacle to peace. If the Germans could see that they are fighting not for the happiness and greatness of their country, but for the advancement of a dozen upstarts, adventurers chained together by their crimes! If this clique is disregarded just for an instant, where is the reason for the life-or-death struggle which Germany now believes it must undergo, and because of which it is sinking from misery to misery? But unfortunately it is not enough that these men be disregarded; they must be discarded, and shaken off, so that a phantom is all that remains of what was never anything but a phantom.

A Day's Work

BY KATHERINE ANNE PORTER

1940

The dull scrambling like a giant rat in the wall meant the dumb-waiter was on its way up, the janitress below hauling on the cable. Mrs. Halloran paused, thumped her iron on the board, and said, "There it is. Late. You could have put on your shoes and gone around the corner and brought the things an hour ago. I can't do everything."

Mr. Halloran pulled himself out of the chair, clutching the arms and heaving to his feet slowly, looking around as if he hoped to find crutches standing near. "Wearing out your socks, too," added Mrs. Halloran. "You ought either go barefoot outright or wear your shoes over your socks as God intended," she said. "Sock feet. What's the good of it, I'd like to know? Neither one thing nor the other."

She unrolled a salmon-colored chiffon nightgown with cream-colored lace and broad ribbons on it, gave it a light flirt in the air, and spread it on the board. "God's mercy, look at that indecent thing," she said. She thumped the iron again and pushed it back and forth over the rumpled cloth. "You might just set the things in the cupboard," she said, "and not leave them around on the floor. You might just."

Mr. Halloran took a sack of potatoes from the dumb-waiter and started for the cupboard in the corner next the icebox. "You might as well take a load," said Mrs. Halloran. "There's no need on earth making a half-dozen trips back and forth. I'd think the poorest sort of man could well carry more than five pounds of potatoes at one time. But maybe not."

Her voice tapped on Mr. Halloran's ears like wood on wood. "Mind your business, will you?" he asked, not speaking to her directly. He carried on the argument with himself. "Oh, I couldn't do that, Mister Honey," he answered in a dull falsetto. "Don't ever ask me to think of

207

such a thing, even. It wouldn't be right," he said, standing still with his knees bent, glaring bitterly over the potato sack at the scrawny strange woman he had never liked, that one standing there ironing clothes with a dirty look on her whole face like a suffering saint. "I may not be much good any more," he told her in his own voice, "but I still have got wits enough to take groceries off a dumb-waiter, mind you."

"That's a miracle," said Mrs. Halloran. "I'm thankful for that much."

"There's the telephone," said Mr. Halloran, sitting in the armchair again and taking his pipe out of his shirt pocket.

"I heard it as well," said Mrs. Halloran, sliding the iron up and down over the salmon-colored chiffon.

"It's for you, I've no further business in this world," said Mr. Halloran. His little greenish eyes glittered; he exposed his two sharp dogteeth in a grin.

"You could answer it. It could be the wrong number again or for somebody downstairs," said Mrs. Halloran, her flat voice going flatter, even.

"Let it go in any case," decided Mr. Halloran, "for my own part, that is." He struck a match on the arm of his chair, touched off his pipe, and drew in his first puff while the telephone went on with its nagging.

"It might be Maggie again," said Mrs. Halloran.

"Let her ring, then," said Mr. Halloran, settling back and crossing his legs.

"God help a man who won't answer the telephone when his own daughter calls up for a word," commented Mrs. Halloran to the ceiling. "And she in deep trouble, too, with her husband treating her like a dog about the money, and sitting out late nights in saloons with that crowd from the Little Tammany Association. He's getting into politics now with the McCorkery gang. No good will come of it, and I told her as much."

"She's no troubles at all, her man's a sharp fellow who will get ahead if she'll let him alone," said Mr. Halloran. "She's nothing to complain of, I could tell her. But what's a father?" Mr. Halloran cocked his head toward the window that opened on the brick-paved areaway and crowed like a rooster, "What's a father these days and who would heed his advice?"

"You needn't tell the neighbors, there's disgrace enough already," said Mrs. Halloran. She set the iron back on the gas ring and stepped out to the telephone on the first stair landing. Mr. Halloran leaned forward, his thin, red-haired hands hanging loosely between his knees, his warm pipe sending up its good decent smell right into his nose. The woman hated the pipe and the smell; she was a woman born to make any man miserable. Before the depression, while he still had a good job and prospects of a raise, before he went on relief, before she took in fancy washing and ironing, in the Good Days Before, God's pity, she didn't exactly keep her mouth shut, there wasn't a word known to man she couldn't find an answer for, but she knew which side her bread was buttered on, and put up with it. Now she was, you might say, buttering her own bread and she never forgot it for a minute. And it's her own fault we're not riding round today in a limousine with ash trays and a speaking tube and a cut-glass vase for flowers in it. It's what a man gets for marrying one of these holy women. Gerald McCorkery had told him as much, in the beginning.

"There's a girl will spend her time holding you down," Gerald had told him. "You're putting your head in a noose will strangle the life out of you. Heed the advice of one who wishes you well," said Gerald McCorkery. This was after he had barely set eyes on Lacey Mahaffy one Sunday morning in Coney Island. It was like McCorkery to see that in a flash, born judge of human nature that he was. He could look a man over, size him up, and there was an end to it. And if the man didn't pass muster, McCorkery could ease him out in a way that man would never know how it happened. It was the secret of McCorkery's success in the world.

"This is Rosie, herself," said Gerald that Sunday in Coney Island. "Meet the future Mrs. Gerald J. McCorkery." Lacey Mahaffy's narrow face had gone sour as whey under her big straw hat. She barely nodded to Rosie, who gave Mr. Halloran a look that fairly undressed him right there. Mr. Halloran had thought, too, that McCorkery was picking a strange one; she was good-looking all right, but she had the smell of a regular little Fourteenth Street hustler if Halloran knew anything about women. "Come on," said McCorkery, his arm around Rosie's waist, "let's all go on the roller coaster." But Lacey would not. She said, "No thank you. We didn't plan to stay, and we must go now." On the way home Mr. Halloran said, "Lacey, you judge too harshly. Maybe that's a nice girl at heart; hasn't had your opportunities." Lacey had turned upon him a face ugly as an angry cat's, and said, "She's a loose, low woman, and 'twas an insult to introduce her to me." It was a good while before the pretty fresh face that Mr. Halloran had fallen in love with returned to her.

Next day in Billy's Place, after three drinks each, McCorkery said, "Watch your step, Halloran; think of your future. There's a straight good girl I don't doubt, but she's no sort of mixer. A man getting into politics needs a wife who can meet all kinds. A man needs a woman knows how to loosen her corsets and sit easy."

Mrs. Halloran's voice was going on in the hall, a steady dry rattle like old newspapers blowing on a park bench. "I told you before it's no good coming to me with your troubles now. I warned you in time but you wouldn't listen. . . . I told you just how it would be, I tried my best. . . . No, you couldn't listen, you always knew better than your mother. . . . So now all you've got to do is stand by your married vows and make the best of it. . . . Now listen to me, if you want himself to do right you have to do right first. The woman has to do right first, and then if the man won't do right in turn it's no fault of hers. You do right whether he does wrong or no, just because he does wrong is no excuse for you."

"Ah, will you hear that?" Mr. Halloran asked the areaway in an awed voice. "There's a holy terror of a saint for you."

". . . the woman has to do right first, I'm telling you," said Mrs. Halloran into the telephone, "and then if he's a devil in spite of it, why she has to do right without any help from him." Her voice rose so the neighbors could get an earful if they wanted. "I know you from old, you're just like your father. You must be doing something wrong yourself or you wouldn't be in this fix. You're doing wrong this minute, calling over the telephone when you ought to be getting your work done. I've got an iron on, working over the dirty nightgowns of a kind of woman I wouldn't soil my foot on if I'd had a man to take care of me. So now you do up your housework and dress yourself and take a walk in the fresh air. . . ."

"A little fresh air never hurt anybody," commented Mr. Halloran loudly through the open window. "It's the gas gets a man down."

"Now listen to me, Maggie, that's not the way to talk over the public wires. Now you stop that crying and go and do your duty and don't be worrying me any more. And stop saying you're going to leave your husband, because where will you go, for one thing? Do you want to walk the streets or set up a laundry in your kitchen? You can't come back here, you'll stay with your husband where you belong. Don't be a fool, Maggie. You've got your living, and that's more than many a woman better than you has got. Yes, your father's all right. No, he's just sitting here, the same. God knows what's to become of us. But you know how he is, little he cares. . . . Now remember this, Maggie, if anything goes wrong with your married life it's your own fault and you needn't come here for sympathy. . . . I can't waste any more time on it. Goodby."

Mr. Halloran, his ears standing up for fear of missing a word, thought how Gerald J. McCorkery had gone straight on up the ladder with Rosie; and for every step the McCorkerys took upward, he, Michael Halloran, had taken a step downward with Lacey Mahaffy.

They had started as greenhorns with the same chances at the same time and the same friends, but McCorkery had seized all his opportunities as they came, getting in steadily with the Big Shots in ward politics, one good thing leading to another. Rosie had known how to back him up and push him onward. The McCorkerys for years had invited him and Lacey to come over to the house and be sociable with the crowd, but Lacey would not.

"You can't run with that fast set and drink and stay out nights and hold your job," said Lacey, "and you should know better than to ask your wife to associate with that woman." Mr. Halloran had got into the habit of dropping around by himself, now and again, for Mc-Corkery still liked him, was still willing to give him a foothold in the right places, still asked him for favors at election time. There was always a good lively crowd at the McCorkerys, wherever they were; for they moved ever so often to a better place, with more furniture. Rosie helped hand around the drinks, taking a few herself with a gay word for everybody. The player piano or the victrola would be going full blast, with everybody dancing, all looking like ready money and a bright future. He would get home late these evenings, back to the same little cold-water walk-up flat, because Lacey would not spend a dollar for show. It must all go into savings against old age, she said. He would be full of good food and drink, and find Lacey, in a bungalow apron, warming up the fried potatoes once more, cross and bitterly silent, hanging her head and frowning at the smell of liquor on his breath. "You might at least eat the potatoes when I've fried them and waited all this time," she would say. "Ah, eat them yourself, they're none of mine," he would snarl in his disappointment with her, and with the life she was leading him.

He had believed with all his heart for years that he would one day be manager of one of the G. and I. chain grocery stores he worked for, and when that hope gave out there was still his pension when they retired him. But two years before it was due they fired him, on account of the depression, they said. Overnight he was on the sidewalk, with no place to go with the news but home. "Jesus," said Mr. Hal-loran, still remembering that day after nearly seven years of idleness.

The depression hadn't touched McCorkery. He went on and on up the ladder, giving beefsteaks and beanfests and beer parties for the boys in Billy's Place, standing in with the right men and never missing a trick. At last the Gerald J. McCorkery Club chartered a whole boat for a big excursion up the river. It was a great day, with Lacey sitting at home sulking. After election Rosie had her picture in the papers, smiling at McCorkery; not fat exactly, just a fine figure of a woman with flowers pinned on her spotted fur coat, her teeth as good as ever.

Oh God, there was a girl for any man's money. Mr. Halloran saw out of his eye-corner the bony stooped back of Lacey Mahaffy, standing on one foot to rest the other like a tired old horse, leaning on her hands waiting for the iron to heat.

"That was Maggie, with her woes," she said.

"I hope you gave her some good advice," said Mr. Halloran. "I hope you told her to take up her hat and walk out on him."

Mrs. Halloran suspended the iron over a pair of pink satin panties. "I told her to do right and leave wrongdoing to the men," she said, in her voice like a phonograph record running down. "I told her to bear with the trouble God sends as her mother did before her."

Mr. Halloran gave a loud groan and knocked out his pipe on the chair arm. "You would ruin the world, woman, if you could, with your wicked soul, treating a new-married girl as if she had no home and no parents to come to. But she's no daughter of mine if she sits there peeling potatoes, letting a man run over her. No daughter of mine and I'll tell her so if she—"

"You know well she's your daughter, so hold your tongue," said Mrs. Halloran, "and if she heeded you she'd be walking the streets this minute. I brought her up an honest girl, and an honest woman she's going to be or I'll take her over my knee as I did when she was little. So there you are, Halloran."

Mr. Halloran leaned far back in his chair and felt along the shelf above his head until his fingers touched a half-dollar he had noticed there. His hand closed over it, he got up instantly and looked about for his hat.

"Keep your daughter, Lacey Mahaffy," he said, "she's none of mine but the fruits of your long sinning with the Holy Ghost. And now I'm off for a little round and a couple of beers to keep my mind from dissolving entirely."

"You can't have that dollar you just now sneaked off the shelf," said Mrs. Halloran. "So you think I'm blind besides? Put it back where you found it. That's for our daily bread."

"I'm sick of bread daily," said Mr. Halloran, "I need beer. It was not a dollar, but a half-dollar as you know well."

"Whatever it was," said Mrs. Halloran, "it stands instead of a dollar to me. So just drop it."

"You've got tomorrow's potatoes sewed up in your pocket this minute, and God knows what sums in that black box wherever you hide it, besides the life savings," said Mr. Halloran. "I earned this half-dollar on relief, and it's going to be spent properly. And I'll not be back for supper, so you'll save on that, too. So long, Lacey Mahaffy, I'm off."

"If you never come back, it will be all the same," said Mrs. Halloran, not looking up.

"If I came back with a pocket full of money, you'd be glad to see me," said Mr. Halloran.

"It would want to be a great sum," said Mrs. Halloran.

Mr. Halloran shut the door behind him with a fine slam.

He strolled out into the clear fall weather, a late afternoon sun warming his neck and brightening the old red-brick, high-stooped houses of Perry Street. He would go after all these years to Billy's Place, he might find some luck there. He took his time, though, speaking to the neighbors as he went. "Good afternoon, Mr. Halloran." "Good afternoon to you, Missis Caffery." . . . "It's fine weather for the time of year, Mr. Gogarty." "It is indeed, Mr. Halloran." Mr. Halloran thrived on these civilities, he loved to flourish his hat and give a hearty good day like a man who has nothing on his mind. Ah, there was the young man from the G. and I. store around the corner. He knew what kind of job Mr. Halloran once held there. "Good day, Mr. Halloran." "Good day to you, Mr. McInerny, how's business holding up with you?" "Good for the times, Mr. Halloran, that's the best I can say." "Things are not getting any better, Mr. McInerny." "It's the truth we are all hanging on by the teeth now, Mr. Halloran."

Soothed by this acknowledgment of man's common misfortune Mr. Halloran greeted the young cop at the corner. The cop, with his quick eyesight, was snatching a read from a newspaper on the stand across the sidewalk. "How do you do, Young O'Fallon," asked Mr. Halloran, "is your business lively these days?"

"Quite as the tomb itself on this block," said Young O'Fallon. "But that's a sad thing about Connolly, now." His eyes motioned toward the newspaper.

"Is he dead?" asked Mr. Halloran; "I haven't been out until now, I didn't see the papers."

"Ah, not yet," said Young O'Fallon, "but the G-men are after him, it looks they'll get him surely this time."

"Connolly in bad with the G-men? Holy Jesus," said Mr. Halloran, "who will they go after next? The meddlers."

"It's that numbers racket," said the cop. "What's the harm, I'd like to know? A man must get his money from somewhere when he's in politics. They oughta give him a chance."

"Connolly's a great fellow, God bless him, I hope he gives them the slip," said Mr. Halloran, "I hope he goes right through their hands like a greased pig."

"He's smart," said the cop, "That Connolly's a smooth one. He'll come out of it."

Ah, will he though? Mr. Halloran asked himself. Who is safe if Connolly goes under? Wait till I give Lacey Mahaffy the news about Connolly, I'll like seeing her face the first time in twenty years. Lacey kept saying, "A man is a downright fool must be a crook to get rich. Plenty of the best people get rich and do no harm by it. Look at the Connollys now, good practical Catholics with nine children and more to come if God sends them, and Mass every day, and they're rolling in wealth richer than your McCorkery's with all their wickedness." So there you are, Lacey Mahaffy, wrong again, and welcome to your pious Connollys. Still and all it was Connolly who had given Gerald McCorkery his start in the world; McCorkery had been publicity man and then campaign manager for Connolly, in the days when Connolly had Tammany in the palm of his hand and the sky was the limit. And McCorkery had begun at the beginning, God knows. He was running a little basement place first, rent almost nothing, where the boys of the Connolly Club and the Little Tammany Association, just the mere fringe of the district, you might say, could drop in for quiet evenings for a game and a drink along with the talk. Nothing low, nothing but what was customary, with the house taking a cut on the winnings and a fine profit on the liquor, and holding the crowd together. Many was the big plan hatched there came out well for everybody. For everybody but myself, and why was that? And when McCorkery says to me, "You can take over now and run the place for the McCorkery Club," ah, there was my chance and Lacey Mahaffy wouldn't hear of it, and with Maggie coming on just then it wouldn't do to excite her.

Mr. Halloran went on, following his feet that knew the way to Billy's Place, head down, not speaking to passersby any more, but talking it out with himself again, again. What a track to go over seeing clearly one by one the crossroads where he might have taken a different turn that would have changed all his fortunes; but no, he had gone the other way and now it was too late. She wouldn't say a thing but "It's not right and you know it, Halloran," so what could a man do in all? Ah, you could have gone on with your rightful affairs like any other man, Halloran, it's not the woman's place to decide such things; she'd have come round once she saw the money, or a good whack on the backsides would have put her in her place. Never had mortal woman needed a good thrashing worse than Lacey Mahaffy, but he could never find it in his heart to give it to her for her own good. That was just another of your many mistakes, Halloran. But there was always the life-long job with the G. and I. and peace in the house more or less. Many a man envied me in those days I remember, and I was resting easy on the savings and knowing with that and the pension I could finish out my life with some little business of my own. "What came of that?" Mr. Halloran inquired in a low voice, looking around him. Nobody answered. You know well what came of it, Halloran. You were fired out like a delivery boy, two years before your time was out. Why did you sit there watching the trick being played on others before you, knowing well it could happen to you and never quite believing what you saw with your own eyes? G. and I. gave me my start, when I was green in this country, and they were my own kind or I thought so. Well, it's done now. Yes, it's done now, but there was all the years you could have cashed in on the numbers game with the best of them, helping collect the protection money and taking your cut. You could have had a fortune by now in Lacey's name, safe in the bank. It was good quiet profit and none the wiser. But they're wiser now, Halloran, don't forget; still it's a lump of grief and disappointment to swallow all the same. The game's up with Connolly, maybe; Lacey Mahaffy had said, "Numbers is just another way of stealing from the poor, and you weren't born to be a thief like that Mc-Corkery." Ah God no, Halloran, you were born to rot on relief and maybe that's honest enough for her. That Lacey— A fortune in her name would have been no good to me whatever. She's got all the savings tied up, such as they are, she'll pinch and she'll starve, she'll wash dirty clothes first, she won't give up a penny to live on. She has stood in my way, McCorkery, like a skeleton rattling its bones, and you were right about her, she has been my ruin. "Ah, it's not too late yet, Halloran," said McCorkery, appearing plain as day inside Mr. Halloran's head with the same old face and way with him, "Never say die, Halloran. Elections are coming on again, it's a busy time for all, there's work to be done and you're the very man I'm looking for. Why didn't you come to me sooner, you know I never forget an old friend. You don't deserve your ill fortune, Halloran," McCorkery told him; "I said so to others and I say it now to your face, never did man deserve more of the world than you, Halloran, but the truth is, there's not always enough good luck to go round; but it's your turn now, and I've got a job for you up to your abilities at last. For a man like you, there's nothing to it at all, you can toss it off with one hand tied, Halloran, and good money in it. Organization work, just among your own neighbors, where you're known and respected for a man of your word and an old friend of Gerald McCorkery. Now look, Halloran," said Gerald McCorkery, tipping him the wink, "do I need to say more? It's voters in large numbers we're after, Halloran, and you're to bring them in, alive or dead. Keep your eye on the situation at all times and get in touch with me when necessary. And name your figure in the way of money. And come up to the house sometimes, Halloran, why don't you? Rosie has asked me a hundred times, 'Whatever went with

Halloran, the life of the party?' That's the way you stand with Rosie, Halloran. We're in a two-story flat now with green velvet curtains and carpets you can sink to your shoetops in, and there's no reason at all why you shouldn't have the same kind of place if you want it. With your gifts, you were never meant to be a poor man."

Ah, but Lacey Mahaffy wouldn't have it, maybe. "Then get yourself another sort of woman, Halloran, you're a good man still, find yourself a woman like Rosie to snuggle down with at night." Yes, but Mc-Corkery, you forget that Lacey Mahaffy had legs and hair and eyes and a complexion fit for a chorus girl. But would she do anything with them? Never. Would you believe there was a woman wouldn't take off all her clothes at once even to bathe herself? What a hateful thing she was with her evil mind thinking everything was a sin, and never giving a man a chance to show himself a man in any way. But she's faded away now, her mean soul shows out all over her, she's ugly as sin itself now, McCorkery. "It's what I told you would happen," said Mc-Corkery, "but now with the job and the money you can go your ways and let Lacey Mahaffy go hers." I'll do it, McCorkery. "And forget about Connolly. Just remember I'm my own man and always was. Connolly's finished, but I'm not. Stronger than ever, Halloran, with Connolly out of the way. I saw this coming long ever ago, Halloran, I got clear of it. They don't catch McCorkery with his pants down, Halloran. And I almost forgot . . . Here's something for the running expenses to start. Take this for the present, and there's more to come. . . ."

Mr. Halloran stopped short, a familiar smell floated under his nose; the warm beer-and-beefsteak smell of Billy's Place, sawdust and onions, like any other bar maybe, but with something of its own besides. The talk within him stopped also as if a hand had been laid on his mind. He drew his fist out of his pocket almost expecting to find green money in it. The half-dollar was in his palm. "I'll stay while it lasts and hope McCorkery will come in."

The moment he stepped inside his eye lighted on McCorkery stand-ing at the bar pouring his own drink from the bottle before him. Billy was mopping the bar before him idly, and his eye, swimming toward Halloran, looked like an oyster in its own juice. McCorkery saw him too. "Well blow me down," he said, in a voice that had almost lost its old County Mayo ring, "if it ain't my old sidekick from the G. and I. Step right up, Halloran," he said, his poker-face as good as ever, no man ever saw Gerald McCorkery surprised at anything. "Step up and name your choice."

Mr. Halloran glowed suddenly with the warmth around the heart he always had at the sight of McCorkery, he couldn't put a name on it, but there was something about the man. Ah, it was Gerald all right, the same, who never forgot a friend and never seemed to care whether a man was rich or poor, with his face of granite and his eyes like blue agates in his head, a rock of a man surely. There he was, saying "Step right up," as if they had parted only yesterday; portly and solid in his expensive-looking clothes, as always; his hat a darker gray than his suit, with a devil-may-care roll to the brim, but nothing sporting, mind you. All first-rate, well made, and the right thing for him, more power to him. Mr. Halloran said, "Ah, McCorkery, you're the one man on this round earth I hoped to see today, but I says to myself, maybe he doesn't come round to Billy's Place so much nowadays."

"And why not?" asked McCorkery, "I've been coming around to Billy's Place for twenty-five years now, it's still headquarters for the old guard of the McCorkery Club, Halloran." He took in Mr. Halloran from head to foot in a flash of a glance and turned toward the bottle.

"I was going to have a beer," said Mr. Halloran, "but the smell of that whiskey changes my mind for me." McCorkery poured a second glass, they lifted the drinks with an identical crook of the elbow, a flick of the wrist at each other.

"Here's to crime," said McCorkery, and "Here's looking at you," said Mr. Halloran, merrily. Ah, to hell with it, he was back where he belonged, in good company. He put his foot on the rail and snapped down his whiskey, and no sooner was his glass on the bar than McCorkery was filling it again. "Just time for a few quick ones," he said, "before the boys get here." Mr. Halloran downed that one, too, before he noticed that McCorkery hadn't filled his own glass. "I'm ahead of you," said McCorkery, "I'll skip this one."

There was a short pause, a silence fell around them that seemed to ooze like a fog from somewhere deep in McCorkery, it was suddenly as if he had not really been there at all, or hadn't uttered a word. Then he said outright: "Well, Halloran, let's have it. What's on your mind?" And he poured two more drinks. That was McCorkery all over, reading your thoughts and coming straight to the point.

Mr. Halloran closed his hand round his glass and peered into the little pool of whiskey. "Maybe we could sit down," he said, feeling weak-kneed all at once. McCorkery took the bottle and moved over to the nearest table. He sat facing the door, his look straying there now and then, but he had a set, listening face as if he was ready to hear anything.

"You know what I've had at home all these years," began Mr. Halloran, solemnly, and paused.

"Oh God yes," said McCorkery with simple good-fellowship, "How is herself these days?"

"Worse than ever," said Mr. Halloran, "but that's not it."

"What is it, then, Halloran?" asked McCorkery, pouring drinks. "You know well you can speak out your mind to me. Is it a loan?"

"No," said Mr. Halloran, "It's a job."

"Now that's a different matter," said McCorkery, "What kind of a job?"

Mr. Halloran, his head sunk between his shoulders, saw McCorkery wave a hand and nod at half a dozen men who came in and ranged themselves along the bar. "Some of the boys," said McCorkery, "Go on." His face was tougher, and quieter, as if the drink gave him a firm hold on himself. Mr. Halloran said what he had planned to say, had said already on the way down, and it still sounded reasonable and right to him. McCorkery waited until he had finished, and got up, putting a hand on Mr. Halloran's shoulder. "Stay where you are, and help yourself," he said, giving the bottle a little push, "and anything else you want, Halloran, order it on me. I'll be back in a few minutes, and you know I'll help you out if I can."

Halloran understood everything but it was through a soft warm fog, and he hardly noticed when McCorkery passed him again with the men, all in that creepy quiet way like footpads on a dark street. They went into the back room, the door opened on a bright light and closed again, and Mr. Halloran reached for the bottle to help himself wait until McCorkery should come again bringing the good word. He felt comfortable and good as if he hadn't a bone or muscle in him, but his elbow slipped off the table once or twice and he upset his drink on his sleeve. Ah, God, McCorkery, is it the whole family you're taking on with the jobs? For my Maggie's husband is in now with the Little Tammany Association. "There's a bright lad will go far and I've got my eye on him, Halloran," said the friendly voice of McCorkery in his mind, and the brown face, softer than he remembered it, came up clearly behind his closed eyes.

"Ah, well, it's like myself beginning all over again in him," said Mr. Halloran, aloud, "besides my own job that I might have had all this time if I'd just come to see you sooner."

"True for you," said McCorkery in a merry County Mayo voice, inside Mr. Halloran's head, "and now let's drink to the gay future for old times' sake and be damned to Lacey Mahaffy." Mr. Halloran reached for the bottle but it skipped sideways, rolled out of reach like a creature, and exploded at his feet. When he stood up the chair fell backward from under him. He leaned on the table and it folded up under his hands like cardboard.

"Wait now, take it easy," said McCorkery, and there he was, real enough, holding Mr. Halloran braced on the one side, motioning with his hand to the boys in the back room, who came out quietly and took hold of Mr. Halloran, some of them, on the other side. Their faces were all Irish, but not an Irishman Mr. Halloran knew in the lot, and he did not like any face he saw. "Let me be," he said with dignity, "I came here to see Gerald J. McCorkery, a friend of mind from old times, and let not a thug among you lay a finger upon me."

"Come on, Big Shot," said one of the younger men, in a voice like a file grating, "come on now, it's time to go."

"That's a fine low lot you've picked to run with, McCorkery," said Mr. Halloran, bracing his heels against the slow weight they put upon him toward the door, "I wouldn't trust one of them far as I could throw him by the tail."

"All right, all right, Halloran," said McCorkery. "Come on with me. Lay off him, Finnegan." He was leaning over Mr. Halloran and pressing something into his right hand. It was money, a neat little roll of it, good smooth thick money, no other feel like it in the world, you couldn't mistake it. Ah, he'd have an argument to show Lacey Mahaffy would knock her off her feet. Honest money with a job to back it up. "You'll stand by your given word, McCorkery, as ever?" he asked, peering into the rock-colored face above him, his feet weaving a dance under him, his heart ready to break with gratitude.

"Ah, sure, sure," said McCorkery in a loud hearty voice with a kind of curse in it, "Crisakes, get on with him, do." Mr. Halloran found himself eased into a taxicab at the curb, with McCorkery speaking to the driver and giving him money. "So long, Big Shot," said one of the thug faces, and the taxicab door thumped to. Mr. Halloran bobbed about on the seat for a while, trying to think. He leaned forward and spoke to the driver. "Take me to my friend Gerald J. McCorkery's house," he said, "I've got important business. Don't pay any attention to what he said. Take me to his house."

"Yeah?" said the driver, without turning his head, "Well, here's where you get out, see? Right here." He reached back and opened the door. And sure enough, Mr. Halloran was standing on the sidewalk in front of the flat in Perry Street, alone except for the rows of garbage cans, the taxicab hooting its way around the corner, and a cop coming toward him, plainly to be seen under the street light.

"You should cast your vote for McCorkery, the poor man's friend," Mr. Halloran told the cop, "McCorkery's the man who will get us all off the spot. Stands by his old friends like a maniac. Got a wife named Rosie. Vote for McCorkery," said Mr. Halloran, working hard at his job, "and you'll be Chief of the Force when Halloran says the word."

"To hell with McCorkery, that stooge," said the cop, his mouth square and sour with the things he said and the things he saw and did every night on that beat. "There you are drunk again, Halloran, shame to you, with Lacey Mahaffy working her heart out over the wash-board to buy your beer."

"It wasn't beer and she didn't buy it, mind you," said Mr. Halloran, "and what do you know about Lacey Mahaffy?"

"I knew her from old when I used to run errands for St. Veronica's Altar Society," said the cop, "and she was a great one, even then. Nothing good enough."

"It's the same now," said Mr. Halloran, almost sober for a moment.

"Well, go on up now and stay up till you're fit to be seen," said the cop, censoriously.

"You're Johnny Maginnis," said Mr. Halloran, "I know you now."

"You should know me by now," said the cop.

Mr. Halloran worked his way upstairs partly on his hands and knees, but once at his own door he stood up, gave a great blow on the panel with his fist, turned the knob and surged in like a wave after the door itself, holding out the money toward Mrs. Halloran, who had finished ironing and was at her mending.

She got up very slowly, her bony hand over her mouth, her eyes starting out at what she saw. "Ah, did you steal it?" she asked. "Did you kill somebody for that?" the words grated up from her throat in a dark whisper. Mr. Halloran glared back at her in fear.

"Suffering Saints, Lacey Mahaffy," he shouted until the whole houseful could hear him, "haven't ye any mind at all that you can't see your husband has had a turn of fortune and a job and times are changed from tonight? Stealing, is it? That's for your great friends the Connollys with their religion. Connolly steals, but Halloran is an honest man with a job in the McCorkery Club, and money in pocket."

"McCorkery, is it?" said Mrs. Halloran, loudly too. "Ah, so there's the whole family, young and old, wicked and innocent, taking their bread from McCorkery, at last. Well, it's no bread of mine, I'll earn my own as I have, you can keep your dirty money to yourself, Hal-loran, mind you I mean it."

"Great God, woman," moaned Mr. Halloran, and he tottered from the door to the table, to the ironing board, and stood there, ready to weep with rage, "Haven't you a soul even that you won't come along with your husband when he's riding to riches and glory on the Tiger's back itself, with everything for the taking and no questions asked?"

"Yes, I have a soul," cried Mrs. Halloran, clenching her fists, her hair flying, "Surely I have a soul and I'll save it yet in spite of you. . . ."

She was standing there before him in a kind of faded gingham wind-ing sheet, with her dead hands upraised, her dead eyes blind but fixed upon him, her voice coming up hollow from the deep tomb, her throat thick with grave damp. The ghost of Lacey Mahaffy was threatening him, it came nearer, growing taller as it came, the face changing to a demon's face with a fixed glassy grin. "It's all that drink on an empty stomach," said the ghost, in a hoarse growl. Mr. Halloran fetched a yell of horror right out of his very boots, and seized the flatiron from the board. "Ah, God damn you, Lacey Mahaffy, you devil, keep away, keep away," he howled, but she advanced on air, grinning and growling. He raised the flatiron and hurled it without aiming, and the specter, whoever it was, whatever it was, sank and was gone. He did not look, but broke out of the room and was back on the sidewalk before he knew he had meant to go there. Maginnis came up at once. "Hey there now, Halloran," he said, "I mean business this time. You get back upstairs or I'll run you in. Come along now, I'll help you get there this time, and that's the last of it. On relief the way you are, and drinking your head off."

Mr. Halloran suddenly felt calm, collected; he would take Maginnis up and show him just what had happened. "I'm not on relief any more, and if you want any trouble, just call on my friend, McCorkery. He'll tell you who I am."

"McCorkery can't tell me anything about you I don't know already," said Maginnis. "Stand up there now." For Halloran wanted to go up again on his hands and knees.

"Let a man be," said Mr. Halloran, trying to sit on the cop's feet. "I killed Lacey Mahaffy at last, you'll be pleased to hear," he said, looking up into the cop's face, "It was high time and past. But I did not steal the money."

"Well, ain't that just too bad," said the cop, hauling him up under the arms. "Chees, why'n't you make a good job while you had the chance? Stand up now. Ah, hell with it, stand up or I'll sock you one."

Mr. Halloran said, "Well, you don't believe it so wait and see."

At that moment they both glanced upward and saw Mrs. Halloran coming downstairs. She was holding to the rail, and even in the speckled hall-light they could see a great lumpy clout of flesh standing out on her forehead, all colors. She stopped, and seemed not at all surprised.

"So there you are, Officer Maginnis," she said, "Bring him up."

"That's a fine welt you've got over your eye this time, Mrs. Halloran," commented Officer Maginnis, politely.

"I fell and hit my head on the ironing board," said Mrs. Halloran. "It comes of overwork and worry, day and night. A dead faint, Officer

Maginnis. Watch your big feet there, you thriving, natural fool," she added to Mr. Halloran. "He's got a job now, you mightn't believe it, Officer Maginnis, but it's true. Bring him on up, and thank you."

She went ahead of them, opened the door, and led the way to the bedroom through the kitchen, turned back the covers, and Officer Maginnis dumped Mr. Halloran among the quilts and pillows. Mr. Halloran rolled over with a deep groan and shut his eyes.

"Many thanks to you, Officer Maginnis," said Mrs. Halloran.

"Don't mention it, Mrs. Halloran," said Officer Maginnis.

When the door was shut and locked, Mrs. Halloran went and dipped a large bath towel under the kitchen tap. She wrung it out and tied several good hard knots in one end and tried it out with a whack on the edge of the table. She walked in and stood over the bed and brought the knotted towel down in Mr. Halloran's face with all her might. He stirred and muttered, ill at ease. "That's for the flatiron Halloran," she told him, in a cautious voice as if she were talking to herself, and whack, down came the towel again. "That's for the half-dollar," she said, and whack, "that's for your drunkenness—" her arm swung around regularly, ending with a heavy thud on the face that was beginning to squirm, gasp, lift itself from the pillow and fall back again, in a puzzled kind of torment. "For your sock feet," Mrs. Halloran told him, whack, "and your laziness, and this is for missing Mass and"— here she swung half a dozen times—"that is for your daughter and your part in her. . . ."

She stood back breathless, the lump on her forehead burning in its furious colors. When Mr. Halloran attempted to rise, shielding his head with his arms, she gave him a push and he fell back again. "Stay there and don't give me a word," said Mrs. Halloran. He pulled the pillow over his face and subsided again, this time for good.

Mrs. Halloran moved about very deliberately. She tied the wet towel around her head, the knotted end hanging over her shoulder. Her hand ran into her apron pocket and came out again with the money. There was a five-dollar bill with three one-dollar bills rolled in it, and the half-dollar she had thought spent long since. "A poor start, but something," she said, and opened the cupboard door with a long key. Reaching in, she pulled a loosely fitted board out of the wall, and removed a black-painted metal box. She unlocked this, took out one five-cent piece from a welter of notes and coins. She then placed the new money in the box, locked it, put it away, replaced the board, shut the cupboard door and locked that. She went out to the telephone, dropped the nickel in the slot, asked for a number, and waited.

"Is that you Maggie? Well, are things any better with you now? I'm glad to hear it. It's late to be calling, but there's news about your father. No, no, nothing of that kind, he's got a job. I said a *job*. Yes, at last, after all my urging him onward. . . . I've got him bedded down to sleep it off so he'll be ready for work tomorrow. . . . Yes, it's political work, toward the election time, with Gerald McCorkery. But that's no harm, getting votes and all, he'll be in the open air and it doesn't mean I'll have to associate with low people, now or ever. It's clean enough work, with good pay; if it's not just what I prayed for, still it beats nothing, Maggie. After all my trying . . . it's like a miracle. You see what can be done with patience and doing your duty, Maggie. Now mind you do as well by your own husband."

Liberty and Action

BY BENEDETTO CROCE

1941

A more special examination is needed of the concept of liberty in relation to action, not now viewed as the criterion of historical interpretation or as general moral direction, but as determinate action in determinate circumstances. If we omit from our survey of the sphere of practice the eternally Vulgar of mankind—those exclusively intent (or intent in the degree of their vulgarity) upon their private business, upon the means of subsistence, upon comfort and pleasure; and if we consider only true men, animated by the earnest search for the common good and so by the moral ideal—those who effectively carry forward mankind with their work—all such are, intrinsically, representatives of liberty. They vary, certainly; they disagree and fight each other on particular issues, but the historical result, which emerges through cooperation, composition, and elision from their different or contrary tendencies, is the creation of a new and richer form of life, and thereby involves the progress of liberty.

The same thing is to be said of the parties which are based upon the variety of men and their problems and tendencies, and designate their changeable groupings. These, provided that they have moral worth and consistency, that is, the will for the common good, and are not mere factions and bands, are also all intrinsically liberal.

Now, if this is how things are, how is it that in the past people have spoken, and even now speak, of a liberal party, specifically liberal, which seems to wish to claim for itself the prestige of liberty? Is there then a party which is not a historical formation or subject to contingency, which champions a philosophical and eternal principle, a philosophical party among political parties, something more and something less than they, and at bottom different, something which therefore does not connect well with them, and like an interloper or intruder becomes tiresome and may seem even ridiculous?

Nothing of the sort. The liberal party is really a party, because it represents a historical situation, and its name, which, like all names, has good etymological rather than logical reasons, is the name of a political party and not of a philosophical school. Its historical character leaps to the eye directly one tries to carry the name to epochs other than its own. Thirst for liberty, fights for liberty, the glory of liberty emerge from every period of history—liberty "which is so dear, as they know who give up their lives for her." Nevertheless, there was no party properly and consciously liberal in the medieval hierarchy, or in the freedom of Greece and Rome, or even in the early centuries of the modern era, when people were working to free themselves from feudalism and theocracy, and fashioning the arms and the rule of the absolute monarchies.

The liberal party came into existence to challenge at one and the same time the outworn and exhausted absolute monarchies and the no less outworn and empty ecclesiastical absolutisms, Catholic or otherwise. Having run through a sort of pre-history in the struggles for freedom of conscience, in the English revolution, in the period of "Illuminism," and in the French Revolution, it took form and consolidated itself after the fall of Napoleonic dictatorship and for a century was the dominating factor in European life. In its days of power, like any other party which wins to office, the liberal party made use of the strong hand: it enjoyed or procured the support of certain economic classes, behaved variously in various countries, from time to time carried out necessary agreements and transactions, customary in the world of affairs and so in the world of political affairs. Yet in so doing it did not lose and squander amid material considerations of circumstances and methods that liberty of which *igneus est vigor et caelestis origo*, liberty which is spiritual and moral strength, operating certainly by means of those circumstances and with those practical methods, but never coinciding with them or resolving itself into them. It was said and it was repeated that, when it had risen to rule and become well established in power, and had passed beyond the danger of counteroffensives by the former regimes, the liberal party then lost its splendid virtues, enthusiasm, dash, self-dedication, readiness to fight and to lose its life for the sake of its soul. And cries of distress and alarm were raised as its accustomed forms, the well-marked political divisions of conservatives and liberals, of right and left, and so on, were seen to disappear and to be succeeded by other more prosaic divisions on special or economic questions. None the less it was natural that all this should happen, and that when the war was over the warlike spirit of the past time should be laid down with the weapons of war. The triumph of the liberal party carried in itself, as its logical correlative, the gradual end of that party itself, which had accomplished its goal, and which in order to be of further service had to become something else, had in fact to yield its place to something else.

It was not properly speaking the liberal party—already in some sort thrust into retirement as the effect of its own victory—that entered, as they say, upon a period of decadence and crisis. It was the liberal settlement, which it had advocated and realized and consolidated, that began to be plotted against, threatened, and undermined by a double range of forces, related to each other but not identical. In the range of the intellect these forces were the check to mental, dialectic, and historical modes of thought, modes which had been initiated toward the end of the eighteenth and the beginning of the nineteenth century, and prevailed in the first half of this latter century, but were now ousted by positivist materialism, and later by a species of irrationalism and mysticism. In the range of social affairs the forces at work were the profound economic changes which robbed certain classes of importance and increased that of others, indeed almost dissolved some while bringing others almost newly into existence or to positions of extraordinary power. This is not the place to describe a process which in its essential lines is clear to everybody's mind, in its past and present development and acceleration.

Questions badly framed and answers worthy of them, solutions which solve nothing, and stupid proposals have followed in the train of this so-called "crisis." The chief and commonest of these brings into doubt the very principle of liberty, and inquires whether human life cannot be better conducted by substituting for thought and criticism an instilled and obligatory belief, and for the deliberations of the will, obedience—an inquiry shown up by the mere formulation of it as unworthy of further discussion. Many, too, are those who resort to the reading of omens to determine whether the future belongs to liberty, or to authority, or to slavery, revealing an anxiety sometimes perhaps not without a hint of nobility. This anxiety, however, directing itself to the solution of a fantastic theoretical problem and vainly circling around it, can but increase to the point of agony and delay recourse to the only means to health, which is to follow the never uncertain path of duty and to nourish in oneself and in others the virtues of liberty.

It is obvious that the great ages of poetry and art are followed, as Dante would say, by the gross ages, and none the less we always long for and desire and prepare with zeal and effort for the coming of the ever-flourishing and classic beauty; so, too, the great ages of thought relax and are succeeded by an age of mere echoers, compilers, or, indeed, by positively forgetful and unintelligent generations, yet the ideal always remains thought, which creates truth, and never becomes not-thought, nor do we devoutly prepare ourselves to become stupid and shortsighted in honor of a stupid and shortsighted century. Not otherwise is it with the ages of liberty, moments of moral brilliance which yield to periods of less splendor and force, of uncertain light, or even of darkness and night. In this extreme case we rediscover the meaning of Vico's *cursus* and *recursus*, and of Goethe's saying that God, when he sees a society increasing in wisdom and understanding, but necessarily ever less energetic because less pugnacious, wearies of it, and breaks the universe into fragments to make room for a new creation. Nevertheless, when periods of barbarism and violence are approaching it is only for the vile and the foolish that the ideal becomes unfreedom and slavery; for others it remains that which alone can be called human, the only ideal which always works. We always tend toward liberty and work for it even when we seem to be working for something else; liberty is realized in every thought and in every action that has the character of truth, poetry, and goodness.

Moral action, then, must not be governed by what is about to happen in the near future, or by what will happen when it happens. For if we suppose that human society enters for one or two centuries, or even for a thousand years, upon a condition of servitude, that is to say, of liberty attenuated and reduced to a minimum, of the least possible creativity, approximating the condition of animals, this incident—an incident as short against eternity as a wink of the eye—does not affect morality, does not interfere with its task, or change it. This task is ever to kindle liberty from liberty, and from time to time to select the means and materials adapted to this end. And since new adversaries have moved against it, taking the place of those that, like the absolute monarchies, had been vanquished, while others, weary but not extinguished, have again scrambled to their feet, or at least to their knees, the liberal party, which had been thrust or had thrust itself into retirement for lack of adversaries, today finds the adversaries and with them the ideal conditions for fresh activity.

But at this point the greatest doubts and objections are usually raised, because, it is argued, a liberal party cannot work effectively when the actual conditions in which it was formed and worked in the past no longer exist. For example, there is no longer the same local life and local autonomy, no longer a landlord class which has the capacity and the leisure to take part in the administration and government of public affairs and to pursue political studies, no longer are there industrialists interested in competition and in free trade among nations. In place of these, we see everywhere the centralization of administration and government, masses of city workers and agricultural laborers with their respective mass leaders, industrial monopolies, and so on. What such noble minds as De Tocqueville, in the middle of the nineteenth century, and Italians of the right after 1870, caught a glimpse of as they reflected on the future of liberty, seems now to have happened, and that in an irreparable fashion. The facts have turned against the liberal settlement, and we are invited to resign ourselves to mass governments and to dictatorships.

Those who make this objection forget, in propounding the material conditions, that the fundamental and sole necessary condition for a liberal party is the rebirth of oppression or tyranny, whether lay or ecclesiastical, whatever its particular forms may be (demagogy, dictatorship, Bolshevism, and so forth)—the thesis which substantially provokes it antithesis. And they forget it because, unaware or ignorant of its *igneus vigor* and its *caelestis origo*, which we have recalled, they fallaciously posit liberty as a material and economic fact among material and economic facts. Hence it is natural that they consider it finished with the material conditions with which at one time it was bound up and consider that it cannot be restored until those conditions are reproduced.

But why should liberty desert the world, and man descend from being a man to being a slave or a sheep, just because, instead of the few roads and the poor communications of other days, human society has now at its disposal railways and airways, telegraphs and telephones and radio, means of understanding which facilitate centralization of government and business? Or because, instead of individual cultivation of land, we are now adopting or may adopt agricultural associations or even state agricultural institutions; and instead of free trade, trade which is more or less regulated? Liberty has no objection to make, in principle, to these or similar economic changes, if calculation and economic experience, which are alone competent in these matters, approve of them, in the given conditions, as more useful and more productive than others. Liberty objects to and opposes only this: nationalization of the soul, the sale of that which cannot be sold; and it accepts or rejects all economic changes only with regard to this, its supreme principle.

The premises having been thus reestablished in their true aspect, the correct conclusion to be reasonably drawn is not that a liberal party has nothing more to do in the world and is henceforth, as the journalists say, an "anachronism," but rather that it has enough and too much to do because the antithesis of its thesis has arisen. But a liberal party cannot do its work with the same means that it once used, because its antithesis has not the same form that it used to have. Therefore it has to look for new means, and, constant in its goal, faithful to its own religion, it must renew itself on the practical side, must study other methods of penetrating into minds and hearts, ally itself with other interests, and give life to a new ruling class.

And if someone asks that the program of the regenerated liberal party should be particularized and that the precise norms for carrying out its intention should be described, the request can be met with a smile at the simple-minded questioner. What he would like is to possess, in a few short rules, what must be a varied and complex movement finding its way as it makes it and its means to action in acting, a labor of good sense, of course, of patience, of practical and political skill, of greater or of smaller scope as it may be, not waiting upon programs but putting itself into action every day and every instant. And, to clear up this assertion by an example, in this very instant the writer of these pages is in his way collaborating toward that end, dissipating the clouds of certain bad political reasonings and allowing to flow in with the rays of the sun a little of that warmth of which the need is great. Strong impulses, the opening of new ways to action, resolutions in moments of crisis are more especially reserved for the apostles and political geniuses. There is no reason to suppose that there will be less of these in a world which has need of them, and by its own efforts and labors strives to call them into existence.

M., W., F. at 10

BY LIONEL TRILLING

1942

Probably few *Nation* readers will have heard of the book I am writing about. It has never been advertised in the literary sections; it may never have been reviewed. It is "A Survey-History of English Literature" by William Bradley Otis and Morriss H. Needleman. Its aim is modest: it undertakes to present all the useful facts and necessary opinions about English literature. Barnes and Noble first issued it as one of a series of review-outlines but it seems to have had an unusual success and it is now being advertised and adopted as a required textbook for college courses. This utilitarian, rather grubby-looking volume is, I think, one of the symptoms of our intellectual condition.

My own interest in it is first of all aesthetic. For me there is a pawky charm in its mysterious critical statements. I like to read of Thomas Carew:

> Gentleman of the privy chamber (1628). Taster-in-ordinary to the King (1630). Friend of Suckling. Brilliant wit, lover of women and rime. Skilfully polished verse, neat and tuneful phrase, mastery of the overlapped heroic couplet. Second only to Herrick, lacking the latter's warmth and love of nature, but possessing a sensuous fancy and a becoming virility. . . . Best of his longer poems is "A Rapture," audaciously amatory and "marred" by unreticent passionate "impurity," emphasizing the physical (and to some the "perverted") side of love much in the way of Aretino and Donne. In the latter poem his expressions, metaphysical either through volition or constraint, are not inappropriately imaginative; e.g. "And we will coyne young *Cupids*," and taste "The warme firme Apple, tipt with corall berry." Two of his most common stanzaic structures are *ababcc* and *ababb*.

230

Of this it is perhaps appropriate to remark, in the cryptic words the authors use of John Webster's work, that its "pornography is endemic rather than deliberate."

Then it is fascinating to read that Bacon's "counsels for the practical life are nucleated by three staple subjects" and to wonder why the authors wrote this rather than "stapled by three nuclear subjects." And there are those mad masterpieces of cautiousness from which we learn of Gibbon that "not only may his anti-Christian arguments be antiquated but his method of historical research may be defective or obsolete," and that his history is "somewhat sneering in its ironical deference toward Christianity." But most engaging of all is the system of parallel opinions, the columns of Suggested Merits balanced by the columns of Suggested Defects. Of "Beowulf" a Suggested Merit is "Broad study of character"; a Suggested Defect is "No minute characterization." Two Suggested Merits of Dr. Johnson are "Teacher of moral wisdom" and "Sonorous words," but a glance to the right discovers that two Suggested Defects are "A moralist in everything he wrote" and "Copious use of Latinized vocabulary." With an apparatus like this it is impossible to go wrong.

For example, under Alexander Pope we find:

Suggested Merits	*Suggested Defects*
2. Heatless, faultless lucidity. Polished and brilliant diction. Unerring choice of right word, incisive.	2. Poor in largeness of imagination. Rhetoric, not poetry. Periphrastic constructions and pretentious expressions.

In every class of English B1 (M., W., F. at 10) some students will take their stand as Merit men or Defect men, but they will be strongminded rather than well-rounded. Well-rounded students with a proper feeling for the nuances of criticism will know how to deal with the problem of Pope's style: "Pope, by his polished and brilliant diction, his periphrastic constructions and pretentious expressions, achieved a heatless, faultless lucidity. As a result of his unerring choice of the right word he produced rhetoric, not poetry."

But literature is not always easy and even the well-rounded student will be stumped by the Wordsworth situation. For no sooner has he absorbed Suggested Merit 1, "Spiritual love of nature, cosmic sympathy for peaceful things," than he has to square it with Suggested Defect 1, "In a strict sense is not always a descriptive poet, nor a great nature poet." The chances are that he will prefer Suggested Merit 2, "Found God in Nature—pantheistic philosophy," to Defect 2, "Philosophy unorthodox, or materialistic, or pantheistic, or mystical"; with Defects so irreconcilable any sensible student will hang on to Merits.

But then he will have to deal with Merit 5, "Love poetry while small in quantity, is important for its personal quality, intensity and significance," as against Defect 5, "Lack of intensity and passion; note the mention but not the expression of sexual passion."

Mr. Otis and Mr. Neddleman lack taste and prose, but they have not been lazy—they have accumulated the facts, they have consulted the treatises and learned journals and they cite their sources assiduously and indiscriminately, so that even graduate students use the "Survey-History" as a cram-book, finding it more efficient than the older discursive histories. Perhaps a moderately intelligent graduate student could make use of the facts and laugh at the opinions—although not all the facts are correct (we are told that Swift in A Modest Proposal "proposes revoltingly that the Irish should fatten and eat their children for food") and although, in the study of literature, it is often hard to separate fact and opinion. But not all graduate students are moderately intelligent and the "Survey-History" is primarily intended not for graduate students but for undergraduate "majors" in English and for those students who are taking a "required" or an "elective" course in literature, perhaps the only one they will ever have. A concise manual of facts is useful, even a cram-book can be recommended if its purpose is properly understood, but the "Survey-History," as I have said, is making its way in some of our colleges as a textbook, a historical and critical account of literature, an approved source of attitudes and ideas. When we have this in mind, the "Survey-History" begins to seem less funny than it is. Of the graduate students and the "majors" in English, a large number become teachers; and it is not at all funny to think of teachers instructing young people in literature out of the opinions and in the style of the "Survey-History."

It is not essential to anybody's education to know anything at all about Chapman's "Caesar and Pompey," but when the student reads of this play, "Ethical reflection. Cato, the protagonist, commits suicide," he has been led to suppose that this nugget of inconsequence is a literary fact or idea. When he has been taught that "not the pitter-patter of hearts is involved" in the novels of Scott, "who apparently has no major purpose of crying in the wilderness" and "is quite blind to the abstract intelligence"; or that Sir Thomas Browne wrote "tassled" prose; or that "The Tempest" is "poetically emotional" although "its character-outlines [have] no particular merit"; or that Milton's "Epitaphium Damonis" is superior to "Lycidas" "in sincerity and purpose"; or that Blake has "intense, esctatic sensitiveness to impressions" but is "unable to depict his sensibilities," he—who is to be a member of the literary public, possibly a teacher—has had thrust upon him every shabby, fusty, third-rate vulgarity of opinion—I have chosen at random—that has ever attached itself to a work of English literature. Education for democracy? Perhaps we ought to begin with education for democracy's first element, simple intellectual decency.

And perhaps that is the element students are looking for when they turn away from literature to science or even social science. The honest student who takes his one course in literature with the help of the "Survey-History" or with a teacher who can use the "Survey-History" will surely be impatient to get it over with and go on to a less cynical subject. Even the literary student, the "major" in English, will surely need to be fortified by a native sense of intellectual honor if he is not to suppose that the study of literature is the jolliest of the disciplines because in literature anything goes.

In academic circles we hear a great deal about the sad estate into which literary studies have fallen and a great deal about what the function of the teacher of literature should be. Well, let us consider that the authors of the "Survey-History" made their book in an apparently successful effort to meet what is presumably an academic need; let us consider too that they made their book, as their footnotes testify, out of the precious essence of academic literary opinion. They have accumulated all the academic ideas, taking the good with the bad, distilling both into silliness, making a negation of common-sense and meaning. I am not trying to absolve the "Survey-History" nor to indict a profession; but clearly the "Survey-History" could not have been written without the connivance of a large number of teachers of English. And what is important is not that a foolish and vulgar book has been produced but that the written word is being treated without seriousness and respect by the very people who are supposed to be its guardians.

So the "Survey-History" is not a funny book after all. It raises grave thoughts. At the moment, however, I can escape the serious reflections by contemplating Defoe's lack of modern conveniences: I have just discovered in the "Survey-History" that one of Defoe's Suggested Defects is "No plumbing of the soul."

Literature of the Third Reich

BY ERIC BENTLEY

1943

"Soll es zu Tod, zu Leben sein:
O nimm uns, Führer, Wir sind dein."
A NAZI POET

The Nazis began getting rid of their literary enemies the moment they came to power. In May, 1933, they publicly burned all the books which good Nazis are not supposed to read. This event is thus described in an official history of literature: "The fire of the pyres which flared up in German lands in May, 1933, is to us a sign and symbol of an inflexible will to purity. . . ." On June 7, 1933, there took place the first meeting of the purged Writers' Section of the Prussian Academy of Arts, of which Heinrich Mann had been president. It seems that Goebbels hoped that Stefan George would accept the presidency, but George declined. Unabashed, the Nazis appointed Hanns Johst, a much safer choice, and changed the name of the section to the "German Academy of Literature." Kulturminister Bernhard Rust was present at the inaugural session to congratulate the academy on its "inviolable independence and freedom of action."

A decree of September 22, 1933, set up the necessary machinery for the state control of literature. And not literature only. Literature, the press, radio, theater, music, painting, and the movies became the seven illiberal arts of Nazism. Each of the seven was incorporated in a division under the jurisdiction of the Ministry of Enlightenment and Propaganda. The German writer had become a civil servant.

The servant did not lack a master. Goebbels reigned. As head of the ministry, the author of "Michael" had at last got the better of his professional rivals. Let them submit or flee. A board of censorship, handsomely named the Office for the Promotion of German Writing, was set up under the direction of Alfred Rosenberg, editor of the *Nationalsozialistische Monatshefte* and the *Völkischer Beobachter*, author of "Der Mythus des 20 Jahrhundert" and ex-czarist spy. A black list of books which might not be published, sold, bought, or lent was issued. Most of the names which Weimar had celebrated were on it, for no man, the New Order proclaimed, could be a good writer if he was the least bit liberal or if even his grandmother was Jewish.

Yet the Nazis did not abolish literature. Hitler and Goebbels are both frustrated artists; they do not wish to eliminate the arts but to canalize them along their own dirty, narrow, and sinuous channels. There are many novelists, poets, and dramatists in Germany today. I shall try to explain what they are like.

The older writers fall into two classes: those who keep their mouths shut except on indifferent subjects; and those who, since they have spent their lives attacking positivism, science, reason, or Marx and defending Kultur, race, heroism, or nationalism, now feel that they have come into their own and might as well collect the dividends. Among the former, Gerhart Hauptmann is the best known. He was for some time ignored by the Nazis—had he not been a radical?—but in 1937 Goebbels attended a performance of "Michael Kramer" at which the poet received an ovation: Hauptmann was part of the New Order. Some writers of the first class attack the Nazis under cover of apparently harmless historical narratives of distant times and places. Ernst Wiechert is one of these. Ernst Jünger, who originally belonged to the second class, has also used this trick. Among the orthodox members of this class are Ernst Bertram, an Aryan member of the George circle who writes about Norns and explains that our conception of free speech is outmoded; Rudolph G. Binding (1867-1938), who defended the Nazi revolution against Romain Rolland's indictment in 1933; Ina Seidel and Agnes Miegel, both elected to the Nazi academy; and, above all, Erwin Guido Kolbenheyer, whom the literary magazines make more of than any other living author. Kolbenheyer is not a great artist, but he writes for the "high-brow" and without prompting from the Nazi Party worked out for himself—before 1933—a philosophy of race and Kultur. The Nazis are doubtless amazed at such disinterestedness.

So much for the older generation. They patronize Nazism and are patronized by it. They are still somewhat pre-Nazi. The real Nazi tone is found chiefly in younger writers, though there is one older man who cannot be ignored. This is Hans Grimm, author of "Volk ohne Raum" (1926), a best-selling novel which sentimentally champions German imperialism in Africa. Grimm had lived in England without liking it: "The Germans," he says in his novel, "must be the allies of every nation that chooses freedom and defies England." This vulgar book is treated as serious literature.

Of the host of younger writers none, I believe, is of much merit. Their work frequently exemplifies the theories of Walther Darré, whose motto *Blut und Boden* led to a school of writers known, apparently in all seriousness, as *Blubo*. Those who emphasize *Boden*—Josef Ponten is a name for those who want one—write sentimental bucolics with the correct anti-rationalist attitudes. Germany is divided into regions, and the critics tell you just who celebrates each *Heimat*: Bavaria has its Billinger, East Prussia its Menzel, and the like. Literature is thus tied to the half-quaint, half-crazy Nazi theories of what will probably soon be called meta-geography. The literary histories link meta-geography with meta-ethnology. The Nordic race is subdivided into a number of *Stämme*, of which the Germans are one. A standard history is "Literaturgeschichte der deutschen Stämme."

The writers who emphasize *Blut* are not so harmless as the Cook's-tour rhymesters of the soil. They celebrate joy of battle; they recall the tribal dawn of the Teutonic race; they appeal to the *Volk;* they praise the Führer. The most famous of these poets is the leader of the Hitler Youth, Baldur von Schirach. Here is one of his poems:

> Ihr sollt brennen!
> Nicht wie Asketen
> die in Gebeten
> sich bekennen,
>
> nein! Wie Soldaten
> die tief in Gräben
> Gebete leben
> durch ihre Taten!

[You should be on fire! Not like ascetics who confess their sins in prayers, no! Like soldiers who, deep in trenches live prayers through their deeds.]

A whole volume of poems in praise of Hitler has been published. It is edited by a Nazi named Bühner, and among the contributors are several writers known before 1933, such as Agnes Miegel and the inevitable Kolbenheyer. Here are some extracts:

> Er war die Antwort, wenn der Zweifel kam
> Mit seinen hundert klugen, feigen Fragen;
> Er war der Antrieb, der, was matt und lahm,
> Stets wieder vorwärts riss zu neuem Wagen. . . .

[He was the answer when doubt came with its hundred clever, cowardly questions. He was the power which always rushed forward to new daring, whatever was tired and lame. . . .]

Die Augen leuchten bergseetief und klar.
Es strömt aus ihnen unsagbare Güte.
Es droht in ihnen Schicksal und Gefahr,
Das eine Kraft die andre stumm behüte.

Die schmale Hand, die Kinder zärtlich hält . . .

[The eyes gleam clear and deep as a mountain pool. Ineffable geniality streams from them. Danger and destiny threaten in them, so that one power may keep the other quiet. The small hand which tenderly holds children . . .]

The pseudo-saga literature of Hans Friedrich Blunck, first president of the Reichsschrifttums Kammer, and Will Vesper, editor of *Die neue Literatur,* is not on a much higher level. Nor are the dramas of President Hanns Johst. The latter's play about Tom Paine is chiefly interesting because of the extraordinary message Johst contrives to extract from Paine's life—that the individual is to be sacrificed to national greatness. Another play, which Johst published in 1933, is a brutal account of the occupation of the Ruhr. Johst is a philistine, and one of several to whom the aphorism is attributed: "When I hear the word 'culture' I reach for my revolver."

Since the outbreak of war in 1939 German writers have been, in F. C. Weiskopf's phrase, either sergeants or sleepwalkers. Dream novels, fantasies, and the like have been written by Max Kommerell, Ina Seidel, Waldemar Bonsels, Gerhart Pohl, Werner Bergengrün, and others, as well as by Ernst Jünger, and these books have sold well. The sergeants include the old Nazi hacks—Johst, for instance, published a volume of poems on the Polish campaign—and a number of younger zealots. What they are zealous about is chiefly war and victory, but the Nazi emphasis upon death and its gruesome splendor is now replacing the anti-plutocratic pseudo-socialism of "blood against gold." A "Songbook for Our Soldiers" opens with the lines:

Auf der Trommel liegt mein Herz,
Tambour schlage drein,
Morgen geht es todeswärts. . . .
[My heart rests on the drum, drummer keep on beating, tomorrow we move toward death. . . .]

Poetry, the Nazis know, is a weapon. Volumes have been published about each phase of the war—Norway, France, Britain, and the rest. About Russia, H. F. Blunck writes:

The eastern clouds burn red over Russian plains,
Where crows cry mournfully and somewhere death
Stands quietly awaiting you. . . .

The official Nazi publishers (Franz Eher Verlag) put out cheap editions for the troops. A special military functionary called Bibliotheks-Feldwebel makes it his business to provide the soldiers with "suitable" reading matter. One cannot know whether these methods are successful. The only concrete result I have heard of is that when one German soldier picked up a broadsheet on the Russian front he promptly gave himself up to the Russians, among whom he met the author of the poem which converted him—Erich Weinert, the German Communist. But so far this example is unrepresentative.

Yet there is abundant evidence that Nazi literature is not popular; the public's preference for escapist mediocrity is proof in itself. Even Goebbels can see that the quality of his writers is not high, and only a month or two ago he was berating them for not playing an adequate role in the New Order. He said they had ample opportunities. And indeed in what other country does the chief executive give an annual speech wholly devoted to culture? For lack of new Nazi writers the party was obliged to hunt through the histories for proto-Nazis. Books appeared with such titles as "Goethe's Mission in the Third Reich," "Schiller as Hitler's Buddy" (*Kampfgenosse*), "Heinrich von Kleist, "Poet of the Folk," "Nietzsche and National Socialism." Probably every classic German writer except Heine has been exploited in this way.

Lists are issued of writers who are specially *volkhaft*. Once again the twentieth-century list is not impressive. The Nazis are not sure of their one great name—Stefan George, who as late as 1938 was applauded by one Nazi and condemned by another. They are on safer ground with Hans Carossa, Max Mell, Hans Franck, Friedrich Schnack, Hermann Stehr, Friedrich Griese, Wilhelm Schäfer, and Paul Ernst, but who, aside from specialists, has heard of these gentlemen? It is obviously better strategy to "interpret" Hölderlin, Kleist, Nietzsche, even Schiller, Goethe, and Lessing. And there is this much justification for Rohan D'O. Butler's "The Roots of National Socialism," the best of the books against German culture: Germany has produced more fascistic literary men than any other country—what other land could produce such queer creatures as Julius Langbehn or Möller van den Bruck? The list of proto-Nazis is therefore very long, and is stretched by the *Nationalsozialistische Monatshefte* to include Kierkegaard and Emerson.

The histories have been, quite literally, rewritten. Hans Naumann's "Die deutsche Dichtung der Gegenwart" is a classic example. Everything was altered in the 1933 edition. For example: the 1931 edition contains an appraisal of Thomas Mann consisting of some strictures followed by a eulogy. In 1933 the eulogy is omitted. In 1931 a sentence began, "And therefore Heinrich and Thomas Mann rendered a higher service. . . ." In 1933 Naumann deleted the words "Heinrich and Thomas Mann" and substituted "they," "they" being a number of other writers. He also changed the following comment on a poem by Fritz von Unruh to the version indicated in parentheses: "Ethically it stands in the service of pure humanity (in the service of the cosmopolitan revolution) as one of the earliest monuments of that revulsion from war which later became so general in our whole literature (in this literature)." The 1933 edition is dedicated to Our Leaders, Hitler and Stefan George.

Revaluation meant praising everything *volkhaft* and denouncing or ignoring every Jewish writer, every liberal, and every Communist. Literary criticism degenerates to this sort of thing:

> He [R. Göring] too seemed to me to have Jewish blood, for in his *Seeschlacht* he makes a sailor addressed as "you Jew" answer "you Christian." His speech melody too seemed to me Jewish.

Or this:

> Max Dauthendey's father was twice married, to a German and to a Jewess. The poet has been described as the son of the first and also as the son of the second. The birth certificate asked for has not been forthcoming.

Both these quotations are from a standard work, Adolf Bartels's "Geschichte der deutschen Literatur."

This reconsidered historiography is not a mere catalogue of authors in two columns, approved and forbidden. There are also ideas, absurd ideas, huge, ugly, sprawling, Germanic generalities. For instance, the whole of cultural history is interpreted as a struggle between the Germanic and the Western, categories that have been passed on by the Nazis to Aurel Kolnai, Lord Vansittart, Butler, and Peter Viereck. But the Nazis differ from these latter about the dominance of the Germanic in Germany. According to the Nazis, Germany has too often been dominated by foreign Western thought. One historian, Walter Linden, declares that this domination lasted about a thousand years (800-1800 A. D.) and that only now are the Germans coming out from under.

Every principle advanced in Franz Neumann's "Behemoth" is horribly confirmed by a study of the German literary scene. On the one hand, regimentation and a purely negative order; on the other, neurotic fantasy, either feeble or febrile, a terrifying chaos. Consider what happened to such literary periodicals as were not banned. *Euphorion* was one of the best. Before 1933 Nazi nonsense was only mentioned in its columns to be ridiculed. In 1933, however, it changed its name to

Dichtung und Volkstum, announced that the *Volk* was the source of all value, and proceeded to devote more and more space to the meta-sciences. First the name of the magazine changes; next the names of editors and old contributors disappear; in 1938 only one editorial name is left out of half a dozen; in 1939 the magazine ceases publication. Comment is superfluous.

Surrealist Painting

BY CLEMENT GREENBERG

1944

I

Surrealism is the only programmatic and more or less compact aesthetic movement aside from Pre-Raphaelitism to affect directly more than one of the arts. The number of parallels between the two movements—already glimpsed by Herbert Read and R. H. Wilenski—are surprising. Both are inspired by an ambition which looked first to change the décor and then the structure itself of industrial society. Dissatisfaction with the state of the arts grew into a more radical dissatisfaction with the very quality of life, which could vent itself only through politics.

Like the Pre-Raphaelites, the Surrealists have gone, although less consciously, in two different directions. Morris and Ruskin made their way to revivalist socialism, while the other Pre-Raphaelites, reconciling themselves to the status quo, became fashionable missionaries of aestheticism and religiosity. The orthodox Surrealists have stood firm on socialism, yet their stand has not kept Surrealism from becoming largely identified with the younger generation of smart international bohemia, to whom the movement has furnished a new principle of taste. The desire to change life on the spot, without waiting for the revolution, and to make art the affair of everybody is Surrealism's most laudable motive, yet it has led inevitably to a certain vulgarization of modern art. The attempt is made to depress it to a popular level instead of raising the level of popularity itself. The anti-institutional, anti-formal, anti-aesthetic nihilism of the Surrealists—inherited from Dada with all the artificial nonsense entailed—has in the end proved a blessing to the restless rich, the expatriates, and aesthete-flaneurs in general who were repelled by the asceticism of modern art. Surrealist subversiveness justifies their way of life, sanctioning the peace of conscience and the sense of chic with which they reject arduous disciplines. Not all the steadfastness of its leader in protesting against corruption wherever he could see it has prevented this ambivalence in the effects of Surrealism from eating back into and corrupting Surrealism itself.

The Pre-Raphaelites, for all Ruskin's insistence on going to nature "in all singleness of heart," looked mostly to the past for inspiration as to motifs, style, and décor. The Surrealists, promoting a newer renascence of the "Spirit of Wonder," have cast back to those periods after the Middle Ages which were fondest of the marvellous and which most exuberantly exercised the imagination: the Baroque, the late eighteenth century, and the Romantic and Victorian nineteenth century. Surrealism has revived all the Gothic revivals and acquires more and more of a period flavor, going in for Faustian lore, old-fashioned and flamboyant interiors, alchemistic mythology, and whatever else is held to be the excesses in taste of the past. Surrealism is "advanced," but its notion of the future is not too unlike the comic-strip fantasies about the twenty-first century.

The effects of Surrealism in art and literature have differed in much the same way as did those of Pre-Raphaelitism. In both cases literature has benefited more than painting—English poetry through the Rossettis and through Swinburne (who was at least influenced by Pre-Raphaelitism); French letters through Eluard, Aragon, Breton, and others. Both movements were essentially literary and placed all emphasis on the anecdotal, notwithstanding that the Pre-Raphaelite movement was made up largely of painters and that both Pre-Raphaelite and Surrealist poetry bears a strong pictorial impress. The pictures of the Pre-Raphaelites form a doubtful contribution, ratifying literary vices habitual to English art; while in the arts and crafts Morris and his followers practiced little more than antiquarianism. A good deal of Surrealist painting has similarly suffered from being literary and antiquarian.

II

Surrealist writing more or less fulfils the Surrealist theory of creation as an automatic procedure uncontrolled by reason or the deliberate consciousness. Inspiration is induced by surrender to immediate impulse and to accident; thus the writer—or painter—reveals his unconscious to himself and to his audience, whose own unconscious is stirred by echoes. But in the practice of painting it is much harder than in that of poetry—though equally difficult in theory—to tell where the unconscious stops and the reasoning will takes over. The poet, subjecting his invention to meter or rhyme or logic, knows that he thereby suspends the automatic process. But the Surrealist painter, beginning with the first thing that comes into his mind—with accidents met in the manipulation of his tools, or with hints from the seams and texture of Leonardo's old wall, finding in these ways suggested resemblances to actual objects, which he proceeds to improve upon—the painter is not so apt to realize that he interrupts the automatic procedure the moment he begins to enhance these resemblances by methods taught in art school. For the trained painter can exercise the consciously acquired habits of his craft while seeming to absent his mind's attention and rely solely on his hand and eye. This, however, is not the same as automatic creation. Rubens had Plutarch and Seneca read to him while he painted, but he did not withdraw his conscious attention from his work, he simply divided it, like any painter one knows who can carry on a conversation while working. There was indeed an element of automatism in Rubens's art, as there is in all successful art, but it was not the primary factor in the process by which it was created.

The difference between automatism as a primary and as a secondary factor is responsible for the two different directions in which Surrealist painting has moved. On the one side are Miró, Arp, Masson, Picasso, and Klee—the last two of whom are claimed by the Surrealists without their ever having formally attached themselves to the movement. On the other side are Ernst, Tanguy, Roy, Magritte, Oelze, Fini, and a myriad more, including Dali, who was several years ago excommunicated by the orthodoxy for political, not artistic, deviations. With the first group automatism may be relatively complete or incomplete, but in either case it is primary as a rule and intervenes decisively—even though it is impossible to determine with any satisfying exactness where in their painting the automatic stops and the conscious begins. The artist may doodle his picture from start to finish, or he may elaborate accidentally discovered representational elements, or he may begin with a definite eidetic image. But he will never use methods learned at art school, and the resemblances to actual phenomena will be schematic rather than realistic. A dog barking at the moon is indicated by certain unmistakable signs, but these are in the nature of provocations to the artist's "painterly" imagination, which seizes upon the signs as excuse for elaborating shapes and colors which do not image anything possible even as an idea off the flat picture surface. The dog and the moon become the springboard, not the subject of the work. Here the reliance upon the unconscious and the accidental serves to lift inhibitions which prevent the artist from surrendering, as he needs to, to his medium. In such surrender lies one of the particular advantages of modern art. Surrealism, under this aspect and only under this, culminates the process which has in the last seventy years restored painting to itself and enabled the modern artist to rival the achievements of the past.

The other direction of Surrealist painting can best be charted by fixing the almost invariable point at which the automatic procedure stops. Here too inspiration is sought by doodling, or in accidents of the medium, but it is found most often in images offering themselves spontaneously and irrationally to the artist's mind before he picks his brush up. Sometimes he claims to do nothing more than transcribe a dream. But even the doodling, the rubbing of pencil on paper over a rough surface, or the observation of Leonardo's old wall is a means primarily of anticipating or inducing images, not of creating the picture itself. Automatism is made a secondary factor; for this type of Surrealist painting wishes to preserve the identifiable image at all costs, and complete automatism goes too far in the direction of the abstract.

Having received his inspiration, the painter most consciously goes to work to clothe the given image in pictorial forms that will produce a strong illusion of its possible existence in the world of real appearances. The subject matter is different, but the result is the same that the nineteenth-century academic artist sought. It makes no difference that the creatures, anatomies, substances, landscapes, or juxtapositions limned by the Surrealist violate the laws of probability: they do not violate the modalities of three-dimensional vision—to which painting can now conform only by methods that have become academic. For all the problems involved in transferring faithfully the visual experience of three dimensions to a plane surface have been solved by this time, and where all the problems have been solved only academicism is possible. The Surrealist represents his more or less fantastic images in sharp and literal detail, as if they had been posed for him. Seldom does he violate any of the canons of academic technique, and he vies with and sometimes imitates color photography, even to the very quality of his paint. Dali's discontinuous planes and contradictory perspectives approximate photomontage. Ernst's volcanic landscapes look like exceptionally well manufactured scenic postal cards.

III

The Surrealist motive for a naturalistic technique is plain. The more vividly, literally, painstakingly the absurd and the fantastic are represented, the greater their shock. For the sake of hallucinatory vividness the Surrealists have copied the effects of the calendar reproduction, postal card, chromeotype, and magazine illustration. In general they prize the qualities of the popular reproduction because of its incongruously prosaic associations and because the reproduction heightens illusionistic effect by erasing paint texture and brushstroke.

Another motive is the desire to sin against decorum, violate all the rules, do the disreputable thing, and attach oneself to whatever seems discredited. Advanced painting since the Impressionists has established a certain decorum, a notion of the aesthetically relevant, which the Surrealists find pompous, as they profess to find all relevancies pompous (this makes another of the possible rationalizations of the disassociated or disconnected image). Dali turned on post-cubist painting, praised Meissonier and commercial illustrations, and asserted his contempt for "formal" values by the deliberate but just as often unconscious negligences of his own painting. Thus he made a virtue of his shortcomings. Granted that irreverence has a necessary function in our time, yet irreverence as puerile and as widely welcome as Dali's is no more revolutionary than fascism. But of course, Dali is not to be taken seriously as anything other than a symptom. He is the Ossian of our day.

IV

The decisive question is whether the Surrealist image, as illustrated in the works of Ernst, Dali, Tanguy and the other painters of their kind, provides painting with a really new subject matter. That is, must hitherto untapped possibilities of the medium be explored in order to accommodate the Surrealist image? As far as painting alone is concerned, does it involve a new way of seeing as well as new things to be seen? For such painters as Miró, Arp, Masson, and Picasso, it certainly does. But not for Ernst, Dali, Tanguy, Oelze, Roy, Magritte, Dominguez, Brauner, Delvaux, Fini, *e tutti quanti*, who do indeed see new things, but no differently in essence than painters of the past would have seen them had they accepted Surrealist notions of subject matter. The Surrealist image is thus a new object to be posed and arranged, but it requires no fundamental change in the conventions of painting as established by the Renaissance. Given the same subjects, Meissonier, Ford Madox Brown, or Greuze would have approached the same effects. There would be the same modelling, shading, and spacing, and the same color schemes, although the hues themselves would be a little less saccharine or brassy and a little less unbroken.

The Surrealist image provides painting with new anecdotes to illustrate, just as current events supply new topics to the political cartoonist, but of itself it does not charge painting with a new subject matter. On the contrary, it has promoted the rehabilitation of academic art under a new literary disguise. The maxim *nulla sine narratione ars* is true enough, now as before, but the Surrealists have interpreted it vulgarly to mean that there can be no picture without an anecdote. The tradition of painting which runs from Manet through Impression-

ism, Fauvism, and Cubism has created the first original art style since
the French Revolution, and the only original one our bourgeois society
has been capable of. All its other styles are revivals. That style is now
threatened for the first time from the inside by Surrealist painters, and
by the Neo-Romantics and "Magic Realists" who bring up their train.
These painters, though they claim the title of avant-garde artists, are
revivers of the literal past and advance agents of a new conformist, and
best-selling art.

The Surrealists have, like the Pre-Raphaelites, reinvigorated academicism by their personal gifts—which are undeniable—and by going to
either a remoter or a more discredited past for guidance; in distinction
from self-confessed academicists, who try to keep abreast of the times
by watering down yesterday's advanced art. Taking their lead and
most original impulse from Chirico—that archaizer who made a small
but valid contribution—the Surrealists prefer Mantegna, Bosch, Ver-
meer, and Böcklin to the Impressionists. This does not make their
painting any the less academic, but it does make it livelier, disturbing,
and more attractive to new talents: adroit talents who read Rimbaud,
have a sense of format, finish, and *mise en scène*—and can at least draw
seriously. (The drawings of Ernst, Dali, and especially Tanguy are
adventurous and original in a way that their paintings are not. The
compelled economy of the line exposes their art to problems which are
on the order of the day and which they otherwise evade by taking
refuge in the ancient arsenal provided by the traditions of oil painting.)

Prompted by a real dissatisfaction with contemporary life, the art of
these Surrealists is essentially one of vicarious wish-fulfilment. Its very
horrors are nostalgic and day-dreamy, having associations with
a more pleasant-seeming past, which is resuscitated in brighter, irides-
cent colors, smoother contours, glossier surfaces, and sharper outlines.
The artist shows us how he would prefer life to look or how—as
children do—he would prefer to be frightened. His wish is painted with
such an illusion of super-reality as to make it seem on the brink of
realization in life itself. The result is indeed a new and interesting kind
of pictorial literature, but it is more literature or document than painting or art.

It is possible, I believe, to construct faithful duplicates in wax, papier
maché, or rubber of most of the recent paintings of Ernst, Dali, and
Tanguy. Their "content" is conceivable, and too much so, in other
terms than those of paint. But the pictures of Picasso and Miró attain
virtuality as art only through paint on a flat surface, and they would
disappear utterly if translated elsewhere. Which is also true of the
works of the old masters.

Films—the Death of President Roosevelt

BY JAMES AGEE

1945

The moving pictures of President Roosevelt made at Teheran and at Yalta and when he reported to Congress after Yalta are, I believe, the best records we have of him. In the first I had fully and with sympathy and deep respect realized, however belatedly, how much that had seemed frivolous and even silly in Roosevelt was the high-pitched nervousness of a vivid, sensitive intelligence, and was inextricable from an extraordinary gallantry, in part created by background and in part limited by it, which I have always venerated. In the Yalta pictures there is not only the frightening thinness and sickness, or portent of sickness, but also much more. President Roosevelt had long been a great and fascinating figure for reasons which seemed mainly external, historical; now beyond any question, it seems to me, he was himself becoming a great man. An exceedingly complex and in many ways devious personality was undergoing profound and very rapid change. It was becoming integrated on a level it had scarcely before approached. In the plainest, simplest senses of the words that I can think of, his face was becoming the face of a religious, even of a seer, without loss of its adroitness and worldly resourcefulness and its singular, triumphant, essential gaiety. I felt in the face an intimacy with death and with tragedy which I had never seen in it before, and through that quiet and resolute, cheerful intimacy, a wonderful kind of recklessness, of all save the best that might be perceived and endeavored for the good of all other men. In this curiously light, shining, calm recklessness, this sense that all personal scores were settled and dismissed, in this quality of heroism emergent at last upon its highest level and its grandest prospect, I felt hope of a kind it was impossible to feel in any other living man, and reverence, regardless of how sure I felt that the best hopes must be proved idle. In the moving pictures made when the President addressed Congress, I saw all these same newly crystallized qualities at ease within the gentleman, and was convinced that nothing could destroy them. Their only impermanence was in their great possible increase; now this possibility has been ended. I will not try to describe with what glacial implacability this fact and the following days corroborated and enhanced my impressions.

If there is any possible excuse for my writing so subjectively, beyond the fact that I can hardly write or think of anything else, it lies in the fact that I was and remain fairly close to political agnosticism; and that if a person of my kind can be so moved by such a man, and such an event, that may be one more measure and one more expression of what the man and the event mean to those who have and who practice political hope and faith. For my own part I continue without much hope. But I doubt that I can ever again think of a man who works in politics, if his effort seems truly disinterested, without deepest respect.

So, too, I think of the new President. It is hard to imagine that history can ever have brought any man into a more terrible predicament. I realize too, as he does and as everybody does, that, forced to stand up and work his best under pressures which would fill the greatest and wisest of men with an annihilating sense of inadequacy, he is not very far, if far at all, from what we too contemptuously describe as mediocrity. But here again I am a sample of alteration which I assume applies still more powerfully in others. I have always believed, and still believe, in gifted individuals, and have trusted chiefly in their performance. But I have also always believed that the best that is in any ordinary man is illimitable; and now when that kind of faith is to be so severely tested, in the President and, just as acutely, in millions of others, I find it greatly fortified. Partly, it is because I know that greatness can emerge only under adequately difficult circumstances and that most people, including the great President who has died, find in themselves not the circumstances but merely the intellectual or still more important the moral adequacy to circumstance if it arises. Just as much, it is because sympathy, responsibility, love, magnanimity, resoluteness, and the obligation to selflessness, now more clearly than before, rest with great and equal weight upon all human beings who can so much as apprehend their existence. The wish that one might be of use is as great at least as the dismay, the shock, and the sorrow. The ways by which ordinary men can be of use are tragically limited, even in a democracy. To a great extent one is forced to fall back on a metaphysical yet very literal faith in unanimity and massiveness of spirit. I believe that this exists, and that if it is known to exist it can have very great power.

This Is Your Fight!

BY WALTER P. REUTHER

1946

DETROIT, *January 3*

In the confusion of peace, much of it carefully planned, we are in danger of losing the clear view of post-war needs which we had during the war. Administrative agencies, Congressional post-war planning committees, and business groups such as the Committee for Economic Development were generally agreed during the war that after the war we must produce and consume at least 50 per cent more than we did in pre-war days to avoid a return to chronic mass unemployment. They were agreed that a return to pre-war levels of production—and consumption—would mean nineteen million unemployed.

This conviction was expressed in the Department of Commerce study "Markets After the War," which became the bible of the C. E. D. It was reiterated by Senators James E. Murray and Harry S Truman in the 1944 year-end report of their War Contracts Committee, in which they proposed a bill to insure full employment. Last July Fred Vinson, then Director of War Mobilization and Reconversion, put it this way: "We are in the pleasant predicament of having to learn to live 50 per cent better than we have ever lived before." In August, before V-J Day, the Board of Governors of the Federal Reserve System published Post-War Economic Study No. 1, "Jobs, Production, and Living Standards," in which these statements were made:

We shall have an opportunity of living better than we ever have in the past, but only if we so manage our economy as to provide markets for a much larger total product than we have ever had in peace time.

Purchases of all classes of goods and services could and should expand greatly. A rise of 40 or 50 per cent above pre-war levels in consumption goods will be possible and necessary. This would mean that people would buy more cars than they did during the 1930's, many more ice-boxes, and several times the amount of some other goods and services. . . . Resources will be available for this rise in national well-being, but it will require a well-planned and vigorous national public and private business policy to realize this unequaled opportunity.

We must not accept the miserable alternative of having our products piling up as surpluses for lack of markets and have their output shrink in consequence. We must not suffer our wealth to be the cause of our poverty, or permit the abundance of our resources to be the basis of our want. . . .

If there is to be a market for the goods and services that will be produced if employment is to be maintained, the nation's income must not be permitted to decline materially.

Four days after V-J Day President Truman announced the national reconversion wage-price policy: free collective bargaining between workers and employers was to be restored, and wage increases were to be approved up to the point where price increases would result.

On the same day, August 18, the United Automobile Workers of the C. I. O. filed with the General Motors Corporation a demand for a 30 per cent increase in hourly wage rates without price increases, asserting that this increase was needed to make up for the loss in take-home pay resulting from abolition of overtime and downgrading in jobs. We said that such an increase in wage rates was directly in the national interest as stated over and over again during the war, that it was in line with the national wage-price policy, that it was necessary to maintain purchasing power during reconversion. We pointed out that to make progress toward a standard of living 50 per cent better than we had ever known it was first necessary to hold our ground, to stay where we were, economically, when the war ended.

It seemed to us that the way to begin was to begin. It was only fair to call upon the General Motors Corporation, the most profitable corporation in the most profitable industry, to lead the way. We were convinced that past earnings, the certain market for capacity production for at least three years, and the lower unit costs of a volume 50 per cent above pre-war days made it possible for the automotive industry generally—and General Motors most conspicuously—to pay 30 per cent higher wage rates without increasing prices, and at the same time to pay dividends higher than the high pre-war rates.

However, our demand was never "30 per cent, or else!" as some editors, politicians, and propagandists have charged. From August 18 up to now we have offered to scale down our demand by whatever amount was proved necessary to prevent an increase in prices. But we said that until and unless G. M. proved it could not pay 30 per cent, we would not reduce our demand by one red cent.

On October 2 G. M. turned down our demand as "unreasonable." No counter-proposal was made.

In dismissing our demand as "unreasonable" and in arguing in page advertisements that higher wages meant higher costs and higher prices —suppressing the basic production fact that 50 per cent greater volume will mean lower unit costs—General Motors was, in our view, pleading inability to pay higher wage rates.

On October 19 we began presentation of an economic brief in support of our demand. We addressed ourselves to the question of G. M.'s ability to pay. We invited, urged, and begged the G. M. representatives to discuss our facts, figures, and arguments as presented. They refused. They said, "Go ahead, and when you're all through, we'll make our answer." We read our case to the soles of their shoes perched on the edge of the negotiating table, and to the back of *Liberty*, which they said was "more interesting than the crap you [the union] are giving us."

When our case was all in, on October 26, Harry Anderson, vice-president of G. M., said they would answer us in ten days. That was at five o'clock in the afternoon. Three hours later, on a nation-wide radio network, he gave G. M.'s answer—a flat rejection.

In the course of the so-called negotiations G. M. shifted its ground from inability to pay to a refusal to discuss the corporation's ability to pay. In our view the change was made because G. M. knows that the arithmetic of our case is taken from its own reports and published government sources, is confirmed by facts hidden in the corporation's books, and is incontrovertible. This was made plain when G. M. made its formal answer to our brief on November 7. G. M. offered the union a wage increase of 10 cents an hour—subsequently increased to 13½ cents—hitched to the right later to use the increase in applying to the OPA for higher prices. (When we asked if G. M. would offer even a 1 per cent wage increase without a price increase, the answer was no.) In addition, G. M. renewed its proposal that the union join the corporation in petitioning Congress to amend the wage-hour act to raise the normal work week from forty to forty-five hours.

The U. A. W.-C. I. O. could have settled this wage dispute long ago, without resort to a strike, if the General Motors workers had been willing to join the General Motors management in a double conspiracy —against American consumers clamoring for eighteen million cars, and against millions of returning veterans and laid-off war workers, including more than one hundred thousand former G. M. workers with seniority rights. We could have agreed to take a wage increase and have kept quiet about price increases which, spreading out from auto-mobiles in spiraling inflation, would have taken fifteen cents or more out of one pocket for every dime put in the other in high wages. We could have joined the corporation in ganging up on Congress to legal-ize a longer normal work week at a time when unemployment of between six and nine million is predicted. We could have drawn down on the head of labor the whole blame for the rising pressures of infla-tion and its disastrous results. We could have focused on labor the justified resentment of millions of unemployed veterans and laid-off war workers. We could have drunk the cup of pure economic poison which the G. M. management poured out and enticingly set before us on the negotiating table day after day.

Instead, faced with the deliberate, contemptuous, and provocative refusal of G. M. to bargain collectively in good faith by discussing the ability to pay, and having vainly offered to submit the dispute to arbitration, the G. M. workers on November 21 went on strike to obtain the demands presented on August 18. The strike, with an appeal to the opinion and judgment of the American people, was their only remaining economic weapon.

Today, with the strike in its second month, and with the G. M. attitude being copied by other employers across the whole country, General Motors workers and their families are the front-line troops in a home-front war to win the very peace that, only five months ago, it was generally agreed we must have if the war aims of the Four Freedoms were to be more than a sour phrase on the lips of apple-selling veterans of World War II. On G. M. picket lines and in U. A. W.-C. I. O. union halls and soup kitchens in a hundred American towns and cities the eyes of G. M. strikers see the post-war needs of this nation as clearly now as when they were stated before V-J Day by our business and political leaders.

They are exercising the right of free collective bargaining. One of these days the G. M. management will agree to move the bargaining back from the picket lines to the conference room and to write a contract with the U. A. W.-C. I. O. which will maintain the purchas-ing power of G. M. and other workers, including the farmers and business men from whom those workers in years to come will buy more or less, depending on the wages they receive.

Until that day, the strike of the G. M. workers is the fight of all Americans who want a lasting peace of full production, full consump-tion, and full employment, year in and year out, spreading beyond the United States, by example, not by conquest, to the rest of this fevered and unhappy world.

French Existentialism

BY HANNAH ARENDT

1946

A lecture on philosophy provokes a riot, with hundreds crowding in and thousands turned away. Books on philosophical problems preaching no cheap creed and offering no panacea but, on the contrary, so difficult as to require actual thinking sell like detective stories. Plays in which the action is a matter of words, not a plot, and which offer a dialogue of reflections and ideas run for months and are attended by enthusiastic crowds. Analyses of the situation of man in the world, of the fundaments of human relationship, of Being and the Void not only give rise to a new literary movement but also figure as possible guides for a fresh political orientation. Philosophers become newspapermen, playwrights, novelists. They are not members of university faculties but "bohemians" who stay at hotels and live in the cafe—leading a public life to the point of renouncing privacy. And not even success, or so it seems, can turn them into respectable bores.

This is what is happening, from all reports, in Paris. If the Resistance has not achieved the European revolution, it seems to have brought about, at least in France, a genuine rebellion of the intellectuals, whose docility in relation to modern society was one of the saddest aspects of the sad spectacle of Europe between wars. And the French people, for the time being, appear to consider the arguments of their philosophers more important than the talk and the quarrels of their politicians. This may reflect, of course, a desire to escape from political action into some theory which merely talks about action, that is, into activism; but it may also signify that in the face of the spiritual bankruptcy of the left and the sterility of the old revolutionary élite—which have led to the desperate efforts at restoration of all political parties—more people than we might imagine have a feeling that the responsibility for politi-

cal action is too heavy to assume until new foundations, ethical as well
as political, are laid down, and that the old tradition of philosophy
which is deeply imbedded even in the least philosophical individual is
actually an impediment to new political thought.

The name of the new movement is "Existentialism," and its chief
exponents are Jean-Paul Sartre and Albert Camus, but the term Existentialism has given rise to so many misunderstandings that Camus has
already publicly stated why he is "not an Existentialist." The term
comes from the modern German philosophy which had a revival immediately after the First World War and has strongly influenced
French thought for more than a decade; but it would be irrelevant to
trace and define the sources of Existentialism in national terms for the
simple reason that both the German and the French manifestations
came out of an identical period and a more or less identical cultural
heritage.

The French Existentialists, though they differ widely among themselves, are united on two main lines of rebellion: first, the rigorous
repudiation of what they call the *esprit sérieux;* and, second, the angry
refusal to accept the world as it is as the natural, predestined milieu of
man.

L'esprit sérieux, which is the original sin according to the new philosophy, may be equated with respectability. The "serious" man is one
who thinks of himself *as* president of his business, *as* a member of the
Legion of Honor, *as* a member of the faculty, but also *as* father, *as*
husband, or as any other half-natural, half-social function. For by so
doing he agrees to the identification of himself with an arbitrary function which society has bestowed. *L'esprit sérieux* is the very negation
of freedom, because it leads man to agree to and accept the necessary
deformation which every human being must undergo when he is fitted
into society. Since everyone knows well enough in his own heart that
he is not identical with his function, *l'esprit sérieux* indicates also bad
faith in the sense of pretending. Kafka has already shown, in "Amerika," how ridiculous and dangerous is the hollow dignity which grows
out of identifying oneself with one's function: In that book the most
dignified person in the hotel, upon whose word the hero's job and daily
bread depend, rules out the possibility that he can make an error by
invoking the argument of the "serious" man: "How could I go on
being the head porter if I mistook one person for another?"

This matter of *l'esprit sérieux* was first touched upon in Sartre's
novel "La Nausée," in a delightful description of a gallery of portraits
of the town's respectable citizens, *les salauds.* It then became the central
topic of Camus's novel "L'Etranger." The hero of the book, the

stranger, is an average man who simply refuses to submit to the serious-mindedness of society, who refuses to live as any of his allotted functions. He does not behave as a son at his mother's funeral—he does not weep; he does not behave as a husband—he declines to take marriage seriously even at the moment of his engagement. Because he does not pretend, he is a stranger whom no one understands, and he pays with his life for his affront to society. Since he refuses to play the game, he is isolated from his fellow-men to the point of incomprehensibility and isolated from himself to the point of becoming inarticulate. Only in a last scene, immediately before his death, does the hero arrive at some kind of explanation which conveys the impression that for him life itself was such a mystery and in its terrible way so beautiful that he did not see any necessity for "improving" upon it with the trimmings of good behavior and hollow pretensions.

Sartre's brilliant play "Huis Clos" belongs to the same category. The play opens in hell, appropriately furnished in the style of the Second Empire. The three persons gathered in the room—"Hell is the Others" —set the diabolical torture in motion by trying to pretend. Since, however, their lives are closed and since "you are your life and nothing else," pretense no longer works, and we see what would go on behind closed doors if people actually were stripped of the sheltering cover of functions derived from society.

Both Sartre's play and Camus's novel deny the possibility of a genuine fellowship between men, of any relationship which would be direct, innocent, free of pretense. Love in Sartre's philosophy is the will to be loved, the need for a supreme confirmation of one's own existence. For Camus love is a somewhat awkward and hopeless attempt to break through the isolation of the individual.

The way out of pretense and serious-mindedness is to play at being what one really is. Again Kafka indicated in the last chapter of "Amerika" a new possibility of authentic life. The great "Nature Theater" where everyone is welcome and where everybody's unhappiness is resolved is not by accident a theater. Here everybody is invited to choose his role, to play at what he is or would like to be. The chosen role is the solution of the conflict between mere functioning and mere being, as well as between mere ambition and mere reality.

The new "ideal" becomes, in this context, the actor whose very profession is pretending, who constantly changes his role, and thus can never take any of his roles seriously. By playing at what one is, one guards one's freedom as a human being from the pretenses of one's functions; moreover, only by playing at what he really is, is man able to affirm that he is never identical with himself as a thing is identical with itself. An inkpot is always an inkpot. Man is his life and his actions, which are never finished until the very moment of his death. He *is* his existence.

The second common element of French Existentialism, the insistence upon the basic homelessness of man in the world, is the topic of Camus's "Le Mythe de Sisyphe; essay sur l'absurde," and of Sartre's "La Nausée." For Camus man is essentially the stranger because the world in general and man as man are not fitted for each other; that they are together in existence makes the human condition an absurdity. Man is the only "thing" in the world which obviously does not belong in it, for only man does not exist simply as a man among men in the way animals exist among animals and trees among trees—all of which necessarily exist, so to speak, in the plural. Man is basically alone with his "revolt" and his "clairvoyance," that is, with his reasoning, which makes him ridiculous because the gift of reason was bestowed upon him in a world "where everything is given and nothing ever explained."

Sartre's notion of the absurdity, the contingency, of existence is best represented in the chapter of "La Nausée" which appears in the current issue of the *Partisan Review* under the title "The Root of the Chestnut Tree." Whatever exists, so far as we can see, has not the slightest reason for its existence. It is simply *de trop*, superfluous. The fact that I can't even imagine a world in which, instead of many too many things, there would be nothing only shows the hopelessness and senselessness of man's being eternally entangled in existence.

Here Sartre and Camus part company, if we may judge from the few works of theirs which have reached this country. The absurdity of existence and the repudiation of *l'esprit sérieux* are only points of departure for each. Camus seems to have gone on to a philosophy of absurdity, whereas Sartre seems to be working toward some new positive philosophy and even a new humanism.

Camus has probably protested against being called an Existentialist because for him the absurdity does not lie in man as such or in the world as such but only in their being thrown together. Since man's life, being laid in the world, is absurd, it must be lived as absurdity—lived, that is, in a kind of proud defiance which insists on reason despite the experience of reason's failure to explain anything; insists on despair since man's pride will not allow him the hope of discovering a sense he cannot figure out by means of reason; insists, finally, that reason and human dignity, in spite of their senselessness, remain the supreme values. The absurd life then consists in constantly rebelling against all its conditions and in constantly refusing consolations. "This revolt is the price of life. Spread over the whole of an existence, it restores its grandeur." All that remains, all that one can say yes to, is chance itself, the *hazard roi* which has apparently played at putting man and world together. " 'I judge that everything is well,' said Oedipus, and this word is sacred. It resounds in the ferocious universe which is the limit of man. . . . It makes of destiny an affair of men which should be settled among men." This is precisely the point where Camus, without giving much explanation, leaves behind all modernistic attitudes and comes to insights which are genuinely modern, the insight, for instance, that the moment may have arrived "when creation is no longer taken tragically; it is only taken seriously."

For Sartre, absurdity is of the essence of things as well as of man. Anything that exists is absurd simply because it exists. The salient difference between the things of the world and the human being is that things are unequivocally identical with themselves, whereas man— because he sees and knows that he sees, believes and knows that he believes—bears within his consciousness a negation which makes it impossible for him ever to become one with himself. In this single respect—in respect of his consciousness, which has the germ of negation in it—man is a creator. For this is of man's own making and not merely given, as the world and his existence are given. If man becomes aware of his own consciousness and its tremendous creative possibilities, and renounces the longing to be identical with himself as a thing is, he realizes that he depends upon nothing and nobody outside himself and that he can be free, the master of his own destiny. This seems to be the essential meaning of Sartre's novel "Les Mouches" ("The Flies"), in which Orestes, by taking upon himself the responsibility for the necessary killing of which the town is afraid, liberates the town and takes the Flies—the Erinyes of bad conscience and of the dark fear of revenge—with him. He himself is immune because he does not feel guilty and regrets nothing.

It would be a cheap error to mistake this new trend in philosophy and literature for just another fashion of the day because its exponents refuse the respectability of institutions and do not even pretend to that seriousness which regards every achievement as a step in a career. Nor should we be put off by the loud journalistic success with which their work has been accompanied. This success, equivocal as it may be in itself, is nevertheless due to the quality of the work. It is also due to a definite modernity of attitude which does not try to hide the depth of the break in Western tradition. Camus especially has the courage not even to look for connections, for predecessors and the like. The good thing about Sartre and Camus is that they apparently suffer no longer from nostalgia for the good old days, even though they may know that in an abstract sense those days were actually better than ours.

They do not believe in the magic of the old, and they are honest in that they make no compromises whatever.

Yet if the revolutionary élan of these writers is not broken by success, if, symbolically speaking, they stick to their hotel rooms and their cafes, the time may come when it will be necessary to point out "seriously" those aspects of their philosphy which indicate that they are still dangerously involved in old concepts. The nihilistic elements, which are obvious in spite of all protests to the contrary, are not the consequences of new insights but of some very old ideas.

Twenty-five Years of American Sensuality

BY JACQUES BARZUN

1948

We have at last entered upon our salad days. This, despite the old belief that we are a young country, does not mean that we are now adolescent. Far from it. We have skipped five stages, and the mixed greens on the menu stand culturally for the sere and yellow leaf. All the fuss about wine vinegar and the right-shaped wooden bowl is like the hobby of an idealist in decline who has given up Agitation for the pleasures of the table.

When I first came to know the United States, in the early nineteen twenties, the nation was still as Europe pictured it and as it liked to picture itself—hustling, bolting its food, crazy about business. Meals were among the harsh necessities of life, and conversation did not turn upon the more exquisite ways of making coffee. In those manly days when the frontier had just been heard slamming shut, the Sunday chicken dinner—with waffle submerged in library paste—was a mere symbol of leisure and luxury, not an actual reward for six days of raw deals and rough diet. Prohibition had just become law, and I remember my surprise on hearing that it was not, as I had childishly supposed, a hygienic measure in force during the hot summer months but a piece of self-denial forever. Except in a few geographical pockets of gluttony the American mortified the flesh both when fasting and when breaking his fast; he remained a Puritan within and without.

But while I was learning my United States, many young Americans whom the war had uprooted were exploring Europe and particularly France. The articulate among them were saying cruel things about their native land and spending the proceeds of unpatriotic literature on the acquisition of a new life of the senses. It was about the same time that the silent movies inculcated the arts of passionate courtship, and that, together with popularizations of Freud, solemn treatises began to appear on the technique of sexual love. "The Sheik," Valentino, and other stars with foreign names became for the younger generation models of conduct quite opposed to the Puritan. Shortly, the expatriates repented and returned, bringing their new habits with them. Yet prohibition was repealed, depression grew worse, raw deals and rough diet gave way to new deals and *PM* recipes. All classes were permanently affected in their tastes; even the poor learned—usually from foreign neighbors—that strange foods were edible.

From that time on the change has been steady, extensive, profound —and its effects have not been limited to the digestive tract. America has been re-Europeanized. It is from the thirties that one can date in this country a recognition that business is not the sole aim of life. This went with an apologetic tone in capitalist utterances and a new self-assurance in cultural affairs—all these, moreover, in a setting neither commercial nor bohemian but elegant, suave, almost arty. The rolltop desk of yellow oak is no more; the ads look like Matisses and Laurencins; the pervasive taste is French impressionist. The historian of manners might say that from Romans we have turned into Greeks, and the psychologists might be tempted to think that French dressing had acted as an emollient on the national character.

In domestic and individual life, certainly, the resurrection of the wine industry, the cultivation of herbs, the popularity of cookbooks, and the tossing of salads have given a new tone to sociability. To one whose earlier impressions are still vivid, it is always amazing, despite frequent occurrence, when a business man of good standing in urb and suburb opens dinner with a harangue on vintage years, when his son home from school overdoes maturity by gargling the claret, and when the *omelette fines herbes* turns out, not a depressed soufflé, but a genuine omelet—though smelling like a *hortus siccus*. In such a household, one soon finds, there are few absolute commandments, but one of them is that "we never, never throw away any bones." It makes the only stock they have faith in, skepticism being rife about Babson's Reports but not about the dicta of Clémentine in the Kitchen. As for the feeling of One World, it expresses itself in an over-valuation of foreign dishes and a virtual rubbing of garlic on the guests.

Follow the husband downtown and you will discover that his lunch hour, which used to be fractional and pinched, is now expansive: the midday meal is the time of contacts and propositions, and as sacrosanct as the former "conference." It is futile to try telephoning a really executive person between 12:30 and 3; he is then as incommunicado as a French shopkeeper.

And yet he is far from having become the Frenchman's counterpart in feeling, for the American in all these new ways is not yet free: he is only emancipated. His gormandizing is still a dutiful pleasure, during which he does business, holds committee meetings, or vaguely improves public relations. Despite the relaxing cocktails and pedigreed dishes, the function is still part of his enormous anxiety. Although it is *his* ulcers that are forming, it is not *his* lunch that he is eating; it is the company's, and it is accounted for, not in his stomach, but in the overhead. In merging two modes of life that had distinct physical and social origins, the old America fears have been diffused and disguised, and the new pleasures have been turned into instruments of guilt or expressions of defiance.

But the disguise and defiance are real enough to have brought about an important change in the conception of American manliness. In the pages of Mark Twain, Henry James, or William Dean Howells the representative American is the ancestral Jacksonian figure—tall, spare, nasal, dry of speech and leathery of surface. Within the last decade he has paled, smoothed out, and softened up until he may be said to be approaching Nero Wolfe as a limit. Here again Europe is visible. In the 1920's the word for Wolfe and his household would have been "sissyfied." Now it is more likely to be "civilized," and quite apart from the unctuous literature of gourmets and cooks, a good deal of popular fiction lets us eat expensively by proxy, for a mere Womrath fee.

There is much distress, no doubt, in this frenzy for seeming civilized, and one could expatiate on the appropriateness of the name Nero, but the vicarious debauchery is a true sign of general abandon. The radio announcers whose words about the role of wine or clothes in human life would have caused them to be run out of town in the days of Teddy Roosevelt now address male listeners who have completely shed the old taboos about tertiary sexual characteristics: they wear wrist watches and suspenders, cultivate their charm, and control their hair cuts. Their summer hats, no longer of the shape of cheese boxes, they wear at discretion during the season and not, as before, within the rigid schedule set by custom and enforced by street boys. Summer and winter, their clothes may border on pastel shades, while their ties emulate flowered chintz and the whole economy of shirt, trousers, sleeve length, weave, and cut bespeaks caprice, looseness, and latitude.

Manners, too, have had the starch taken out of them. The first Roosevelt shook hands with the engineman, but condescension still lurked in the very trouble he took. It was the second Roosevelt who truly leveled ranks and brought upon this continent the baptismal brotherhood of man: "I'm sorry, John, but I didn't quite catch your last name." The family name as a mode of address is reserved for occasions of ultimate contempt, just as "sir" remains an angry expletive or the mark of the mild sycophant. Meanwhile, the common greeting of the common man has reached its final simplification in the monosyllable "Hi"; so that to the youth of today the humorist whom I heard twenty-five years ago gravely murmuring as he shook hands, "How do you do, I'm sure," would not sound comic but quaintly polite and old-fashioned.

Almost all formalities, within recent years, have followed into oblivion the dropping of cards and the paying of dinner calls. The rate of disuse is very rapid. When a famous and quite simple-mannered English author visited this country last summer, he found and relished the warm and easy human relations which his books had long urged on his own compatriots. But here his imagination was quickly outdone by reality. Going up to his host at the end of a pleasant evening, he uttered his thanks in a few direct words, only to find another guest at his elbow who waited until he had finished and then chimed in with an emphatic "Check!"—whereupon their host acknowledged the double courtesy with: "Take it easy, boys!"

It is all very winning, disarming, "human"—like the sloppy clothes, the love of good food, and the downtown conviviality. But then how is it that with every step in the breakdown of restraints business has become more irritating, sociability more difficult, and friendship more precarious? Is it not because the relentless search for what is "natural" and "easy" is itself cramping and exhausting? The trouble seems to be not only that each perpetually competes with all in simplicity, under-bidding his neighbor in word and act until it seems as if the only democratic garb were the figleaf and unkempt hair, and the only un-affected discourse a few grunts of varied pitch; the trouble also is that the normal desire to shine and to accomplish is now forced to take the same collective path. Individuality seems eccentric, offensive, and is repressed. The result is that to be a friend is no different from being an acquaintance; to do business is no different from having a party; to act as host is no different from advertising and selling the latest facilities; to taste and enjoy is no different from squaring one's mind with public opinion.

In striving to be no one in particular, the common man has turned into an absolute being who neither enshrines nor recognizes any distinctions and who tries to behave like an interchangeable unit. Youth and age, sex and status, are obliterated in the effort to be "human." But being human in this fashion imposes the heroic discipline of daily altering one's temperature to jibe with the average so as to avoid giving offense by the mere fact of difference. When all barriers are down, every situation requires tact, and the absence of "signals" to denote courtesy makes a perpetual drain on good-will. This is the extreme we have reached through a just criticism of Puritan manners and a repudiation of the frank free-for-all of business.

Our European imports have failed us. The love of food, leisure, and gay dress, the desire to please and to avoid wounding our multitudinous peers, should have made us into Chesterfieldian personalities. The release from asceticism and greed should have made us into Emersonians, or Nietzscheans—generous because energetic and free. Instead, we remain anxious in our weak depravity and suffer the neuroses of an unfeatured grain of tapioca in a pudding. No doubt we can cheer and inspire ourselves by reading Rabelais or Thomas Love Peacock or John Cowper Powys, or more lately the Kinsey Report. But how many quarter-centuries will it be before we achieve with our own means the balance of sense and soul?

Cities Fit to Live In

BY LEWIS MUMFORD

1948

What kind of cities do we want? We Americans have never asked ourselves this question, during the last century, in terms of the needs of human living. We have asked for big cities, for skyscraper cities thronging with traffic and rife with trade, sometimes for monumental cities with great civic centers to express a dignity denied by every other activity. More lately we have asked for cities whose blighted areas and partly emptied slums have been converted back again into profitable investments or done over into hygienic "housing developments."

American cities, to a large degree, have been the products of the private land monopolist, the speculative builder, the too canny banker and insurance administrator, the centralizing business bureaucrat, bent on seizing and displaying power. With profit, prestige, and power the controlling influences in city development, more rational and humane ends have become secondary. Accordingly, if we dare to ask ourselves what kind of cities we want, we must be prepared to liquidate many of our present financial activities and to transform the remainder into social enterprises.

Is that too drastic a demand upon our social conscience, our political intelligence, our economic competence? Perhaps it is, but in that case there is no use asking what kind of cities we want. Whatever we may privately yearn for, we shall get the product of the same forces that have been operating in the past; and such modifications as public-housing authorities may make will be subservient to those forces. At best, they will do reasonably well what private enterprise has done badly, to the undermining of its own long-term interests.

Admittedly, the present is a bad time to frame more human demands, since while the housing shortage prevails people will put up with any kind of city so long as it incidentally puts a roof over their heads. That condition, however, is a temporary one. Our great metropolises are overcrowded, financially topheavy, environmentally lopsided; and the excessive costs of the congestion they promote are rivaled only by the costs of the remedies for alleviating it. Even our smaller cities, which have imitated the metropolitan pattern, likewise fall short of any adequate human goal. In the long run our civilization, just because it has already become predominantly urban, cannot afford to misdirect its energies in this fashion. It did not take the atomic bomb to prove that the present form of our cities is doomed. Though decentralization is no answer whatever to the practice of genocide, it is a first step toward building up a sound, life-centered civilization.

The tendency of population movements during the last century has been to heap people into spreading metropolitan districts, dominated by cities with over a million people; some quarter of the population of the entire country lives in such metropolitan areas—suburban in almost every sense. Do we want this movement to continue? If it does, it will produce two unfavorable results: it will wipe out the local balance between city and country and require those who seek recreation in rural areas to travel ever greater distances to have even a glimpse of nature. But even more fundamentally, if metropolitan standards prevail, it will bring about a premature stabilizing of the population, indeed, probably cause it to recede, since the big cities do not biologically reproduce their population and an ever smaller rural group remains to compensate for this lack of urban fertility. Theoretically, the great cities of the Eastern seaboard and the Great Lakes region might continue their growth until they merged into one another, as Minneapolis merges into Saint Paul, in one vast undifferentiated urban mass. But before that point was reached, the urban population would begin to dwindle, for with immigration restricted, its supply would be cut off at the source.

As between big cities and small cities, then, every biological argument backs the small city as more favorable, despite its lack of highly organized medical services, to life. The problem of population is too complicated to be disposed of in an aside; but if we wish to achieve even stability at present levels, we shall have to make it possible for more people to live in towns of fifty thousand or less, because they produce an environment and a routine of life more favorable to family life and reproduction. Does this mean that we must abandon the city altogether, as Frank Lloyd Wright has proposed? No, it means something quite different—namely, that we must drain away its population steadily into smaller centers until the metropolitan areas themselves can be reconstituted into a constellation of relatively self-contained communities, built on a more open pattern and separated from one another by parks and green belts.

London already has plans to remove a million people from its central areas into New Towns of some sixty thousand people each, not suburbs but complete and balanced communities, with factories and workshops for the local population. There can be no adequate rebuilding of our congested centers until the pressure that produces this congestion is thus removed. Hence housing and slum clearance, even if undertaken by public authorities, without industrial decentralization, are the most superficial of palliatives. But one must not minimize the cost of such a radical form of urban redevelopment. Since it involves cutting down present urban land values on a colossal scale, it will require heavy state and federal aid to make even the first steps possible: otherwise, merely to avoid bankruptcy, our municipalities—to say nothing of our banks and insurance companies—will fight it tooth and nail.

In short, we must plan and build new communities, on a large scale, before we can adequately replan and rebuild our old centers. Our present policy of replacing slum areas with grim monumental structures of the kind favored by the New York City Housing Authority changes the existing pattern of congestion but does not alter the fact itself, nor does it lower the land values which make congestion inevitable. A housing policy that purposes to rebuild American cities in this fashion is in the long run the most extravagant possible: it builds the wrong thing, in the wrong order, in the wrong place.

To achieve a better result, we must use governmental means to carry farther the tendency toward industrial decentralization which was fostered in many industries during the war. Regional planning, industrial decentralization, housing, and city development are four aspects of a single process which must be unified if it is to be effective. Administratively, this program cannot possibly be handled from Washington. If we wish to achieve it, our first step must be a political one: we must create regional authorities, on the model of the New York–New Jersey Port Authority or the Tennessee Valley Authority, capable of planning, building, developing, and holding these new communities till they are ready to take over the tasks of self-government. In an article as brief as this I cannot particularize all the political and economic measures that will be necessary: what I would emphasize is that the controlling factors in city building are no longer of a local nature; and that even the most farsighted municipality cannot by itself take the measures necessary to establish a better social structure.

The main point I would make is simple: there is no use asking ourselves what sort of city we want unless we are ready to deal energetically with the forces that have been automatically piling up congestion, disorder, and human depletion. Once this fact is realized, the next thing to understand is a fundamental theorem about city development first put forward by Ebenezer Howard exactly half a century ago. Howard pointed out that there were essentially two methods of city development: one is by continued agglomeration and extension, without any essential change in form; and the other is by reproduction. With the first method growth is unlimited and unbalanced. With the second method, which Howard reinvented, the city has a norm of growth: its area and population are limited. When the city reaches the limits of its growth, another community must be formed, on the same lines, to carry on the social and economic processes. Howard placed the optimum number of people for a relatively self-contained community at 32,000, some two thousand of whom were to be occupied by agricultural pursuits in the surrounding rural area. This was a reasonable guess; though by now, with the increase of facilities for transportation and communication, the upper limit is probably around sixty thousand. What is important to understand about Howard's conception of the garden city as he called it is not merely the limitation of area, or the collective ownership of the land, or density and numbers, but the even more essential principle of cellular growth and cellular division.

Ideally speaking, a city is a group of cells each of which has a social nucleus which furthers the common life, and the city as a whole is the larger organ of that common life. The principle of cell division applies to every part of a city's activities. If 100 beds is the right number for a well-organized general hospital, then when 500 beds are required, they should not be combined into a single gigantic institution but into five self-contained units distributed through the city or region. If 250 pupils is the desirable number for an elementary school, the neighborhood unit must be scaled and planned to that size. From the smallest housing group to the city as a whole, the aim is to create a balance of activities, in a varied and balanced environment. Instead of fostering growth by agglomeration, we must foster growth by reproduction.

The kind of city we want, accordingly, is one adequately planned and equipped for the fulfilment of life at every stage from cradle to grave. A city might be composed of houses and open spaces of the most excellent design, from one end to the other, without meeting this requirement. Consider the life of an ordinary city neighborhood today. We are happy when such a neighborhood has adequate playgrounds for the young: too easily we forgo the possibilities of swimming pools and gymnasiums, health clinics and maternity clinics, reading rooms and game rooms, where the members of the family would, even outside the home, find a common life. Despite the fact that an ever larger part of the community now lives beyond the age of sixty, what provisions have we made, in new housing communities, to enable the old to continue their normal social relationships? We either shift the aged into overgrown institutions, already cramped for space, or we condemn them to a state of dependency in the insufficiently roomy quarters of their own families. By building special quarters for old folks, scattered about a residential unit, we would give them the care, the stimulus, and the neighborly companionship they need.

None of the essential needs of a well-planned neighborhood, from nursery schools to special quarters for the aged, will be provided by private enterprise, seeking profit, except in the most limited and grudging manner. If we want better cities, we must look forward to the resolute extension of public enterprise, not as at present to rescue bankrupt investments but to rehabilitate a bankrupt life. Free enterprise in a democracy means, among other things, freedom to socialize.

Whatever changes toward more efficient administration take place in the political organization of the country at large, the most important task of all is to rebuild the essential unit of spontaneous cooperation and voluntary effort in the local community and, to begin with, in the neighborhood unit. We must rebuild and reequip the essential cell of community life. All large-scale planning will be inadequate until we have such units to work with. Once we have such units, we can build up balanced cities and draw them together in larger schemes of cooperation; so that eventually we shall have regional units capable of performing effectively all the functions that our metropolitan areas now perform at such a heavy cost.

What kind of cities do we want? Cities in which man is at home again—at home in an orderly and comely environment cut to the human measure: cities where every function necessary to growth and development, biological and cultural, has an appropriate place in the plan and an appropriate structure. To bring such cities into existence, we cannot continue to follow the line of least resistance. Quite the contrary, we must alter our present life-denying goals and lay down the foundations for a new civilization—not a money economy but a life economy.

Writers in America

BY STEPHEN SPENDER

1949

A certain frustration accompanies attempts of Britishers to write about Americans and of Americans to write about the British. This is in itself a significant fact of the Anglo-American situation. We are each of us hypersensitive about our nation in relation to this particular other nation. Therefore many things which a Britisher could say about Britain would cause annoyance if they were said by an American, and vice versa. It seems, then, important to say at the outset that I am not hostile to America.

In fact, I love America in the only way in which it seems to me real to love a country. That is to say, I regard America as a country where opposition to bad institutions, commercialization, exploitation, vulgarity, and other obvious evils is, after all, real. It is possible to be an American and yet oppose the bad things which are American, and there is nourishment in the climate and the institutions of America for such opposition. There are few countries in the contemporary world to which one can pay such a compliment.

The greatness of American literature is that it derives from this opposition—the best American writing today is a living body of protest against the vulgarity and commercialization which many people think of as most characteristic of America. In fact, contemporary American literature suggests what the last American election suggested —that there is an America more real and more alive than the America which pollsters, advertisers, Hollywood, and news editors know about.

The most striking difference between Europe and America as far as writing is concerned is probably that the American writer does not belong to a community of literature. In France, to be a young writer is to seek entry into a community. The symbol of this community is the Parisian cafe where students and young writers meet to discuss their literary problems, admire one another's work, and decide that their "movement" is the last revolution of the word. The literary review, like the cafe, is a meeting place, which is also a battleground, of generations.

In England contemporary literature is not such a conscious community as in France. However, to a great extent Oxford and Cambridge provide a literary tradition which widens later into Bloomsbury, the twenties, the thirties, the New Romantics, and in which the lives of writers who have not been educated at those universities merge, albeit sometimes rebelliously. Even a writer like D. H. Lawrence became, by way of meetings with other writers at Lady Ottoline Morel's house at Garsington, an Oxford rebel, belonging far more to this tradition than to the Nottingham coal mines. Periodicals such as *Horizon*, the *Cornhill Magazine*, and *New Writings* are meeting places of generations. Apart from the tendency of older and more successful English writers to petrify into public monuments during their lifetime, a general consciousness of shared values which can be maintained or betrayed informs English literary life.

The young American writer is in an entirely different situation from the young French writer going to the cafe or the young English writer at Oxford or Cambridge or at some intellectual suburb of these centers. There is no cafe in which he will meet Hemingway, Dos Passos, Faulkner. There is no periodical in which his name will be "accepted" among the great reputations of older writers who are known throughout the world.

If he happens to meet older writers, he will be meeting them across, as it were, an enormous gulf of grandiose success, Hollywood success, *Life* magazine success, which raises writers socially out of the sphere of literature and into that of film stars or successful journalists. Or perhaps he meets them across a gulf of bitter failure within which the older writer is isolated, embittered—and fortified.

The pathology of literary success would make an interesting study. The dangers are twofold: first, that success may separate the writer physically and spiritually from his most fertile material of felt experience, which may well be associated with his childhood and early strivings; second, that it may consign him to the enthusiasm of an audience which appreciates qualities having little connection with literature. In America there is the third danger that the writer's economic position may rest almost entirely on by-products of his purely literary activity —on films, on articles in high-paying magazines, even on exploitation of his name by advertisers (recently an advertisement displayed a high-minded sentiment about world peace in the handwriting of Ernest Hemingway, using a Parker pen). Above all, there is the danger that the publicized personality of the writer, with his four wives, his big-game hunting, his knocking-down-of-other-writers-at-parties, tends to eclipse his ever more modest activities in his study. Nor does the working of this machinery by which the loaded ore of writing is transformed into glossy, expensive-seeming by-products of reputation —just as the by-products of coal tar are turned into miscellaneous articles such as aspirin tablets, artificial silk, and film for cameras— delay until the writer has attained middle age. One has only to follow the whizzing comets of Truman Capote and Gore Vidal to see how quickly and effectively this transforming, diluting, disintegrating machinery can work.

In America the only way to escape the consequences of great success is to escape literally and physically. This is doubtless why William Faulkner is inaccessible in his Southern home, why John Steinbeck is elusive, why Hemingway now lives in Cuba. Paradoxically, the publicizing of contemporary American literature contributes to the disruption of any community of letters in America. The successful writer, dazed by the irrelevances of a success which has little to do with recognition of his best qualities and which robs him of his deepest experiences, escapes somewhere, if he is sensible, hugging his precious talent. Instead of being now the boy from the Middle West with the hard-luck story, he becomes the poor rich boy clinging to his aesthetic conscience. Alcoholism, the occupational disease of the successful American writer, can surely be explained at least in part as an effort to restore contact with the dionysiac, the violent, the real, the unconscious level of experience by those who have been cut off by success from their roots.

But failure is perhaps even more disastrous than success in America. In Europe, after all, success and failure are comparative terms, particularly failure. One has the feeling that the European failure is often a kind of secret success, at any rate among a small group. It is possible to envy Keats the position he enjoyed in Leigh Hunt's circle, or Gide his reputation when his publishers had sold only a few copies of "Paludes," or Rilke when he commanded the attention of only a few princesses. But in America there are seldom these public failures who are private, highly superior successes. There is a lack, within a civilization which is changing and expanding so rapidly, of a sense that if one misses one's time, one will be discovered by another time. Failure, therefore, like success, has something definite and final about it. It creates a gulf which separates the unsuccessful writer from America.

The young writer is confronted with a dramatic choice between success, with the kind of gigantic systematic exploitation of misunderstanding which it involves—success of one's inferior qualities through the medium of one's best ones—or failure, which leads to an isolation almost as complete as that of success. The fact that certain writers deliberately refuse success and even choose failure does them enormous credit. Yet by making this choice they sacrifice more than reward. For the vitality of America is so enormously absorbed into the success story that to reject success is to reject a great part of the experience of America. There is a bitterness of the rejecting and the rejected about American literary failures.

Probably I have oversimplified in drawing this black-and-white contrast between success and failure, and I shall qualify the picture in a moment. What is important, however, is to emphasize that the American writer is confronted by a number of choices any one of which tends in the long run to isolate him, to dramatize his position within a society where there are writers—some good, some bad, some successful, some unsuccessful—but no literary life, no considerable public sustainedly and discriminatingly interested in seeking out the best, a kind of jury of middle-class middling readers to whom the European writer, after all, continually addresses his appeals, restates his case, and on whose judgment he is prepared to wait for twenty years if necessary. Also I wish to show that the choice between success and failure is not a simple choice between corruption and integrity, although the writer who refuses success would maintain that it is. Failure means putting oneself outside the preoccupations of the greater part of American life and placing oneself within perhaps an embittered Greenwich Village group, or perhaps a sophisticated university group. It may mean withdrawing into a voluntary exile in some part of the country and issuing from time to time those vituperative messages against the whole of America which characterize the work of Henry Miller and his followers. Success also means isolation, but it is the experience of a form of loneliness which is the lot of a great many successful Americans. The successful American writer at least can and sometimes does absorb into his work some of the dynamism of American materialism.

The qualifications which rather modify my picture of the writer who rejects success is that he can to some extent exploit his by-products, just as the successful one can. In many universities today there are "poets in residence": for example, Paul Engel at Iowa, Karl Shapiro at Baltimore; and other writers, besides poets, are coming more and more to seek work at colleges and universities. Another way of tiding over unsuccess is to be supported by some trust or obtain one of the many literary awards offered by the great foundations, such as the Rockefeller and the Guggenheim.*

The American universities are to a large extent subsidizing American contemporary literature. In fact, one can foresee a day when American literature may be divided into two channels—the commercialized success and the subsidized commercial failure. Such a development might not be entirely bad, but it would tend to accentuate a division of American writing which is already apparent: on the one hand writing which can be exploited by the book clubs and Hollywood, transformed into something which sells to a wide public for other than literary reasons; and on the other hand writing which is highly intellectualized, critical in spirit, hermetic, self-conscious, writing by writers for writers communicating with each other in a highly allusive idiom. The popular work adapted to popular misconceptions might well sometimes prove to be a masterpiece, as might also the exclusive and literary. But between the two extremes of commercialization and academic exclusiveness the communication of literature with a wide cultivated public would not exist.

The universities, like the trusts, render a great service to the best American writers. But nevertheless a university post tends to isolate a writer within his academic surroundings. And surely one of the results of turning writers into university teachers is the immense and massive concentration on literary criticism which fills so large a space in the literary periodicals. Some of this criticism is excellent. Yet the enormous energy devoted to producing volume after volume of research into Henry James by now resembles one of the great American industries. A good deal of talent which might be creative is diverted into critical channels by a situation which makes critical research a "safe" subsidized literary task, and in which published criticism is a good way of gaining advancement in the universities.

* The Rockefeller Foundation also does much to help young English writers in their present difficulties. Last year it gave thirty-four of them Atlantic Awards.

Halfway to What?

BY REINHOLD NIEBUHR

1950

The embattled American plutocracy, finding political power slipping from its hands and seeing little in the whole world to give it comfort, has invented a nice little theory to scare its enemies and quiet its own apprehensions. This is that the policies of the New Deal or the Fair Deal are a halfway house to socialism, even as socialism is a halfway house to communism and totalitarianism. Any nation, therefore, which uses its sovereign power to extend the general welfare is starting down the slippery slope which ends in the abyss of totalitarianism. At a recent convention of the National Association of Manufacturers almost every speaker reiterated this idea until it became a kind of liturgy. It was not quite clear whether the business community hoped to regain political power by emphasizing the danger or was assuring itself of its own virtue as the defender of a lost but sacred cause.

The politicians of the right, as distinguished from the business men, have not yet achieved such a degree of unanimity. They must win elections, and they have learned through bitter experience that the American people are not impressed by the allegedly inexorable logic of history, which is supposed to deliver them into the arms of communism if they decide to use their political power to guarantee their basic economic security. Mr. Dewey complained after his defeat that the critics of his "me-tooism" did not know what it took to win an election in a modern industrial community, but his complaint did not prevent him from trying the other tack in the recent senatorial election. That was not successful either. Governor Dewey's dilemma is typical of that which the Republican Party is bound to face for some time to come, and which need not detain us here.

American business men, much less hesitantly than the politicians, assert that the same America which from the perspective of an impoverished Europe and Asia seems to cling to an almost neolithic economic theory is already on the way to communism. John T. Flynn has recently invented a variant of the theory. British socialism, he declares, is a halfway house to *either* fascism or communism. It has no other choice.

The idea is too implausible to have much political effect. The danger is that it may so blind American business men to real trends that they will understand the world they live in as little as the bosses of the Kremlin, who wear another set of blinders. Our business men, to be sure, are not so powerful as the Communist oligarchs, but they are not impotent, and they might in their blindness become dangerous. We ought to do our best, therefore, to enlighten them.

In this task the first point to emphasize is that no nation in modern history has ever lost its liberties by inadvertence. No people has ever used a free election to annul the power of its suffrage. Totalitarian systems are forced upon nations in times of social convulsion, when minorities of either the right or the left have found it possible to seize control of the government. Aware that a free election would never validate their authority, these minorities have destroyed democracy, either with the complete cynicism of the Nazis or the combined cynicism and illusion of the Communists.

It must be noted, in the second place, that the Socialist and quasi-Socialist regimes which seek to control economic life through the democratic process have impaired the liberties of their peoples so little that two such governments, in Australia and in New Zealand, have just been defeated in an election. In Great Britain the coming election will probably be close; if the Tories are defeated, it will not be because they were unable to reach the ear of the electorate but because they failed to persuade its mind and conscience. They will lose the election, if they do, for the same reason that the Republicans lost in 1948.

This does not mean that every detail of democratic socialism is defensible or that the successive steps toward the political control of economic processes in America are always justified. But whatever the differences between the United States and the Socialist and quasi-Socialist nations of the Continent, we have in common the will to use political power to mitigate the injustices which arise from the increased centralization of economic power inherent in a technical society. Thus political movements driven solely by the resentments of the defrauded and intent upon a revolutionary overthrow of society are not required. Society moves from point to point toward a more tolerable justice.

The nostalgia of the American business community for the "never-never land" of pure laissez faire is doubly ironic. In the first place, the business community sought, as long as it could, to bend political power to its ends, violating every principle of free enterprise. The tariff policy of the Republican Party is certainly not in harmony with the principles of laissez faire; nor were such devices as the Reconstruction Finance Corporation, which, originally conceived in the Hoover era, was designed to bail out some of the weakest units of American business. Protests rose against the use of political power in economic life when the masses began to use it to broaden their economic opportunities, to check the centralization of economic power, and to assure basic economic security. The American business community tried desperately to prove the truth of the Marxist theory that political power is always the slave of the dominant economic power. The theory was refuted through the discovery by the common people that their political power could be used to redress economic imbalances.

Business nostalgia is also ironic because the movement away from the pure theory and the impure practice of free enterprise actually saved modern democratic nations from the social convulsions with their totalitarian outcome which occured in less democratic nations. This movement invalidated not only the Marxist dogma of the inevitable subservience of political to economic power but the ancillary doctrine that an imperiled privileged class would inevitably embark on fascist adventures to destroy the democracy which endowed the people with dangerous political power. No fascist adventures were resorted to in Britain, or in Norway or Sweden, or in Australia or New Zealand. It is possible, in short, for nations to have so strong a sense of community beyond and above the class conflict that a minority will yield its privileges without seeking to destroy the majority's political power. The minority submits in healthy democratic nations partly because it has a sense of justice beyond its class interests and partly because the authority of government is great enough to make a rebellion of either the right or the left too precarious.

In America no full-fledged Marxist movement has ever developed. If the lack of one retarded the political development of the working classes here, it also freed American labor from many Marxist illusions which European labor parties carry as so much excess baggage. The highly pragmatic and not very consistent policies of the New Deal first showed the American people how to use political power for correcting economic abuses. But the election of Truman was more instructive than anything which happened in the Roosevelt era. For here a candidate, seemingly doomed to defeat, saved himself by embracing the cause of the common man more unambiguously than Roosevelt ever did.

The movement toward basic economic security for the common man in America is too pragmatic to satisfy British Socialists, even as the British have always been too lax in their dogmas to satisfy their more orthodox colleagues on the Continent. But the British and Scandinavian Socialists have carried the national communities with them, while the orthodox Continental parties have never succeeded in gaining any great mass of adherents outside the industrial workers. The democratic middle ground on the Continent must therefore be held by an uneasy alliance between working-class parties encumbered with Marxist dogma and middle-class parties controlled by ecclesiastical interests. No one can doubt the sincerity of the Socialist devotion to freedom and opposition to communism. But the Socialists regard Stalinism as a corruption of the original Marxist dream. They do not fully recognize that this corruption is the natural fruit of certain Marxist illusions. The most grievous of these illusions is the expectation that the proletarian state will wither away, for this inclines men toward an uncritical acceptance of an allegedly temporary dictatorship.

Pragmatism as such has no particular virtue. There must be a proper framework of values in which pragmatic decisions are reached. The democratic movement, whether Socialist or non-Socialist, finds this framework in devotion to justice and freedom and in a recognition that while every form of power, whether political or economic, must be made to serve the cause of justice, the very exercise of power imperils justice.

Many modern democracies which have placed checks upon economic power have sacrificed no essential freedom, not even the freedom of the nation to reverse the tendency toward greater control of economic life. It does not follow, however, that the indeterminate extension of political control over life is necessarily wise. On the contrary, it may be unwise, not because a tyrannical state is thus inadvertently created, as the conservatives maintain, but because bureaucratic decisions can never anticipate all the economic contingencies which a free market holds in some kind of harmony. A nation might preserve all its essential political liberties and yet become economically sterile. Society will always face the problem of "achieving the harmony of the whole without destroying the vitality of the parts." We don't know exactly how to achieve this end and must therefore proceed circumspectly. We only know that a completely free market lacks the self-regulating power once ascribed to it, and that too inclusive planning destroys the flexibility which a healthy economy requires.

The extension of political control over economic life may also be unwise if it rests upon the assumption that man's social needs, whether for basic security, housing, education, or health, are determinate. All human needs are indeterminate. As a consequence inordinate demands are bound to be made upon any political scheme which offers "free" services. A modern democracy must provide health insurance for all of its citizens; that is one way in which the sovereign power of a government ought to be used. It may well be, however, that the British health scheme contains too many Marxist assumptions about the determinate character of human needs. The health schemes of our most progressive unions are more circumspect, and we may hope that state-supported schemes will be equally so.

The highly pragmatic type of progressive democracy developing in America, which is condemned by the reactionaries as a halfway house to communism and criticized even by British Socialists as lacking in dogmatic rigor, may prove better able to preserve democratic justice in a technical society than any of the alternatives of right or left. This can be our answer to Europeans who criticize the ambiguities of our political life. To our own reactionary critics we must emphasize the common elements in the democratic life of Europe and America. The democratic movement in America is not slipping into totalitarianism. It is the only effective safeguard against totalitarianism.

The First Fifty Years

BY HAROLD J. LASKI

1950

LONDON, *February 13*

The British Labor Party was born on February 27, 1900, in the Memorial Hall, Farmington Street, London, at a conference summoned by the Trades Union Congress of the previous year. Some of its members were notable men—Keir Hardie, Ramsay MacDonald, Bernard Shaw, Will Thorne, J. R. Clynes. Most of them were not Socialists, and the unions from which they came would not have joined the new party then formed if it had been given that complexion. Some of them were Tories, others were devoted followers of Gladstone, a few did not see that trade unions had political interests of any kind. But the Socialist group in the conference, led by Keir Hardie, knew what they wanted, were shrewd enough to realize the virtue of waiting, and, though from different groups, acted with a persuasive unity. An executive committee was set up, and Ramsay MacDonald, already widely known as a journalist of competence and a rhetorician with a voice like music, was chosen secretary without salary. Organizations could affiliate to the new party and nominate parliamentary candidates under its auspices; they must agree to abide by the decisions of the new party where working-class interests were involved but were free on other matters. The Labor Representation Committee had no doctrine; it was thoroughly respectable; and its income in its first year of life was just over two hundred pounds. Obviously, it had little to lose; perhaps it might have a world to win.

The Labor Party hardly began auspiciously. In the "khaki" election of 1900 it sponsored fifteen candidates, of whom Keir Hardie alone was successful; the noise of the guns in South Africa drowned, even in trade-union ears, the harsh verdict of the Court of Appeal in the famous Taff Vale case, in which the judges hoped they had found a way to jeopardize the very existence of trade unions. But in the next four years the party won four by-elections, in one of which Arthur Henderson, who was to become its greatest organizer as well as the outstanding British Foreign Secretary of modern times, was sent to Parliament. At the general election of 1906 it profited from the great shift of British opinion to the left. Twenty-nine of its members were returned, including men like MacDonald, Clynes, Snowden, and Will Thorne, all of whom were to be great figures in its history for a generation or more; it could, moreover, usually count upon the support of twenty-five other trade-union members elected as Liberals. Arthur Balfour, the defeated Prime Minister, said at once that the Labor Party victories marked a new era in the history of Great Britain.

In the Parliament of 1906 the Labor Party did two things. It secured from the Liberal government the repeal by statute of the Taff Vale decision, which the House of Lords had upheld in 1901, and it gave national standing in the Commons not only to Keir Hardie but to MacDonald, Snowden, Clynes, and Henderson. Its policy was not very original—it accepted most of the doctrine and measures of the Liberal government. It did, indeed, take a firm stand for peace, and it was suspicious of the foreign policy of Sir Edward Grey. Socialist ideas were swiftly permeating the rank and file of its supporters, though a careful analysis of the attitude of MacDonald and Snowden would have shown that if they wore red ties, their shirts were the product of a Liberal factory. The Labor members, with occasional exceptions, did not really do much more than emphasize Liberal measures. Now and again, especially in the epoch of great strikes in 1911-12, when Winston Churchill first showed his natural attitude to trade unions by sending troops to shoot down striking miners in Tonypandy, South Wales, there was a vigorous outburst from a handful of members in which there was a recognizably Socialist note; and Keir Hardie, Snowden, and MacDonald, all protested vigorously against repression in India and Egypt. But it is on the whole true to say that up to 1914 most Labor M. P.'s could be described as Liberals emphasizing with 15 per cent more urgency the need to grapple with working-class questions.

The great turning point in the history of the Labor Party was the war of 1914. The larger part of the membership accepted it on the ground that German militarism was a threat to democracy, and of these Arthur Henderson was the chief; others opposed it, like Keir Hardie and Philip Snowden, either on pacifist grounds or because they thought it, in essence, an imperialist war. MacDonald took a somewhat ambiguous attitude: he criticized the policy of making war but wrote letters supporting the recruiting effort. The great achievement of Arthur Henderson, who had become the general secretary of the party, was that he maintained its unity, even though the two major groups were in fierce conflict. Partly through his influence the party, by a majority, decided to enter the first coalition government in 1915; and when in December, 1916, Lloyd George replaced Asquith as Premier, Henderson became the Labor member of the War Cabinet. But he did not remain there long. In February, 1917, the Russian Revolution began, and its complexities made the War Cabinet decide to send Henderson to Moscow to report upon the vast issues to which it gave rise. He returned convinced not only that the revolution must be safeguarded but also that all European Socialists should meet to see whether some common formula of peace could not be found. But Lloyd George and his other colleagues were insistent on unconditional surrender and emphatic that the Russian withdrawal from the war was a betrayal. After a decisive quarrel Henderson resigned—though with the party's approval other Labor men remained in office—and began to devote his gifts for organization to preparing the Labor Party for the outbreak of peace.

It was at this point that he found his great partner in the famous Fabian sociologist, Sidney Webb. In association with Webb, he persuaded the party to accept the new constitution of 1918, which with some minor changes remains the constitution today. They not only secured for the constitution the support of all the important trade unions and chief Socialist societies but gained the acceptance of the ideas, first, that every parliamentary constituency should have its local party, with both individual members and affiliated trade-union branches, and second, that the national party should boldly declare itself a Socialist party and make the acceptance of Socialist principles a necessary condition of membership. They then got the agreement of the reorganized party to a declaration of war aims which stands out still as one of the two or three most remarkable documents of the war, being built on the realization that the age of international organization had arrived and that national egotism, if written into the peace treaty, would sow the dragon's teeth of new wars. Thirdly, they secured acceptance of the famous document "Labor and the New Social Order," mainly written by Webb. There is still no better statement of the principles of democratic socialism; and it remains the foundation of all subsequent Labor Party efforts.

In the midst of these great achievements the election of 1918, skilfully maneuvered by Lloyd George as a tribute to himself before the war excitement had died down, was a disappointment; the Labor Party obtained only fifty-seven seats. But within a year the tide began to flow the other way. In 1920, under the joint leadership of George Lansbury and Ernest Bevin—the latter had just emerged as a national figure—the Councils of Action were formed and succeeded in putting an end to the ugly policy of armed intervention in Russia, of which the Lloyd George Cabinet, including Winston Churchill, approved. Two years later the Tories separated from Lloyd George, and their leader, Bonar Law, became Prime Minister. In the general election which followed, all the well-known Labor leaders retained their seats, and with them came a famous group from the Clydeside, of whom James Maxton was the most beloved and John Wheatley the ablest figure. A number of these—Attlee, Greenwood, Shinwell, Sidney Webb— entered the House for the first time. With 142 seats, Labor became for the first time the official Opposition. Within a year Bonar Law was dead, and Stanley Baldwin had become Prime Minister. As a strong protectionist Baldwin dissolved Parliament in the hope that he could get a mandate for abandoning free trade. Labor members now numbered 191, and in conjunction with the Liberals they turned out the Baldwin government as soon as the new House met. On January 21, 1924, Ramsay MacDonald became the first Labor Prime Minister.

He had been elected leader of the party in 1922 by the solid vote of the Clydesiders, who believed that he held strongly left-wing Socialist opinions. That was a completely mistaken judgment. MacDonald was in fact an ambitious charlatan who clothed all his opinions in a mass of metaphysical rhetoric; he disliked the left, feared opposition, and was far too timid even to dream of embarking upon a determined program of Socialist legislation. He was vain beyond words and easily captured by the glamor of "society" in London. His government lasted just over ten months, during which Wheatley, as Health Minister, put through an admirable housing act and Ponsonby, the Under Secretary for Foreign Affairs, obtained, in spite of MacDonald, both the recognition of Soviet Russia and a promising trade treaty with its government. Then the Labor Ministry fell, over the issue of a withdrawal of proceedings for sedition undertaken against an ex-soldier who combined a fine war record with strong Communist leanings. MacDonald lied to the House about his part in the whole affair, made the question one of confidence, and when beaten secured a dissolution of Parliament. In the election, which the Tories won by the well-timed "discovery" of the Zinoviev letter, the Labor Party lost forty seats.

The new Tory government was to hold office for nearly five years. Baldwin made Winston Churchill his Chancellor of the Exchequer, and the latter, whose ignorance of economics was one of the most remarkable features of his political equipment, at once returned to the gold standard, with immense deflation as a result. This caused widespread unemployment and a general lowering of wages. The miners, betrayed in 1919 by Lloyd George over their claims for nationalization, were hit with particular severity. They refused to accept either an increase of hours or a decrease of pay. Mr. Baldwin bought them off for some months by a subsidy while his hand-picked Royal Commission reexamined the industry, reported against nationalization, and recommended a decrease in wages. The miners refused to accept this and appealed to the Trades Union Congress, which decided on May 1, 1926, to support them by a massive general strike. The economic life of the country was brought to a standstill for ten days. At the end of them, as the result of some curious half-official negotiations with Sir Herbert Samuel and the fear, whipped up by Sir John Simon, that the congress's action was both unconstitutional and illegal, the unions capitulated, though the miners themselves, with typical courage, remained out for six months longer until they were beaten by sheer starvation. The Baldwin government took its revenge by passing the Trade Union Law Amendment Act of 1927, which, broadly speaking, was an English version of the Taft-Hartley act.

Labor had its revenge in 1929, when the Tory government dissolved and went to the country with a slogan which consisted of Mr. Baldwin smoking a pipe and asking for the confidence of the people. It was not much to offer; and the electorate returned 289 Labor members—only twenty short of an absolute majority. Baldwin resigned, and Mac-Donald became Prime Minister, with Arthur Henderson, to the Prime Minister's chagrin, as his Foreign Secretary. Henderson's handling of the office was the one outstanding success the second Labor government, beset by its own lack of courage and the growing economic depression, could claim.

As unemployment grew, MacDonald set up an Economy Committee which reported in favor of large cuts, even in unemployment relief. When the Cabinet would not accept such proposals, he proposed resignation. He had long thought of coalition government as the way out of his difficulties, and he now, to most people's amazement, formed a new Cabinet for the purpose of "saving the pound." Baldwin and Sir Herbert Samuel entered this Cabinet; Snowden and Thomas, with fourteen other Labor members, followed MacDonald into the prison camp where he hoped to find peace. Twelve days later his "National Government" went off the gold standard it was intended to preserve, and knowing that there was no way back for him, he decided on a general election, the necessity of which he had denied a few weeks before. MacDonald gained an immense victory. Of the best-known

Labor front benchers only George Lansbury, C. R. Attlee, and Stafford Cripps remained to lead the 56 who were left from 289. Mac-Donald remained the nominal Prime Minister until 1934, when Baldwin took over the power that had, all along, been his. In the three years 1931-34, despite furious opposition from Labor and the loss of its Liberal members, the MacDonald government abandoned free trade, cut down all the social services, compelled a reduction in wages, and treated the unemployed as, in MacDonald's own word, "scrap." The Cabinet also turned away from Geneva and the chance of disarmament to the policy of the Stresa front, which led inexorably first to appeasement and then to the isolationism which came to full fruition later.

The Labor Party recovered only slowly from the crisis of 1931. At the general election of 1935 it returned 154 members, but the Tory power was overwhelming. When Neville Chamberlain succeeded Baldwin as Prime Minister in 1936, the Labor Party entered one of the unhappiest periods of its history. George Lansbury's absolute pacifism compelled his resignation of the leadership, C. R. Attlee taking his place. But the party had to watch helplessly while Chamberlain acquiesced, first, in the conquest of Abyssinia, then in Hitler's annexation of Austria, then in the hypocrisy of non-intervention in Spain. Chamberlain went forward, despite the resignation of Eden and the passionate hostility of Churchill, with pride and complacency to the disaster of Munich. Neither dissension nor denunciation could turn him from his goal, until in March, 1939, Hitler devoured the last remnants of Czechoslovakia and got ready for an attack on Poland. At long last, and too late, the Labor Party was able to lead public opinion in Great Britian to make continuation of appeasement impossible. Chamberlain made a last-minute and half-hearted effort to come to terms with Russia, but he was too late. His choice now lay between a super-Munich and a war to preserve what was left of freedom and democracy in Europe. The whole nation responded to the Labor Party's lead in the House of Commons. On September 3, 1939, Chamberlain was compelled to ask for a declaration of war against Germany in the worst possible conditions. By the following May his futility and incompetence were decisively shown in the failure of the Norwegian campaign. He sought earnestly Labor support; the party replied with emphasis that it would serve only under Winston Churchill as Prime Minister, and then upon the vital condition that it was a full partner. The Churchill government was formed, with Attlee as Deputy Prime Minister, Bevin as Minister of Labor, and Herbert Morrison, after a brief period at the Ministry of Supply, as Home Secretary and Minister of Home Security. If Churchill was the leader—and a great war leader—the debt he owed to his Labor colleagues was immeasurable.

None but they could have won for him the confidence of the common people, and without that confidence he could not have become the architect of destiny.

After its famous victory in 1945 the history of the British Labor Party is too well known to require detailed analysis. It is more useful to sum up, on the eve of the election, the party's general characteristics.

1.   It has become a genuinely national party. Though the trade unions remain an integral part of it, it has the support of the Cooperative Union and of members of all trades and professions. Its M. P.'s represent a good cross-section of the national life.

2.   Though as in all political parties leadership counts for much, in no political party in Great Britain is the influence of the rank and file so clear or so obviously recognized.

3.   The party is strongly democratic and has consistently refused to have any dealings with organized communism. It is Socialist, but its socialism has varied shades. Unity is achieved by the program of the party, which is laid down by the Annual Conference.

4.   The members of the party in Parliament, though broadly bound by the policy of the conference, have a large freedom of maneuver in the House, whether in government or in opposition. They are, however, expected to consult the National Executive Committee; this last body, moreover, controls the discipline of the party. Subject to the will of the conference, it endorses the nomination of candidates, may expel members of the party who refuse to accept its decisions, and decides whether or no the circumstances make it desirable to accept the task of government. The parliamentary party elects the leader of the party each session, but the program of the party for a general election is formulated by the National Executive Committee.

5.   While the party has now a considerable staff of paid officials both in London and in the provinces, it relies for by far the larger part of its work on the voluntary efforts of individual members of local constituencies, among whom the women's sections make a particularly notable contribution.

Looking back on the last fifty years, one is struck by how the Labor Party, starting as a small group of trade unionists, Socialists, and cooperatives, has become the greatest Socialist party in Europe, strongly democratic, empirically rather than dogmatically internationalist. It is conscious of the reality of the class war but rejects the Marxian theory of a community which can only be made Socialist by a revolution to establish the dictatorship of the proletariat, which then, by repressing all opposition, passes into the classless society. Since 1917 it has sought with great energy to come to a full understanding with Russia, but the Kremlin, after a brief effort to achieve a united front, has shown little interest in the Labor Party, preferring to support the British Communist Party. At present this situation seems unlikely to change.

The inspiration of British socialism is a compound of various elements, some of which go back to the Great Revolt of 1381, others to the civil wars of the seventeenth century, others to the Chartist movemen of the nineteenth century. It has by no means been uninfluenced by Marx and Engels, by Lenin, and even by Henry George. But the outcome is a peculiarly English one, and the tradition of progress by constitutional consent lies at its roots. That tradition would be difficult to destroy unless it were attacked by the power of wealth or threatened by a third world war. It suffers, probably, by its insufficient attention to Socialist philosophy, which makes it excessively empirical, and by its geographical position, which makes it excessively insular. But nowhere is there a party in which the spirit of fellowship is more profound and the reserve of practical wisdom more remarkable. It may still save Europe by its energy, as it is likely to triumph over the difficulties of its economic position. With all their faults its leaders are notable both for their integrity and their sagacity; its rank and file for their acute sense of fair play. It may lack any figure with the romantic dash and color of Winston Churchill, but it is at least aware that it has to operate in the twentieth and not in the eighteenth century.

The Uses of Translation

BY MARK VAN DOREN

1950

One piece of pedantry we have with us always—a book is not read well unless it is read in its native tongue. Some go farther and say that only then is it read at all: Homer in English has nothing left of his greatness. And so with Dante. And so, presumably, with Cervantes, Rabelais, Montaigne, Pascal, Voltaire, Rousseau, Stendhal, Balzac, and Proust; so with Tolstoy and Dostoevsky; so with Ibsen; so with Goethe; so with Plutarch; so with Lucretius; so with Plato and Aristotle; so with Herodotus and Thucydides; so with St. Augustine and St. Thomas; so with Machiavelli and Molière. So too, of course, with the Bible. If you cannot read Hebrew you will never know anything about Abraham, and if you are not a master of first-century Greek you will have no notion of what Jesus said.

The list, which could be longer, itself reveals the pedantry. Many a person, speaking thus, forgets in his pride of knowing Greek that he knows no Hebrew; or, if he knows some Russian, that he did as a matter of fact first feel Raskolnikov's force through the English of Constance Garnett; or, granting that he reads Russian as Russians do, that he did once, in a moment of inadvertence, enjoy Li Po by way of Ezra Pound. But this is not the biggest mistake he makes. His true crime—the word is scarcely too strong—consists in his ignorance of how the literature of the world has exerted its power. It has exerted it—in the world—by being translated. Only great writers, to be sure, can be translated without deadly loss; the others, having at best a minor, a local virtue, die promptly in foreign air. But it is the great writers that count in the great world; for the great world understands, as none other does, the language of literature. There is the English language, but a few who have used it wrote also in the human tongue,

287

and that tongue—witness Shakespeare—can be comprehended any-where. Even we who are most vain of our knowledge that Shakespeare wrote English as no one else ever has can also take pleasure in contemplating that the Germans once did, and the Russians now do, consider him their best poet. To insist that he is only ours would be to deny his ultimate distinction. It would be, in fact, to expose our incapacity to see what that distinction is. It would prove that we read him badly even in English, as many classical scholars read Homer badly in Greek. They read him, that is to say, without suspecting his immense, his humorous, his natural, his wise, his temperate, his courageous power.

A recent translation of "Don Quixote" has been recommended as the first such translation to render in English the true meaning of that tremendous masterpiece. Those who say this, and by a certain logic they should add that "Don Quixote" should not have been translated at all, tell us that only now can we know—well, what the whole world has known about Cervantes for three hundred years. Comedy at its deepest and best is not a Spanish thing, it is a human thing, it is an intellectual and emotional thing, and somehow neither Fielding nor Dickens missed it; not to speak of a million other readers in whose minds the influence of Cervantes will never be traced. The influence of great literature is universal, and in the course of things works through translation. The Romans did not understand all the Greek they turned into Latin, but without the part they did understand they would have had no literature at all. The Elizabethan Age was ushered in by translations of Plutarch, Montaigne, Seneca, Ovid, and many another ancient or foreign writer without access to whom Shakespeare, for instance, would have been poorer. I have never heard it seriously suggested that he should not have tried his hand at "Julius Caesar" and "Antony and Cleopatra" because North's Plutarch was the only Plutarch he could read. Dryden's Virgil and Pope's Homer created an age of English poetry, just as French translations of English books caused 1789, and just as English translations of German books caused Transcendental-ism.

I am told that I cannot know what Aristotle is saying in his "Po-etics" unless my Greek is perfect, but I must refuse to believe this. I must admit, to be sure, the difficulty of rendering each term precisely as that greatest of literary critics intended it. But another sort of preci-sion in him nobody can miss. It is the precision that guards his mind against the blunder of leaving any important consideration out as he decides what poetry—we would say story—at its fullest is. A complete story, he certainly is saying, will be good in its language, its characters, its scene, its sentiments, its ideas, and its plot—most of all its plot, which is its very soul, and indeed is always the thing an unwise poet manages worst. Modern criticism can praise a novelist or a playwright for one of these virtues alone, and regularly does. To do so is not to ask him for enough, and in the long run is not to get enough. Literature dries up without a living memory of what it is that happens when it uses all its power. Here, finally, is the one use of translation that outmeasures the others. It keeps us open to greatness wherever it may be, and it may be anywhere. As one literature withers another revives it; as one nation of writers forgets its chief business another nation shows it has remembered. Translation keeps literature going in the world. It always has, and it always will unless the pedants have their way. Of course they will not have their way.

Revolution Is Our Business

BY WILLIAM O. DOUGLAS

1952

There is much talk these days of war. I, of course, am not in a position to know, but I have a feeling that the fears of America are often misplaced. I have a feeling that we have misinterpreted and misjudged some of the forces in the world.

Soviet Russia, with its hungry appetite for imperialistic expansion, is a military threat, and America must be prepared, of course. But I don't think there is going to be war with Russia at this time. And why?

I think the stakes involved, the immediate stakes are the stakes of Asia and the Middle East. I think that Soviet Russia will not move in a military way until it has on its side the balance of the people of the world. Freedom and justice and equality are the bulwark against any form of totalitarianism, the most virulent of which is communism. . . .

The great struggles for the world today are at the political level. The battle for Asia is at the political level, and in that sense, I think we in America have misinterpreted the signs of the times. It is my deep conviction that the peoples of Asia cannot be won by guns or by dollars. The peoples of Asia must be won, if they are to be won, with ideas.

I suppose that each of us projects into his personal relationships and into his community relationships, the conflicts he has within himself.

That is inevitable because, after all, we are all human beings. If you do not believe in free speech, if you are afraid of new ideas, of course, you will be panicky and alarmed at people like Nehru of India, who believes in experimentation.

If you are suspicious that every one who has a new idea may be a secret Communist agent representing the Kremlin, of course, you will be suspicious of the peoples of the Middle East who are speaking and working and striving for a higher standard of living for themselves. And, if you practice racial discrimination, if you do not believe that a man is entitled to the same opportunities, whatever his religion, whatever his race, whatever his creed, when you turn to the colored people of Asia, you will be confused and in trouble, because you who are not able to recognize equality at home will not be able to recognize equality abroad.

The worst provincialism of which America can be guilty is the provincialism of prejudice, racial prejudice, prejudice against new and challenging ideas. . . .

The most powerful things in the world are ideas, more powerful than all of the atomic bombs, all of the big guns, all of the airplanes. They are the most dangerous things in the world too.

What is this hold that communism has on people? Mostly ideas, and rather shabby ones at that—ideas borrowed from the West and perverted to the Communist goal.

What is the great, powerful thing of which we are proud in America? What is it that we represent? . . . It is our Declaration of Independence, it is our Constitution, it is our Bill of Rights. Those are the things that set us apart, not our television sets, not our bathroom facilities, not our motor cars, not our buildings, and paved streets. And when the atomic dust settles, if it ever does, we will still have our ideas of brotherhood and freedom and justice and we will go on from there and not turn back.

There are revolutions that are sweeping the world and we in America have been in a position of trying to stop them. With all the wealth of America, with all of the military strength of America, those revolutions cannot be stopped. Those revolutions are revolutions against a form of political and economic organization in the countries of Asia and the Middle East that are oppressive. They are revolutions against feudalism. It is feudalism that is feeding the fires of communism in the Middle East and Asia.

When I say feudalism, I mean a system of economic organization in which a few men own the wealth of the country, where a few men run the politics of a country and where there is a government of the landlords and by the landlords and for the landlords. We do not have that in America. We have in America a broad base for participation in all affairs by everyone. We in America are not perfect. We have much to do, but our standards are right and our ideals are good, and we are striving to live up to them.

But out there in the Middle East and Asia, people like us who have come from the bottom of society, as all of us have, would not have any opportunity.

We would have no schools for our children; we would have no doctors or dentists to take care of ourselves or our families; we would have no hospitals; our income would be barely enough to live on.

We would be tied into a farm-tenancy system in which the owner of the land would get a net return of about 90 per cent or 95 per cent on the crop and we would get 5 per cent or 10 per cent—a bare subsistence. He would own our land, our houses, our oxen, our plows, our water. He would own our souls.

That kind of a system is not going to survive.

People are on the move. I did not fully appreciate that until I got to the Middle East and spent three summers there and saw what was happening in the villages. People are on the march.

Who are their champions today? The underground Communist Party. Why aren't we their champions? Why aren't we in America standing in the villages of the Middle East and Asia and saying we are for economic justice and social justice and we are going to help you, the peasants, achieve your revolution? Not by throwing bombs, of course. Not by smuggling in guns, not by leading armed insurrections. But through revolutions in the political sense.

What do we do instead? We have been supporting corrupt reactionary regimes, putting money behind governments that are vicious governments, reactionary governments, wasting the wealth of America, trying to underwrite the status quo, trying to stabilize the situation, as our officials sometimes say.

The situation cannot be stabilized with all the wealth of the world, with all of the guns of the world. Things are on the move. Revolutions are in the making. The stakes are civilization. Russia is not going to move in a military way, in my opinion, until the balance of power politically swings to Russia in Asia. So I say, let us concentrate our thinking upon Asia and the Middle East and decide, as a result of our own soul-searching, what we do really stand for. . . .

This is a great country and the people are generous and warmhearted and idealistic. There is today, I think a great groping for something that is constructive and positive. There is a growing feeling in this country of utility, of frustration. What we are doing is not succeeding while Russia seems to be having political success after political success.

Russia has been winning by default. With very few exceptions, there is no such thing in the Middle East as political parties as we know them. The only political alternative that the people have had, who have been trying to escape from their misery and their poverty, has been the Communist Party. There are exceptions, but the exceptions are not many. We, in our generosity, go to these countries with a vast Point Four program from a technical point of view. With all our medical skills and public-health services, we can move into the Middle East and Asia and we can improve conditions substantially.

In many parts of the Middle East and Asia, eight out of ten babies die before they reach the age of one; and it would not take very many American technicians to move through that part of the world and to stop that, by cleaning up water supplies, by teaching vaccination, and so on.

But if that is all that is done, if all you do is keep the babies from dying before they reach the age of one, you have done nothing but increase the number of people among whom you will have to ration the poverty.

You can move in to your agricultural areas of Asia and the Middle East with our wonderful Point Four program and increase the production of the land. But if the net return to the tenant is still only 5 per cent, all you are doing is making a few landlords richer.

I am not exaggerating. I do not think we have any idea of the extent to which the feudal system has fastened itself upon that part of the world. It is about the way Europe was before 1000 A. D.

I met men out there who own farming land greater in acreage than the entire state of Switzerland. One man owned 1,600 villages lock, stock, and barrel. Go into those villages with your Point Four program and increase the production of the land and if the owner takes 95 per cent, what have you gained in the struggle against communism?

There are many raw materials in Asia and the Middle East. There are tremendous industrial possibilities there. Those industrial possibilities fill men like Nehru with alarm and deep concern. Why? Your unskilled labor in that part of the world gets around 25 cents a day. Your skilled labor in that part of the world gets about $1 a day.

The standards are not the same as they are here. Conditions are vastly different. Of course, Asia needs industrialization. Of course, the Middle East does too. But it will take years and years to get it, in the American sense, unless there is going to be tremendous exploitation.

It cannot be done quickly. It cannot be done in the typical American way of doing things. It must be slow. One of the things that must be imported along with capital is the organization of unions for the protection of the rights of labor. . . .

When one sees how far back in the train of things the peoples of Asia are, industrially speaking, one begins to appreciate the wisdom of Gandhi when he was arguing for the development of home industries and village industries, rather than these tremendous social cancers that would fasten themselves on Asia and India for the benefit of a few men.

Yes, we must go to the Middle East and we must go to Asia. We must help them. We must go with technical programs. We must also go with social and political ideas. If we do not go with social and political ideas, our technical program will be of little value in saving that part of the world from Soviet imperialism.

Abraham Lincoln said that the Declaration of Independence was an instrument forged not only for the benefit of Americans on this continent, but one destined to lift the weight off the shoulders of men the world around. That is what people in the backward areas think.

Let us be true to our great traditions. Let us go to the world with ideas of freedom and justice. Let us make the revolutions. Let us make sure that when our technical people go into the villages of the Middle East and Asia the people of the villages know on which side America stands.

You cannot go into those villages and be there a week without taking sides. You are either for the landlord or you are for the peasants. Before we go, let us make up our mind whom we are for; and if we cannot make up our mind, we should not go. If we can hitch the few dollars that we have and the much knowledge that we have to a few simple ideas of economic democracy and political democracy and social justice, and be heard in that part of the world as the advocates of economic and social and political democracy, the red tide of communism will turn. Then we of the West will make a political victory; we will have Asia and the Middle East on our side; we will save those people from the curse of Soviet imperialism. Those are things that we must go to the world with.

We have been hesitant, we have been afraid. We have poured billions of dollars into Europe, and we did necessarily, I think; but we have never hitched much of our European dollars to ideas.

Why do you think the number of Communists have been increasing in France and in Italy? Why do you think they have been growing? Because we have not hitched our dollars to ideas. Unless we hitch our few dollars to ideas, unless we are forthright in our dealings in the Middle East and in Asia, we are going to go down in history as identified with the worst reactionary imperialistic forces, apart from Soviet Russia, that the world has known. That is not fair to America nor to her people, because America is not made up of people who want to do that kind of thing.

We believe not in terror, but in tolerance; we believe in justice for everyone, regardless of his political faith, his racial origins, or his religious creeds. Those are the strongest ideas that have ever been let loose in the world.

Gogol: The Demon in the Overgrown Garden

BY EDMUND WILSON

1952

The centenary of Gogol's death, February 21, was celebrated by Russians both here and at home and made the subject of a conference at Columbia, but it has not, so far as I know, brought forth any writing in English except a small book by Janko Lavrin, a professor of Slavonic languages at Nottingham University in England: "Nikolai Gogol: A Centenary Survey" (Sylvan Press, distributed by Macmillan). Professor Lavrin is not much of a critic and not much of a master of English, but in his unpretentious way he has been doing useful work in introducing Russian writers to the English-speaking world, and this book has its value for us because it treats certain phases of Gogol's life more satisfactorily than either D. S. Mirsky in his "History of Russian Literature" or Vladimir Nabokov in his own little book on the subject. Both these writers give a rather blurred picture of Gogol's depressing later years, but Professor Lavrin follows, stage by stage, his subject's agonized attempts to find in religion a force that would lift him to the level of the mission—the mission, as he conceived it, of the great Russian writer—of which he had tormenting glimpses but which he never felt confident of being able to fulfil.

The present writer proposes to make use of Professor Lavrin's book as a pretext for adding his own word to the current commemoration of this very great writer, the least read and understood in English of the five Russian masters of fiction. It should be noted that an excellent edition of Gogol in six small and cheap volumes has recently been published in the Soviet Union, so that most of his work is now more accessible than it had been for many years, during which the pre-Soviet sets were bringing enormous prices. This new edition is not quite complete, for it omits, along with a number of lesser things, almost the whole of Gogol's last published book, "Selected Passages from Correspondence with Friends," in which he expressed his reactionary views, but the volumes are well printed and handy, equipped with adequate notes, and full of curious illustrations from the old editions. (Constance Garnett's six-volume translation is unfortunately out of print, but Mr. Nabokov speaks well of B. G. Guerney's more recent translation of "The Overcoat," "The Inspector General," and "Dead Souls.") The writer has been using this Soviet edition to fill up the gaps in his reading of Gogol and has now been through all his principal works in Russian; so to this extent, at least, he is qualified to write on the subject. It is always rather dangerous for a foreigner who has to work at reading an author to argue about the classics of another country with people who have known them all their lives. (Though Professor Lavrin is a Slovene, he is evidently at home in Russian.) There are sometimes extremely important things about relative rank and quality that the foreigner cannot know, because he has read only scattered works and does not see the whole development of a literature. I have tried to bear in mind, in this connection, a remark that Jean Cocteau once made to me: "Maupassant is a great writer in Russian." Yet the very necessity for the foreigner of paying close attention to every sentence may prevent the story from carrying him along so fast that he fails to notice exactly what is being said and how the author is saying it; and to come fresh to an accepted classic with a mature and unprejudiced mind may make it possible for him to see certain things that have been obscured for readers to whom the language is native, by childhood associations or conventional interpretations. One sometimes has this experience with the works of one's own literature—as when one only discovers in later life the beauty and the meaning of some play of Shakespeare's that bored one when one read it at school.

Apropos of the first of these points and before going on to the second, a word about the impression made by Gogol's style on the reader who attacks him with a dictionary. None of the other Russian classics, so far as my experience goes, presents so many obstacles to the foreigner. The paragraphs confront one like solid walls; the sentences seem to go on for pages. The vocabulary is queer and enormous. In Gogol's Ukrainian stories, the Ukrainian dialect is a factor that has to be reckoned with, as one has to reckon with Scottish in Scott, and the glossaries provided by Gogol himself fall far short of being complete—though the new editors have done something to supplement them. Then, Gogol was fond of collecting the vocabularies of special occupations and classes as well as the local dialects, and he liked to invent words. You should not be disheartened when you meet, for example, on the threshold of the brilliant fragment "Rome" the rebarbative

word *ishcher*, which is not given in the most comprehensive dictionary, and learn at last from the notes of this new edition that we have
only Gogol's assurance that this is an "authentic Russian word" meaning "live coal." If you persist, Gogol's spell will conduct you over all
these stumbling blocks; I know of no equally demanding writer who
will give you more for your trouble. Gogol rarely produced a sentence
that was not interesting from the literary point of view—that is, from
the point of view of the special use of language to create impressions—
and any one of his far-stretching paragraphs will contain so much
poetry and humor, apt phrasing and unexpected imagery, that it makes
one's slow-going delightful. It is as if one were steadily consuming a
big bowl of Ukrainian soup, full of cabbage and beets and potatoes,
chunks of sturgeon and shreds of beef or duck, with a foundation of
sour cream—not that I know of any such Russian soup (they usually
have fewer ingredients), but then there is no other writer who seems
so to have mixed in everything.

Gogol's style is a variety of that viscous prose which—for reasons
rather difficult to understand—was so popular in the early nineteenth
century. The plum cake of Charles Lamb is a typical example; so, in a
different field, is the maddeningly impeded narrative style of a Hawthorne or a Herman Melville. This style allows no rapid progression. A
paragraph seems a mere clot of words, which might almost as well be
read backward as forward and in which the contrived rhythms have
the air of being ends in themselves, since they are always forcing the
reader to stop and pay attention to them instead of carrying him along.
This style must have been due to some very strong pressures, for it is
shared by a relatively careless writer who worked on a big scale, like
Balzac; and even by a popular writer, like Scott, who did want to tell a
story. The settings of the stage in Balzac, the antiquarian preliminaries
of Scott, are often mare's-nests of this littered non-functional style,
which combines the facetious with the pompous, clumsily handled
actualities with jaunty mythological allusions. Now, Gogol is the master of the mare's-nest. Though he may seem to be merely stirring
round and round his thick and nutritious pages, as if they were the
strawberry boiled preserve, or the *kasha* to be eaten with currants or
honey, or the dough full of hazelnuts and poppy-seeds for one of the
fancier forms of the rich polymorphous Ukrainian bread that his country people are always eating, this invariably results in a finished dish,
which contributes to a well-arranged dinner. The Russian genius for
movement, which is one of the great features of Russian literature—I
make no apology in this connection for continually changing the
metaphor—never allows Gogol's prose to get really stuck; there is
always a drama on foot that you know will not let you down, and in

the meantime the rhapsodies, the inventories, the interpolated anecdotes, and the huge, Homeric similes that are whole short stories in
themselves are managed with a great sense of rhetoric, so that they do
not hold anything up, and they always become in some curious way
organic parts of the story. With so much that might be stifling or
stagnant, like the life that Gogol depicts, there is always something
else that creates suspense—an element of the passionate, the *détraqué*,
that may startle us at any moment. In these pages, which in style
resemble the tangled forests and the overgrown gardens that are a
recurrent motif in Gogol's work, from his earliest goblin tales to
Plushkin's estate in "Dead Souls," astounding transformations take
place: a devil will suddenly appear at the turn of a paragraph, a treas-
ure will be revealed—though the treasures are mirages arranged by the
devils—but, as is not always the case with the Gothic novels or the
Hoffmannesque tales from which Gogol derived, these visions have a
force of emotion, and intense identity and life of their own, that make
even Poe seem cerebral and such fancies of Hawthorne's as the "Minister's Black Veil" and the "Black Sabbath of Young Goodman Brown,"
mere phantoms of woven words.

I am still speaking of the early Ukrainian stories—"Evenings on a
Farm Near Dikanka" and its successor, the "Mirgorod" series—and this
brings me to my second point: the chance that a foreign reader may be
able to grasp certain things more readily than a native one. I am going
to presume to register dissent from some of the accounts of these tales
that we have had from Lavrin, Nabokov, and Mirsky. This is the
department of Gogol's work that is most taken for granted by Russians. They first read these stories as fairy tales or farces about comic
villagers. "It was . . . this kind of stuff," says Nabokov, "the juvenilia
of the false humorist Gogol, that teachers in Russian schools crammed
down a fellow's throat. . . . After a lapse of perhaps twenty-five years I
forced myself to reread the 'Evenings'—and I remained as unmoved as
I had been in the days when my teacher could not understand why
'The Terrible Vengeance' did not make my flesh creep or 'Shponka
and His Aunt' did not make me rock with laughter." "Taras Bulba,"
the longest of the Mirgorod stories, is apparently prescribed to Russian
children somewhat as "Ivanhoe" is, or was, prescribed to ours—as an
exciting historical romance. It celebrates the exploits of the Cossacks at
a period, rather vaguely indicated, in the sixteenth or seventeenth century when they were fighting the Poles and the Tartars. Yet if one
comes to these stories after reading "Dead Souls," one sees that they are
a good deal closer to Gogol's later work than Mr. Nabokov, for example, is willing to admit. Taras Bulba himself has a good deal in

common with the boorish and maniacal landowners encountered by Chichikov in "Dead Souls." In spite of the heroic element, in spite of Gogol's interpolation of passages that imitate the language of the folk ballad or the epic, he cannot help making his Cossack chieftain—who gratuitously starts a war in order to give his two sons a field for exhibiting their prowess, then unhesitatingly shoots down one of them when, infatuated with a Polish princess, the boy has gone over to the Poles, and avenges the death of the other, who has been captured and executed by the enemy, by laying waste the whole of Poland—less a hero than a comic monster. If Pushkin exclaimed over "Dead Souls," "God, how sad Russia is!" he might have said of this earlier epic, "How horrible old Russia was!" And the arrival of Taras in the Warsaw ghetto in which he is to hide for a time launches Gogol on a characteristic but quite non-heroic episode of magnificent comic squalor.

Nor is the household in "The Old-World Landowners," the first of the Mirgorod stories, really so different from the households of "Dead Souls" as one would gather from the descriptions of this story by Mirsky and Lavrin (and Mr. Nabokov quotes Mirsky with approval). The first of these critics says of it that "the vegetable humors of the old pair, their sloth, their gluttony, their selfishness, are idealized and sentimentalized, and pathetic sympathy is the main emotion evoked in the reader." Gogol, says Lavrin, "disgusted by the noise and whirl of a big town," had turned this old man and his wife "into an embodiment of his own idea of peace and of that unruffled pastoral world which he had known in his childhood." The chronicle of their gluttony, he continues, conveys "no implication of moral censure, since the whole of it is but an example of man's 'return to nature,' to the contentment of the vanishing or vanished patriarchal ways," etc. But is it true that this old-world couple are much idealized by Gogol? Does he really approve of their plantlike life? The climax of the story comes when the old lady's cat is lured away by the outlaw cats that live in the woods but creep in through a hole under the barn. The pet comes back to be fed (as the old man is always being fed); then, when her mistress reaches out to stroke her, she escapes to freedom again. The old lady takes this at once as a sign that death has come for her. She feels, no doubt, that the cat has deserted her, but an impression is also created that this life of peace, comfort, and overeating, which is not enough for the cat, is not enough for her either. Yet she cannot slip away like the cat, she can only escape by dying. Over the old man's grief at her death Gogol is certainly eloquent but hardly sentimental; the author makes it plain that his mourning for his wife is also a vegetable affair, that he misses her out of "habit," not "passion." The quickly spent emotions of youth seem childish, the author says, beside this long and slow habituation to another human being on the part of a man "who has never been moved by any strong feeling but whose life has simply consisted of sitting in a high chair, eating dried pears and mushrooms, and taking part in amiable conversations." But we do not get the impression that Gogol would be satisfied with such an existence. No: this household, too, is a jungle, a condition stuffed with sensual gratifications that can never be enough for the soul, a way of life in which, sooner or later, things are bound to take a queer turn. A wild impulse, an unearthly summons, may suddenly upset everything. The cats from the forest have crept in like devils. The widower, walking in the orchard, by whose fruit trees with their succulent fruit he, too, has been overgrown, thinks one day that he hears his wife calling him, and this proves to be an omen of his death. Gogol tells us here that sometimes in his childhood he has imagined, on a bright and quiet day, that he heard a voice calling his name and has fled to find some other human being who would relieve him of his sense of desolation. No night of raging storm, he says, in the heart of a pathless forest could have frightened him so much as that terrible silence in the midst of a cloudless day. This is a subtle and disturbing story, of which the *Gemütlichkeit* is not the author's but a part of the subject; yet Marc Slonim, in his recent book "The Epic of Russian Literature," seems to be the only critic in English who has gone even so far as to mention that "under the surface" of it "there lurks Gogol's usual dread of insignificance and triviality."

As for the celebrated "Quarrel of the Two Ivans," as Lavrin abridges the title, it seems to me a typical example of the classic which everybody knows so well—it is invoked by Russians like the "Alice" books—that no one any longer pays attention to it. It is assumed to be a hilariously funny story—though with a famous sigh and shrug at the end—that exploits a ridiculous quarrel between two queer and crotchety old men, one of whom has called the other a goose. Russians refer to it with the ready-made grin that we have for Tom Sawyer painting the fence or old Weller telling the court to spell his name with a "we." Neither from Lavrin's account of this tale nor from that of any other of these critics would one be able to get any idea of what it is really about, for they all make the quarrel appear meaningless. Lavrin does make it clear that the story is fundamentally bitter but tells us only that the issue between the two old cronies is that "Ivan Ivanovich wanted to buy from his friend an old gun the latter would not part with." Actually, the trouble is that Ivan Ivanovich cannot bear the feeling of inferiority inflicted by the sight of his neighbor's maid hanging out on the line a whole wardrobe of old uniforms, old dress clothes, and other signs of his friend's superior rank, and that he begs Ivan Nikophorovich to give him the gun in order to induce the latter to confer on him some sign of equality. The quarrel could never be healed because Ivan Nikophorovich could never refrain, in a crisis, from treating Ivan Ivanovich *de haut en bas*, and Ivan Ivanovich could equally never forgive this. It is a tragedy of provincial snobbery destroying good human relations in a community so dismal and dull that one might think people would try to preserve them—though the point is, of course, that it was inevitable that Ivan I.'s vulgar insistence should incite Ivan N. to insolence and that, for men with nothing to do, a war of spite that involves a class issue may, by stimulating a certain excitement, prove more satisfactory than a peaceful friendship. In any case, the two Ivans, in their humble way, are monsters, too, that lead up to the more formidable monsters to be later encountered in "Dead Souls."

From "Dead Souls" all the glory has departed of ancient Ukrainian legend as well as the amusing mythology of Ukrainian peasant lore, and even the gentleness and decency of the comfortable "old-world landowners." We are submerged in the messy and stuffy and smelly and run-to-seed life of landowners who are drunken and quarrelsome, moping and ineffective, brutal and self-assertive or crazily acquisitive or stupidly grasping. After an opening almost Pickwickian, with a man putting up at an inn, this strange book, which never ceases to be humorous, leads us into a domain of horror: another and ranker jungle that is also a stagnant morass. Gogol wallows, like his characters, in the paragraphs of a cluttered, apparently phlegmatic style that has now been brought to perfection; yet this style has a persistent undercurrent of sadness, of disgust, of chagrin; it condemns and it undermines. There is still the same queer suspense that is sometimes disrupted by violence but is never completely relieved. What, we ask ourselves, is meant by this chronicle of Chichikov, the empty soul, who buys up the names of serfs (referred to as "souls" in old Russia) that have died since the last census, in order to pretend he owns them and borrow money on them? Are not the souls of their masters also dead? Are these landowners really devils who appear to Chichikov or is he himself a devil who has come for *them*? Exposed in the district he has been working, he is last seen driving away in his carriage. There is a moment of respite and open horizons—the troika dashing off with its cheerful bells. In this torpid and moldy Russia, something has been set in motion, and Gogol has a moment of exaltation. But where is it going? he asks, and the horizon returns no answer. Nor is he able to escape from this world that is tedious as well as mad; nor has he power to redeem his hero through the Purgatory he plans to succeed this Hell. In the fragments that have come to us of the Second Part, the adventurer Chichikov, though sent to jail, seems to emerge just as much of a scoundrel, and the supposedly virtuous characters are the victims of obsessions like those of the First.

Gogol's life was full of absurdities, and Mr. Nabokov takes advantage of them, rather cruelly, to make his last phase ridiculous. It becomes somewhat more comprehensible in the account of it by Mr. Lavrin. Poor Gogol, who felt it his duty to supply his public with something more positive, to answer himself the question he had sent after the flying troika, now resorted to a sort of sham fanaticism, set up as a preacher and teacher, and published the "Selected Passages from Correspondence with Friends," in which he glorified the Russian land-owner as the agent of God on earth and opposed the education of the peasants, who, he said, should not be allowed even to know of the existence of any book but the Bible. But the indignant retorts of his friends, toward whom he had adopted a didactic tone, seem seriously to have shaken his self-confidence. He came to feel that, for all his pretensions, he had not really yet found God. He visited Palestine in the hope of a new revelation but could not find Him even there, and he finally came under the influence of a strong-minded Russian priest who, bigoted and ignorant of literature, tried to persuade him to give up writing. Ten days before his death—at the insistence, perhaps, of this priest—he burned up the Second Part of "Dead Souls," on which he had spent years of work, then declared that this had been a mistake, that the Devil had induced him to do it.

The typical situation in Gogol is the sudden falling-out of the bottom of some impressive construction that we have watched being elaborately built. You have, thus, the dissolution of the old-world landowners; the loss of Taras Bulba's sons; the explosion between the two Ivans; the theft of the overcoat in the famous later story; the cataclysmic discoveries, too late, in the plays, of the large-scale imposture of "The Inspector General" and of the confidence game in "The Gamblers," the abject jumping out the window of the fiancé of "Marriage" at the moment when, with infinite difficulty, his betrothal has been achieved; the breakdown of Chichikov's fraudulent traffic just in his hour of triumph when he is fêted as the toast of the town. So Gogol and his great book, at the moment when Turgenev says that all attention in Russia was centered on him and it, unexpectedly collapsed together.

Gogol presents an unusual case of a frustrating impasse of the spirit, a hopeless neurotic deadlock, combined with a gusto for life, an enormous artistic vitality. So vigorous and so rich is this talent that it must have been difficult for his friends and his readers to foresee that it was doomed to be choked. Lavrin suggests that the trouble may be traced to an Oedipus complex, an explanation suggested so often that it is coming to seem rather suspect. There is, however, no doubt that Gogol's defeat was bound up with his lifelong failure to arrive at any satisfactory sexual life. Fear of marriage is made the comic theme of the story of "Shponka and His Aunt," deliberately left unfinished, and of the rather inferior comedy "Marriage," and Gogol's difficulties in this connection appear in another kind of theme, which he never succeeds in developing: that of the ideal woman, seen briefly and adored from afar—the maidenly *pensionnaire* who makes such an impression on Chichikov; the Italian beauty who gleams in the crowd for the hero of the projected novel on Rome. The magnificent opening of this novel has far more of positive inspiration than anything that has survived from the Second Part of "Dead Souls." Gogol's longing for a feudal world becomes somewhat more sympathetic when it is dramatized in the person of an Italian prince returning from impoverished exile to discover for the first time his native Rome, but at the moment when it at last becomes necessary, after the long, the monumental buildup, to bring the prince into direct relations with the dazzling Annunziata, the story abruptly breaks off. In "Viy," of the Mirgorod series, the traveler and the beauty—both Gogol and his heroes are always traveling—do engage, but with a fatal result, and that this fatal result was inevitable to Gogol's vision of life is shown by the turn that he seems to have given to the folk tale from which he derived the story. This is a version of the vampire legend in which a young man must stand watch for three nights by the body of a dead woman, who at midnight comes to life and attacks him. Gogol says that he has followed the folk tale exactly, but in the versions of this story included in the collection of Afanasiev, the Russian Grimm, the young man is always able to defend himself with the Psalter and the sign of the Cross, and finally defeats the witch; and, from these and from the habits of folk tales in general, we may assume that it is Gogol himself —the solid Ukrainian background, more or less realistically presented, is certainly very much Gogol's—who is responsible for making his student succumb at the third vigil and fall dead with fright when the vampire calls in the reinforcements of Hell (just as, in "Taras Bulba," the young Andréy is destroyed through the irresistible spell that has been cast on him by the Polish princess). It should be noted that the girl is revenging herself. She had fastened herself first on the student in the shape of an old hag, and he had only got rid of her by beating her to death, at which point she had been forced to reveal herself as the typical Gogolian beauty, intimidating and unattainable. In a final ironic scene, the boy's former companions on the walking trip that has had for him this tragic end—back in college now and warming over their cups—are discussing his fate at their ease. Not having had to share his ordeal, they decide that if he had not been yellow, the witch could have done him no harm: "You've only got to cross yourself and spit on her tail, and nothing can happen to you!" But this rite had never worked for Gogol. It was always the Devil who appeared to him, never the Savior he hoped for, and when the feminine apparition toward whom he aspired comes at all close to any of his heroes, she proves to be a devil, too.

It was only to Dostoevsky, in the next generation, that the Christian revelation came. It is one of the striking features of the continuity of Russian literature that Dostoevsky should not only show strongly the literary influence of Gogol but that he should even give somewhat the impression of being haunted by Gogol's devils and even of saving Gogol's soul.

The Irregular Right

BY C. P. SNOW

1956

The other night I was standing in the bar of a London club and some-one mentioned a book about the Spanish Civil War. The club happens to be one for professional men, in particular for writers: most of those in the bar that night had been friends or acquaintances of mine for a long time. As we talked, I was thinking what we had been doing politically twenty years ago. Without exception—there were half a dozen men present, all between forty and fifty—we had been passionately on the Left in that war. One had fought in the anti-Franco armies; the rest had worked on committees, lobbied M. P.'s, marched in what used to be called "Demo's"—all of us totally committed.

Now, twenty years after, there was a change. It was not so much that they had denied their past; they believed they had been right, and in the same circumstances would have done the same again. But, as it was, in the England of 1956, the dividing line had vanished; there did not seem to be a fighting-point anymore. Several of these men had last year voted Conservative for the first time in their lives. Not with enthusiasm, not with the ruthlessness of converts; it did not seem to matter much.

Well, there is nothing surprising in middle-aged men moving to the Right. In itself that is just commonplace and would not be worth mentioning. What is surprising is that my acquaintances are still the last relics of the radical intellectuals. Despite their changes, despite the softening effect of the English official embrace (the most subtle, the least conscience-disturbing, of all the official embraces in the world), these men are still far more radical and opposition-minded than the intellectuals who have grown up after them. In England the middle-aged may have moved to the Right: but the young have started there. At the moment the intelligensia is less rebellious than it has been for two centuries.

I do not mean anything so trivial as that a large proportion of young intellectuals would now call themselves Tories, though that is true. The major point is that they accept the Establishment and on all fundamental issues feel in their fibres that it is both satisfactory and certain to persist. It is because this state of affairs is so manifest that the concept of the Establishment had to be invented. One has to live in the English air to know by instinct and in detail what the Establishment means—but broadly, it is an agreement, entirely unspoken and very largely unconscious, to preserve substantially the present web of power-relations. It extends at least as much to the cultural and educational status quo as to the political; prominent agencies of the Establishment are both Front Benches, the General Council of the Trade Union Congress, vice-chancellors of universities, anyone engaged in running public (i.e., private) schools, the BBC, the administrative class of the civil service, all bodies and persons connected with what, twenty years ago, was *avant garde* art, the entire respectable press.

Like all Establishments, ours reveals itself more clearly in little things than big. You can tell it when, without any prearrangement, it does not argue so much as sing in unison. There was a curious example last year. That old malcontent Richard Aldington—who is not the easiest of men, and has always been an anti-Establishment writer—produced an intemperate and denigratory biography of T. E. Lawrence. Before it was published, any of us could have written the reviews—the moral indignation, the seemly rebukes, the herding-together round the cultural totem against this rude voice from outside. That was the public voice everywhere. The Establishment voice. Yet in private, it is now tacitly assumed that in at least 80 per cent of his case, Aldington was right.

Only three sizeable groups of intellectuals stand outside the Establishment. The first, and by far the most important in functional terms, are the scientists, or at least a sizeable slice of them: but their curious place in English intellectual life is another subject. Then there is a collection of young literary people, often teachers of English, brought up under the influence of F. R. Leavis, who do not exactly oppose the Establishment so much as passively contract out. In literature they are building up a new school of analytical criticism, at the same time high-spirited, puritanical and disrespectful (they also include at least two creative writers of real talent, Kingsley Amis and Philip Larkin). Culturally they are very far from negligible; but politically they go in for a kind of rough-neck neutralism, mitigated only by outbursts on questions of social manners: for example, the abolition of hanging.

The only genuine anti-Establishment group comes, however, from the irregular Right. Henry Fairlie, the political columnist of *The Spectator* (which used to be the staidest of the Conservative weeklies and has suddenly gone in for a wild eccentric fling) is the most bitter enemy of all the Establishment stands for. So is Malcolm Muggeridge, the anarchical editor of a similarly renovated *Punch*. Another enemy is John Raymond, the most brilliant of the young journalists. Yet he, with some ambivalence, and Fairlie and Muggeridge without any ambivalence at all, would claim to be men of the Right. Now I do not believe much in any kind of irregular Right. People starting there are liable to finish at best in the seedier kinds of invitation-hunting, at worst in Maurrasism and its crueller counterparts. Nevertheless, the interesting thing is that men like Raymond possess a generous social feeling; in temperament and outlook they are much more like the left-wing rebels of twenty years ago than any other group of their contemporaries.

It is time someone examined why the Establishment has come to sit so firmly, why the English intellectuals have suddenly become domesticated. I suspect it is the pattern of intellectual behavior in a social democracy, particularly in a social democracy which is getting internally tidier at a time when its external power is, relative to the outside world, going down. From the little I know of Sweden, I believe something not dissimilar happened there earlier in the century.

There are, of course, advantages in a society where the intellectual differences have been damped down: a lot of frictions and fears disappear when there is such a homogeneity of mood. The English society of today is probably more miscellaneously tolerant than any large one has ever been, particularly (not in law but in climate of opinion) in sexual matters. In the autumn debate of Burgess and Maclean, the speeches both of Harold Macmillan and Eden were models of tolerant humanism. There was nothing surprising in that from Macmillan, who is exceptionally intelligent and liberal-minded, a good deal of a sport among Tory politicians. But to hear a Prime Minister speaking in the gentle accents of E. M. Forster was something I, for one, never expected to witness.

But what we have gained on those swings we have lost on other roundabouts. Our transition to the welfare state has sometimes been called a peaceful revolution; but in a profound sense it was the reverse of a revolution. It has not loosened the social-power relations, but stiffened them; the forms of society have been rigidifying under our eyes. Any revolution triggers free the energy of an emerging class; in our transition, far from any such energy being released, it has been confined and has only found an outlet in a kind of play, a newly-invented fashion of triviality.

There is one example which shows how intellectuals have shifted to the Right and how they are driven to occupy themselves. For months past, one topic of conversation has been springing out all over the place: which speech usages are Upper Class (U) or non-Upper Class (non-U)? You will hear intelligent men from the social origins of Newton and Rutherford and Dickens hurriedly correct themselves after saying "mirror" (which is non-U) and substitute "looking-glass." I have several times recently been asked to "luncheon" by people who have never before used the word in their lives. In the kind of home where I was brought up, no one would have dreamed of talking of anything but a "mantlepiece" but I find acquaintances from identical homes—who ought to know better—proving their social knowledge-ableness by bringing into the conversation "chimneypiece" (which, according to the researches of Professor A. S. C. Ross, is most emphatically "U").

It is a joke, but it is not a very good joke. In the twenties and thirties, intellectuals would have had something less ant-like to talk about. There are plenty now, of course, who are getting impatient. We are writing some good books. But I am looking for a cruder sign of returning health. The one I should welcome most is a serious intellectual row.

Post-Stalin Shock

BY G. D. H. COLE

1956

It is obviously much too soon to make any definitive estimate of the effects of recent changes in the Soviet Union on either the Socialist Parties of the West or the Communist Parties which dispute with them the allegiance of the working class in the Western countries. It is still far from clear whether the Russians themselves have now moved as far as their leaders are minded to go, or whether the momentum of the decisions already taken will speedily carry them a long way further, whether they will or no. No more can be attempted at present than a highly provisional estimate of the impact on Western Communists and Socialists of the dethronement of Stalin.

I had better stress most what I feel I know most of—the personal reactions of Communists and left-wing Socialists with whom I have had some individual contact. I should explain first of all my own record and attitude in relation to communism. I need hardly say that I have never been either a Communist or what is called a "fellow-traveler," because the socialism I have always believed in is of a sort in which great stress is laid not only on personal freedom of speech and organization, but also on the need for diversity and for the widest possible diffusion of power and responsibility. In social philosophy I have been always a *pluralist*, rejecting the notion that absolute sovereignty belongs to any single person or group and insisting that the proper basis for the organization of a free society must be *functional*, with power and responsibilities split up and shared between co-operating but autonomous agencies, so as to leave the individual free to choose his own primary allegiance instead of being subjected more than is unavoidable to a centralized authority over which he is too weak to have any effective control. I am still, in fact, what is known as a "Guild Socialist"; and I can imagine no kind of Socialist more entirely immune from the contagion of the "power" concepts which underlie Communist doctrine.

Nevertheless, I have always regarded, and continue to regard, the Bolshevik Revolution in Russia as a tremendous and admirable achievement, and have recognized that, given the conditions of Czarism and the enmity shown towards the revolution by the capitalist world, it was unavoidable for it to take a highly authoritarian form. It would have been quite impossible to carry through the revolution in Russia, or to maintain it against its adversaries, without the presence of a highly disciplined party prepared to take strong, and even ruthless, action and to gather power into its own hands with little regard for those liberal values of which the Russian peoples have had no experience at all. To deny the right to such action is equivalent to saying that the Russian Revolution either ought not to have happened at all or ought to have allowed itself to go down to defeat at the hands of its enemies, who were certainly no less ruthless than the Bolsheviks were forced to be. I have therefore always refused to join in denunciations of the Communists based on ignoring or denying these hard necessities; and I have no patience with those so-called Socialists who are first and foremost anti-Communists—and Socialists, if at all, only a long way after. I try, however, to distinguish between those evils which arose unavoidably out of the condition of Czarist Russia and the perversions which I think could have been avoided without lessening the prospects of revolutionary success.

The danger that such perversions would occur was, I feel sure, inherent in the fundamental doctrine of the Communist Party as it was worked out by Lenin well before 1917. This danger is indeed inherent to some extent in all revolutionary action directed to bringing about fundamental changes in the structure of society; for such revolution involves both destroying the old order root and branch and building up the new order under circumstances in which it is out of the question to observe the niceties of democratic behavior. In a revolutionary situation—above all, in such a situation as existed in Russia in 1917—great concentration of power was inescapable; and it is always much easier to concentrate power than to disperse it afterwards.

In my view, two things went wrong in Russia from an early stage. The first was the attempt to impose the Russian pattern of revolution on the whole world, to be pursued everywhere by the same methods. This was Lenin's error as much as it was anyone's; and it led directly to the splitting of the world Socialist movement so as to destroy its chances of victory in the West—above all, in Germany. The second error was not Lenin's, but primarily Stalin's. It consisted of what Trotsky at once denounced as the "bureaucratization" of the Communist Party under Stalin's manipulative control, with the effect of destroying the interior democracy of the party and replacing "*democratic* centralism" by centralism without democracy. Trotsky saw this degeneration of the party being brought about well before Lenin's death, and denounced Stalin for it in his famous booklet, *The New Course;* but he was unable to affect the trend and became the first of Stalin's victims.

The present leaders of the Soviet Union have advanced some way towards a denunciation of both these errors. They are now admitting the possibility of alternative roads to socialism—though it is still by no means clear how far this admission extends; and they are attacking the "cult of personality," for which the bureaucratization of the party laid the foundation, but have so far failed to trace the growth of the cult back to its origins in the middle twenties, when Stalin was busy converting the party into his personal power-machine.

In reacting to the attacks on Stalin launched by Khrushchev and others at the Twentieth Congress, Western Communists and Socialists alike have been almost compelled to consider first of all what attitude to take up towards the blackguardly features now admitted to have been present in the Stalinist regime, at any rate during its later stages. The anti-Communists have naturally tended to say, first of all, "We told you so," and to suggest that the official "repentance" has not yet gone nearly far enough, in that what has been most at fault has been not Stalin's personal shortcomings as a moral being, but rather the infection of the entire Soviet society with a deep-seated disease of totalitarian immoralism inseparable from the basic concepts of centralism and the one-party state. The Communists, no less naturally, have for the most part not seen the matter at all in this light, but have in many cases been deeply revolted by the revelations of trumped-up charges leading to the shameful liquidation of good, honest revolutionaries whom Stalin felt to stand in his way. Such Communists have experienced, first and foremost, a sense of personal shame in having allowed themselves to be deceived into defending the indefensible— and in the process telling a great many lies it now hurts them to remember. In effect, these Communists have relapsed into a condition which less sensitive-minded comrades regard as contemptible bourgeois or petit-bourgeois moralizing, quite unworthy of being entertained by anyone who sets out to guide his course by the star of historic determinism.

These tough-minded Communists may regret that Stalin made serious "mistakes"—which were mistakes because they harmed the revolutionary cause—but feel no moral reprobation, even if the "mistakes" led to the wrongful condemnation, execution and disgrace of good comrades, whom they regard as having suffered in a good cause. Stalin's sins are thus reduced to mere errors of judgment; and no conclusions are drawn except that it is necessary to avoid endowing any individual with the arbitrary power which made such immense "mistakes" possible. It is assumed that collective leadership will somehow provide an assurance of better sense—*not* that there was anything in the system of centralism and one-party government that accounted for them. Thus, there are two sharply opposed reactions; one of which rests on moral revulsion, whereas the other, rejecting such a revulsion as "bourgeois" moralizing, admits mistakes, but does its best to minimize their seriousness by insisting on the greatness of Stalin's revolutionary contribution.

So far, the signs of moral revulsion have been clearest of all in Poland, and least clear of all in France. The French Communists, indeed, appear to be standing pat and to be going as near as they dare to ignoring the whole matter; whereas the Poles seem to have reacted very strongly, not so much against Stalin personally as against the entire concept of centralized discipline and suppression of freedom of speech. The Italians seem to stand between these extremes. Togliatti has pertinently observed that the present leaders of the Soviet Union cannot be allowed to evade their share of responsibility for the occurrences they have now been moved to denounce, and has thus thrown doubt on the view that collective leadership can be relied on to correct the errors now attributed exclusively to the cult of personality. This attitude may well be due in part to the fact that the Italian Communist Party is much closer to the main Italian Socialist Party—that of Nenni —than other Western Communists are to their Socialist Parties: so that Togliatti has to take account of the likelihood of defections to the Nenni party unless he tries honestly to face the reality of what has been disclosed.

The Yugoslav Communists are placed in a quite different situation from either the French or the Italians. During their quarrel with the Comintern they went a long way not only in relaxing the control of free speech and of personal freedom but also in decentralizing the regime by a real diffusion of power, functionally as well as locally, into the hands of committees and councils representing the "common man" —or at all events the local citizen and rank-and-file producer. The Yugoslav leaders had good reason to know the truth about Stalin long before the Twentieth Congress, which actually took place at a moment when they were busily engaged in restoring good relations with the Soviet Union and therewith emphasizing their differences with the Western "democracies." They were accordingly not at all minded to extend their case against Stalin into a general case against the political system of the Soviet Union.

In comparison with the parties so far mentioned, it is of small account how the Communist Party of Great Britain reacts, because it has so little working-class backing and counts for so little in influencing the course of events. Nobody outside the narrow ranks of the CPGB cares much what line it takes. But of course its members do care a great deal; and there is every sign that they are sharply divided among themselves. Of their most notable leaders, Harry Pollitt, who has been removed from his post as general secretary, has ceased to count; and his successor, John Gollan, is still something of a dark horse. Palme Dutt, the outstanding intellectual of the party, belongs unquestionably to the amoralist wing which wishes to play down Stalin's "mistakes" and is opposed to any major change in the party's attitude or policy; but even he, taken to task by many of his former admirers for his first public expression of his views in the *Labour Monthly*, has been forced into a most confusing half-retraction which still amounts to a comprehensive defense of Stalinism, barely modified by an admission that Stalin did make certain serious errors of judgment. There is, however, good evidence that Dutt's hold on the party, though by no means shaken off as yet, is being strongly challenged, and that the challenge comes mainly from those who feel most deeply the moral aspect of the questions raised by the recent revelations and are conscious of their personal share in the deceits. The British—Communists no less than others—are a moralizing people, accustomed to conduct their affairs—including the class struggle—mainly within the limits of decent, civilized behavior without drawing sharp distinctions between bourgeois and proletarian standards or being ready to argue that the revolutionary end is enough to justify the means. For a number of British Communists whom I know personally the outstanding effect of the recent revelations has been that of a deep moral shock; and most of these men and women have, I think, not yet had time to move on from this initial reaction to any renewed consideration of future policy—except that the shock has made many of them eager to diminish their feeling of isolation from other left-wing Socialists and has taken away much of the pride they used to feel in being of the true "vanguard" of the historic movement towards the coming Socialist society. It has become possible, as it was not until now, for left-wing Socialists such as I to converse freely with Communists of this type, with a sense of assurance that each of us is doing his best to speak out honestly about what he believes, without holding anything back for fear of damaging our respective "causes" or seeking to score points rather than to follow the argument where it leads.

I do not profess to know what will come of this ferment of minds, which so far seems to have spread hardly at all to the official Socialist Parties of the West—or at all events to their official spokesmen. But recently at an unofficial Paris gathering of non-Communist, left-wing Socialists from a number of countries—at which we set up a new organization, the International Society for Socialist Studies—I was deeply impressed by the extent of the change that seemed to have come about in the attitude of most of those present on the issue of Socialist-Communist relations. None of those present, I believe, re-garded it as possible in the near future to achieve any formal rap-prochement between Communist and democratic Socialist Parties in the West; but most of us did seem to believe that the time had come for individuals from both camps, instead of merely abusing one an-other or remaining entirely apart, to begin discussing our differences in an amicable way and to look out for points of agreement. That was the spirit in which the new society—ISSS—was founded: behind it lay a conviction that the changes now going on in the Soviet Union and in the entire Communist movement cannot possibly stop short at the point they have reached so far, but are the beginning of a long, and probably checkered, course of re-thinking and adaptation that will, in the long run, react no less profoundly on the democratic socialism of the West than on the communism which is only now beginning to face the fundamental challenge thrown out by its own outstanding leaders.

The Heretic's Coat

BY BERTOLT BRECHT
Translated by Helmut W. Bonheim

1957

Giordano Bruno, the man of Nola, was burned at the stake in 1600 by order of the Roman Inquisition. He is generally considered a great man—not only for his daring hypotheses on the motion of the planets (since proven to be true) but also for the courage he showed before the Inquisition. To the Inquisition he said: "You pass your sentence on me with perhaps greater fear than I have in receiving it." And a glance at his writings and at the reports of his public appearances makes it impossible to doubt his greatness. But another story may increase our respect for him even more.

It is the story of his coat.

First we must learn how he fell into the hands of the Inquisition.

A Venetian, a patrician by the name of Mocenigo, invited the learned man into his house, asking to be taught physics and skills of memory. For a few months Mocenigo accepted the stipulated lessons as payment for his hospitality. But he was tutored in physics instead of in the black magic he had hoped for. Physics seemed to him to be of no use at all: very dissatisfied, he regretted the expenses occasioned by his guest. Several times he earnestly urged the man of Nola to impart the secret and lucrative information which such a famous man must surely possess. When this did not help he sent a letter of denunciation to the Inquisition. He wrote that this evil and ungrateful man had, in his presence, spoken ill of Christ, said that the monks were asses and misled the people, and moreover he claimed that there existed, contrary to the teaching of the Bible, not just one sun but countless suns, etc., etc. He, Mocenigo, had therefore locked him into his attic and requested that the authorities fetch him as quickly as possible.

315

And so in the middle of the night between a Sunday and a Monday the authorities came to take the scholar to an Inquisition dungeon.

This was 3 o'clock, Monday, the 25th day of May, 1592. The terrible trial lasted for eight long years. Although he fought unceasingly for his life, the fight he conducted that first year in Venice against his extradition to Rome was, perhaps, the most frustrating part of the long difficult process.

In this period occurred the affair of his coat.

In the winter of 1592, while still living in a hotel, the man of Nola had a heavy coat fitted by a tailor, Gabriele Zunto. When he was arrested he had not yet paid for the coat.

Hearing of the arrest the tailor rushed to the house of Mocenigo in the neighborhood of St. Samuel to present his bill. It was too late. A servant of Mocenigo showed him to the door. "We have paid out enough for that swindler," he shouted so loudly from the doorstep that several passers-by looked around. "Perhaps you would care to run to the tribunal of the holy office and announce that you have business with this heretic."

Frightened, the tailor stood in the street. A group of alley-boys had heard it all and one of them, a bepimpled and ragged urchin, threw a stone at him. Although a meanly dressed woman emerged from a door and gave the boy a slap, Zunto, an old man, already felt the danger of "having business with this heretic." After glancing timidly about he ran around the corner and took a wide circuit home. He told his wife nothing of this ill fortune, and for a week she was puzzled by his depressed behavior.

But on the first of June she made out the bills and discovered that payment was still due for the coat of a man whose name was on everybody's tongue, for the man of Nola was being talked about all over town. The most fearful rumors of his evil nature were noised about. He had not only dragged marriage through the mud in books as well as in conversation, but had even called Christ a charlatan and made the most insane statements about the sun. That he had not paid for his coat fitted in very well. The good woman was not in the least inclined to suffer this loss. After a violent quarrel with her husband, the seventy-year-old woman went to the building of the holy office in her Sunday best and, in great anger, demanded the 230 skudi which the arrested heretic owed her.

The official whom she addressed wrote down her demand and promised to look into the matter.

And soon Zunto received a summons; trembling and wobbling, he reported at the feared building. To his surprise he was not cross-examined. He was simply told that his demand would be considered in the settlement of the arrested man. To be sure, the official indicated that not much would come of it.

The old man was only too glad to come off so cheaply and he showed his gratitude most obsequiously. But his wife was not satisfied. It was not enough that her husband make good the loss by giving up his evening pint and stitching into the night. What about the debts to the cloth-merchant? She cried out in the kitchen and in the courtyard that it was scandalous to arrest a criminal before he had paid his debts. If need be she would go to the holy father in Rome to get her 230 skudi. "He won't need a coat to burn in!" she cried.

She told her father confessor what had happened. He advised her to request that at least the coat be released to her. Herein she saw the admission by a churchly authority that her claim was just and she declared she would in no way be satisfied with the coat, which had probably been worn already and besides had been made to measure. She had to have the money. As she waxed a bit loud in her zeal, the father threw her out. That brought her to reason a little and she was quiet for a few weeks. No further reports on the arrested heretic emerged from the palace of the Inquisition. Yet everywhere one heard it whispered that the examinations were bringing monstrously shameful deeds to light. The old woman kept her ears wide open for all such gossip. It tortured her to hear that the case of the heretic stood so badly. He would never be free and able to pay his debts.

She could not sleep a single night now, and in August, when the heat altogether ruined her nerves, started to present her complaint with great loquacity where she shopped and to the customers who came for fittings. She pointed out that the fathers committed a sin if they so carelessly refused the justified demands of a minor workman. The taxes were oppressive and bread prices had just shot up again.

One morning an official summoned her to the building of the holy office, where she was sternly warned to give up her malicious chatter. She was asked if she were not ashamed to dirty a very serious and holy proceeding with her grumbling for a few skudi. She was given to understand that all manner of means were at hand for dealing with people of her sort.

This helped for a while, even though the thought of the phrase "for a few skudi" in the muzzle of the well-fed brother brought a flush of anger to her face. But in September it was heard that the head inquisitor in Rome had demanded the extradition of the man of Nola. The matter was being negotiated in the signory.

The citizenry briskly discussed this application for extradition, and feeling was generally against it. The guilds did not care to hear Roman judgments on themselves.

The old woman was beside herself. Did they really intend to let the heretic go to Rome before he had settled his debts? That was the limit. She had barely received the unbelievable news before she ran, without even taking time to change into a better skirt, to the palace of the holy office.

This time she was received by an official of higher rank and he proved strangely more conciliatory than the former officials had been. He was almost as old as she and quietly and attentively heard her complaint. After a slight pause when she had done, he asked if she wished to speak to Bruno.

She agreed immediately. A meeting was arranged for the next day.

On this morning, in a tiny room with barred windows, a lean man with a sparse dark beard approached her and courteously asked her what she desired.

She had seen him at the time of the fittings, and although she had remembered his face very well she did not recognize him immediately. The excitement of the examinations must have changed him.

She said hastily: "The coat. You never paid for it."

He looked at her for a few seconds in astonishment. Then he remembered and asked in a low voice: "What do I owe you?"

"Two-hundred-thirty skudi," said she. "You got the bill."

He turned to the large fat official who guarded the conference and asked him if he knew how much money was with his belongings in the building of the holy office. The man did not know, but he promised to find out.

"How is your husband?" asked the prisoner, turning again to the old woman as though the affair were now so ordered that normal relationships were again established, and the circumstances of an every-day visit created.

And the old woman, confused by the friendliness of the little man, mumbled that he was well and even added something about his rheumatism.

She waited two whole days before returning to the building of the holy office, for it seemed to her proper to leave the gentleman time to make inquiries.

She actually received permission to see him again. Admittedly she had to wait more than an hour in the tiny room with barred windows, for he was being examined.

He came and seemed quite exhausted. For lack of a chair to sit on, he leaned against the wall a little. Yet he spoke to the point at once.

With a weak voice he told her that he was unfortunately not in a position to pay for the coat. No money had been found with his belongings. Yet she did not need to give up all hope. He had thought about it and recollected that there must be money held for him by a man in Frankfurt who had printed books of his. He would write to him if granted permission and he would ask for the permission the next day. He had felt at the examination that day that they were not too well disposed toward him at the moment. So he did not wish to ask at once and thus possibly ruin all.

The old woman looked searchingly at him as he spoke. She knew the evasions and excuses of tardy debtors. They were devilishly concerned about their responsibilities, and when one came to grips with them they acted as though they were trying to move all heaven and earth.

"What did you need a coat for if you had no money to pay for it?" she asked coldly.

The prisoner nodded to show her that he followed her line of thought. He answered:

"I had always earned something with my books and my teaching. So I thought I would earn something now. And I had expected to use the coat—I thought I would still be going about in the open air." This without a touch of bitterness, clearly so as not to owe her an answer.

Again the old woman inspected him from top to bottom, full of scorn; but feeling that she was getting nowhere with him, she turned without a word and ran out of the room.

"Who would send money to a man in the claws of the Inquisition?" she angrily declared to her husband when they lay in bed that night. He felt more comfortable about his relation to the holy office now, but did not care for his wife's tireless efforts to rake in their money.

"I guess he has other things to think about now," he grumbled.

She made no answer.

The following months passed without any fresh news of the unpleasant affair. Early in January it went about that the signory was weighing the idea of bowing to the wish of the Pope and extraditing the heretic. And then a fresh summons to the building of the holy office was received by the Zuntos.

Since no particular time was specified, she went one afternoon. She came at an awkward moment. The prisoner was expecting a visit from the procurator of the republic, whom the signory had ordered to work out a report on the problem of extradition. She was received by the higher official who had arranged her first interview with the man of Nola. The old man told her that the prisoner had asked to speak to her but that she should consider if this time was a favorable one to choose, since the prisoner was about to enter into a highly important conference.

She said curtly that they only needed to ask him.

An official left and returned with the prisoner. The interview took place before the older official.

Before the man of Nola, who was already smiling at her from the door, could say a word, the old woman burst forth:

"Then why do you behave that way, if you really want to go about in the open air?"

The little man seemed puzzled for a moment. He had answered so many questions in that quarter-year that he hardly remembered the conclusion of his last interview with the tailor's wife.

"No money has come for me," he finally said; "although I wrote about it twice, it did not come. I wondered if you would take the coat back."

"I knew it would come to that," she said scornfully. "And it was made to measure and too small for most people."

The man of Nola looked at the woman in embarrassment.

"I did not think of that," he said, and turned to the holy man.

"Could not all my belongings be sold and the money given these people?"

"That is not possible," put in the official who had fetched him, the big fat one. "Mocenigo lays claim to that. You lived for a long time at his expense."

"He invited me," the man of Nola replied wearily.

The older official raised his hand.

"That is really out of place here. I think the coat should be returned."

"What am I to do with it?" said the old woman stubbornly.

The old man got a little red in the face. Slowly he said:

"My dear woman, a bit of Christian charity would not suit you ill. The accused waits an interview which may mean life or death to him. You can hardly expect that he concern himself greatly with your coat."

The woman looked at him uncertainly. She suddenly remembered where she stood. She was thinking of leaving when she heard the prisoner behind her say in his low voice:

"I believe she can expect it."

And when she turned to him, he added: "You must excuse all this. In any case do not think that your loss is immaterial to me. I will submit a petition on the matter."

Upon a nod of the old man the big fat one left the room. Now he came back, spread out his arms and said: "The coat was not delivered with the other articles at all. Mocenigo must have kept it."

The man of Nola gave an obvious start. Then he firmly declared: "That is not just. I will bring action against him."

The old man shook his head.

"Rather concern yourself with the interview that you must undertake in a few minutes. I cannot permit you to argue further here about a few skudi."

The blood streamed to the old woman's face. While the man of Nola spoke she had been silent, grumpily looking into a corner of the room. But now again her patience was stretched beyond bounds.

"A few skudi!" she cried. "That is a month's earnings! It is easy for you to be considerate. You suffer no loss!"

At that moment a tall monk stepped into the doorway.

In a monotone he said: "The procurator has come," and he cast a wondering look at the screaming old woman.

The big fat one took the man of Nola by the sleeve and led him out. The prisoner looked back at the woman over his narrow shoulder until he was led over the threshold. His lean face was very pale.

Troubled, the old woman descended the steps of the building. She did not know what to think. After all, the man was doing what he could.

A week later, when the big fat one delivered the coat, she did not go into the shop. But she listened at the door and heard the official say: "He has actually spent all his last days here bothering about the coat. Twice in between the hearings and interviews with the local authorities he submitted a petition, and several times demanded an interview with Nuntius on this matter. He fought it through. Mocenigo had to give up the coat. As a matter of fact, Bruno could have made good use of it, for he is being extradited and is to go to Rome this very week."

That was so. It was late January.

He Never Had a Chance

BY FRED J. COOK AND GENE GLEASON

(A section from a special issue of *The Nation*, "The Shame of
New York," by Fred J. Cook and Gene Gleason.)

1959

A light flashed on the central switchboard of the New York Telephone
Company office in Forest Avenue, West Brighton, S.I., at precisely
2:04 A.M., Sept. 2, 1958. Mrs. Catherine B. Thompson, one of the
operators on duty, plugged in on the line. She heard the sound of
heavy breathing. "Hello," she said, "hello." There was no answer, just
that heavy, breathing sound. Mrs. Thompson turned to another operator, Mrs. Florence Parkin, and asked her to trace the call. Mrs. Parkin
quickly found that it was coming from a house at 242 Vanderbilt
Avenue. Then she cut in on the line, holding it open, while Mrs.
Thompson notified police that something appeared to be wrong.

Even as Mrs. Thompson was speaking to the desk sergeant at the St.
George police station, Mrs. Parkin heard the labored breathing on the
line turn into a voice. A woman gasped : "I've been stabbed."

The operator immediately cut the police in on the conversation, and
both she and the desk officer heard the woman repeat: "I've been
stabbed. I've been attacked with a knife." A second later, the voice
added: "My husband has been stabbed, too."

Then there was silence. It lasted only a second. Then a new voice,
a little boy's voice, came on the wire.

"My mother is bleeding," the voice said.

Mrs. Thompson told the boy police already were on the way.

"I'll wait for the police outside," he said.

"No," she told him, "you better stay with your mother."

Such was the beginning of a drama that was to shock the nation.

THE CURTAIN LIFTS

Just six short minutes after that first warning light flashed on the Staten Island switchboard, at exactly 2:10 A.M., Patrolmen Vincent J. Meli and Henry Tyson pulled up before the two-story house at 242 Vanderbilt Avenue in the Fox Hills section, an area that in olden days had been known as "The Witches' Field." The house sat on a steep little hill. The patrolmen climbed seven steps, went up a ten-foot walk, climbed three more steps and entered the front door. Waiting to greet them, clad only in pajamas, was a small, slender, tow-headed boy, Melvin Dean Nimer, aged eight. Behind him in the silent house was a scene of blood and brutality.

The patrolmen found the boy's father, Dr. Melvin A. Nimer, thirty-one, a physician at the nearby Marine Hospital of the U.S. Public Health Service, sprawled on the kitchen floor, covered with blood from deep stab wounds. In the master bedroom upstairs, they found Mrs. Lou Jean Nimer, thirty-one, slumped on the floor between the bed and the wall where she had collapsed while telephoning. She, too, had been badly stabbed.

An emergency call went out for an ambulance and detectives. The ambulance arrived promptly, and at 2:18 A.M., Mrs. Nimer was placed in it to be taken to the Marine Hospital, just three blocks away. She was still conscious. Significantly, in the light of future developments, she still retained her presence of mind. As she was being placed in the ambulance, her thoughts obviously turned to her younger children still asleep in the house—Melvin Dean's brother, Gregory, two, and his sister, Jennifer Jean, just five months. The baby especially was on the mother's mind, for she told police: "Please feed the baby plain milk. No formula."

Even as the ambulance left, in the house, on the kitchen floor, Dr. Nimer was dying. Blood was welling up from his wounds. "I'm choking, I'm choking," he moaned. But he, too, still retained his faculties. He warned police against moving him or raising his head, and told them simply to brace his feet against the wall until the ambulance returned. When it did, within a few minutes, he too was rushed to the hospital, and there he died shortly after he was admitted.

Mrs. Nimer lived a few hours longer. An emergency operation was performed in a desperate attempt to save her life, but at 5:30 A.M. she died while still on the operating table.

Staten Island authorities had a sensational double murder on their hands, and investigative forces were quickly marshaled. District Attorney John M. Braisted, Jr. and his assistant, Thomas R. Sullivan, were notified. Deputy Chief Inspector Edward W. Byrnes and Inspector Carl I. Blank assumed command of the police investigation. Detectives and technical experts swarmed over the house at 242 Vanderbilt Avenue. From the outset, they had one thing going for them. They had an eye-witness—Melvin Dean Nimer, known as Deany.

DEANY'S STORY

The boy told this story:

He had been asleep in his bedroom across the hall from his parents' room when he was awakened by something touching the bed, disturbing the bed clothing. Startled, Deany woke, looked up, saw a man looming above his bed. The man, he said, wore a white mask, like a sheet, that covered his entire head. Deany screamed.

The masked man grabbed him by the throat, tried to choke him. Across the hall, Mrs. Nimer, hearing her son scream, rushed to his aid.

"Mommy came and the man hit her with something and she started bleeding," Deany told police. "Then Daddy ran in and they started fighting and Daddy started bleeding."

The struggle between his father and the masked intruder took place in the hall outside his bedroom, at the top of the stairway, the boy told detectives. The prowler, he said, was "a little bigger than Daddy," and he broke away and ran downstairs with Dr. Nimer in pursuit.

Mrs. Nimer had gone to her bedroom and sat down on the edge of the bed to use the telephone and call for help. She slid off the bed, moaning faintly, "I'm dying. . . ."

This was Deany Nimer's story. Based upon it, police sent out a thirteen-state alarm for the prowler who had slain Dr. Nimer and his wife: "Unknown male, white, wearing blue dungarees and blue-striped shirt. May have blood on his clothing."

THE CLOTH STRIPS

Right at the start there was one bit of undeniable physical evidence that seemed to lend substantiation to the story Deany Nimer had told. Only vague hints of this appeared in the press at the time, and its significance was quickly forgotten. It was mentioned that police had found a piece of cloth (some accounts said two pieces) that had been left folded on the boy's bed. Actually, we are told, there were about half-a-dozen strips of cloth torn into handy lengths that suggested they had been intended for gags or bonds. The cloth was a faded, odd-colored, cotton ticking—the kind of coarse, heavy material that was often used for old mattress covers—and the strips, according to those who tested them, were strong. The material matched nothing else found in the house, and police at first thought that the strips might have been ripped from an old hospital mattress. The nearby Public Health Service Hospital was checked on this supposition, but the cotton ticking evidently hadn't come from there. It never was traced and identified.

Indeed, the mysterious cloth strips soon were forgotten as investigators concentrated on two other elements of the mystery. How had the prowler entered the home? And where was the murder weapon?

Again these key questions were never to be answered, but the first one, from a combination of circumstances at the murder scene, appears to have assumed from the early moments of the investigation an exaggerated importance in official minds. An examination of the house showed that a cellar window had been left open. A water hose led out the window into the driveway, where Dr. Nimer had washed the car the day before he and his wife were murdered. An intruder could have slipped into the house through this window, but technical experts examined the window sill and quickly discounted the possiblity. Minute particles of dust and dirt on the sill had been undisturbed, and this would hardly have been possible had a full-grown man squeezed through the comparatively narrow opening.

Yet this appeared to be the only easy means of entrance. Elsewhere in the house, a screen on one of the downstairs windows was unhooked, but again there was nothing to indicate an intruder had crawled through the window. The inside front door had been partially open when the first patrolmen arrived, but the aluminum screen door had still been latched and Deany himself had released the catch to admit police. It almost seemed as if no one could have entered the house—and, especially, that no one could have departed in the kind of hasty flight that Deany Nimer had described, *if* Deany's story were true.

BEGINNINGS OF MYSTERY

This, it became obvious later, was the first fork in the road the investigators were to take. A second element involved the location of Deany's Boy Scout knife. In searching the house for the murder weapon, detectives discovered that apparently none of the kitchen ware had been used. But Deany's Boy Scout knife was missing. The boy was positive it had been in a pocket of his trousers, hanging on the knob of his bedroom door. Detectives looked, but the knife wasn't where Deany had said it was. A thorough search of the house finally turned up the potential weapon, hidden between the covers of the Mormon magazine *Era*. A laboratory analysis—the kind of minute examination that can reveal droplets of blood not perceivable by the human eye—soon established that the knife was absolutely unstained. Still, could the knife have been cleaned? Could it still be the murder weapon?

These questions were hovering unasked in the air, unknown as yet to press and public, when the first reporters converged upon the murder scene. Even though the early roadblocks, the early forks in the investigative pathway, were not clear, there was about this investigation from the start a disturbing overtone. One of the first reporters on the scene was scrambling for information when he was elated to receive a high-sign from a high-ranking detective whom he knew. The detective drew him aside, and the reporter was all anticipation.

"I thought he had something he wanted to tell me," the reporter recalled later. "But do you know what he said? He pointed to District Attorney Braisted, and he asked me: 'You've been around quite awhile. You've seen Hogan work. How do you think he compares with Hogan? Is he as good?' "

This early, it would seem, some minds were already more preoccupied with the question of the reflected public image, the question of their own reputations, than they were with the baffling details of the horrible crime that cried out for solution.

FINGER ON THE BOY

In the succeeding days, the investigation followed the usual frenetic course of sensational headline crimes. A number of suspects were picked up, questioned, released. The ground around the Nimer house, the streets in the area, were searched and searched again. In all of this just two discoveries were made that seem of significance now. Detectives disclosed that they had found two footprints—the footprints of a man—in the soft earth at the left rear side of the Nimer house. Plaster casts were taken of them in the hope that they might ultimately serve to identify the foot that had made them. The second discovery involved a knife. About 6 P.M. on Sept. 3, the day after the murders, two patrolmen found a sharp-pointed knife, with a five-inch blade and a wooden handle, in a hedge about 1,000 feet from the Nimer home. Under laboratory analysis, the knife revealed traces of blood, but they were so faint that it could not be scientifically determined whether the blood was animal or human.

Both of these discoveries, if they meant anything at all, seemed to point away from the suspicion that already had taken root in the minds of officials. This suspicion involved Deany Nimer. Newsmen, under a pledge of confidence, were told that the boy was a suspect in the murder of his parents. He was undergoing psychiatric examination.

While the public still had no suspicion of the sensation that was about to burst, journalists who had been given the tip dug energetically into the background of the Nimer family. The parents had been Mormons. They had been married in September, 1946, in the culmination of a childhood romance that had begun back in their home town of Orem, Utah. Dr. Nimer had received his medical degree from the University of Utah, had served in a Public Health Service Hospital in Seattle, Wash., and had come to Staten Island only a few months before to start a three-year surgical residence at the Marine Hospital. Intimates of the family had considered their home life ideal. There had never been a hint, prior to the murders, of any mental problem involving Melvin Dean Nimer. He was an open-faced, smiling, attractive boy. Indeed, he and his father had seemed to have great affection for each other. Neighbors recalled how, when Dr. Nimer came home from the hospital, Deany would run up to him and throw his arms around him.

Was it possible that such a boy, at so young an age, could be a veritable Dr. Jekyll and Mr. Hyde? Even if he were possessed by a dark soul-demon hiding under the smiling face, was it physically possible for such a tiny lad to murder *both* of his parents? After all, Deany was only 4 feet 4; he weighed only sixty pounds.

The authorities obviously decided that he could. Relatives of the Nimers had been notified promptly of the tragedy. Mrs. Bertha Park, mother of Mrs. Nimer, and Dr. Harold Nimer, Deany's uncle, had flown to New York immediately. With Dr. Harold Nimer's consent, District Attorney Braisted sent the boy on Friday, Sept. 5, three days after the murders, to the Staten Island Mental Health Center for analysis. The clinic, under the direction of Dr. Richard M. Silberstein, examined the boy on just two days, Friday and Saturday. It was after these examinations, it was to be disclosed later, that Deany changed his original story and gave a statement confessing that he had committed the murders. This was still not known, even to reporters, when Deany left on the weekend, accompanied by his uncle and Detective James Cox, to fly to the funeral of his parents in Orem, Utah.

THE TURNING POINT

The funeral was held on Tuesday, Sept. 9, and on Wednesday, Sept. 10, as Deany was returning to New York with his uncle and Detective Cox, the New York *Journal-American* broke the story and announced in sensational headlines that the boy was a suspect in the murder of his parents. What happened next has to be considered of the greatest significance. For this was the crossroads, the point at which the life and the future of an eight-year-old boy were going to be protected—or he was going to be pilloried in public.

The *Journal-American*'s story was damaging, but it was not official. Other newspapers did not touch it until District Attorney Braisted had been given an opportunity to comment, and on what he said depended the extent to which the story would be used, the credibility that would be attached to it. The district attorney, quite obviously, had several courses of action open to him. He could have denounced the published story as a violation of confidence and refused to confirm it; he could have refused flatly to comment, as district attorneys often do, because the case was under investigation and still unsolved; or he could have confirmed the fact that the boy had been under suspicion—and at the same time pointed out all of the solid facts in the case (as yet unknown to the public) that seemed to negate that suspicion.

District Attorney Braisted did none of these things. He gave the impression of a public official who was glad the story was out. He refused to be quoted on the fact that he had required a pledge of silence from newspapermen about the suspicions that had been focused on Deany; he refused to criticize publication of a story that had tarred an eight-year-old boy as a suspect in the murder of his parents. He said, on the contrary, that preliminary psychiatric examination to which Deany had been subjected had shown the boy was suffering "from a paranoid type of schizophrenia and that the boy's illness and basic personality were compatible with the commission of a crime of violence."

While thus throwing the prestige of his office behind the most horrible and harrowing suspicion that could be leveled at a child, the district attorney left himself an out in carefully expressed reservations. He pointed out that the boy's uncle, Dr. Harold Nimer, was not satisfied with "the statement"—he refused to say confession—that Deany had made. He added, "I am not satisfied, either," and said the boy would be subjected to more extensive and more thorough psychiatric tests.

DRAWING THE NET

The district attorney's statement made the story official. Press services spread it nation-wide. And in the next hours it seemed that the last room for doubt had been banished. On the evening of this day of horrible revelation, little Deany was taken back to the house of tragedy on Vanderbilt Avenue, and there, in a pattern reminiscent of the one followed with all-but-convicted criminals, he "re-enacted" the crime, authorities said. The next day, Thursday, Sept. 11, he was sent to Bellevue Hospital in New York for psychiatric examination. And that same day, in an extended press conference, District Attorney Braisted was subjected to searching questions by reporters about the circumstances that pointed to young Deany Nimer's guilt or innocence.

On the side of innocence, District Attorney Braisted listed just one theoretical proposition. "The one important thing that would negate" the idea of guilt, he said, was that the statement came from an eight-year-old boy. On the side of guilt, he listed an impressive array of supposedly solid facts.

The most important factor pointing to the boy's guilt, he said, "is the statement by the Medical Examiner that the wounds, their location, etc., could indicate they were received while the victims were in a prone position in bed." The first autopsy report (it was later revised) by Assistant Medical Examiner Dr. Dominick DeMaio disclosed that Dr. Nimer had a superficial wound on the back of the left shoulder and a fatal wound "in the upper abdomen under the left chest cage." Mrs. Nimer, Dr. DeMaio's report said, had a superficial wound of the right breast and "a lethal wound of the upper abdomen under the right chest cage." The medical report added that "the thrusts all were direct downward thrusts," supporting the theory that the Nimers were surprised and stabbed while lying "in a prone position in bed."

This scientific documentation seemed to offer a rational explanation for the incredible. Conceivably, even an eight-year-old, 4 foot 4, 60-pound boy *could* stab both of his parents to death if he surprised them as they slept and stabbed them in the soft flesh of the abdomen before they were aware of what was happening. The medical report seemed almost to explain how the crime *had* happened; but even so—and even though there were vital facts in this case that were still being kept from the press and public—there were a few obvious pieces that did not fit into this almost-final solution.

SOME AWKWARD FACTS

One dealt with Deany's person. Authorities said he had admitted he had washed his hands, and so, of course, there was no blood upon them. But what of his pajamas? They had, according to Dr. DeMaio's report, only "one or two" small bloodstains on them. Then there was the peculiar matter of the bedclothing. The murder night had been an exceptionally cool one when, almost certainly, the Nimers would have had covers over them. Yet there were no knife rips, no tears at all in the bed sheets.

These minute flaws in the case did not seem too significant at the time, but reporters questioned District Attorney Braisted closely. And everything he said built one picture, a dark picture for Deany Nimer.

Asked about reports that the boy had changed his confession, the district attorney said: "No, he has not changed his story." Then he admitted that the boy, in answer to a question from his uncle, had said that his original story about an intruder was the true one. The district attorney was asked whether there were discrepancies in the boy's story. He said flatly: "No discrepancies." He added that Deany had had a motive and that it lay in "an attitude he had toward his parents." He explained, "I would be inclined to say they (the Nimers) were very strict." Of Deany, he said: "He has never shown any remorse."

Braisted was questioned about the absence of blood on any of the knives in the house, especially on Deany's Boy Scout knife. Assuming that the knife had been washed off, had detectives examined the drain traps to see if they could find any traces of blood? They had—and they found no blood. Only six minutes had elapsed between the first winking alarm light on the telephone switchboard and the arrival of police. Could Deany have rushed downstairs, washed off the knife so perfectly that it retained no trace of blood and hidden it in that short time? "It is possible," said District Attorney Braisted. "The time limit is conceivable?" he was asked again. "It is possible," he said.

THE BOY'S "CONFESSION"

The effect of all this was to accuse and damn Melvin Dean Nimer in the public eye without accusing him in court. The story touched a sensitive nerve of the times and was a sensation across the nation. Parents everywhere have been concerned in recent years about the increasing frequency of violent and bloody youth crimes, and the case of Melvin Dean Nimer seemed to touch a new nadir. If so young and so attractive a boy could have committed so heinous a crime, then there were no limits to youthful depravity. No New York crime case in our experience caused such deep and wide-spread agitation among parents.

Yet all the time there were vital elements of the case that had been kept secret—elements that did not fit into the picture of a little boy's seemingly almost-certain guilt. They were vital facts that supported the story Deany originally had told about a masked intruder. For the plain truth was this: *virtually every word that he had uttered had been corroborated from the mouths of his dying parents.*

Though District Attorney Braisted had been questioned with the utmost thoroughness, he had given no hint of this. The district attorney had insisted there were "no discrepancies" in the boy's confession —nor, presumably, in the case against the boy. It was left for newsmen to drag the truth out into the light of day. One Friday, Sept. 12, Vincent E. Sorge, a painstaking and tireless reporter for *The New York World-Telegram and Sun*, broke through the veil of official reticence. He revealed the verbatim question-and-answer exchange between a detective and Mrs. Nimer before Mrs. Nimer died. This was the exchange:

Q. Can you tell me anything about the case? A. A mask . . . a mask.
Q. Can you tell me anything else?
A. A hood . . . a hood.
Q. What kind? A. White.
Q. Slits in the eyes? A. Yes, covered full head.
Q. How tall? A. Tall as my husband, same build.
Q. Why did you get up? A. Heard boy scream.

District Attorney Braisted was in the midst of another press conference, discussing Deany's motives, when *The World-Telegram and Sun* broke the story. Asked if Mrs. Nimer had made a statement before she died, Braisted said he understood she had described the killer as about the size of her husband and added: "We believe she might have seen her husband and no one else, but this matter is still being investigated."

Thomas Sullivan, Braisted's assistant, came into the room at this point, leaned over and whispered into the district attorney's ear. Braisted paled noticeably. Then he turned to reporters and said: "Mrs. Nimer did mention the words 'white mask and hood' to Detective John Morgan, but you must remember that she was in shock and was put under sedation . . . and [her statements] were made in dribs and drabs. . . . She also said, 'tall as my husband, same build.' " Pressed for further details, he said abruptly: "I will make no comment on any published statement attributed to victims of this crime. I am declining comment because I sincerely believe that comment would impede our investigation."

The lid had been lifted. Answers that did not answer no longer satisfied. More and sharper questions were asked. What about Dr. Nimer? He had lived for some time after the stabbing. Had he, like his wife, identified his assailant? "He didn't give us anything you would call useful information," one high police source said. "He made no positive identification of the assailant," said District Attorney Braisted. It took reporters three days to pierce this screen of non-answering answers; but finally, on Monday, pressed again and pressed harder, District Attorney Braisted admitted that Dr. Nimer, too, before he died, had used the words "prowler" and "mask."

FIRST VERSION SUBSTANTIATED

The picture that then developed was this: Little Melvin Dean Nimer's first story that he had been awakened by a masked prowler, that he had screamed, that his parents had come to his aid—all of this had agreed in exact detail with the statements his dying parents had made to police. His description of the mask, his description of the intruder as a man "about Daddy's size," agreed perfectly with his mother's dying statement. Why, in the face of all this, had authorities concentrated such strong and harrowing suspicion upon the boy?

The answer may be found, perhaps, in District Attorney Braisted's admission of official investigative frustration. Three things, he said, led authorities to suspect Deany, and he listed them: "1. Our inability to establish with any certainty that there had been an entrance to and an exit from the house. 2. Motive—we couldn't settle on a motive. 3. A few statements by the boy which did not conform to the facts. Adding it all together—though we, like many other people, just couldn't believe it—we had no choice."

The only way, seemingly, that the positive statements of the dying parents could be explained away lay in the assumption that, to protect the son who had stabbed them, they had conferred and concocted the story of the masked intruder. Yet Mrs. Nimer had collapsed in the upstairs bedroom, Dr. Nimer in the downstairs kitchen, and there was absolutely no proof that they could have talked with each other in those six short minutes before police arrived. Anyway, in logic, the whole idea appeared preposterous, and in an analytical article on Sept. 19, 1958, the writing half of this team tore into the case against Deany Nimer and asked this question:

> Is it conceivable that a dying mother who thought enough of her children to warn about her daughter's formula would make up a story about a prowler and a mask to protect her son—and endanger the other two children—if he were a killer?

The day that question was asked District Attorney Braisted was not available to reporters, and Sullivan, his assistant, said: "No comment."

And with that story, the Nimer case virtually died. Melvin Dean Nimer's psychiatric examination at Bellevue was concluded. The report, as relayed to the public, was vague. Psychiatrists said they found evidence of "a personality disorder predating the tragic occurrence on Staten Island." Deany needed continued psychiatric treatment, they said; but clear evidence that the boy was not considered dangerous was seen in the fact that he was released and allowed to go to his grandparents' home in Orem, Utah, there to attend school and mingle with other children. Deany left New York for Orem on Oct. 23, 1958, and on Nov. 3, the forty detectives who had been working on the mystery were called off. The case was as good as dead.

AT LAST THE ANSWER

But the damage had been done, and a haunting, horrible suspicion still remained—the suspicion that Melvin Dean Nimer, only eight, might have committed one of the most horrible crimes of the century. Everywhere a reporter went, even in towns miles away from New York, he was asked: "What is the truth about the Nimer case? Did the boy really do it?" It was a question to which there was no official answer, but one to which we can, we feel, give a positive answer now.

It is an answer that was obtained by the reporting half of this team only after weeks of exhausting and meticulous leg work. Every inch of the murder scene was re-examined. Every person who would talk, even many who didn't want to talk, was questioned. The picture that emerged grew more shocking every step of the way. For as we dug more deeply into the mystery, it became apparent that there wasn't a chance, *there never had been a chance*, that Melvin Dean Nimer could have committed the murders. Only the most incredibly slipshod investigation that proceeded in blind defiance of some facts and in blind ignorance of others could have resulted in even the vaguest suspicion being cast upon the boy.

THE BLOOD CLUES

We began with the house at 242 Vanderbilt Avenue. Any supposition of Deany's guilt rested upon the belief—in all logic, the only possible belief—that he had surprised his sleeping parents in bed and stabbed them there. But once we got into the master bedroom and examined the mattress on the bed, we found this: there was just one splotch of blood on the entire mattress and that was on the side of the bed on which Mrs. Nimer sat when she used the telephone.

The traces of blood still discernible in the house indicated clearly that the crime had been committed elsewhere. Across the hallway, there was a splash of blood on the door jamb of Deany's room, and there was a large amount of blood around the light switch in the hall nearby—an indication perhaps that Dr. Nimer, his hands already bloody from his wounds, had fumbled desperately for the switch in an effort to turn on the light so that he could see his assailant already fleeing down the stairs. It was significant to us that signs of blood in massive quantities appeared first in the hallway and trailed down the stairs through the house—just as would have been the case if the first story Deany told were the right one.

Downstairs, we faced the problem of the front door. It was obvious that a key angle had been the conclusion by the police and the district attorney that no one could have come in—or, even more significantly, could have left in haste—through the aluminum door with its spring lock. Yet aluminum doors with this kind of latch often give under pressure. Gene Gleason set the catch, then gave the door a slight tug—and open it came, easily, without damaging door or lock.

MRS. NIMER'S EVIDENCE

Turning from the mute evidence of the house, we sought information of a more positive kind in the records of the Marine Hospital, where the Nimers had been taken. Mrs. Nimer, the records showed, had been placed in a recovery room at 3:05 A.M. Personnel of the hospital who knew her had talked with her. She was fully conscious, fully coherent. When a nurse giving Mrs. Nimer oxygen mistakenly placed the mask on backwards, Mrs. Nimer reached up with one hand and said: "It's on backwards." This was not a woman, obviously, who was in such a state of shock or under such sedation that she did not know what she was saying when she talked about a prowler and a mask.

The vital questioning of Mrs. Nimer had been overheard by hospital personnel. Two detectives were present, and they questioned her gently, carefully, hospital personnel said. They heard Mrs. Nimer tell about the mask-hood, the slits for the eyes; heard her describe the intruder as "about the size of my husband." And they heard her say: "I met the man in the hall."

Every effort was made to save Mrs. Nimer's life. Dr. Norman Tarr, deputy chief of surgery, was summoned to perform an emergency operation. He knew Mrs. Nimer personally, and she recognized him. Before he operated, the records show, he examined her carefully and turned her body over gently so that he could see if she had any wounds on her back. Mrs. Nimer told him that she had not been stabbed there and, indeed, she had not—a sequence again that seems to demonstrate that this was a woman still in possession of her faculties.

In his examination of his patient, Dr. Tarr discovered that she had three wounds. There was a slight knife wound on the heel of her right hand, received apparently when she had tried to ward off a blow. She had a one-inch stab wound in the upper right chest above the breast. And she had a mortal wound, not in the abdomen as the official medical examiner's report had said, but in the right chest between the sixth and seventh ribs.

The location and nature of this last wound assume vital importance. The presumption of Deany Nimer's guilt had been based to a large extent upon the autopsy report that placed the wound in the abdomen and described it as a direct downward thrust. This enabled officials to envision a boy stabbing his parents in bed, *but Dr. Tarr's reports show conclusively that this was a completely inaccurate impression, that the stabbing did not and could not have happened that way at all.*

POWERFUL THRUST

The blade of the knife had been driven through the rib cage and muscles with terrific force. It had gone in at an angle, slanting down and towards the center of the body. So vicious was the thrust that the blade had penetrated about five inches, and there was evidence that the blow had been struck by an experienced knife-wielder. The wound on the outside was small, only about the width of the knife blade; but there was evidence that the knife tip had been flicked on an arc inside the body, the trick of an experienced killer. The flicking tip had slashed through the diaphragm, had severed the major blood vessel going into the vena cava, and had inflicted a cut about five inches long and very deep in the liver.

Dr. Tarr knew that only a miracle could save Lou Jean Nimer, but he attempted to perform that miracle. He made an incision, beginning approximately at the navel and proceeding upward to the bottom of the breast plate. He mopped up the blood and tried to staunch its flow. His patient was sinking fast. Her pulse and breathing faded. She was only a whisper away from death. Dr. Tarr reached into her chest cavity and tried frantically to massage her failing heart. He tried for twenty minutes, but he failed as he had known, almost from the first, that he must fail.

All during this grim drama of the operating room, Dr. Tarr detailed every step in operative notes that he dictated as he went along. Realizing that he would have to cut through the original wound, he was careful to describe its location, its size, its depth. All of this detail, so vital to any understanding of the murder case, was in Dr. Tarr's operative notes when Mrs. Nimer's body was released to the city morgue for autopsy at 7:05 A.M., Sept. 2, 1958.

What happened next seems fairly obvious. The medical examiner, Dr. DeMaio, confused the incision which Dr. Tarr had made with the fatal wound. Only so could the wound have been erroneously located in the abdomen instead of between the sixth and seventh ribs; only so could it have been described as a direct downward thrust when Dr. Tarr, the only man who could know, described it emphatically as an angled, downward-slanting blow. How could this confusion have occurred? Quite simply. The autopsy report was ready the day after the murders, but Dr. Tarr's operative notes were not transcribed and forwarded to authorities for four days! And in the meantime, nobody asked. It was not until "about ten days" after Mrs. Nimer's death that detectives came around to question Dr. Tarr and hospital personnel—and learned, presumably for the first time, one of the most elemental facts about the crime they were investigating: the nature of Mrs. Nimer's fatal wound.

DEANY'S THROAT MARKS

This sequence, revealing enough, is not quite so shocking as one other medical fact that until now has been buried from the public. Deany, it will be remembered, had told authorities originally that the intruder had grabbed him by the throat and tried to strangle him. During the period when suspicion was being focused on the boy, District Attorney Braisted had been asked about this. Had there been marks on Deany's neck? He had replied: "There might have been one or two little marks on the boy's neck. There were no lacerations or deep marks. The boy was examined superficially on the night of the murders, but was not given any medical treatment."

This account simply does not agree with specific reports that show conclusively that a man *had* tried to strangle Deany Nimer!

The story of the evidence that was plainly visible on Deany's throat comes from Dr. William Smith, an associate of Dr. Nimer and a neighbor and friend of the family. He hurried to the Nimer house early on the morning of the tragedy. Deany had already been questioned, had been sent back to bed to sleep and had only just reawakened. Dr. Smith and Ralph L. Perkins, administrator of Marine Hospital, were present when detectives began to question the boy again about 6 A.M. Even then, police were saying that the boy's "story doesn't conform with the facts." And even then the trend of the questioning indicated that they suspected Deany. The questioning went on and on for nearly two hours, and considering the circumstances, the age of the boy and the horror of the night, it impressed observers as excessive, as constituting a virtual verbal third degree.

Finally, about 8 A.M., in the kitchen of the Nimer home, police asked Dr. Smith to examine Deany's throat. The doctor turned a sun-lamp on the boy, and this is what he found:

> On the right side of the boy's neck—to the rear of the midway point—four fingerprints. On the left side, in approximately the same position, a thumb print and the curvature of a thumb nail mark. Clusters of petechia, more commonly known as pinpoint hemorrhages caused by the rupturing of the capillaries.

Dr. Smith said he told police and the D.A.'s men present: "The marks are more than halfway back. He could not have done it himself. The hand was too big."

This positive finding, it would seem, should have put an end to all suspicions of Deany Nimer. But as the sequel was to show, it did nothing of the kind.

Obviously, police and investigating officials were not listening to facts that they did not want to hear. Their attitude even at the time, even when one could not know what was to come, must have been obvious; for Dr. Smith, when he left the house and took Deany home with him, was so worried that he did an unprecedented thing. He discussed the situation first with his wife, then he called in a second doctor to examine Deany's throat again. This second examination corroborated Dr. Smith's findings, and both doctors wrote out formal reports of what they had found and filed them in the hospital records.

"A ROTTEN DEAL"

It was not until some weeks later that Detective James Cox, who appears to have taken a more realistic view of the case than some of his superiors, came around rechecking evidence and discovered that two formal medical reports establishing beyond doubt Deany Nimer's innocence, showing that a man *had* tried to strangle him, were reposing in hospital files like a couple of concealed time bombs. Cox was visibly disturbed. But no one else appears to have been. At least no one in official position to this day has had the grace publicly to admit the horrible sequence of blunders that ended in the pillorying of an eight-year-old boy. The pretense has been maintained publicly that the investigation is still open; that anyone, including Deany Nimer, could conceivably still be a suspect. *But privately a high police official has since admitted to the reporting half of this team, "We know that the boy could never have done it."*

Out in Utah, Deany went back to school last winter like any other eight-year-old boy. According to his grandfather, Dean E. Park, he appeared normal and bright in every way. There had been no trouble, no need even for Deany to make regular trips to a psychiatrist. But, understandably, there was bitterness. Dean Park, speaking of New York, put it well. He said: "We think we got a rotten deal back there."

Quiet, Please!

BY J. B. PRIESTLEY

1963

One reason why life is difficult today is that many of us are compelled to live in two quite different worlds. Moreover, it costs us about a thousand times as much to live in the world we don't trust, don't like, don't believe in, as it does to live in the other world that has our liking and confidence. Another thing is that while one world, the expensive one, cannot have a future, because it must soon either fade away or end itself—and us—with a bang, the other world already shows us a possible and promising future. It can do this because it is very much *our* world, belonging to our age, and not a dubious legacy from the past, a monstrously magnified inheritance.

This world, the one that doesn't cost much and never makes the headlines, is known to most artists, scientists, scholars, technologists, athletes. It is a world of coexistence and cooperation. It covers the round earth, and is peculiarly suited to a time in which jet aircraft can cross any frontier in a few hours. It does not think in terms of good people versus monsters. It talks instead of screaming hysterically. It is not secretive and enjoys swapping pictures and passing out information, but is not engaged in propaganda. It is not moving towards war, but always away from war; not talking about Peace as if it were a golden egg a mile long as people in the other world do, but creating peaceful conditions, the global civilization of the near future, simply by going along with what interests it.

Because it is flexible and easy, I shall call this the Loose World. And now that it has a name, I can reveal one remarkable fact about it. Intelligent young people *in all countries* accept and try to live in this Loose World. This is the one they believe in, not the other. They move into it and around in it quite naturally and easily. It is their

world. And this I believe to be true of the intelligent and most promising young people, whether they live in Baltimore or Odessa, Manchester or Belgrade, St. Louis or Tiflis, Kiev or Lyons, Chicago or
Warsaw. They are all, so to speak, Loose-minded.

The other, the magnified inheritance, I shall call the Stiff World. It
costs us about ten dollars for every cent we spend on Loose. It could
easily cost us everything we have and are. But though it demands so
much and could kill us all, somehow it is far more unreal and fantastic
than Loose, which is one reason why the young turn away from it. In
this Stiff World, everything is out of scale and proportion. It is as if an
old game were being played in an immensely exaggerated form, baseball teams a hundred strong playing with immense steel bats and explo-
sive balls on a field sown with mines. It is crowded with tough-minded
realists who are, in fact, more than half-crazy.

The Stiff World never stops declaring that it is guarding democracy.
But the democracy it guards never allows people to vote on anything
important to the Stiff World. This is in fact a strangely secretive,
authoritarian, liberty-removing kind of democracy, which tells most of
us to keep quiet and mind our own business. And indeed, some of us
are sufficiently cynical to believe that many Stiff types, although they
pretend to deplore the state of the world, cannot help enjoying the
authority and importance lent them by the Stiff setup, and would not
know what to do if we stopped having so many crises. They are
themselves power-hungry types, and so they cannot help seeing everything in terms of power. It is a weakness of our age, which has largely
rejected any inheritance of power, that we are led by men who have
been hungrily ambitious for years. I have often thought that our international affairs might be better managed by any random collection of
chess players or bird-fanciers.

The Stiff World is forever announcing that it is looking for a lasting
peace; but this is just a tape-recording. It maintains, at our expense,
huge state departments working day and night to make mischief.
Sometimes they are trying to put into effect policies that are not only
out-of-date now, but were shaky and dubious fifty years ago. The new
foreign secretaries start where their predecessors left off. They are all
too busy and anxious, as one crisis follows another, to ask themselves
and their staffs what the hell they think they are doing. No flexibility
is tolerated; all is rigid; this is the Stiff World.

Here the characters are as fixed and typed as they were in the
crudest old melodramas. They are seen in black and white. It is sheer
goodness defying appalling wickedness. It is Truth versus The Lie.
This is, of course, the world of propaganda. And most of this propa-

ganda is curiously rigid, pedantic and unreal, for in it are opposed a communism that the East hasn't got and a capitalism that the West hasn't got, as if we were all staking our lives on a debate on a ouija board between Adam Smith and Karl Marx. It is only if we go into the Loose World that we can begin to discover what West and East really have got.

But then of course the chief product of Stiff World propaganda is fear. And some curious things have happened. In the old world, from which the Stiffs inherited their power complex, armaments had to be increased to meet a new danger. But in the Stiff World this has been reversed. Because, once we were in the atomic age, the new armaments were so terrible, so monstrous, that the danger, the menace, had to be hugely magnified to match them. Clearly if we had such things, then we *must* be in a desperate situation. And now indeed we are, though we weren't when all this nonsense began. What was unthinkable has now become thinkable—that is, if you call it thinking to suggest that a nation halved by nuclear casualties can still function as a nation, and begin organizing itself for World War IV. It would, in fact, consist of a lot of radioactive lunatics, not ready to organize anything except the immediate lynching of any World War III experts they could find.

To show what propaganda can do, I take an example from behind the iron curtain, as the Stiffs like to call it. We were recently in Soviet Armenia and Georgia, where my wife, an archaeologist, was visiting digs and sites and ruins, and I was tagging along, trying to capture some of the mountain scenery in *gouaches*. Our guide and interpreter was an extremely intelligent, youngish anthropologist, who knew several oriental languages as well as sufficient English to interpret for us. He was in nearly everything a Loose World man, but as soon as disarmament came up as a topic, the shadow of the Stiff World fell on him. He said if the Soviet Union took a unilateral disarmament risk— "Tomorrow, American paratroopers would be in our streets." This is what propaganda can do to a nice, quiet, intelligent scholar, quite sure his own people had no intention of attempting world conquest, suddenly turning up with machine guns in Dallas or Cleveland, Ohio.

Sometimes I read those stories of international espionage and counterespionage that exist entirely in a Stiff World atmosphere. They are often the work of men who know something about Intelligence, spycatching and whatever else makes for what is called "security." And nearly always, reading these stories, I feel I am being given a glimpse and a whiff of hell. It is not only the inhumanity, the ruthlessness, the cruelty, that make me feel this; it is also their suggestion of an appalling underlying idiocy. The harder you look at the Stiff World, the more you realize that behind its solemnity, its unceasing activity, its dark secrets, its daily waste of millions, there is nothing but a bad mental legacy and a few false assumptions. If it kills us, as it easily might, we shall not have died for freedom, for our country, for our children's sake, only for silliness—tragic figures in a planetary farce.

Now I believe that the Stiff World, which is organized for conflict and war and not for understanding, mutual help and peace, has no future to offer us and our children. It is bound for nowhere except catastrophe. It has been given a good run, together with more money than all the tyrants in world history have demanded, and all it can offer for tomorrow is a lot more of what we dislike today. This is why all intelligent young people—and, I repeat, *in all countries* —want no part of it, are already rejecting it by the millions, are turning hopefully towards the other, the Loose World. And with them, I believe, are nine-tenths of the most gifted persons on earth, the real public benefactors. So now I will venture a suggestion on their behalf.

It is this. The Stiff World, which has been laying it on, thick and hard and fast, for years, should now consent to lay off for a year or so, just to give the Loose World and the future a chance. If only as an experiment, it should instruct its huge mischief-making departments to stop plotting and planning. It should give its spies and counterspies a sabbatical. It should arrange for its pet maniacs to take a twelve-month narcotic treatment. It should lend some—let us say, a fifth—of the money it wastes annually to the Loose World, to help finance better coexistence and more cooperation, the start of real global civilization. But even if it refuses to lend anybody or anything a cent, it can benefit us all just by laying off for a spell, by trying not to whisper for six months in order to shout and scream for the next two crisis weeks, by behaving for a year as if it was not important and did not do what it had been doing.

Anyhow, it has been working too hard; let it give itself a holiday. For even with such a brief respite, the Loose World, the real world, the only one with a future, might begin to take over. It seems to me worth trying.

POETRY

Mr. Flood's Party

BY EDWIN ARLINGTON ROBINSON

1920

Old Eben Flood, climbing alone one night
Over the hill between the town below
And the forsaken upland hermitage
That held as much as he should ever know
On earth again of home, paused and observed.
The road was his with not a native near;
And Eben, having leisure, said aloud,
For no man else in Tilbury Town to hear:

"Well, Mr. Flood, we have the harvest moon
Again, and we may not have many more;
The bird is on the wing, the poet says,
And you and I have said it here before.
Drink to the bird." He raised up to the light
The jug that he had gone so far to fill,
And answered huskily: "Well, Mr. Flood,
Since you propose it, I believe I will."

Alone, as if enduring to the end
A valiant armor of scarred hopes outworn,
He stood there in the middle of the road
Like Roland's ghost winding a silent horn.
Below him, in the town among the trees,
Where friends of other days had honored him,
A phantom salutation of the dead
Rang thinly till old Eben's eyes were dim.

Then, as a mother lays her sleeping child
Down tenderly, fearing it may awake,
He set the jug down slowly at his feet
With trembling care, knowing that most things break;
And only when assured that on firm earth
It stood, as the uncertain lives of men
Assuredly did not, he paced away,
And with his hand extended paused again:

345

"Well, Mr. Flood, we have not met like this
In a long time; and many a change has come
To both of us, I fear, since last it was
We had a drop together. Welcome home!"
Convivially returning with himself,
Again he raised the jug up to the light;
And with an acquiescent quaver said:
"Well, Mr. Flood, if you insist, I might.

"Only a very little, Mr. Flood—
For auld lang syne. No more, sir; that will do."
So, for the time, apparently it did,
And Eben evidently thought so too;
For soon amid the silver loneliness
Of night he lifted up his voice and sang,
Secure, with only two moons listening,
Until the whole harmonious landscape rang—

"For auld lang syne." The weary throat gave out,
The last word wavered; and the song being done,
He raised again the jug regretfully
And shook his head, and was again alone.
There was not much that was ahead of him,
And there was nothing in the town below—
Where strangers would have shut the many doors
That many friends had opened long ago.

Death of Little Boys

BY ALLEN TATE

1925

When little boys grown patient at last, weary,
Surrender their eyes immeasurably to the night,
The event will rage terrific as the sea;
Their bodies fill a crumbling room with light. . . .

Then you will touch at the bedside, torn in two,
Gold curls now deftly intricate with gray
As the window-pane extends a fear to you
From one peeled aster drenched with the wind all day.

And over his chest the covers, in an ultimate dream,
Will mount to the teeth, ascend the eyes, press back
The locks—while round his sturdy belly gleam
The suspended breaths, white spars above his wreck:

Till all the guests, come in to look, turn down
Their palms; and delirium assails the cliff
Of Bedlam where you ponder, and your quiet town
Reels like a sailor drunk in a rotten skiff. . . .

The bleak sunshine shrieks its chipped music then
Out to the milkweed amid the fields of wheat.
There is a calm for you in the street where men
Unroll the chill precision of moving feet.

Dark Summer

BY LOUISE BOGAN

1926

Under the thunder-dark, the cicadas resound.
The storm in the sky mounts, but is not yet heard.
The shaft and the flash wait, but are not yet found.
The apples that hang and swell for the late comer,
The simple spell, the rite not for our word,
The kisses not for our mouths, light the dark summer.

Hurt Hawks

BY ROBINSON JEFFERS

1928

I

The broken pillar of the wing jags from the clotted shoulder,
The wing trails like a banner in defeat,
No more to use the sky forever but live with famine
And pain a few days: cat nor coyote
Will shorten the week of waiting for death, there is game
　　without talons.
He stands under the oak-bush and waits
The lame feet of salvation; at night he remembers freedom
And flies in a dream, the dawns ruin it.
He is strong and pain is worse to the strong, incapacity is
　　worse.
The curs of the day come and torment him
At distance, no power but death the redeemer will humble
　　that head,
The intrepid readiness, the terrible eyes.
The wild God of the world is sometimes merciful to those
That ask mercy, not often to the arrogant.
You do not know him, you communal people, or you have
　　forgotten him;
Intemperate and savage, the hawk remembers him;
Beautiful and wild, the hawks, and men that are dying,
　　remember him.

II

I'd sooner, except the penalties, kill a man than a hawk;
　　but the great redtail
Had nothing left but unable misery
From the bones too shattered for mending, the wing that
　　trailed under his talons when he moved.
We had fed him six weeks, I gave him freedom,
He wandered over the foreland hill and returned in the
　　evening, asking for death,
Not like a beggar, still eyed with the old

349

Implacable arrogance. I gave him the lead gift in the twilight.
  What fell was relaxed,
Owl-downy, soft feminine feathers: but what
Soared: the fierce rush: the night-herons by the flooded
  river cried fear at its rising
Before it was quite unsheathed from reality.

The Bear

BY ROBERT FROST

1928

The bear puts both arms round the tree above her
And draws it down as if it were a lover
And its choke-cherries lips to kiss goodby,
Then lets it snap back upright in the sky.
Her next step rocks a boulder on the wall.
(She's making her cross-country in the fall.)
Her great weight creaks the barbed wire in its staples
As she flings over and off down through the maples,
Leaving on one wire tooth a lock of hair.
Such is the uncaged progress of the bear.
The world has room to make a bear feel free.
The universe seems cramped to you and me.
Man acts more like the poor bear in a cage
That all day fights a nervous inward rage,
His mood rejecting all his mind suggests.
He paces back and forth and never rests
The toe-nail click and shuffle of his feet,
The telescope at one end of his beat,
And at the other end the microscope,
Two instruments of nearly equal hope,
And in conjunction giving quite a spread.
Or if he rests from scientific tread,
'Tis only to sit back and sway his head
Through ninety-odd degrees of arc it seems,
Between two metaphysical extremes.
He sits back on his fundamental butt
With lifted snout and eyes (if any) shut
(He almost looks religious but he's not),
And back and forth he sways from cheek to cheek,
At one extreme agreeing with one Greek,
At the other agreeing with another Greek,
Which may be thought but only so to speak.
A baggy figure equally pathetic
When sedentary and when peripatetic.

Prelude

BY CONRAD AIKEN

1932

And there I saw the seed upon the mountain
but it was not a seed it was a star
but it was not a star it was a world
but it was not a world it was a god
but it was not a god it was a laughter

blood red within and lightning for its rind
the root came out like gold and it was anger
the root came out like fire and it was fury
the root came out like horn and it was purpose
but it was not a root it was a hand

destructive strong and eager full of blood
and broke the rocks and set them on each other
and broke the waters into shafts of light
and set them end to end and made them seas
and out of laughter wrung a grief of water

and thus beneath the web of mind I saw
under the west and east of web I saw
under the bloodshot spawn of stars I saw
under the water and the inarticulate laughter
the coiling down the coiling in the coiling

mean and intense and furious and secret
profound and evil and dispatched in darkness
shot homeward foully in a filth of effort
clotted and quick and thick and without aim
spasm of concentration of the sea
and there I saw the seed upon the shore
but it was not a seed it was a man
but it was not a man it was a god
magnificent and humble in the morning
with angels poised upon his either hand.

The Men That Are Falling

BY WALLACE STEVENS

1936

God and all angels sing the world to sleep,
Now that the moon is rising in the heat

And crickets are loud again in the grass. The moon
Burns in the mind on lost remembrances.

He lies down and the night wind blows upon him here.
The bells grow longer. This is not sleep. This is desire.

Ah! Yes, desire . . . this leaning on his bed,
This leaning on his elbows on his bed,

Staring, at midnight, at the pillow that is black
In the catastrophic room . . . beyond despair,

Like an intenser instinct. What is it he desires?
But this he cannot know, the man that thinks,

Yet life itself, the fulfilment of desire
In the grinding ric-rac, staring steadily

At a head upon the pillow in the dark,
More than sudarium, speaking the speech

Of absolutes, bodiless, a head
Thick-lipped from riot and rebellious cries,

The head of one of the men that are falling, placed
Upon the pillow to repose and speak,

Speak and say the immaculate syllables
That he spoke only by doing what he did.

God and all angels, this was his desire,
Whose head lies blurring here, for this he died.

Taste of the blood upon his martyred lips,
O pensioners, O demagogues and pay-men!

This death was his belief though death is a stone
This man loved earth, not heaven, enough to die.

The night wind blows upon the dreamer, bent
Over words that are life's voluble utterance.

Long-Legged Fly

BY WILLIAM BUTLER YEATS

1939

That civilization may not sink
Its great battle lost,
Quiet the dog, tether the pony
To a distant post.
Our master Caesar is in the tent
Where the maps are spread,
His eyes fixed upon nothing,
A hand under his head.

Like a long-legged fly upon the stream
His mind moves upon silence.

That the topless towers be burnt
And men recall that face,
Move most gently if move you must
In this lonely place.
She thinks, part woman, three parts a child,
That nobody looks; her feet
Practice a tinker shuffle
Picked up on the street.

Like a long-legged fly upon the stream
Her mind moves upon silence.

That girls at puberty may find
The first Adam in their thought,
Shut the door of the Pope's Chapel,
Keep those children out.
There on that scaffolding reclines
Michael Angelo.
With no more sound than the mice make
His hand moves to and fro.

Like a long-legged fly upon the stream
His mind moves upon silence.

Matthew Arnold

BY W. H. AUDEN

1939

His gift knew what he was—a dark disordered city;
Doubt hid it from the father's fond chastising sky,
Where once the mother-farms had glowed protectively
Spread the haphazard alleys of the neighbors' pity.

Yet would have gladly lived in him and learned his ways,
And grown observant like a beggar, and become
Familiar with each square and boulevard and slum,
And found in the disorder a whole world to praise.

But all his homeless reverence, revolted, cried:
"I am my father's forum, and he shall be heard;
Nothing shall contradict his holy final word,
Nothing." And thrust his gift in prison till it died.

And left him nothing but a jailor's voice and face,
And all rang hollow but the clear denunciation
Of a gregarious optimistic generation
That saw itself already in a father's place.

The Mind Is an Enchanting Thing

BY MARIANNE MOORE

1943

is an enchanted thing
  like the glaze on a
katydid-wing
    subdivided by sun
    till the nettings are legion.
Like Gieseking playing Scarlatti;

like the apteryx-awl
  as a beak, or the
kiwi's rain-shawl
    of haired feathers, the mind
    feeling its way as though blind,
walks along with its eyes on the ground.

It has memory's ear
  that can hear without
having to hear.
    Like the gyroscope's fall,
    truly unequivocal
because trued by regnant certainty,

it is a power of
  strong enchantment. It
is like the dove-
    neck animated by
    sun; it is memory's eye;
it's conscientious inconsistency.

It tears off the veil, tears
  the temptation, the
mist the heart wears,
    from its eyes—if the heart
    has a face; it takes apart
dejection. It's fire in the dove-neck's

357

iridescence; in the
        inconsistencies
of Scarlatti.
            Unconfusion submits
            its confusion to proof; it's
not a Herod's oath that cannot change.

The Dead Wingman

BY RANDALL JARRELL

1945

Seen on the sea, no sign; no sign, no sign
In the black firs and terraces of hills
Ragged in mist. The cone narrows, snow
Glares from the bleak walls of a crater. No.
Again the houses jerk like paper, turn,
And the surf streams by: a port of toys
Is starred with its fires and faces; but no sign.

In the level light, over the fiery shores,
The plane circles stubbornly: the eyes distending
With hatred and misery and longing, stare
Over the blackening ocean for a corpse.
The fires are guttering; the dials fall,
A long dry shudder climbs along his spine,
His fingers tremble; but his hard unchanging stare
Moves unacceptingly: *I have a friend.*

The fires are gray; no star, no sign
Winks from the breathing darkness of the carrier
Where the pilot circles for his wingman; where,
Gliding above the cities' shells, a stubborn eye
Among the coaled and ashen nations, achingly
Tracing the circles of that worn unchanging *No*—
The lives' long war, lost war—the pilot sleeps.

The Injury

BY WILLIAM CARLOS WILLIAMS

1946

From this hospital bed
I can hear an engine
breathing—somewhere
    in the night:

—Soft coal, soft coal,
    soft coal!

And I know it is men
    breathing
shoveling, resting—

—Go about it
the slow way, if you can
find any way—
            Christ!
who's a bastard?
            —quit
and quit shoveling.

A man breathing
    and it quiets and
the puff of steady
work begins
          slowly: Chug.
Chug. Chug. Chug. . . .
          fading off.
Enough coal at least
    for this small job

To Juan at the Winter Solstice

BY ROBERT GRAVES

1946

There is one story and one story only
That will prove worth your telling,
Whether as learned bard or gifted child;
To it all lines or lesser gauds belong
That startle with their shining
Such common stories as they stray into.

Is it of trees you tell, their mouths and virtues,
Of strange beasts that beset you,
Of birds that croak at you the Triple will?
Or of the Zodiac and how slow it turns
Below the Boreal Crown,
Prison of all true kings that ever reigned?

Water to water, ark again to ark,
From woman back to woman:
So each new victim treads unfalteringly
The never altered circuit of his fate,
Bringing twelve peers as witness
Both to his starry rise and starry fall.

Or is it of the Virgin's silver beauty,
All fish below the thighs?
She in her left hand bears a leafy quince;
When with her right she crooks a finger, smiling,
How may the King hold back?
Royally then he barters life for love.

Or of the undying snake from chaos hatched,
Whose coils contain the ocean,
Into whose chops with naked sword he springs,
Then in black water, tangled by the reeds,
Battles three days and nights,
To be spewed up beside her scalloped shore?

361

Much snow is falling, winds roar hollowly,
The owl hoots from the elder,
Fear in your heart cries to the loving-cup:
Sorrow to sorrow as the sparks fly upward.
The log groans and confesses
There is one story and one story only.

Dwell on her graciousness, dwell on her smiling,
Do not forget what flowers
The great boar trampled down in ivy time.
Her brow was creamy as the long ninth wave,
Her sea-blue eyes were wild
But nothing promised that is not performed.

New Year's Day

BY ROBERT LOWELL

1946

Again and then again . . . the year is born
To ice and death, and it will never do
To skulk behind stormwindows by the stove
To hear the postgirl sounding her French horn
When the thin tidal ice is wearing through.
Here is the understanding not to love
Our neighbor or tomorrow that will sieve
Our resolutions. While we live, we live

To snuff the smoke of victims. In the snow
The kitten heaved its hindlegs, as if fouled,
And died. We bent it in a Christmas box
And scattered blazing weeds to scare the crow
Until the snake-tailed sea-winds coughed and howled
For alms outside the church whose double locks
Wait for St. Peter, the distorted key.
Under St. Peter's bell the parish sea

Swells with its smelt into the burlap shack
Where Joseph plucks his hand-lines like a harp,
And hears the fearful *Puer natus est*
Of Circumcision, and relives the wrack
And howls of Jesus whom he holds. How sharp
The burden of the Law before the beast:
Time and the grindstone and the knife of God.
The child is born in blood, O child of blood.

Faustina, or, Rock Roses

BY ELIZABETH BISHOP

1947

By and by the whisper
says *"Faustina, Faustina ..."*
"¡Vengo, Señora!"

On bare scraping feet
Faustina nears the bed.
She exhibits the talcum powder,
the pills, the cans of "cream,"
the white bowl of farina,
requesting for herself
    a little coñac;

complaining of, explaining,
the terms of her employment.
She bends above the other.
Her sinister kind face
presents a cruel black
coincident conundrum.
    Oh, is it

freedom at last, a lifelong
dream of time and silence,
dream of protection and rest?
Or is it the very worst,
the unimaginable nightmare
that never before dared last
    more than a second?

The acuteness of the question
forks instantly and starts
a snake-tongue flickering;
blurs further, blunts, softens,
separates, falls, our problems
becoming helplessly
    proliferative.

There is no way of telling.
The eyes say only either.
At last the visitor rises,
awkwardly proffers her bunch
of rust-perforated roses
and wonders oh, whence come
    all the petals.

Tended by Faustina
yes in a crazy house
upon a crazy bed,
frail, of chipped enamel,
blooming above her head
into four vaguely rose-like
    flower-formations,

the white woman whispers to
herself. The floor-boards sag
this way and that. The crooked
towel-covered table
bears a can of talcum
and five pasteboard boxes
    of little pills,

most half-crystallized.
The visitor sits and watches
the dew glint on the screen
and in it two glow-worms
burning a drowned green.
Meanwhile the eighty watt bulb
    betrays us all,

discovering the concern
within our stupefaction;
lighting as well on heads
of tacks in the wall paper,
on a paper wall-pocket,
violet-embossed, glistening
    with mica flakes.

It exposes the fine white hair,
the gown with the undershirt
showing at the neck,

the pallid palm-leaf fan
she holds but cannot wield,
her white disordered sheets
        like wilted roses.

Clutter of trophies,
chamber of bleached flags!
—Rags or ragged garments
hung on the chairs and hooks
each contributing its
shade of white, confusing
        as undazzling.

The visitor is embarrassed
not by pain nor age
nor even nakedness,
though perhaps by its reverse.

On the Pilots Who Destroyed Germany
in the Spring of 1945

BY STEPHEN SPENDER

1947

I stood on a roof top and they wove their cage
Their murmuring throbbing cage, in the air of blue crystal.
I saw them gleam above the town like diamond bolts
Conjoining invisible struts of wire,
Carrying through the sky their geometry
Woven by senses delicate as a shoal of flashing fish.

They went. They left a silence in our streets below
Which boys gone to schoolroom leave in their playground.
A silence of asphalt, of privet hedge, of staring wall.
Through the glass emptied sky their diamonds had scratched
Long curving finest whitest lines.
These the day soon melted into satin ribbons.
Falling over heaven's terraces near the sun.

Oh that April morning they carried my will
Exalted expanding singing in their aerial cage.
They carried my will. They dropped it on a German town.
My will expanded and tall buildings fell down.

Then, when the ribbons faded and the sky forgot,
And April was concerned with building nests and being hot
I began to remember the lost names and faces.

Now I tie the ribbons torn down from those terraces
Around the most hidden image in my lines,
And my life, which never paid the price of their wounds,
Turns thoughts over and over like a propeller
Assumes their guilt, honors, repents, prays for them.

Lunas Are Tempting to Old Consciousness

BY DELMORE SCHWARTZ

1950

Dear Citizens,
You are a summer people, all year long,
The seashore is the lyric of your lives,
And all hearts quicken when the breaker strives
To curve and fall, like love, forever wrong.

The strong rocks also serves the fickled soul,
The sand is rough with goodness like a towel.

Cartoons, come true, run forth in bathing suits
Cheery as flutes, spontaneous as brutes.

The self-enjoyment of the flesh is full,
The nakedness is warm and admirable.

Nevertheless the Luna Park is near,
The roller-coaster soars and dives to fear.

Hark, from the coiling track come screams like jazz,
As if they jumped from brinks of a burning house.
How much some love the gross and plunging shock
As if the screeching broke the block to luck!
        Why do they hate their lives?
        Why do they wish to die?
        Believing in vicious lies,
        Afraid to remember and cry.
Nearby in little caves a little train
Seeks mystery and darkness like a vine.
Upon a wheel the couples are revolved,
As if tomorrow's blank had been resolved.

Not far, before a door, and with a roar,
A girl's skirt is blown up! showing her hips,
Her drawers, her giggles, her belly and—surprise!
Panic like rape shudders and shakes her eyes.

Soon at the boardwalk sandwiches are rich.
Apples and cones are sticky, licky, lush.
The sated summer people now may look
At abnormality's crude picture book.

Perversity attacks the mind like a storm,
Seeing the fat lady's gashouse form.
And as the Sunday wanes, and the flesh tires,
How the unconscious stretches, yawns, rises, wanders,
                    aspires and admires!

A Negro's face appears, to grin, if hit,
And hurt by baseballs, sublimation sweet!
Last is the gallery where the guns are neat,
The hearts not satisfied and still denied
Can win a mamma doll with a good shot.

This is the Luna of the heart's desire,
This is the play and park we all admire.

The Plain Sense of Things

BY WALLACE STEVENS

1952

After the leaves have fallen, we return
To a plain sense of things. It is as if
We had come to an end of the imagination,
Inanimate in an inert savoir.

It is difficult even to choose the adjective
For this blank cold, this sadness without cause.
The great structure has become a minor house.
No turban walks across the lessened floors.

The greenhouse never so badly needed paint.
The chimney is fifty years old and slants to one side.
A fantastic effort has failed, a repetition
In a repetitiousness of men and flies.

Yet the absence of the imagination had
Itself to be imagined. The great pond,
The plain sense of it, without reflections, leaves,
Mud, water like dirty glass, expressing silence

Pastorale

BY THEODORE ROETHKE

1953

The bank swallows veer and dip,
Diving down at my windows,
Then flying almost straight upward,
Like bats in daytime,
And their shadows, bigger,
Race over the thick grass;
And the finches pitch through the air, twittering;
And the small mad siskins flit by,
Flying upward in little skips and erratic leaps;
Or they sit sideways on limber dandelion stems,
Bending them down to the ground;
Or they perch and peck at larger flower-crowns,
Springing, one to another,
The last-abandoned stalk always quivering
Back into straightness;
Or they fling themselves against tree trunks,
Scuttling down and around like young squirrels,
Birds furious as bees.

Now they move all together!—
These airy hippety-hop skippers,
Light as seed blowing off thistles!
And I seem to lean forward,
As my eyes follow after
Their sunlit leaping.

Melancholy in the Families

(From the Spanish of Pablo Neruda)

BY CLAYTON ESHLEMAN

1961

I keep a blue flask,
inside it an ear and a picture.
When the night closes
the feathers of the owl,
when the rough cherry tree
destroys lips and threats
with shells perforated by ocean winds,
I know there are great expanses and wastes,
quartz in ingots.
pigments,
blue waters waiting for a storm,
heavy silence, veins running backwards, camphor
and fallen things, medals, tenderness,
parachutes and kisses.

It is no more than a step from one day to another,
a lone bottle walking over the sea,
a dining room where roses come,
an abandoned dining room like a fishbone.
I look at a broken glass, a curtain,
at a river dragging pebbles through a deserted hall.
It is a house built in a rain bed,
a house with boarded windows,
entangled with vines.

I go there in the afternoon,
I arrive full of mud and death,
dragging the earth and its roots,
its vague belly where corpses sleep in wheat,
where there are metals and fallen elephants.

But over all of this there is a terrible dining room,
a terrible abandoned dining room

with broken cruets
and vinegar running under the chairs,
a thin ray of the moon,
something dark . . .
and I search for a comparison inside of me.
Maybe it is a store surrounded by the sea
with its torn cloths dripping brine.

It is only an abandoned dining room
and all around there are expanses . . .
submerged factories, lumber,
which I alone know
because I am sad and old,
and know the earth, and am sad.

Pigeons

(For Hannah Arendt)

BY ROBERT LOWELL

1961

Rilke: *Taube, die draussen blieb*

The same old flights, the same old homecomings,
dozens of each per day,
but at least the pigeon gets clear of the pigeon-house . . .
What is home, but a feeling of homesickness
for the flight's lost moment of fluttering terror?

Back in the dovecote, there's another bird,
by all odds the most beautiful,
one that never flew out, and can know nothing of gentleness . . .
Still, only by suffering the rat-race in the arena
can the heart learn to beat.

Think of Leonidas perhaps and the hoplites,
glittering with liberation,
as they combed one another's golden Botticellian hair
at Thermopylae, friends and lovers, the bride and the bridegroom—
and moved into position to die.

Over non-existence arches the all-being—
thence the ball thrown almost out of bounds
stings our hands with the momentum of its drop—
body and gravity,
miraculously multiplied by its mania to return.

Junk

BY RICHARD WILBUR

1961

Huru Welandes worc ne geswiceth
monna aenigum thara the Mimming can
heardne gehealdan. —WALDERE

Truly, Wayland's handiwork — the
sword Mimming which he made — will
never fail any man who is able to wield it
bravely.

An axe angles
         from my neighbor's ashcan;
It is hell's handiwork,
         the wood not hickory,
The flow of the grain
         not faithfully followed.
The shivered shaft
         rises from a shellheap
Of plastic playthings,
         paper plates,
And the sheer shards
         of shattered tumblers
That were not annealed
         for the time needful.
At the same curbside,
         a cast-off cabinet
Of wavily-warped
         unseasoned wood
Waits to be trundled
         in the trash-man's truck.
Haul them off! Hide them!
         The heart winces
For junk and gimcrack,
         for jerrybuilt things
And the men who make them
         for a little money,
Bartering pride
         like the bought boxer

Who pulls his punches,
              or the paid-off jockey
Who in the home stretch
              holds in his horse.
Yet the things themselves
              in thoughtless honor
Have kept composure,
              like captives who would not
Talk under torture.
              Tossed from a tailgate
Where the dump displays
              its random dolmens,
Its black barrows
              and blazing valleys,
They shall waste in the weather
              toward what they were.
The sun shall glory
              in the glitter of glass-chips,
Foreseeing the salvage
              of the prisoned sand,
And the blistering paint
              peel off in patches,
That the good grain
              be discovered again.
Then burnt, bulldozed,
              they shall all be buried
To the depth of diamonds,
              in the making dark
Where halt Hephaestus
              keeps his hammer
And Wayland's work
              is worn away.

Three Dream Songs

BY JOHN BERRYMAN

1964

GENERAL FATIGUE

General Fatigue stalked in, & a Major-General,
Captain Fatigue, and at the base of all
pale Corporal Fatigue,
and curious microbes came, came viruses:
and the Court conferred on Henry, and conferred
                            on Henry
the rare Order of Weak.

—How come dims *one* these wholesome elsers oh?
Old polymaths, old trackers, far from home,
say how thro' auburn hair   titbits of youth's grey climb.
I have heard of rose-cheekt but the rose is here!
I bell: when pops her phiz in   a good crow.
My beauty is off duty!—

Henry relives a lady, how down vain,
spruce in her succinct parts, spruce everywhere.
They fed like muscles and lunched
after, between, before. He tracks her, hunched
(propped on red table elbows) at her telephone
white rear bare in the air.

HENRY'S PENCILS

I figure with this grey upon this yellow
pencil on paper in my super-pad,
nurses flying to & fro,
he could a new it dredge forth like a billow
forsaking them diseases Henry had
and pull the nurses down O.

I figure on these yellow with my blue—
why ever did one pass the Second Grade
to shoal up mis'able,
forlorn typewriting—I can make it too,
wining his colleagues where he will not fade.
I figure it over; I mull.

I haunt my fate of yellow with sweet green:
let me not yet have mustered all in vain,
but suffer war (I wish)
yellow the breaking sky: he attack, lean
& mean, with crazed laughs intervalling pain,
and do you know what? he flourish.

DONNYBROOK

Henry of Donnybrook bred like a pig,
bred when he was brittle, bred when big,
how he's sweating to support them.
Which birthday of the brighter darker man,
the Goya of the Globe & Blackfriars, whom—
our full earth smiled on him

squeezing his old heart with a daughter loose
(hostages they are)—the world's produced,
so far, alarms, alarms.
Dig the fatigue & cold four hundred years
award a warm one. All we know is ears.
My slab lifts up its arms

in a solicitude complete, too late.
Of brutal revelry open your mouth to state:
Front back & backside go bare!
Cats' blackness, booze, blows, grunts, grand groans.
Yobad yom i-oowaled bo v'ha'l-lail awmer h're gawber!
—Now, now, poor Bones.

INDEX

Index